LEARN
TEACH
PREVENT

Holocaust Education
in the 21st Century

The National Catholic Center for Holocaust Education, Seton Hill University

The National Catholic Center for Holocaust Education (NCCHE) was established on the campus of Seton Hill University in 1987. Seton Hill initiated this national Catholic movement toward Holocaust studies in response to the urging of Pope John Paul II to recognize the significance of the *Shoah*, the Holocaust, and to "promote the necessary historical and religious studies on this event which concerns the whole of humanity today." The NCCHE has as its primary purpose the dissemination of scholarship on the root causes of antisemitism, its relation to the Holocaust, and the implications of both from the Catholic perspective for today's world. Toward this end, the Center is committed to equipping scholars, especially those at Catholic institutions, to enter into serious discussion on the causes of antisemitism and the Holocaust; shaping appropriate curricular responses at Catholic institutions and other educational sites; sustaining Seton Hill's Catholic Institute for Holocaust Studies in Israel through a cooperative program with Yad Vashem, the Isaac Jacob Institute for Religious Law, and the Hebrew University; encouraging scholarship and research through conferences, publications, workshops for educators, and similar activities; sponsoring local events on the Holocaust and related topics in the University and the community; and enhancing Catholic-Jewish relations.

LEARN
TEACH
PREVENT

Holocaust Education
in the 21st Century

Carol Rittner, R.S.M.
Editor

Wendy Whitworth
Managing Editor

LEARN TEACH **PREVENT**

Holocaust Education in the 21st Century

Editor, Carol Rittner, R.S.M.
Managing Editor, Wendy Whitworth

Published in the United States by
Seton Hill University
National Catholic Center for Holocaust Education
1 Seton Hill Drive
Greensburg, Pennsylvania 15601-1599
724-830-1033
ncche@setonhill.edu
http://ncche.setonhill.edu

ISBN 978-0-9830571-0-9

Funding from The Ethel LeFrak Holocaust Education Conference Endowment made possible both The Ethel LeFrak Holocaust Education Conference and publication of The Ethel LeFrak Holocaust Education Conference Proceedings.

The papers contained in this publication express the opinions of the individual authors and do not necessarily represent the views of the National Catholic Center for Holocaust Education or Seton Hill University.

Cover: Photographs of The Question Mark/er Project, Harlan Gallery, Seton Hill University, 2009. Carol Brode © Seton Hill University

Design and artwork by Glen Powell Graphic Design
Printed by Laurel Valley Graphics, Inc., Latrobe, Pennsylvania 15650

Table of Contents

Learn. Teach. Prevent.

Carol Rittner, R.S.M.

Distinguished Professor of Holocaust & Genocide Studies,
Dr. Marsha Raticoff Grossman Professor of Holocaust Studies,
The Richard Stockton College of New Jersey, Pomona, NJ

"Today we understand that the future we are shaping now is the past we will share tomorrow."
Prime Minister Göran Persson,
The Stockholm International Forum on the Holocaust, 2000

When he opened The Stockholm International Conference on the Holocaust in January 2000, Prime Minister Göran Persson of Sweden welcomed an assembly of diplomats, politicians, scholars, teachers, historians, survivors, and witnesses of the Holocaust from more than fifty countries around the world. They had come to Sweden at the Prime Minister's invitation to participate in the first international Holocaust conference of the new millennium. For three days, in plenary and workshop sessions, they grappled with four major questions:

- What can we learn from the Holocaust?
- How can its study alert contemporary society to the dangers of racism, antisemitism, ethnic conflict and other expressions of hate and discrimination?
- Can we predict the conditions that create persecution and genocide, and can we prevent their reoccurrence?
- What can and should political, civic and religious leaders do to promote education, remembrance and research?[1]

1

These are perennial questions, asked during every conference on the Holocaust, if not directly, then indirectly. And these questions, in one way or another, also provided the impetus for the 2009 Ethel LeFrak Holocaust Conference at Seton Hill University. Those who presented papers, directed workshops, performed music, created works of art, and participated in the conference examined and discussed similar questions: What can we learn from the Holocaust? How can we teach about genocide? What can we do to prevent genocide in the future? These are important questions because:

> The Holocaust was no accident of history. The systematic murder of the Jews did not happen by chance. Nor the genocide of the Roma. Nor the mass murder of disabled persons and the persecution and murder of homosexuals and dissidents. It occurred because people willed it, planned it and carried it through. It occurred because people made choices which allowed it to happen. It occurred, not least, because people remained silent.[2]

The Holocaust happened once, but it must not happen again. Education about the Holocaust is important, not simply as "horrible history," but to make everyone aware, teachers no less than students, clergy no less than politicians, that it was human beings – people like us – who "willed it, planned it and carried it through." Education about the Holocaust is fundamental to learning from history, fundamental to seeing the connections between what is happening in our world today and what happened before and during the Holocaust: the rise of anti-democratic forces in Germany and elsewhere, the exclusion of minorities from society, the massive violations of human rights, and the silence of so many onlookers.

The theme of the 2009 Ethel LeFrak Conference was *Holocaust Education in the 21st Century: Religious and Cultural Perspectives*, and the message was clear: **Learn** the lessons of the past. **Teach** a new generation. **Prevent** such things from happening again – to anyone, anywhere, at any time. And yet, if truth be told, how successful have we been when it comes to teaching about the Holocaust, learning from it, and preventing genocide? Have we, in fact, learned from history? The evidence that we have learned anything useful in this regard seems scant indeed. Why? Because, as Koïchiro Matsuura, Director-General of UNESCO, once said, "The Holocaust may have been the apogee of state-sponsored genocide in our time, but campaigns of genocide have erupted in our contemporary world: Rwanda, Bosnia and Herzegovina, Kosovo and East Timor,"[3] Congo and Sudan, to name a few places in the world where such horrors have happened *after* 1945, the end of World War II, Nazi Germany and the Holocaust.

UNESCO's Matsuura was not, and is not, the only one to call into question humankind's "learnings" from the Holocaust. In January 2000, Dr. Haris Silajdžić,

Co-Chairman of the Council of Ministers of Bosnia Herzegovina, told participants at the Stockholm International Forum on the Holocaust that:

> ... the brave words that were spoken after the Second World War, when the full horrors of the Holocaust became known – the words "Never Again!"... these words were not properly heeded as former Yugoslavia began to disintegrate; and we in Bosnia and Herzegovina paid a heavy price for the failure to learn from the Holocaust... How loud must the cry of the victims be before the world will hear us?[4]

This, despite the fact that hundreds of thousands of students in educational institutions worldwide – at every level: primary, secondary, tertiary – study and learn about the Holocaust and other genocides; that hundreds of institutions – colleges and universities, museums, and other cultural institutions – sponsor lectures, organize conferences, and publish papers, monographs, and books about the Holocaust and other genocides; and literally thousands of movies and television programs about the Holocaust and other genocides are made and shown in theaters and viewed in homes worldwide. What is one to make of all this information disseminated and floating on the airwaves around the world?

If this is not revelatory enough, consider that in June 2010, at the Salzburg Global Seminar on Holocaust Education and Genocide Prevention held in Austria, former United Nations Secretary-General Kofi Annan told participants that "it is surprisingly hard to find education programs that have clearly succeeded in linking the history of the Holocaust with the prevention of ethnic conflict and genocide in today's world."[5] A few weeks later, Aleksander Kwasniewski, former president of Poland (1995–2005), commenting on Kofi Annan's Salzburg presentation in an op-ed piece in *The International Herald Tribune*, wrote, "The younger generations commonly view the Holocaust with indifference. Born in the early 1990s, they tend to view World War II as irrelevant to their everyday lives," even though, according to Kofi Annan, "in our increasingly diverse and globalized world, educators and policy-makers believe Holocaust education is a vital mechanism for teaching students to value democracy and human rights, and encouraging them to oppose racism and promote tolerance in their own societies."[6] What is one to make of all this?

Are those of us who teach about the Holocaust – and increasingly about other genocides as well – wasting our time, whistling in the wind, so to speak? Are we fooling ourselves when we claim that teaching about the Holocaust helps to "sensitize people, raise awareness of the other, help identify the preliminary warning signs of genocide, and put the brakes in place"[7] to prevent future genocides? Is this all wishful thinking? Is teaching about the Holocaust and other genocides just another fad in an already overcrowded curriculum that advances some pressure group's agenda, but has little real effect on how people live their lives in our complex, confusing, and increasingly violent world?

Learn. Teach. Prevent.

What do students in our Holocaust and Genocide Studies courses really **learn** beyond the facts, figures, and historical context of the Holocaust, or the other national, ethnic, religious, and racial conflicts that they study? Are we simply teaching "horror history" to students who are inured to human suffering as a result of compassion fatigue? What is it that we **teach** students when we **teach** Holocaust and Genocide Studies? Do our students only **learn** about the last steps in extreme genocidal evil – the mayhem and murder – or do we also **teach** about the first steps leading in that direction – that a dangerous increase in nationalist sentiments, a rising tide of intolerance against minorities (ethnic, racial, religious, sexual), the entrenchment of racism, antisemitism, the teaching of contempt of those who are not us, not ours, or not "able" can lead to the slow disintegration of conscience? All of this over time can desensitize peoples, plant "in the minds of a whole chain of subordinates the idea that it is possible to kill women, men and children in extermination camps, but impossible to disobey the order of a superior."[8] Do we help our students to understand that the Holocaust did not begin with Auschwitz, that the genocide in Cambodia did not begin with "the killing fields," and that the genocide in Rwanda did not begin with thousands of Hutus hacking their Tutsi neighbors to death? Do we **teach** our students that "every act of racism or of intolerance toward minorities may be the beginning of an onslaught on the very foundations of human civilization"?[9] Do they **learn** that genocide is not the work of devils, monsters, or animals but of human beings like ourselves?

What kind of Holocaust and Genocide Studies education can help students grapple with these kinds of questions? What kind of Holocaust and Genocide Studies education can enable students to **learn** and commit themselves to putting into practice not just the Ten Commandments given to us by the Jewish people, but also the three additional commandments given to us by the Israeli scholar, Yehuda Bauer: "Thou shall not be a perpetrator; thou shall not be a victim; and thou shall never, but never, be a bystander."[10] What kind of Holocaust and Genocide Studies education can prepare students in a democratic society to more than simply *know* about genocide, but also, if and when faced with genocide, *empower them to act* to **prevent** genocide?

These are not easy questions, but if we think that more research about the Holocaust – or any other genocide, or genocidal event in history – will provide us with answers about why human beings inflict horror on other human beings; if we think that Holocaust and Genocide Studies education will give us clear-cut, ready-made solutions about how to **prevent** future genocides, we are mistaken.

Does this mean that because we have not yet discovered how to link education about the Holocaust to genocide prevention that we should give up, that we should stop teaching about the Holocaust and other genocides, stop organizing lectures and conferences, stop putting our efforts into developing courses and programs in Holocaust and Genocide Studies? No! What we must do is try harder, be more creative, focus on the human story within the facts of history, ask more questions, engage students intellectually and affectively. As Sam Totten and Bill Parsons have written, "Each generation… has a desire to shape a more humane world," and even though we "seem to be in the Stone Age when it comes to mass killings and atrocities… there are thousands upon thousands of individuals throughout the world who are pushing back on the perpetrators of mass atrocities…[11] As a student of mine once wrote in a final examination for a course on the Holocaust, "Genocide has shown me the darkest part of humanity, but I shall strive to be the light that drives back the darkness."[12] Our task as educators is to fuel that "light," however delicate and fragile it may be.

Education for Freedom

The late Bart Giamatti, President of Yale University, used to say that what students need in general is an education for freedom,[13] an education that places an emphasis on questions rather than answers, for answers aim to settle things while questions keep us open to continuing inquiry, further dialogue. Giamatti's ideas about education in general, in my view, also apply to Holocaust and Genocide Studies education in particular. More than ever, students need a critical education that addresses why we make wars, destroy lives, brutalize and devalue others, following those who lead us into the blind rage of ethnocentrism or other forms of social hatred. Such an education aims to develop in students the ability to question assumptions, to challenge what is taken for granted, and to approach knowledge and truth as the stuff of human invention. Without such an education, people simply will "follow the herd," do whatever they are told, even murder men, women, and children who are perceived as "different" from themselves. Giamatti's education for freedom aims to **teach** the common humanness of "the other" – whether gay or straight, black, white, yellow, or brown, Muslim, Christian, or Jew, of one religion or no religion – and it stresses the values of caring, personal responsibility, and compassion. In my view, Giamatti's education for freedom is the pedagogical approach that we need in teaching Holocaust and Genocide Studies courses, whether introductory or more advanced, whether at the primary, secondary, or tertiary level, whether undergraduate or graduate.

We who teach courses in Holocaust and Genocide Studies need to remind students as well as ourselves that evil and goodness are enacted by ordinary men and women, not by villains wearing ugly masks as in medieval allegories. To characterize people who engaged in, or engage in, genocidal evil as villains – people like Hitler, Himmler, Eichmann, and Stangl; Pol Pot, Slobodan Milosevic, Jean-Paul Akayesu, or

President Bashir of Sudan – is misguided. Such people need to be presented in all their humanness, as fallible agents, human beings who constantly are making choices – choices guided by their views of "the other," choices motivated by an ideology that includes some people as part of their universe of moral obligation, and excludes others.

But even with such an education for freedom, the question is still open as to whether or not it would enable students to move from studying about the Holocaust – studying about any genocide – to moving to the point of trying to **prevent** genocide, a position that is easier to affirm in principle than to bring about in reality,[14] as Samantha Power discovered and wrote about in *"A Problem From Hell": America and the Age of Genocide.*[15]

Teaching about the Holocaust and other genocides is in many ways like wading into a minefield: One has to be very careful and cautious. To paraphrase slightly something written by Dalia Ofer, the teacher must try to convey to her/his students "the enormity of the crimes committed without leading them to lose hope in humanity or become cynical about the condition of the world".[16] Does teaching about the Holocaust, does teaching about any genocide, whether recent or more distant, lead to genocide prevention? Based on our history since 1945, it does not seem so; and yet, we cannot desist from engaging in the task of trying to teach in a way that can lead toward the prevention of genocide now, and in the future. To quote two survivors of the Holocaust, one of whom, Primo Levi, ended his own life, but initially believed the Holocaust could not happen again,[17] later changing his mind and warning his readers:

> We must be listened to: above and beyond our personal experience, we have collectively witnessed a fundamental unexpected event, fundamental precisely because unexpected, not foreseen by anyone. It happened, therefore it can happen again: this is the core of what we have to say. It can happen, and it can happen everywhere.[18]

The other, Hédi Fried, who lives in Stockholm, Sweden, still maintains, despite all she knows about the human condition and its dark side, that:

> We have to make people aware, young and old, that we are all vulnerable, and that we all have a responsibility also for what is going on elsewhere in the world. We should not rely on our leaders to change the world, we all have to do whatever we can, small as it may be, in order to keep this world a better place to live in.[19]

Can we, in fact, **teach** students such awareness? Can they **learn** such responsibility? Does such behavior, such action on the part of individuals help to **prevent** genocide?

These are not questions that I can answer, but what I know is that we must try – and we must keep trying. We must never think the task is completed, for "Learning the lessons of the past is a task without end. There will always be a new generation to win over to knowledge, democracy and human dignity."[20]

Ethel LeFrak Holocaust Education Conference 2009
The 2009 Ethel LeFrak Holocaust Conference, "Holocaust Education in the 21st Century: Religious and Cultural Perspectives," held at Seton Hill University, October 25–27, 2009, gave particular attention to interreligious dialogue, recent genocides, and new technologies in an effort to encourage Holocaust scholars and teachers, clergy and students, Holocaust survivors and others from the civic, religious, and academic community to think about, discuss, and suggest ways in which the university can help prevent genocide. The papers that follow in this volume of proceedings, in one way or another, all address the overall theme: **Learn. Teach. Prevent.** Each paper includes Questions for Discussion, as well as a Bibliography of readings for further study. The Editor and Managing Editor of this book, Carol Rittner, R.S.M., and Wendy Whitworth, as well as the Director and Associate Director of the National Catholic Center for Holocaust Education at Seton Hill University, Gemma Del Duca, S.C., and Wilda Kaylor, extend their thanks to the 2009 LeFrak Holocaust Conference presenters who so graciously cooperated with them by completing their papers and meeting every deadline. Our hope is that those who read this volume will **learn** from the past, **teach** their students what they have learned, and join in the never-ending task to **prevent** genocide now, and in the future.

Notes

1. See further, *The Stockholm International Forum on the Holocaust Proceedings* (Stockholm: Swedish Government Publications, 2000) p. 6.
2. Göran Persson, "Opening Address, 26 January 2000," *The Stockholm International Forum on the Holocaust Proceedings*, p. 29.
3. Koïchiro Matsuura, "Written Message by UNESCO," *The Stockholm International Forum on the Holocaust Proceedings*, p. 147.
4. Haris Silajdžić, "Message of the Co-Chairman of the Council of Ministers of Bosnia and Herzegovina at the Closing Plenary Session, 28 January 2000," *The Stockholm International Forum on the Holocaust Proceedings*, p. 90.
5. Kofi Annan, "The Myth of 'Never Again,'" *The International Herald Tribune*, June 18, 2010, http://dev.kofiannanfoundation.org/newsroom/news/2010/06/myth-never-again.
6. Aleksander Kwasniewski, "On Holocaust Education," *The International Herald Tribune*, June 28, 2010, http://www.nytimes.com/2010/06/29/opinion/29iht-edcounter.html.
7. Kofi Annan, "The Myth of 'Never Again,'" op.cit., *The International Herald Tribune*, June 18, 2010.
8. Lionel Jospin, "Message by the Prime Minister of the French Republic at the Ceremonial Opening, 26 January 2000," *The Stockholm International Forum on the Holocaust Proceedings*, p. 44.
9. Václav Havel, "Message by the President of the Czech Republic at the Ceremonial Opening, 26 January 2000," *The Stockholm International Forum on the Holocaust Proceedings*, p. 43.

10. Professor Yehuda Bauer, "Speech at the Ceremonial Opening of the Forum, 26 January 2000," *The Stockholm International Forum on the Holocaust Proceedings*, p. 36.
11. Sam Totten and Bill Parsons, "Introduction," *Century of Genocide: Critical Essays and Eyewitness Accounts*, Third Edition in Samuel Totten and William S. Parsons eds. (New York: Routledge, 2009), p. 12.
12. Student Comment on a Final Examination, The Richard Stockton College of New Jersey, December 2001.
13. See further, A. Bartlett Giamatti, *A Free and Ordered Space: The Real World of the University* (New York: W. W. Norton, 1988).
14. Bridget Conley-Zilkic and Samuel Totten, "Easier Said than Done: The Challenges of Preventing and Responding to Genocide," *Century of Genocide: Critical Essays and Eyewitness Accounts*, Samuel Totten and William S. Parsons eds., op.cit., p. 609.
15. Samantha Power, *"A Problem from Hell": America and the Age of Genocide* (New York: Basic Books, 2002).
16. Dalia Ofer, "Holocaust and Education: Where are we going?" in *The Stockholm International Forum on the Holocaust Proceedings*, p. 167.
17. Gerry Caplan, the Canadian scholar, asserts this in an online essay published in AfricaFiles, "Some Things We Know about Genocide – 10 Years, 10 Lessons." See further, http://www.africafiles.org (accessed August 20, 2010).
18. Primo Levi, *The Drowned and the Saved* (New York: Simon & Schuster, 1988), p. 199.
19. Hédi Fried, "Holocaust and Education," *The Stockholm International Forum on the Holocaust Proceedings*, p. 165.
20. Göran Persson, "Opening Address, 26 January 2000," *The Stockholm International Forum on the Holocaust Proceedings*, p. 30.

Tribute to Ethel LeFrak

■ ■ ■ ■ ■ ■ ■ ■ ■ ■ ■

Gemma Del Duca S.C.

Co-Director (Israel), The National Catholic Center for Holocaust Education,
Seton Hill University, Greensburg, PA

September 2009 marked the 70th anniversary since the outbreak of World War II. During the 8th Holocaust Education Conference, presenters and participants remembered, reflected on, and responded to the Holocaust, the *Shoah*, as a cataclysmic event in Jewish and human history.

A distinguishing feature of this conference was that it bore the name of Ethel LeFrak of New York, benefactor and friend of Seton Hill University. When the war broke out, Ethel LeFrak was a young student at Barnard College. The memory of those years stayed with her. It was during this time that she met and later married Samuel J. LeFrak, who became the founder of one of the largest private building firms in the world. Ethel LeFrak, loving wife and devoted mother of four, became with her husband a distinguished philanthropist, dedicating her time and resources to cultural, educational, and medical institutions. She has served as a trustee of the Cardozo Law School and of the Albert Einstein Medical College, as a member of the Council of the Salk Institute, vice-president of the Little Orchestra Society, and patron of the Asia Society. A member of the Metropolitan Opera's "Golden Horseshoe" and "Opera Club," Ethel LeFrak has also been a patron of the Lincoln Center.

In her efforts to reach out to as many fellow New Yorkers as possible, she became a conservator of the New York Public Library. Her interest in international affairs moved her to become a member of the Board of the United Nations International Hospitality Committee. This Committee was instrumental in having her and her husband, the late Dr. Samuel J. LeFrak, honored in 1994 with the United Nations "Distinguished Citizens of the World" Award. The LeFraks co-edited and published two books on their family art collection: *Masters of the Modern Tradition* (New York: LeFrak Organization, 1988; catalogue by Diane Kelder) and *A Passion for Art* (New York: Rizzoli, 1994; text by Diane Kelder). In 1996, Ethel LeFrak was awarded a Doctor of Humane Letters, *honoris causa*, by Seton Hill University.

In 2008, with a munificent gift, Ethel LeFrak endowed the triennial conference of the Seton Hill University National Catholic Center for Holocaust Education, which will henceforth be known as The Ethel LeFrak Holocaust Education Conference. Ethel LeFrak conveyed a message to the Conference participants in October 2009, expressing her hopes for them and for the world. Her words were sensitive and to the point: "Simply to think of the Holocaust and all genocides sends shivers down one's spine. It is inconceivable that during the twentieth century these horrors occurred. Nevertheless, it is now up to us to continue the fight against bigotry and ignorance by inspiring worldwide understanding and tolerance, by educating the educators to probe and dissect, to publish and disseminate the reasons behind the Holocaust and all genocide, so that abominations like that will never happen again, at any time, to anyone."

Seton Hill and the National Catholic Center for Holocaust Education presented Ethel LeFrak with the Saint Elizabeth Ann Seton Woman of Courage Award in October 2009, in recognition of her commitment to the work of the Seton Hill University Center and her noble efforts to foster friendship, peace, and reconciliation among people of different backgrounds. Nobel Prize Laureate Elie Wiesel commented on Ethel LeFrak's life's work, "You have done so much for so many people of different faiths that all of us, your friends, rejoice in this very merited recognition."

What could one add to Ethel LeFrak's commitment, to her accomplishments, to her generosity? The poetic words of the Book of Proverbs seem to come alive through her:

> An accomplished woman, who can find her? Her value is beyond pearls,
> She is like the merchant ships; she brings her bread from afar.
> She extends her hands to the poor, and reaches out her hand to the needy.
> She opens her mouth in wisdom and the lesson of kindness is on her tongue.
> (Proverbs 31: 10, 14, 20, 26)

With praise and admiration, the Proceedings of the 8th Holocaust Education Conference are dedicated to Ethel LeFrak.

Ethel LeFrak
Photo by Gregory Partanio © ManhattanSociety.com

INTERRELIGIOUS DIALOGUE

CHALLENGES AND OPPORTUNITIES

Interreligious Dialogue since the Holocaust:
Turning Points and Next Steps

■ ■ ■ ■ ■ ■ ■ ■ ■ ■ ■

Victoria J. Barnett

Staff Director, Church Relations, United States Holocaust Memorial Museum, Washington, D.C.

I am grateful for the chance to contribute to this volume, published as a result of the Ethel LeFrak Holocaust Education Conference at the Seton Hill University National Catholic Center for Holocaust Education in Greensburg, Pennsylvania. The work of Sister Gemma and her staff at Seton Hill – and the work of all those in the field of Holocaust education – is an inspiring model for many things that are fundamental for interreligious dialogue and understanding: compassion, education, honesty, and integrity in confronting a painful history.

This work is more important than ever before. For a number of reasons, this is not an easy time in history for interreligious dialogue – between Jews and Christians, between Jews, Christians and Muslims, and sometimes even between members of one religion within their own tradition. Even within my own denomination, there are sharp differences of opinion on social as well as theological issues. So it should not surprise that there are people in different faith communities who view the Holocaust as a stumbling block for dialogue, a problematic history that should be avoided. They do not know how to talk about it, and because it is such a painful conversation, and because Christian complicity is so deeply a part of this history, some would rather "move on." In my own life and work, the event of the Holocaust and the questions it raises – for all people of faith, but especially for Christians – is central to how I approach issues relating to faith and interreligious understanding. I grow increasingly convinced of its importance. But that is not true for everyone, and I have come to realize that many things that are self-evident to those of us who teach about the Holocaust are not self-evident to everyone.

For a number of reasons, we are at a turning point, both in teaching about the Holocaust and in the post-Holocaust conversation. The generation of survivors and witnesses is passing from the stage. To many younger people, the Holocaust seems to be simply one terrible historical event among many. And that means we need to make the case for why the Holocaust is such a central, world-changing, faith-changing event, particularly for Christians. We need to articulate why it is important to study the Holocaust, and why the lessons of post-Holocaust dialogue between Jews and Christians have something very important to teach us today.

I found myself thinking about this last year after a lecture I gave at a university. A young student approached me afterward and said he wanted to ask me something. He began by saying that he was taking his first course on the Holocaust, but it was a literature course, and he did not know much of the history. The first book they had read was Elie Wiesel's book *Night*. His question to me was: "Is *Night* a true story? Did this really happen as Wiesel describes it?" He had been reading it as a novel, really – as a symbolic reflection on evil loosely based on some past event. He knew a little bit about National Socialism, the war, and the concentration camps, but he had not yet connected the dots between the world Wiesel described in *Night*, the event we describe as the Holocaust, and the history that I had just covered in my lecture about the patterns of prejudice and complicity in German Protestant churches under Nazism.

The conversation struck me because he was being so honest. He was not a denier; he was not on the attack or the defensive. He was being honest about his lack of knowledge – and clearly he had been quite moved by the program that day, which in addition to my talk had also included an interview with a survivor. I had the sense that he came up afterward and asked me privately because he was a bit embarrassed. It is easy to forget that everyone has to start somewhere in examining this history, and the personal impact of the starting point can be life-changing.

The Holocaust ended more than sixty years ago. For today's generation of students, that is ancient history, and the window for an immediate personal connection to this history – especially through the presence and testimony of the survivors – is rapidly closing. And yet: it is heartening and moving for me to see that when students hear the basic facts, or read a book like *Night*, they instinctively recognize the significance of this event. It is striking that at the heart of this historical event there is something so crucial, so troubling, and so universal that millions of people around the world are moved, feel a deeper connection, and many of them try to change something in the way they live, teach, and believe as a result of their encounter with the Holocaust.

This holds true for interreligious dialogue as well. The Holocaust itself was a turning point, a *tremendum*, as Arthur Cohen put it in the title of his book, an event that altered something very profound – as Cohen puts it, an event that "discloses something new about our relation to God and God's relations to creation."[1] In the wake of the Holocaust, we know something new and terrible about the human potential for evil, for depravity, and for many people of faith there are new and terrible questions about God. Where was God as the millions of innocent Jews – children, infants, the elderly, women, and men – were murdered? Can we still think of an all-knowing, all-powerful God at all?

These are troubling questions for people of any faith, but there is an added level of complexity here. Christians can explore these hard questions within their traditions, and Jews can do the same, but in interreligious conversation with one another that hard history is on the table. National Socialism was not an explicitly Christian movement, and many of the factors that brought and kept the Nazis in power had nothing directly to do with religion. And yet there are two facts about the history of Nazi Germany and the Holocaust that are very much related to religion, and they are central to understanding this history and its particular relevance for Christians and Jews. The first is that while the Nazis targeted many groups and there were millions of dead by 1945, the persecution and genocide of the Jews stands apart. It was not a side-effect of something else, but an intentional program of persecution that culminated in an intentional genocide. In Wiesel's words: "Not all victims were Jews, but all Jews were victims." The second fact is that the persecution and genocide of the Jews of Europe had its roots and precedents in the persecution of Jews throughout the history of Christian Europe. All too often this persecution was perpetrated in the name of the Christian tradition. The precedents for the Aryan laws, the ghettos, the pogroms, and the antisemitic rhetoric and imagery that permeated Nazi propaganda begin much, much earlier. The origins of the targeting of Jews in Christian Europe are to be found in the language of some of the gospels and the early church fathers, and the language of prejudice and the rationale for violence reflected that in the centuries that followed. Related to this fact is the actual historical record of Christian responses – in Germany, throughout Europe, and in the USA – between 1933 and 1945 as the Holocaust unfolded. The Holocaust was perpetrated by a nation that was civilized, highly educated, and predominantly Christian (over 95 percent). It unfolded on a continent that was predominantly Christian.

The sheer scope of this genocide, particularly the widespread patterns of complicity between 1933 and 1945, raise profound questions about human beings and what we are capable of, about what it means to be a citizen, about how to prevent our civil society from such a descent into barbarity. But it is worth reviewing the very particular questions this history raises for Christians. These questions are both theological and political, but they need to be addressed from the foundation of the history itself. An overview of the history of Protestant and Catholic responses to National Socialism (both from within Germany and internationally) is clearly beyond the scope of this essay, but the main points raised by this history are:

- **The legitimization of the Nazi state by Church cooperation and statements of support**
  Both the Protestant and Catholic leadership in Nazi Germany made agreements with the state and cooperated with the new regime. While in some cases Church leaders may have viewed this as a strategically necessary step that did not reflect a full embrace of National Socialist ideology, the bottom line was that such agreements – as well as photographs of Church leaders meeting with Hitler, giving the Nazi salute, etc. – served to legitimize this regime in the eyes of the average believer. Moreover, there were open and early statements of support for National Socialism, particularly from within the Protestant Churches. Even where they disagreed with the state on something, Protestant leaders were quick to emphasize their patriotism and basic loyalty to the regime. In 1934, the Protestant theologian Dietrich Bonhoeffer wrote: "We are immediately faced with the decision: National Socialist or Christian."[2] But very, very few Christians drew this clear choice.
- **The lack of Church protest against the persecution of the Jews**
  Certainly the most shameful aspect of this history is not only the lack of protest, but the statements by German Protestant Church leaders that actually defended the Nazi anti-Jewish laws, and the numerous statements that rationalized National Socialist policies.[3] Where the Churches spoke out in protest at all, it was usually on behalf of Christians of Jewish descent and Jews who had converted to Christianity. While there were protests against Nazi antisemitism that came from abroad, notably from Protestant ecumenical leaders in the United States and Great Britain,[4] these were exceptions that drew little support from the broad membership of those Churches.
- **Involvement of practicing Christians in the genocide**
  The persecution and genocide of the Jews covered a number of years and spanned an entire continent. It would not have been possible without the complicity and active involvement of numerous populations, predominantly Christian, throughout Europe.
- **The question of how we understand and interpret the phenomenon of rescue and resistance**
  There were clearly individuals and groups that attempted – some on the basis of their beliefs – to resist National Socialism and save its

victims. These people illustrate that rescue and resistance were possible, and they highlight the much more widespread phenomenon of complicity and cooperation. Particularly in Nazi Germany, they had to act alone, often without the support (and sometimes even with the opposition) of Church leaders.[5] This history must be included in its full complexity when we look at the role of Christianity and its followers during this period.

The historical particularity of these questions shapes the particularity of post-Holocaust interreligious dialogue. These historical challenges underscore the challenges to rebuilding the Christian-Jewish relationship and addressing this event from within the context of faith. In the wake of the Holocaust, Christians who enter the interfaith conversation face numerous challenges:

- Integrating a post-Holocaust understanding as we address contemporary issues;
- Articulating an internal Christian critique and new readings of difficult texts;
- Confronting the larger ethical and theological questions;
- The question of guilt and how it is addressed, both historically and theologically;
- Articulating post-Holocaust understandings of "evil," "forgiveness," and "reconciliation";
- The theodicy question: where was God during the Holocaust? How does this historical event challenge our traditional understandings of God?
- The issue of evangelization and recognition of other religions.

Thus, Christians and Jews after 1945 had an unprecedented task if they wanted to engage in interreligious dialogue. In 1947, the post-Holocaust question was not a generalized one about the role of religion in violence, but a very specific one about the persecution of one religious group and the complicity of another. Inevitably, however, people in dialogue move from these particular issues to profound universal ones that are important in any interfaith conversation. In the aftermath of the Holocaust, the particular challenge for the Jewish-Christian relationship was twofold: 1) to establish and acknowledge the historical record of what happened; 2) to explore honestly what this history meant for the interfaith relationship.

In other words, history always needs to be on the table. It was on the table at the 1947 conference in Seelisberg, Switzerland, which was a remarkable meeting of Jews and Christians in the immediate aftermath, and marked the founding of the International

Council of Christians and Jews (ICCJ). The opening sentence of the Seelisberg Declaration was stunning in its honesty:

> We have recently witnessed an outburst of antisemitism which has led to the persecution and extermination of millions of Jews…This would have been impossible if all Christians had been true to the teaching of Jesus Christ on the mercy of God and love of one's neighbour. But this faithfulness should also involve clear-sighted willingness to avoid any presentation and conception of the Christian message which would support antisemitism under whatever form. We must recognise, unfortunately, that this vigilant willingness has often been lacking.[6]

Along with this blunt assessment of Europe's recent past and its present, the Seelisberg authors spoke directly to the issues confronting Christians in the wake of the Holocaust. It was not enough, they said, for Christians to be more faithful to their teachings about loving and showing mercy to their neighbors. In the wake of the Holocaust, Christian Churches needed to "show their members how to prevent any animosity towards the Jews which might arise from false, inadequate or mistaken presentation or conceptions of the teaching and preaching of the Christian doctrine…" This introduction was followed by the "Ten Points of Seelisberg," which specifically cited the most common aspects of Christian doctrine and tradition that have historically been used against the Jews and their faith.

The story of Seelisberg is a remarkable story[7] and the Seelisberg Declaration was a groundbreaking document for many reasons – but the primary one is its early recognition of what the key issues were, and the fact that these remain the key issues today. The Seelisberg authors pinpointed exactly what the challenges are for Christians in a post-Holocaust Jewish-Christian conversation. Sixty-two years later, these challenges remain, and they have surfaced again and again in the intervening decades. The conversation is never easy. If we Christians take these issues seriously, we are called to rethink interpretations of our texts and our faith, and revise the way we worship, our liturgies, our hymns. We are compelled to look at aspects of our history that should provoke deep shame.

There is abundant evidence for the difficulty of this process in the intervening sixty-two years – but there has also been remarkable progress. We now have a solid foundation of scholarship on the Holocaust across the different disciplines – such as history, philosophy, theology, sociology – that has established a firm academic foundation for discussing these issues. In many places, this scholarship has emerged in a larger context of Christian and Jewish scholars coming together to address the Holocaust.

Just as importantly, there now exists a huge number of statements and reflections by the leadership of different Churches, as well as interreligious statements that attest both to the profound nature of the Holocaust and the serious questions it poses for people of faith. If you go to the ICCJ website (www.jcrelations.net), you will find the list and texts of all the corresponding statements that have been made, beginning with Seelisberg, as well as a number of articles and other documents that lend insight not just into the post-Holocaust conversations, but into the topic of interreligious dialogue in general. This list includes some momentous turning points:

- The section on Judaism in the 1965 statement titled *Nostra Aetate* from the Second Vatican Council, which redefined the relationship between Catholics and Jews;
- The 1981 Rhineland synod statement within the Evangelical Church of Germany, in which that Church for the first time acknowledged the enduring validity of God's covenant with the Jewish people;
- The repudiation in 1994 of Martin Luther's anti-Jewish writings by the Evangelical Lutheran Church of America (made after a visit to the Holocaust Museum in Washington by the leadership of that Church);
- The numerous statements in 1995 by the European Churches of Poland, Germany, France, and elsewhere on the fiftieth anniversary of the liberation of Auschwitz;
- The 2009 declaration (the "Twelve Points of Berlin") made by the International Conference of Christians and Jews as a reaffirmation of the Seelisberg Declaration.

Not all the turning points have been in the form of statements. Some of them are crucial symbolic acts, such as the visits to Auschwitz and Jerusalem by Pope John Paul II. And while there have been a number of turning points, there have also been stumbling blocks. These stumbling blocks arise, I think, when history is taken off the table – when the lessons of the Churches' history during the Holocaust are bypassed, when antisemitism is tolerated or ignored. This was particularly evident during 2009 in the controversy about Bishop Richard Williamson.

This reminds us that Holocaust history and interfaith dialogue are interconnected – one can only have an honest, productive conversation when there is agreement on what has happened – but the second, interfaith dialogue, is the most difficult. A central reason that it is so difficult is that interreligious dialogue is not just about faith questions. It is always very much a part of larger conversations about how people of different faiths live together in the world, how they shape their societies, and how they address the big questions of their time. The turning points for post-Holocaust Christian-Jewish dialogue include Vatican II, the 1981 Rhineland Synod, and the numerous Church declarations in 1995 on the anniversary of the liberation of Auschwitz. But there are other turning points – some of them very specific events –

that are not "religious" events, but they have a profound, and sometimes damaging, impact on the interfaith conversation. Any statement today on Jewish-Christian relations comes not only in the wake of the Holocaust, but in the wake of other world events and whatever crises and controversies have arisen in the meantime. That list is very long indeed, but it includes specific controversies over the Mel Gibson film, *The Passion of the Christ*, and the ongoing discussion over the role of Pius XII during the Holocaust. It includes larger world events, such as the painful and protracted conflict in the Middle East, the end of the Cold War, and of course the events of September 11, 2001. The very term "interfaith dialogue" today means something different than it meant fifty years ago, for throughout the world, but especially in North America and in Europe, it has expanded to include members of all faiths, particularly Muslims.

There are numerous contentious issues that test the potential, flexibility, and durability of interfaith dialogue while at the same time proving the absolute necessity of such dialogue. We often think of the primary goal of interfaith dialogue as "understanding" one another, but an equally important but oft-overlooked aspect is *that it facilitates the process of change within traditions*, and this is certainly proven by the post-Holocaust dialogue. Partners in a dialogue cannot be honest without being changed – and this is true both for individuals and institutions. In that context, one sees that all the post-Holocaust statements – from Seelisberg to Berlin – are simply marking points within that process. To some extent they build upon each other; sometimes they even argue with each other. If we examine the trajectory of the statements on the ICCJ website (www.jcrelations.net), we see arguments emerging. The 1998 Vatican statement *We Remember: A Reflection on the Shoah*, for example, elicited statements from the Jewish community that were both affirming and critical. This is all part of the process.

And it is precisely that aspect of the interfaith process that makes us and our religious bodies capable of addressing the important issues. As the delegates in Seelisberg knew, when something crucial is kept off the table – because it is going to be a difficult issue, or it is going to be a hard sell because it may challenge an integral aspect of tradition – the dialogue suffers. The most divisive and contentious issues are the ones we most need to talk about. And the other thing is that the voices of those who have suffered must be there. The truth cannot come out if we are talking *about* someone but not *with* them.

We know these things, especially if we are in the field of Holocaust education. The process begun at Seelisberg is farther down the road. Interfaith dialogue, even between Christians and Jews, is about many things, not just the Holocaust. And the interesting thing is that when we look at the "Twelve Points of Berlin," we see how the foundation of post-Holocaust dialogue laid at Seelisberg has laid the groundwork for Jews and Christians to address current crises – from the Middle East to environmental issues – together and in a new way.

Turning Points and Next Steps

Interfaith dialogue is about many things, and even Jewish-Christian dialogue is about other things besides the Holocaust. In the decades to come, this will be more and more the case. Those of us whose work is in Holocaust study and education need to recognize that, but we also need to find ways to ensure that knowledge of the Holocaust, and an understanding of the centrality of its legacy, is a cornerstone of working on this relationship. We know why the Holocaust is important to us. But we need to remember that the importance of the Holocaust is not self-evident to people who are first encountering it. And yet, if we teach it correctly, if we find a way to articulate why it is important, and why the Holocaust must be understood in its uniqueness, particularly with regard to interfaith issues, then we will have ensured that our students approach the big issues of their times with integrity and respect for this history, and in a way that honors those who died in the Holocaust.

Questions

1. *What are some of the "turning points" in religious consciousness that have occurred as a result of the Holocaust?*

2. *What does a "post-Holocaust" understanding mean for you?*

3. *Looking at the different post-Holocaust statements (at http://www.jcrelations.net/en/?area=Statements), where in your opinion do they "succeed"? Where could they be improved? What issues do they address? What issues don't they address?*

4. *Why is the study of the Holocaust important today, when there are so many other pressing issues that create interreligious tension?*

Bibliography

Boys, Mary C., ed. *Seeing Judaism Anew: Christianity's Sacred Obligation*. New York: Rowman and Littlefield Publishers, Inc., 2005.

Boys, Mary C. and Sara S. Lee. *Christians and Jews in Dialogue: Learning in the Presence of the Other*. Woodstock, Vermont: Sky Light Paths Publishing, 2006.

Frymer-Kensky, Tikva, with David Novak, Peter Ochs, David Sandmel, and Michael Signer, eds. *Christianity in Jewish Terms*. Boulder, Colorado: Westview Press, 2000.

Pawlikowski, John T. and Eugene B. Korn, eds. *Two Faiths, One Covenant? Jewish and Christian Identity in the Presence of the Other*. New York: Rowman & Littlefield Publishers, Inc., 2005.

Notes

1. Arthur Cohen, *The Tremendum: a Theological Interpretation of the Holocaust* (New York: Crossroad Publishing Company, 1981), p. 52.
2. Dietrich Bonhoeffer, *London: 1933–1935* (Minneapolis: Fortress Press, 2008), p. 192.
3. See, for example, Victoria Barnett, *For the Soul of the People* (Oxford University Press, 1992); Doris Bergen, *Twisted Cross* (University of North Carolina Press, 1996); Wolfgang Gerlach, *And the Witnesses were Silent* (University of Nebraska Press, 2000).
4. See two features about this on the USHMM website: http://www.ushmm.org/research/center/presentations/features/details/2006-04-27/ and http://www.ushmm.org/research/center/church/kristallnacht/.
5. See, for example, chapters 6, 7, and 9 in my book, *For the Soul of the People*.
6. This and the following quotations are from the Seelisberg Declaration, the full text of which can be found at http://www.jcrelations.net/en/?item=983.
7. There are two articles about the Seelisberg conference in the online journal, *Studies in Christian-Jewish Relations:* http://escholarship.bc.edu/scjr/vol2/iss2/.

The Memory of the Holocaust: Challenges to Twenty-First Century Christians and Jews

■ ■ ■ ■ ■ ■ ■ ■ ■ ■ ■ ■

Michael Berenbaum

Professor of Jewish Studies and Director of the Sigi Ziering Institute:
Exploring the Ethical and Religious Implications of the Holocaust,
American Jewish University, Los Angeles, CA

We live at a transitional moment for the entire field of Holocaust Studies, and most especially for Jews and Roman Catholics. As everyone who works in this field knows, survivors are all too rapidly passing from the scene and after they are gone, the Holocaust will move from living memory into historical memory. And for Jews and Roman Catholics, the generation that went through the revolution of Vatican II, who instinctively grasped the important and transformative character of *Nostra Aetate*, are swiftly entering the years of retirement. What was once at the forefront of religious consciousness is now receding as other issues have come to take its place.

Fundamentalism without Demonization

The issue that I want to examine is perhaps the central religious issue of our age, perhaps also the contemporary world's most important political issue that may well decide our fate in the new millennia: *Can we embrace fundamentalism within our own tradition and still accept the "other" as "brother/sister"?* Can we use the tools of our own tradition to move beyond the notion of tolerance into acceptance of an underlying religious embrace of the "other"? Or must we resort to those parts of our tradition – each of our traditions – that demonize the "other," that deny the "other," that cannot recognize in the "other" one of God's creation? I know of no issue more central to the world today, one that may well determine our collective future.

In my own work, I have written time and again that the post-Holocaust Roman Catholic Church is the model of how a religious tradition can use its own tools of interpretation to transform long-established religious teaching.[1]

The Guilt of the Innocent

There is a paradox of the post-Holocaust world: the innocent feel guilty and the guilty innocent. Let me illustrate. First, there is a well developed literature of survival guilt, far more developed than the psychological literature of perpetrators who have their dreams disrupted at night and who feel plagued by pangs of guilt over their wartime behavior.[2] Secondly, there is no generation more innocent than the third generation of Germans, grandchildren of perpetrators; they did not perpetrate the Holocaust. They were born long after, yet they – unlike their grandparents – feel responsible for the Holocaust and want to learn about it. Three out of four Germans who attended *Schindler's List* were under the age of thirty. German college students flocked to hear Daniel Jonah Goldhagen's lectures after he wrote *Hitler's Willing Executioners*, which blamed the antisemitism of the German people, and not only its Nazi leadership, for the slaughter of the Jews. They visit the death camps and study the event.

In the Roman Catholic Church, the greatest strides in Catholic-Jewish relations in the entire two millennia of that relationship were made by the initiative of two popes who were innocent during the *Shoah* and yet who felt responsible for the Holocaust – Pope John XXIII and Pope John Paul II.

A word about Pope John XXIII: As Apostolic Delegate in Istanbul, the then Archbishop Angelo Roncalli worked with the delegates of the Yishuv, the Jewish leadership in Palestine – the name of pre-state Israel – to warn the Jews of Hungary and to rescue some who could be rescued. He established direct communication with its formal leaders in Turkey and even met with clandestine operatives. He did not, as widely rumored, offer false baptismal certificates, but rather something a bit more clever – letters indicating that the holder of this certificate was a "co-religionist and fellow countryman of Jesus" and "*should be* entitled to Vatican protection." Notice the language – co-religionist and fellow countryman is another reference to Jews. "*Should be*" entitled to Vatican protection does not mean that the holder is entitled to Vatican protection. It suggests a tone of aspiration rather than actual fact. He wrote to Bulgarian leaders, where he had previously served, urging them to protect their Jews.[3]

Elected as an interim, caretaker pope in January 1959 after the long pontificate of Pope Pius XII, Pope John XXIII met with the French historian Jules Isaac in June 1960 and studied the history of antisemitism. He then took the bold initiative of placing a consideration of the Church's teachings regarding the Jews before Vatican

II, and among its important initiatives were *Nostra Aetate*, which used the tools of Catholic teaching to revamp the Church's teaching on the Jews. He then institutionalized that transformation by changing Good Friday liturgy and its scriptural reading.

In essence, Vatican II taught what critical historical scholarship had established long ago – that Jews were not responsible for the crucifixion of Christ. Sin was. If Christ died for our sins, if his death were a sacrificial atonement, then without human sin, there would be no need for such atonement. Furthermore, Good Friday liturgy eliminated the reference to perfidious Jews and Matthew 27:25, in which Jews are said to have accepted responsibility on themselves and their children for the crucifixion.

Teaching was combined with gesture, doctrine with human contact. Pope John XXIII stopped at the great synagogue of Rome and greeted its worshipers leaving Sabbath prayers, wishing them a "good Shabbat."[4] It was an unprecedented step for the Bishop of Rome, the heir of St. Peter, to visit the Jews of Rome. It had simply never been done before.

Thus, Pope John XXIII came to terms with 1,878 years of Jewish life in exile – the years from 70 C.E. when the Second Temple was destroyed to 1948 when the state of Israel was established. He stopped short of recognizing the state of Israel, the most visible form that Jewish life had taken in the post-Holocaust era. During the papacy of Pope Paul VI, the statements of Vatican II were promulgated, including *Nostra Aetate*, and much of the work implementing these transformations made its way down Church bureaucracy and into Roman Catholic education. Pope Paul VI visited the Holy Land in 1964, but took every conceivable step not to recognize the state of Israel. He even entered the country by a non-border crossing – a special path was created on Mt. Zion – and scrupulously avoided addressing its political leadership by title.

Pope John Paul II

Pope John Paul II took the transformations initiated by Pope John XXIII another series of steps further.

A word of biography is in order. John Paul II is probably the first pope who could truthfully say that "some of my best friends are Jewish," and mean it literally. He was in direct contact with Jews during his pre-priesthood days and knew them from the soccer fields, where he often played on the Jewish side when they were short of a player, to the university and the theater; one local was among his closest friends and remained a friend throughout the pontiff's long life.[5]

Yaffa Eliach has documented in legendary form that when still a parish priest, Karol Józef Wojtyła refused to baptize Jewish children who had been saved by Polish – Roman Catholic – families when their parents were deported in 1942–43, unless they were informed that their biological parents had been Jews. This was an act of singular integrity and, in fact, it was not quite in keeping with the instructions of the post-war Church that was interested in saving the souls of all people – including, perhaps even especially, Jewish children. It was also an act of courage, as his parishioners must have felt this conversation burdensome.[6] Allow me to explain.

If you trusted a neighbor with your child's life and your child had a certain type of appearance, meaning that they did not look "too Jewish" and they were pre-verbal, Jewish parents might ask a Polish family to take care of their child while they were about to be deported. The child could not be told that he or she was Jewish then, as the information would be lethal to the child and also to the family that was sheltering him/her. If the parents returned, the child might not remember them or even recognize them. Often the child had been treated with love and responded in kind, feeling his/her parents to be strangers who had abandoned him/her – remember, feelings are not logical – and loving his adopted family. Even if the parents survived, the child often wanted to stay put. Even after the war, it became dangerous to reveal to a child that he or she was Jewish as this might lead to the parents being labeled as "Jew lovers" and to their ostracism. As a result, such information was not easily revealed, but Father Wojtyła insisted.

As Pope, Father Wojtyła, now John Paul II, visited the Roman synagogue and met with the community and its Chief Rabbi who was attired in the traditional Jewish prayer shawl. In his remarks Pope John Paul said:

> All that remains for me now, as at the beginning of my address, is to turn my eyes and my mind to the Lord, to thank Him and praise Him for this joyful meeting and for the good things which are already flowing from it, for the rediscovered brotherhood and for the new and more profound understanding between us here in Rome, and between the Church and Judaism everywhere, in every country, for the benefit of all.

He recited part of a psalm in the original Hebrew:

> *hodû la-Adonai ki tob*
> *ki le-olam hasdô*
> *yomar-na Yisrael*
> *ki le-olam hasdô*
> *yomerû-na yir'è Adonai*
> *ki le-olam hasd. (Ps. 118:1–2.4)*

> O give thanks to the Lord for He is good,
> His steadfast love endures for ever.
> Let Israel say,
> "His steadfast love endures for ever!"
> Let those who fear the Lord say,

"His steadfast love endures for ever!"
Amen.

Pope John Paul II treated the synagogue as a house of God and the Chief Rabbi of Rome as a fellow religious leader. He established diplomatic relations with Israel and went to Israel in 2000, visiting both Yad Vashem and the Western Wall. At Yad Vashem, he condemned antisemitism in the name of the Church. He said: "As bishop of Rome and successor of the Apostle Peter, I assure the Jewish people that the Catholic Church, motivated by the Gospel law of truth and love, and by no political considerations, is deeply saddened by the hatred, acts of persecution and displays of anti-Semitism directed against the Jews by Christians at any time and in any place."

A man of the theater, he well understood that "the media is the message" and that his words would echo throughout the Christian world. His letter inserted into the Western Wall bears reiteration:

> *God of our fathers,*
> *You chose Abraham and his descendants*
> *to bring Your name to the Nations:*
> *we are deeply saddened*
> *by the behaviour of those*
> *who in the course of history*
> *have caused these children of Yours to suffer,*
> *and asking Your forgiveness*
> *we wish to commit ourselves*
> *to genuine brotherhood*
> *with the people of the Covenant.*
>
> *Jerusalem, March 26, 2000*
> *Signed: John Paul II*

Though he did not say everything I would have liked him to have said, what he said was all important, and the place from which he uttered these statements was even more symbolic. Pope John Paul II visited the Western Wall, the holiest site of Judaism, and by his visit recognized the form that Judaism took after the destruction of the Second Temple in the year 70 C.E. He placed a prayer into the wall, as is the custom of the devout. His visit to the office of the Chief Rabbinate, certainly not the most ecumenical of religious offices in the world, was also compelling. Prepared by Jewish history and memory, the rabbis expected polemics, great disputations. Instead, he greeted them as one religious leader to another. The rabbis were shocked at how moved they were by the Pope's visit. Not all problems were solved, not all issues were settled, but there was tremendous progress and unprecedented warmth in Jewish-Roman Catholic relations.

We should note that the progress in Jewish-Catholic relations has been marked by a severe degradation of Jewish-Muslim relations, and also an equally serious lack of understanding within the Muslim world of the transformations that have taken place in Jewish-Christian relations. This was nowhere more evident than in the welcoming remarks to Pope John Paul II by Syrian President Bashar Al-Assad, who said on May 5, 2001: "They [Israelis and Jews] try to kill all the principles of divine faiths with the same mentality of betraying Jesus Christ and torturing Him and in the same way that they tried to commit treachery against Prophet Mohammad."[7] The London-educated Syrian President had no idea that the Roman Catholic Church had changed its teachings.

For me, the most important impact of all these changes has been their institutionalization, including the changes of liturgy and of educational instruction. An anecdote may suffice as an illustration. I was giving a lecture on the history of antisemitism some twenty-five years ago when a student interrupted me and asked me what I meant by "Jews as Christ-killers." I paused for a moment and asked her to tell me about her background, which consisted of twelve years of Roman Catholic parochial school education and two years at Georgetown University. Sensing something important, I asked the class how many other students were graduates of Roman Catholic parochial schools, and about forty students raised their hands. I asked them, "How many of you have heard of Jews as Christ-killers?" To my amazement, no one raised their hand. I then asked the class for Jewish students to raise their hands – something I had never done before. Ten students raised their hands. And I asked them, "How many of you have heard of Jews as Christ-killers?" All raised their hands. I was startled, for it seemed as if within one generation, an entire tradition that I had assumed was basic to Roman Catholic teaching had no longer been transmitted. That was the impact of *Nostra Aetate* and its institutionalization within the Church.

I met the venerable President of Georgetown, the late Tim Healy S.J., and related the story excitedly to him. He responded: "Michael, hold your enthusiasm for a moment and go ask your students how many of them have heard of Martin Luther. And I can assure you that the Church has not changed its teachings regarding Luther."

Thus, for me, the Roman Catholic Church is the most important model of what a religious institution can do when it confronts a religious teaching that could be used to vilify the "other" and decides to de-emphasize those teachings, however central, to re-interpret them and re-emphasize other parts of the tradition that embrace the "other." By deed, by gesture, by proclamation, by catechism, by human relationship and, above all, by religious conviction, that is what the Roman Catholic Church has done in the last third of the twentieth century.

A New Generation Has Arisen

So much for the good news. Why the concern today? Why the unease?

A new generation of leadership has arisen within the Roman Catholic Church; a new pope has come to the throne of St. Peter and, with his ascension, a new religious agenda. The generation shaped by *Nostra Aetate* is slowly passing from the scene, and certainly from the position of institutional power, we are hard pressed to think of their replacements. Who will replace my friend Father John Pawlikowski O.S.M., or Professor Carol Rittner R.S.M.?

I will speak frankly; in truth I know of no other way of speaking. After the papacy of Pope John Paul II, Jews were bound to be disappointed in the election of any new pope. Few had, and few could have, Pope John Paul II's feel for the Jewish experience.

Jews are concerned about the papacy of Pope Benedict XVI, not because he is not Pope John Paul II, not because he is German, and not because he seems to be charting a religious agenda and a new Orthodoxy, but because that religious agenda has become primary and the initiatives of outreach to the Jews have receded into the background.

As a Jew who prays daily in Hebrew and who routinely attends religious services in synagogues throughout the world, I well understand the importance of the Latin Mass and the desire of a new generation to return to this traditional liturgy. Even the most liberal and least Orthodox of Jewish denominations have returned to the Holy Tongue for prayer, understanding full well that while the vernacular provides accessibility, it comes with the loss of mystery. The debasement of language in our day makes it ever more difficult to pray in the vernacular tongue, ever more difficult to hear the sacred in a language that has been profaned. Wherever I pray, I pray in Hebrew, so I well understand the needs of a universal Church that must provide prayers accessible to parishioners wherever they travel in our global universe. I admire the return to tradition and the attempt to reach out to the more devout, more traditional of believers. And yet the return to the prayer for the conversion of the Jews deeply offends Jews, perhaps even in ways that we should not be offended.[8]

Conversion today is the option of free men and women seeking to understand God and tradition, and to find an institution that makes God's presence manifest and a tradition that is meaningful and accessible. It was not so for millennia when conversion had the feel of coercion and came with rewards for the convert as the handicap of Jewish restrictions were broken and at least partial acceptance was possible. Yet we believing Jews feel our faith and our tradition are disrespected by those seeking to convert us. Seemingly, they say to us that our path to God is not legitimate; our Torah is not the word of God, and our faith inadequate, inferior.

John Cuddihy once wrote of the ordeal of civility as the cost of modernity.[9] There are things we believe that we cannot say, and in the interreligious sphere that means muting some of each tradition's most divisive teaching: for Jews the idea of chosenness is muted in the public sphere, de-emphasized, re-interpreted, by some even abandoned.

Before the events and the interreligious progress of the past half century, it was commonplace even in mainline Protestant faith to teach that "there is no path to the Father save through the Son," and in Roman Catholicism, what is best left unsaid is that "there is no salvation outside the Church."[10]

We can well understand the desire of Pope Benedict XVI, a traditionalist pope, to heal the divide in the Church caused by the followers of Archbishop Lefebvre; that is his prerogative. But we all now know that welcoming the schismatic, Holocaust-denying Bishop Richard Williamson back into the Church was a mistake by the Vatican. The Vatican seemed to be caught off guard by Williamson's history of Holocaust denial that was readily available on the Internet and was seemingly unaware of the variety of peculiar statements that he has made.[11]

I am not a veteran Vatican-watcher by any means. But Bishop Williamson's statements were available to anyone who could use Google. His record is long and his comments, not only with regard to Holocaust denial, have been explosive. So we are left with three choices:

- The Pope knew of his record and was insensitive to its importance, which would be a mistake of monumental proportions; or
- Someone in the Vatican knew and was so interested in the return of the traditionalists that he chose not to inform the Pope lest it endanger the agenda he was advancing;
- That no one in a position of responsibility in the Vatican did his homework is simply impossible to believe. This last possibility should be far more worrisome to Roman Catholics than to Jews.

We should note that the Pope and the Vatican took all the right moves and made all the proper statements regarding Holocaust denial after the Williamson problem emerged. Jews are quite mindful that it was done not in response to Jewish pressure, but immediately after German Chancellor Angela Merkel made her important comments and virtually insisted that the Pope act. His actions had the feel of damage control rather than proper positive action. I think what happened is deeply troublesome. This problem was quite unexpected, especially since the previous pope had made explicit reference to the Holocaust and had been most sensitive to Jewish suffering.

Holocaust Denial

We have seen a variety of forms of Holocaust denial in the contemporary world. I am ordinarily less concerned by the hard-core denial represented by Bishop Williamson, precisely because it has been discredited completely, most especially in the self-inflicted defeat of David Irving in Irving v. Lipstadt in London.[12] There is a more prevalent form that morphs into antisemitism, the all too facile comparisons of the

Israelis to the Nazis, and what happened in Gaza or Jenin before that to the "Final Solution." For the Europeans, it is an alleviation of guilt and a soft-core denial of the Holocaust. If Israelis are Nazis, then the behavior of Europeans a generation ago is less objectionable, less morally reprehensible.

Holocaust denial in the Muslim world is different from Holocaust denial in the West. The latter seek to rehabilitate the good name of Hitler and to cleanse fascism of its bad name. In the Islamic world, denial of the Holocaust seeks to undo what they regard as the most important outcome of the Holocaust, the establishment of the state of Israel. Their Holocaust denial is not about history; it is about wishing away, imagining away, a country that some would wish out of existence. It combines two of the three elements that distinguish legitimate objections to Israeli policies from antisemitism – delegitimization and demonization. If Israel is Nazi-like, it is demonic; if the Israelis are the new Nazis, then Israel itself is illegitimate.

There is an old Hasidic story about a town whose drinking water was poisoned. Anyone who drank the water went mad. The town came to its rebbe and asked him: "What are we to do? If we do not drink the water, we die; yet if we drink the water, we go mad."

The rebbe pondered the question for a moment and then turned to his *gabbai*, his closest disciple. He said: "Give me a brush and some paint." His disciples were startled but complied with his request. He quickly drew a circle on the forehead of his *gabbai* and insisted that the *gabbai* paint a circle on the rebbe's forehead. He turned to the community and said: "Drink the water! But when you look at him, and when you look at me remember, we are mad."

If you want to know the condition of our world today: remember we are mad. The President of Iran, whose country was innocent and the behavior of his countrymen compassionate during the Holocaust – no Jews were harmed and Iran was a way station on the path to safety in Palestine – says that the Holocaust did not happen; and the President of Germany, whose country perpetrated the Holocaust, responds: "Oh yes, it did, and we know because we did it and we cannot face our future without admitting the crime of our past."

Who should deny the Holocaust: the President of Iran or the President of Germany?

Clearly, it would serve the President of Germany to lie; after all, his nation is still tainted by that crime. And who has no stake in denying the Holocaust? The President of Iran! After all, his nation was untouched by the evil that enveloped Europe and his people provided relief for some Jews; Iranian Jews continued to live in peace while the Jews of Europe were decimated. If Christian Europe killed its Jews, what is the stake of a Muslim in Iran in denying what happened? Holocaust denial in the Muslim world is different from Holocaust denial in the West. There are two different denials, two very different agendas. We would be wise to distinguish between the two and not to forge a common alliance between the two.

Canonization of Pope Pius XII

Ordinarily, those of another faith have no right to enter into a discussion as to whom the Church chooses to canonize. It is no secret between us that Jews oppose the canonization of Pope Pius XII. The historical record is incomplete; the archives are still closed to independent researchers who can have unhindered access to its contents. I for one would like to know the answer to the famous Watergate questions: What did Pope Pius XII know and when did he know it? Priests were present in each sector of the war, in the communities throughout Europe from which Jews were deported, and even in the vicinity of the death camps. The German Army had Roman Catholic chaplains. Neutral throughout the war, the Vatican had a diplomatic presence everywhere that could report information back to the Holy See. Pope Pius XI had left an unsigned and unissued encyclical explicitly condemning antisemitism when he died in 1939. It became known as the Hidden Encyclical.[13] It remained unissued by his successor Pope Pius XII, who made but two public and elliptical references to the fate of the Jews during the war. Even when Jews were being deported from Rome, the Vatican did not publicly condemn the deportations. It did provide shelter to some. Other Roman Catholic institutions behaved far more courageously.

With Vatican archives closed, Susan Zuccotti[14] tried to track what local Church leaders sent to the Pope – presuming correctly that local Church archives kept copies of all such correspondence – and what correspondents received in turn from the Vatican. Individual priests and nuns behaved courageously and rescued Jews. They did so without Vatican sanction. Papal nuncios who acted against the Jews were never formally disciplined, as were diplomats from other countries. The President of Slovakia was a Roman Catholic priest and Slovakia, under his leadership, not only deported the Jews to the death camps but paid the Germans to take them.

For most Jews, Pope Pius XII failed the test in our greatest hour of need. I know of few who would not celebrate the canonization of Pope John XXIII or Pope John Paul II. The canonization of Pope Pius XII is truly not about the Jews; it is about the Church and the moral leadership it admires. Still we feel that it is about the Jews; and therefore, we are pained by the intensification of the pace of his canonization. It seems – and we may be wrong – that it is a race against time to make him a saint before the archives are opened, before the truth can be told.

I do not envy any political or religious leader who must follow the long and successful career of a charismatic predecessor. In the rabbinate, such successors usually leave their congregations disappointed. So while I deeply admire the intellectual depth and sophistication of Pope Benedict XVI, I must observe that even where he has followed the path of his predecessor, it was not quite the same. Benedict XVI went to Israel. He visited Yad Vashem. His words were carefully chosen, appropriately chosen. His condemnation of Holocaust denial should have been warmly welcomed, as the words condemning antisemitism by Pope John Paul II were so very well received. Yet coming after the Bishop Williamson flap, the pontiff's words had the feel of damage control; coming after Pope John Paul II's visit to Israel at the turn of the millennium, they were somewhat of a disappointment. But we must all understand that religious leaders with the charisma and charm, media presence, and historical smarts of Pope John Paul II do not come along often. So, too, Pope Benedict XVI's visit to the Rome synagogue, which came after the conversion controversy. We should welcome such visits, even welcome their becoming routine.

Our Common Task

I have outlined the problems afflicting Catholic-Jewish relations, with a brief aside to the history and the opportunities that were created by the last generation. But we are in a transitional moment and we – those gathered at this conference and those who will read its proceedings – must make that transition happen and minimize the loss of a passing generation. Your work is all important. You have understood the importance of the Holocaust, its educational power in the classroom. You have understood how vital the strides have been over the past generation in Jewish-Catholic relations, and our hosts at Seton Hill have had the foresight and the imagination to institutionalize these changes in their widely respected Center for Holocaust Education.

Your work – our work – is vital precisely as the pioneers leave the scene, and as we, the successor generation, must stand in their place. Together, there is much that can be done, much that must be done. And we must do it together. We have a legacy to protect and a task to perform.

The survivors have been the example of how to transform suffering into witness. We must be the witnesses of the witnesses and transform division and hatred into recognition that the "other" is our brother and sister, that we can be true to our faith and embrace all of God's creatures. Our students need to learn that as counter-testimony to the hatred and rage of our time.

Questions

1. *How can religious leaders and teachers help their congregants and students to develop "faith without prejudice"?*

2. *In addition to* Nostra Aetate, *what are some of the other major documents issued by the Vatican that encourage better understanding among Roman Catholics about Jews and Judaism? Are there any documents issued by Protestant traditions that also encourage better understanding among Protestant Christians about Jews and Judaism?*

3. *Does your diocese or local synod have statements for congregants and students in Sunday schools and religious education classes that encourage better relations between and among Jews and Christians, both Roman Catholic and Protestant Christians?*

Bibliography

Accattoli, Luigi. *When A Pope Asks Forgiveness: The Mea Culpa's of John Paul II*. Boston: Pauline Books & Media, 1998.

Berenbaum, Michael, ed., *Not Your Father's Antisemitism: Hatred of the Jews in the 21st Century*. St. Paul, MN: Paragon House, 2008.

Cunningham, Philip A. *A Story of Shalom: The Calling of Christians and Jews by a Covenanting God*. Mahwah, NJ: Paulist Press, 2001.

Dulles, Avery S.J. and Leon Klenicki, eds. *The Holocaust, Never to Be Forgotten: Reflections on the Holy See's Document 'We Remember'*. Mahwah, NJ: Paulist Press, 2000.

Fisher, Eugene. *Faith Without Prejudice: Rebuilding Christian Attitudes Toward Judaism*. New York: Paulist Press, 1977.

Zuccotti, Susan. *Under His Very Windows: The Vatican and the Holocaust in Italy*. New Haven and London: Yale University Press, 2000.

Notes

1. "The Cross and the Crescent: Antisemitism in Contemporary Islam," in Michael Berenbaum, ed., *Not Your Father's Antisemitism: Hatred of the Jews in the 21st Century* (St. Paul, MN: Paragon House, 2008), pp. 153–154. See also Michael Berenbaum, *The World Must Know: The History of the Holocaust As Told in the United States Holocaust Memorial Museum* (Baltimore, MD.: Johns Hopkins University Press, 2006), pp. 153–165.
2. See Jean Amery, *At the Mind's Limit* (New York: Schocken Books, 1986); Zev Harel, Boaz Kahana, and Eva Kahana, "The Effects of the Holocaust: Psychiatric, Behavioral, and Survivor Perspective," *Journal of Sociology and Social Welfare* 11 (1984): 915–929; J. Hassan, "Survivors," *Community Care* (June 1984): 11–14; Henry Krystal, ed., *Massive Psychic Trauma* (New York: International Universities Press, 1968); Lawrence L. Langer, *Holocaust Testimonies* (New Haven and London: Yale University Press, 1991).
3. Michael Bar-Zohar, *Beyond Hitler's Grasp: The Heroic Rescue of Bulgaria's Jews* (Holbrook, MA.: Adams Media Corporation, 1998), pp. 202–203. See also Victoria Barrett, *Desperate Hours: Turkey and the Holocaust* [a film, 2001], interviews with Teddy Kollek and Yehuda Bauer.
4. John Borellis, "Witnessing by Prayer," *America* (October 23, 2006) wrote: "In 1962 Rabbi Toaff had seen Pope John XXIII outside the synagogue in his car blessing Jews as they left services; now he had seen another pope enter the synagogue to pray. In Assisi, John Paul would host an interreligious day of prayer."
5. Gian Franco Svidercoshi, *Letter to a Jewish Friend: The Simple and Extraordinary Story of Pope John Paul II and his Jewish School Friend* (New York: Crossroads, 1994).
6. Yaffa Eliach, "The Tale of a Young Priest," in *Hasidic Tales of the Holocaust* (New York: Oxford University Press, 1982), pp. 142–147.

7. Alessandra Stanley, "Pope, Arriving in Syria, Hears Its Leader Denounce Israel," *New York Times*, May 6, 2001: 1.

8. Editor's Note: The universal permission given to priests by Pope Benedict XVI in 2007 to celebrate the so-called "Tridentine" liturgy resulted in complaints from Jewish groups and some Catholic leaders over what they perceived as a return to a supersessionist theology. In February 2008, Pope Benedict XVI amended the Good Friday prayer for the Jews contained in the Roman Missal of 1962, a prayer many Catholics find as offensive as do Jews.

9. John Murray Cuddihy, *The Ordeal of Civility: Freud, Marx, Levi-Strauss, and the Jewish Struggle with Modernity* (New York: Basic Books, 1974).

10. John Murray Cuddihy, *No Offense: Civil Religion and Protestant Taste* (New York: Seabury Press, 1978); see also Michael Berenbaum, "The Problem of Pluralism in Contemporary Orthodoxy, Policy and Politics," in *After Tragedy and Triumph: Modern Jewish Thought and the American Experience* (Cambridge University Press, 1990), pp. 101–116.

11. See J. Christopher Pryor, "Taken to the Extreme: The Legacy of Bishop Richard Williamson," *The Journal of Antisemitism* (Vol. 1, No 2.), forthcoming.

12. Richard J. Evans, *Lying About Hitler: History, Holocaust, and the David Irving Trial* (New York: Basic Books, 2001); Robert Jan van Pelt, *The Case for Auschwitz: Evidence from the Irving Trial* (Bloomington, IN: Indiana University Press, 2002); Deborah Lipstadt, *My Day in Court with a Holocaust Denier* (New York: Ecco, 2005).

13. George Passellecq and Bernard Suchecky, *The Hidden Encyclical of Pius XI* (New York: Harcourt Brace and Company, 1997).

14. Susan Zuccotti, *Under His Very Windows: The Vatican and the Holocaust in Italy* (New Haven and London: Yale University Press, 2000).

Coming of Age During the Holocaust, Coming of Age Now:[1] Challenges, Opportunities, and Necessities Related to Interreligious Dialogue

■ ■ ■ ■ ■ ■ ■ ■ ■ ■ ■

Elizabeth Edelstein

Director of Education, Museum of Jewish Heritage,
A Living Memorial to the Holocaust, New York, NY

Elena Procario-Foley

Driscoll Professor of Jewish-Catholic Studies, Iona College, New Rochelle, NY

The Curriculum

Holocaust educators are familiar with the many questions they receive concerning age-appropriate Holocaust education. Among these questions, the two that frequently stand out concern the youngest age at which Holocaust education may begin and the materials that can be used at that age. While the question about how early in life Holocaust education should begin will always be debated by parents, educators, and religious leaders, the Museum of Jewish Heritage in New York City – A Living Memorial to the Holocaust has provided an accessible curriculum for young people preparing for a bar or bat mitzvah.[2]

Questions of identity, community, and responsibility are central to any religion. Moreover, Judaism and Christianity share an embattled history concerning these questions that no two other religions share. What if the *Coming of Age* curriculum were used in a Christian context or in a dialogue between Jewish and Christian teenagers? This question prompted us to present the *Coming of Age* curriculum in a workshop setting to educators from both traditions to glean some initial responses. The following will describe the curriculum and offer a perspective on it from the point of view of Catholic religious education and the need for dialogue.

The *Coming of Age* curriculum was created in response to requests from parents and teachers to the Museum to provide a meaningful curriculum for bar and bat mitzvah students. In preparing for a bar or bat mitzvah, a young person is preparing to become a fully recognized member of the Jewish community. What does it mean to be a part of the Jewish community? What responsibilities are involved? These are important questions to consider as one comes of age. One way of being part of a community is to identify with its history and to appreciate its values. By examining how members of our community have responded in moments of great challenge in our communal history, we discover values that will make us stronger individuals and more knowledgeable members of our extended faith community. A threefold outcome is intended by the *Coming of Age* curriculum. First, students reflect deeply on questions of their religious identity, community, and responsibilities in a historical context that will assist them as they engage their journey to become a full member of the Jewish community and a mature, responsible adult in the wider world. Secondly, they learn about the Holocaust – in a particular and dialogic (not comprehensive) key. Lastly, "students will feel that their bar or bat mitzvah experience is enriched."[3]

The method of the curriculum is to stimulate through biography. Students encounter up to thirteen children who were of bar/bat mitzvah age during the Holocaust. Museum staff thought that contemporary bar/bat mitzvah students would benefit from learning about how young people who came of age during the Holocaust dealt with issues of identity, community, and responsibility. There is a workbook particular to each survivor who tells his/her story, and an accompanying DVD that includes interviews with each survivor (some clips are in English – accents vary – while others are in Hebrew with English subtitles).

Coming of Age, however, is not a curriculum that intends to teach about the Holocaust in all of its political and historical dimensions. Rather, in developing it, the Museum worked from the premise that the individual, personal stories about young people would give a focus to students' learning and help make a very broad topic more accessible. Students learn about the Holocaust from people who were their own age when they had to learn to respond to life and death situations, and in so doing decide what their faith community meant to them. One indication of the focus on the personal experiences of the young people whose stories are told throughout the curriculum is the fact that the curriculum uses historically accurate language. In the *Coming of Age* stories, the word "Holocaust" is not used – except in the suggestions in the "for further research" sections. Likewise, the words "survivor" and "rescuer" are not used in the stories when describing the youngsters' own experiences during the war. Although the stories *describe* what we now call the "Holocaust" or "survival" or "courageous acts of rescue by Christians," the language used in the personal narratives and biographical descriptions is historically contemporaneous to the individual survivor's experience. Eschewing the familiar terms of Holocaust studies – survivor, rescuer, bystander, etc. – allows the focus to remain on the individual's personal journey as he or she came of age in horrific circumstances. Today's student is thus able to enter into "conversation" with that individual's experiences and choices almost as a peer, and not as a distant observer of a faraway history. One generation, a generation soon to leave us, teaches lessons to a new generation trying to connect to its tradition, claim its identity, and fulfill its responsibilities in new circumstances.

The thirteen stories that comprise the curriculum reflect a range of experience among Jewish young people during the war. Deliberate choices were made to include the experiences of both boys and girls. People were chosen from a variety of countries because geography, or the social-political history of particular countries, determined to a great extent the wartime experience of individuals. Family religious practice before the war, from orthodox to secular, is represented. The stories also demonstrate some of the different possible experiences of Jewish children during the war – life in a ghetto, life as a partisan, or life as a hidden child saved by a Christian.

Adaptability characterizes the curriculum, allowing for the different circumstances of congregational programs, teaching staffs, and students. While a teacher facilitates logistics and choices and provides a guiding voice, students can work individually, in pairs, or in small groups. Parent participation is also possible. While thirteen workbooks are available, experience has demonstrated that choosing a smaller number of biographies based on the number of students for a semester-long program works best. The seventeen-page workbooks are divided into five "chapters" with "watch and listen" indicators telling students when to view the DVD video clips. Educators and students can choose from a variety of activities located throughout the chapters and at the end of each workbook. Chapters have multiple "think and write" as well as "for your research" boxes. The activities section at the end of each workbook features a mapping exercise, a timeline exercise, a glossary, and a "for further reference" page, all specific to the life of the survivor featured in the story. There are multiple opportunities in each workbook for the student to learn more about the period while reflecting deeply on the choices each featured person encountered as he or she came of age during the Holocaust. The active learning engendered by the curriculum creates an environment for students to integrate profoundly the hard-won lessons of their elders into their emerging young adult identities and into their understanding of community, communal responsibility, and global responsibility.

Finally, it is important to understand the interpretative horizon of the curriculum. The workbooks are organized according to the logic that determines the layout of the permanent exhibit in the Museum. Like visitors to the Museum, readers of the workbook first learn about life before the war. Students get to empathize with the quotidian details of the life a young person led in pre-war Europe – familial, educational, economic, and religious. The narrative then leads the reader into the effects of the war on the individual and the individual's family. The student reads (and listens to) what happened to the survivor during the war years. Lastly, students discover what happened to the young person after the war.

The Possibilities for Interreligious Dialogue

Can this curriculum be used in an interreligious setting? When this question arose, the immediate intuitive response of the present authors was, "Yes!" Though developed to enhance bar/bat mitzvah preparation, the curriculum is poised to provide fruitful opportunities for interreligious dialogue. *Coming of Age* asks bar/bat mitzvah students to probe their moral development as they simultaneously and more thoroughly learn the theology, religious rituals, and expectations of their religion. A similar type of learning is expected of Christian confirmation candidates in general. Since the age for confirmation varies greatly across Christian denominations, this brief review of the issue will focus on Roman Catholicism.

Even within Roman Catholicism, the age of confirmation varies greatly across dioceses. The age may fluctuate slightly within a single diocese. In areas where parishes sponsor confirmation programs for seventh or eighth graders, however, joint synagogue-parish programs could be developed with the *Coming of Age* curriculum.

It has become rather familiar to hear, "[T]here can be no peace among the nations without peace among the religions. There can be no peace among the religions without dialogue between the religions."[4] Since 1965 and the Second Vatican Council's promulgation of *Nostra Aetate*, the Catholic Church has frequently condemned antisemitism, told Catholics that they must learn about Judaism, and acknowledged the shameful history of Christian behavior toward Jews.[5] Courageous Jewish scholars and religious leaders have engaged the dialogue with Catholicism for close to a half century.[6] Yet this effort to strive for peace between the two religions is rarely taught to school-age children and the dialogue is left to academic specialists and religious leaders.

From a Catholic perspective, the situation is perplexing since the highest levels of authority call for Catholics to be educated about Judaism (as for example in the documents listed in note 5), but such education is haphazardly achieved, if at all.[7] For instance, the *National Directory for Catechesis* issued by the United States Conference of Catholic Bishops in 2005 lists only five pages under the entry "Judaism" in the index. There are no entries for "Jews," "Jesus' Judaism," "Holocaust," or "*Shoah*." The one extended treatment is on parts of pages 213 and 214 under the subtitle: "Catechesis in Relation to Jews." The section is a strong statement calling for education that removes ignorance and prejudice from Christian understanding of Judaism. It cites several of the Roman documents, previously noted in this essay, to great effect. The directory asserts that "special care" should be taken when teaching about the relationship between the two faiths. We can be grateful for this clear section in the directory that footnotes important sources.

A comparison of the *National Directory*, however, with the *Guidelines for Catechesis: Grade Seven and Grade Eight* (rev. 1998) of the Archdiocese of New York reveals the fault line between policy and practice. The guidelines for pre-kindergarten through grade six have a tendency toward a fulfillment theology.[8] While the notes for the grade four curriculum state that Jesus "reaffirmed the commandments of the Old Covenant," it also says that Jesus gave a *new* commandment of love. In addition, page forty states that "true freedom comes from following Jesus' law of love." Such a statement is a far too familiar echo of past teaching. By contrast, the 1974 document *Guidelines and Suggestions for Implementing the Conciliar Declaration Nostra Aetate* (no 4) warns against a dichotomy of law and love (see part three, bullet three). The two pages recall the old teaching of contempt that Christianity is a religion of love while Judaism is a religion of law. The stated objective of the sixth-grade curriculum is "to understand the Old Testament as the revelation of God in history of a people, a revelation *fulfilled* in the New Testament" (57, emphasis added). The guidelines do not adequately take up the charge from the *National Directory* to teach substantively and accurately about Judaism. The *Guidelines* for the seventh and eighth grades simply do not appear to address Judaism at all. Even in the history section of the curriculum, no mention is made of Jesus' Jewish life; only Muslims are mentioned with regard to the Crusades, and the Holocaust is not mentioned at all. This very initial review of the *Guidelines for Catechesis* serves to demonstrate how easily the appearance of an older, discredited theology can arise in a text and, more importantly, how difficult it is for religious bodies to find space in their curricula for the type of learning and dialogue that, in this case, the Catholic Church at its highest levels has directed.

The actual textbooks used by Catholic religious education programs may fare much better in their presentation of the relationship between Judaism and Christianity than the *National Directory* and the *Guidelines for Catechesis* from the Archdiocese of New York might indicate. The sixth-grade book of the *We Believe* series published by Sadlier (2004) presents accurate information about Judaism scattered through the text and it distinguishes between Second Temple Judaism and the contemporary practice of Judaism. One might yearn for a more systematic and in-depth treatment, but the index does at least provide two entries ("Jewish faith" and "Jews") with multiple listings. The text provides enough of an introduction to serve as a basis for a dialogue between young Catholics and their Jewish grade-level peers.

Clearly, the challenge of interreligious dialogue at the level of youth programs falls squarely on the shoulders of the educators in charge of parish and synagogue education and the materials they choose to use. Herein is the opportunity presented by the *Coming of Age* curriculum: Jewish and Catholic children need to know more about each other's faiths than attending each other's confirmation and bar/bat mitzvah parties! If they spent a portion of their preparation time for these religious milestones reflecting together on what constitutes a mature religious identity, important strides would be taken in understanding each other's community. With the highly adaptable curriculum of *Coming of Age*, young Jews and Christians could explore together what being Jewish meant to their peer group during the Holocaust. Christians would begin to understand that Christianity had a role to play in the success of Hitler's Final Solution, and articulating this piece of their religious community's identity face to face with their Jewish friends will become part of their mature and responsible Christian faith. Jewish young people will learn that there were a few Christians at least who were "righteous among the nations." Together in a new moment, Jewish and Christian young people will think together about what global responsibility means for contemporary genocides, or how one's identity, faith, and community factor into coping with personal tragedies.

The opportunities for effective use of *Coming of Age* in an interreligious dialogue setting are many. The challenges (beyond the practical issues of a religious education schedule) all become "teachable moments." For instance, the early stages of a joint study of the curriculum will more than likely reveal areas of knowledge that the two groups of students do not share. Opportunities for learning more about Christianity and Judaism will arise and the students will grow in appreciation for each other. Further, students will need to discuss that the relationship of asymmetry in Jewish-Christian dialogue is not a theological reality. The asymmetry of numbers that so negatively affected the history of the two communities and the history of Christian contempt for Judaism does not mark the present moment as irredeemable. The challenge of asymmetry becomes yet another opportunity for joint learning and growth. Both sets of students will realize that dialogue with the other is a necessity for Jews and Christians who wish to embrace their traditions with integrity.

Questions

1. Coming of Age *was designed in response to specific requests to the Museum for material that could support bar/bat mitzvah preparation. Based on what you have read in this essay, do you envision other contexts for a successful use of this curriculum?*

2. *As adolescents strive to craft their personal and communal identities, will reflection on their peers in the Holocaust help them to make connections to contemporary situations – societal or personal? Will it stimulate empathy and social action in the world at large?*

3. *Jewish-Christian dialogue functions always with the awareness that the relationship historically is one of asymmetry: majority/minority; persecutor/persecuted. Given this reality, what are the challenges of using* Coming of Age *in a joint Jewish and Christian religious education setting?*

4. *Do you think that Jewish and Christian students preparing for bar/bat mitzvah or confirmation will be weakened or strengthened in their respective faiths by studying the Holocaust together in an interreligious context?*

Bibliography

Documents on Jewish-Christian Dialogue

A Sacred Obligation: Rethinking Christian Faith in Relation to Judaism and the Jewish People. Christian Scholars Group on Christian-Jewish Relations, 2002. http://www.ccjr.us/dialogika-resources/documents-and-statements/ecumenical-christian/568-csg-02sep1.

Dabru Emet: A Jewish Statement on Christians and Christianity. National Jewish Scholars Project, 2000. http://www.ccjr.us/dialogika-resources/documents-and-statements/jewish/319-dabru-emet.

Books on Jewish-Christian Dialogue

Boys, Mary C. *Has God Only One Blessing? Judaism as a Source of Christian Self-Understanding.* New York: Paulist Press, 2000.

Boys, Mary C., ed. *Seeing Judaism Anew: Christianity's Sacred Obligation.* Lanham, MD: Rowman and Littlefield, 2005.

Boys, Mary C. and Sara S. Lee. *Christians and Jews in Dialogue: Learning in the Presence of the Other.* Woodstock, VT: Skylight Paths Publishing, 2006.

Cunningham, Philip A., Norbert J. Hofmann, SDB, and Joseph Sievers, eds. *The Catholic Church and the Jewish People: Recent Reflections from Rome.* New York: Fordham University Press, 2007.

Flannery, Edward H. *The Anguish of the Jews: Twenty-Three Centuries of Antisemitism.* New York: Paulist Press, 1985.

Greenberg, Irving. *For the Sake of Heaven and Earth: The New Encounter between Judaism and Christianity.* Philadelphia: The Jewish Publication Society, 2004.

Sandmel, David F., Rosann M. Catalano and Christopher M. Leighton. *Irreconcilable Differences?* Boulder, CO: Westview Press, 2001.

Notes

1. *Coming of Age During the Holocaust: Coming of Age Now* was developed with a generous gift from the Conference on Jewish Material Claims Against Germany: Rabbi Israel Miller Fund for Shoah Research, Documentation and Education.
2. *Coming of Age During the Holocaust: Coming of Age Now: A Holocaust Curriculum for Bar and Bat Mitzvah Students* is a project of the Museum of Jewish Heritage, A Living Memorial to the Holocaust in New York, in collaboration with Yad LaYeled – The Ghetto Fighters' Holocaust and Jewish Resistance Heritage Museum in Israel. For funding see note 1. For more information on the curriculum, see: http://www.mjhnyc.org/teach_students_c.htm. For more information on Yad LaYeled, see: http://www.gfh.org.il/Eng/?CategoryID=62.
3. See page 1 of the "Teacher's Guide" workbook of the *Coming of Age* curriculum for a very brief statement of the three goals.
4. Hans Küng, *Global Responsibility: In Search of a New World Ethic,* (London: SCM Press, 1991), p. 105.
5. The four documents that form the core of current teaching are: *Nostra Aetate: The Declaration on the Church's Relationship to Non-Christian Religions*, 1965, Vatican II; *Guidelines and Suggestions for Implementing the Conciliar Document Nostra Aetate, No 4, 1974*, from the Commission for Religious Relations with the Jews; *Notes on the Correct Way to Present Jews and Judaism in Preaching and Catechesis in the Roman Catholic Church*, 1985, from the Commission for Religious Relations with the Jews; and *We Remember: Reflections on the Shoah*, 1998, from the Commission for Religious Relations with the Jews. For a very useful, open-access library of documents, statements, and current events concerning Jewish-Christian dialogue see www.ccjr.us/dialogika-resources.
6. Of particular interest in the past decade is the statement *Dabru Emet: A Jewish Statement on Christians and Christianity*; see http://www.ccjr.us/dialogika-resources/documents-and-statements/jewish. For Jewish and Christian scholars demonstrating the state of the dialogue in the early twenty-first century, see David Sandmel, Rosann M. Catalano, and Christopher M. Leighton, *Irreconcilable Differences: A Learning Resource for Jews and Christians* (Boulder, CO: Westview Press, 2001); Tikva Frymer-Kensky et. al., *Christianity in Jewish Terms* (Boulder, CO: Westview Press, 2000); Mary Boys, ed., *Seeing Judaism Anew: Christianity's Sacred Obligation* (Lanham, MD: Rowman and Littlefield, 2005); Irving Greenberg, *For the Sake of Heaven and Earth: The New Encounter between Judaism and Christianity* (Philadelphia: The Jewish Publication Society, 2004).
7. It should be noted, however, that improvements to Catholic textbooks concerning the treatment of Jews and Judaism have continued ever since the pioneering work of Sr. Rose Thering was continued by Eugene Fisher, and most recently by Philip A. Cunningham, *Education for Shalom: Religion Textbooks and the Enhancement of the Catholic and Jewish Relationship* (Philadelphia: The American Interfaith Institute, 1995).
8. The authors wish to make it clear that the Archdiocese of New York and the Museum of Jewish Heritage – A Living Memorial to the Holocaust have a long history of fruitful and constructive collaboration. The Archdiocese supports the Museum's interfaith work in many substantive ways and the Museum values its partnership with the Archdiocese.

Education of Peacemakers: Challenges and Opportunities in Interreligious Dialogue in Undergraduate Education

■ ■ ■ ■ ■ ■ ■ ■ ■ ■ ■

Diane Bliss

Professor of English, SUNY Orange County Community College, Middletown, NY

Margaret Murphy, O.P.

Associate Professor of Religious Studies, Mount Saint Mary College, Newburgh, NY

When examining the causes of such horrific events as the Holocaust, genocide, and other forms of mass violence against the "other," one is likely to look at political events, economic conditions, even religious competition. However, needing to impress upon today's college students the idea that we must strive to achieve the goal of "Never Again," one comes to the realization that our attitudes towards the "other" are often born out of ignorance as well as fear. As noted in a recent *U.S. News & World Report* interview with Stephen Prothero, while "roughly 9 in 10 of [United States'] citizens [claim] to believe in God or a Supreme Being… it ranks among the most ill-informed" about religion.[1] In fact, "in a land of growing religious diversity, only 10 percent of U.S. teenagers can name the world's five major religions."[2] What our students lack is both appropriate language for, as well as experiential exposure to, the "other" in order to broaden their understanding and respect for the "other" in a way that promotes tolerance and peace over the ignorance, fear, and violence that can lead to genocide. College courses teaching the basics of world religions are one way of providing our students with that language and experience. Two teaching approaches to these courses are described here. In the case of the public community college course described below, the emphasis of the teaching method is on providing students with the appropriate language by first making them aware of how they currently describe or discuss the "other" and then moving them towards more open-minded inquiry and understanding. In the case of the private four-year college, the emphasis is on providing students with an awareness of the need for better knowledge and with experiential learning opportunities geared towards promoting greater understanding and tolerance of the "other." Both approaches are geared towards the education of peacemakers that will counter the ignorance that leads to violence and genocide.

A Community College Experience – SUNY Orange Professor Diane Bliss

As a public community college English professor who also teaches our world religions course, Religious Concepts, I see language as key to my pedagogical approach to world religions, with its emphasis on philosophical concepts and modes of expression. Indeed, Schwartzman confirms the importance of language, particularly as a major factor leading up to the conditions conducive to the Holocaust. He claims, "The perceived Jewish menace was not merely a postulate; it was actively built and reinforced through language."[3] Schwartzman posits that the Nazis engaged in a conscious use of language, particularly derogatory towards Jews, through concerted propaganda campaigns and the supposed objectivity of the language of science and logic, to build a cultural mindset conducive to violence towards the "other." Looking at "key metaphors – in this case biological and medical – can reveal how linguistic resources that foster bigotry and genocide persist before becoming manifest in overt violence."[4] In other words, Schwartzman suggests that "language paves a path to genocide."[5] Anne Bartlett concurs, noting in her article, "The Power to Name in Darfur," that "Labels… are not an afterthought: they define and make real a situation and its consequences."[6]

For the Religious Concepts course I teach, then, one of my goals is to impress upon students the power of language in coloring our perceptions of others. Their understanding of this is important because students are often lacking in the language and knowledge of cultures or traditions other than their own, and in some cases even of their own. Our community college students are overwhelmingly "local," and the vast majority remains in the area after graduating. They come mainly from lower to mid socioeconomic ranges, and the average age is declining to the mid-lower 20s as the college draws in more traditional-age students in hard economic times. The diversity of students is fairly reflective of the Hudson Valley area; of our student population who self-identify, approximately 67 percent identify themselves as White, approximately 11 percent as Black, approximately 16 percent Hispanic, approximately 2.6 percent Asian/Pacific Islander, and 0.5 percent Native American. At the beginning of the course, when asked where they have gained their "knowledge" of other religions or religious traditions, many admit that it is primarily from the media, especially television. An additional factor for our students is the proximity of the county and college to New York City and the impact of September 11, 2001, since many of their parents, relatives, neighbors or friends work in New York City, and many lost family members or people they knew during that terrorist attack. The religious traditions of the students vary but are for the most part Christian, perhaps evenly divided between Roman Catholics and non-Catholic Christians. Other major religious traditions have included Jewish, Buddhist, and Muslim, as well as others. However, since the course is taught in a public community college, I do not ask students specifically to identify their religion, nor do I ever reveal mine.

The fact that students are in need of such a course and a basic understanding of other religions and cultures becomes evident in the first exercise I ask them to do, an "Initial Perceptions" survey. I hand out a paper on which are listed the ten major religious traditions we will be studying. While students have often encountered some of these religions in high school classes such as Global Studies, the answers they provide on this survey are telling. Among some of the "worst" responses students have provided: Hinduism – "the five pillars" (Nice try but wrong religion); Buddhism – "worship a happy, fat guy with a bald head"; Daoism – "That yin yang thing"; Zoroastrianism – "worship a guy with a mask whose sidekick is Tonto" (This earned the creativity award and was admittedly an attempt at humor by a student who had no idea what it was); Judaism – "don't believe in Jesus"; Christianity – "believe in Jesus"; Islam – "suicide bombers who get lots of virgins when they die." The simplistic views of the religions, the resort to humorous but derogatory terms in the face of ignorance, and the number of totally blank answers left on the survey sheets bespeak the need for these students to take this course. However, some students also shine on this survey and occasionally I have students who ask for more paper and time, despite my reminder that this is just a quick "initial perceptions" survey to see what the class does or does not know, so I can adjust the course accordingly.

The next step is to expose students to language that is meant to color their perceptions of a particular culture, before I provide the summary of Initial Perceptions responses for discussion. Students are assigned Horace Miner's essay, "Body Ritual among the Nacirema," and asked to think about the culture he describes.[7] What students aren't told is that this prominent social anthropologist wrote this essay as something of a criticism of nineteenth-century anthropologists and their superior, ethnocentric way of describing "other" cultures as inferior or primitive. They also aren't told that "Nacirema" is "American" spelled backwards. In other words, the culture Miner describes is their own American culture (although mid-twentieth century). In the essay, he describes Americans' preoccupation with, and negative perceptions of, their own bodies. He includes rituals such as teeth brushing, toilet training, shaving, hairdressing (where women bake their heads in ovens once a month), visiting a hospital and seeing a psychiatrist. Although one or two students catch on, for the most part the students do not, and the discussion in the next class inevitably begins with comments about how strange and primitive this culture's rituals are. After allowing students the chance to express their feelings of repulsion towards this culture and its body rituals, I write the word Nacirema on the board and then write American under it. The proverbial light bulbs begin to go on and students have a good laugh at themselves for being taken in by Miner's rhetoric. The real work then begins. Students are asked what made them think of this culture as primitive, backwards, disgusting, or whatever their conclusion. Ultimately we look at Miner's use of language in describing familiar habits or "rituals" of our society in a way that makes us assume that our own societal habits or rituals are superior and different from those he describes. Miner uses words such as "magic," "primitive," "superstitious," "potions," "ritual," "shrine," "secret," "initiation," "medicine men," and "holy mouth men" to create a sense of mystery and backwardness that makes most students feel repulsed about what ultimately describes their own society. Potions were medical prescriptions, shrines were bathrooms, the initiation was toilet training, holy mouth men were dentists. Students begin to see language about the "other" turned upon themselves. At this point, I turn to their Initial Perceptions surveys and we talk about the language they used to describe something unfamiliar to them.

As students become more conscious of the language they use to frame the cultures, religious practices, and concepts that are unknown to them, they also begin to understand the importance of asking more productive and thoughtful questions about the "other." Students are now asked to write three questions about religions other than their own that they would like to attempt answering by the end of the semester, and the difference in the language used is telling. For example, in the Initial Perceptions survey, one student wrote that Islam is a religion of "suicide bombers who get lots of virgins when they die." After the exercise with the Miner essay, the same student wrote as one of his questions: "How is the clash of Christianity, Judaism, and Islam going to affect our children's generations and so on?" Additionally, the difference is marked between the student comment that Buddhists "worship a happy, fat guy with a bald head" and the student question: "Why is the denial of material possessions, and necessities even, so important in Buddhism?"

These exercises in language in the Religious Concepts course are effective in raising students' awareness of the impact of negative language on perceptions about, biases towards, and the denigration of the "other." The remainder of the course provides students with the language of the religions themselves and a basic understanding of their concepts, provided in a non-judgmental exploration of their religious concepts, rituals, practices, and sacred literature. All this is meant to counter the type of language and "hate speech" arising from ignorance and fear, that "incites or encourages physical violence toward minorities" or the "other."[8] For, as Dorfman challenges us, "You want to free the world, free humanity from oppression? Look… at the hidden violence of language. Never forget that language is where the other, parallel violence, the cruelty exercised on the body, originates."[9] Educating people and providing them with more appropriate language, a language of understanding to replace or displace the language of ignorance, hate, and violence, is one initial step in creating societal conditions necessary to the realization of that "Never Again."

A Four-Year College Experience – Mount Saint Mary College, Margaret Murphy, O.P.

When Stephen Prothero, Chair of Boston University's Department of Religion, discussed the issue of religious literacy at the Pew Forum's biannual Faith Angle Conference in Religion, Politics, and Public Life in December 2007, his points were a mixture of humor and poignancy. Having surveyed undergraduates about their religious literacy, he gathered some amusing responses: Joan of Arc was Noah's wife, for instance. However, we have all become aware of the serious consequences of this illiteracy. Prothero cites the impact of religious illiteracy on foreign policy and its significance, arguing that he does not think we understand Iraq as a place where people are, in many cases, primarily motivated by religion.[10]

Dr. Prothero began to realize that his students at Boston University did not seem to get the references to religion he was making as much as he expected they would. In the last six years, he started noticing a shift. When he would say, "This is in Matthew…" he realized the students did not know what he was talking about and discovered they were thinking of Matthew Perry from the sitcom *Friends*. He then began to explain very basically: Matthew, which is one of the four Gospels, which are books in the New Testament, which is a scripture in Christianity, which is one of the world's religions. He then began to give his religious literacy quiz, which I have also given in my classes, and which is available online. Prothero recounts an early student's response: "*Jesus* parted the Red Sea – somebody must have been able to do that. It was probably Jesus, you know." In my own attempts to show the impact of the Bible on Western civilization and our everyday lives, I tell my four-year college students that they may see a reference to David and Goliath in the *Wall Street Journal* in articles about company takeovers. However, most of my students would not know the reference to David and Goliath.

Prothero writes of an Austrian colleague at Boston University who was teaching a course on Orthodox-Catholic relations. He had assumed that students would know the information about the history of Christianity. He said, "Americans are very strange. They all go to church – and they know nothing about Christianity… I have to begin with 'there once was a man named Jesus.'" This helps illustrate the central paradox in Prothero's book, *Religious Literacy: What Every American Needs to Know*. Prothero sees religious illiteracy not as a strictly religious problem, but as a civic problem.[11] We now have politicians on both sides of the spectrum who connect their public policy and initiatives to religious ideas. Hillary Clinton now, when she talks about immigration, is quite likely to talk about the Good Samaritan story. The international aspect is even more urgent. Madeleine Albright, in her book *The Mighty and the Almighty*, stated that when she was Secretary of State under President Clinton, she had a dozen economic advisors upon whom she would call to explain the economics or political situations of Middle Eastern countries. But she had no one to call on to explain the impact of Hinduism or Islam. She also observed that there was neither a prerequisite nor a policy for U.S. ambassadors to Middle Eastern countries to have any training in Islam, or for the Ambassador to India to know anything about Hinduism. These notions grew, in my discussions with my community college counterpart about the relevance of courses in world religions, and resulted in our presentation title, "Education of Peacemakers." Despite the differences in our colleges – one a public community college and the other a private four-year college – and the different socioeconomic populations that attend them, we found ourselves confronted with the same religious illiteracy among our students. Given these examples and Prothero's work, the relevance of offering world religions courses as part of undergraduate education becomes clear.

Our real goal in this presentation, then, is to share how we have seen the importance of religious literacy education lived out with our students. While the concentration in Professor Bliss's presentation has been on the importance of language, mine is on providing students with real-life stories and experiences of diverse religious believers. In my own course at Mount Saint Mary College, several examples are relevant. For instance, in my class presentation on Judaism, I include an excerpt from an interview with Connecticut State Senator Joseph Lieberman, found in our textbook, *Living Religions*, by Mary Pat Fisher. Lieberman spoke of his Orthodox practice and his love of the weekly ritual of Sabbath from sundown Friday to sundown Saturday, noting that it "is the time when the worldly concerns of the rest of the week are put on hold so that we can focus on appreciating all that God has given us." He shared, "I don't even wear a wristwatch on Sabbath."[12] One of my undergraduate students responded, "I'm amazed that religion could play such a part in people's lives." As another example, one of my guest lecturers for Hinduism, Dr. Suparna Bhalla, Assistant Professor of Biology, shared her home altar and her practice of daily *puja* (home worship). Seeing this respected scientist discuss her belief system was an important life-giving experience for my students. Another guest speaker, Mohamed El Filali, Director of the Passaic New Jersey Islamic Center, spoke openly and candidly with my students. The students consistently mentioned their surprise at his encouragement to them to ask any question, noting that there are no politically incorrect subjects. His openness to discussions of the status of women, jihad, and his own practice added tremendously to students' understanding of ethnicity and religious practice. His candor in sharing the struggle of the 5 a.m. prayer period teaches more than any text can about self-discipline and devotion. Personal stories and guest speakers have proven quite effective.

As an experiential assignment, one of the assignments for my course is a visit to a worship service other than the student's own. Students who attend mainline Protestant or non-denominational services consistently report surprise at the welcome, inclusion, and acceptance they experience. Four students attended the evening service at Congregation Shir, a Reform Jewish temple in Poughkeepsie, New York, and had the experience of helping the children's group to construct a *sukka* (booth) for Sukkot in the backyard of the temple. They described for the class their experience of participation, and their growth in respect for Scripture and the customs of Judaism. The fragile "booth" home reminds the faithful that their real home is in God, who sheltered their ancestors on the way from Egypt to the Promised Land of Canaan. "Sitting in the temporary shelter reconnects modern people to the natural order, and to the transitory nature of our carefully constructed forms of material security."[13] For students, the experience of a religion other than their own expands their knowledge and their willingness to respect the "other," rather than to construct negative judgments based on ignorance.

Many are familiar with the film *Paper Clips*, which describes the Holocaust education experience of a Junior High School class in Whitwell, Tennessee. In one of the opening scenes, the school principal remarks, "We're not too multicultural here. Most of our students have never seen a Catholic or a Jewish person." This school population was transformed by Holocaust education and tours of their exhibit continue to be given by eighth-grade students to elementary groups from many neighboring states. I have shown this film each semester in World Religions as we discuss the Holocaust. A significant learning occurs when, after viewing the film, my students are shocked to realize that in attending a Catholic college and being primarily of Roman Catholic background, they are the "other" in other areas of our country.

My young adult students also respond significantly to the story associated with the Holocaust Memorial in Miami Beach, Florida, a photo of which appears in their textbook, *Living Religions*. In Treister's book about the memorial, *A Sculpture of Love and Anguish*, the story that students find so touching is related by a Catholic priest and a teacher who took their high school seniors to the memorial. After instructing them to walk alone and in silence around the memorial, they studied the reactions of their students, mostly Cuban-Americans. The author tells of one girl who stood motionless in front of the sculpture of a nude elderly couple saying their last goodbyes: "It was a cold day, and after minutes of rapt staring, she took off her jacket and covered the bare shoulders of the woman."[14] Such a symbolic act motivated by compassion and understanding in today's society truly resonated with my students.

Finally, students in the Mount Saint Mary College course, World Religions, are reminded that on the tragic day of the World Trade Center bombing in 2001, we witnessed the work of countless heroes, many of whom were our neighbors here in the Hudson Valley. As those firemen went up to assist in the buildings as others were coming down, no one asked, "Are you Jewish?" or "Are you Muslim?" We were human beings together. As one measure of that, each year the students of Mount Saint Mary College sing with a large group of senior citizens and families of all ages from the Newburgh, NY, Jewish Community Center during the annual Yom Ha Shoah commemoration at the College. This is our hope for peacemakers of the future. The commemoration ends with this song, sung in Hebrew and English:

Jerusalem of Gold

The olive trees, they
Stand in silence
Above the hills of time.
We hear the voices
    Of the city
As bells of evening chime.

The Shofar sounding
From the temple
Calling the world to prayer
So many songs,
    So many stories.
We pray for peace everywhere.

The Hope That Follows

Our presentation title – Education of Peacemakers – has become more real to us as we reflect on the hope that we both experience as we share observations and ideas about our courses and students' responses. Students truly grow in understanding and respect for the "other" as they gain the language and experiences necessary to discuss and interact with the "other" in more positive ways. Our use of assignments, activities, and experiences that increase students' awareness of the impact of language in describing the "other," and of common elements of humanity while appreciating cultural and religious uniqueness, work towards that end. Equally important is the creation of a learning atmosphere that is non-judgmental and open to questions and discussion. Through the courses we teach on world religions, our students become more open and willing to learn about the "other." That in turn gives us hope that we can accomplish a small step towards the goal of "Never Again," by educating peacemakers that bear witness to the encouraging words of Pope John Paul II, "Hatred will never have the last word in this world."

Questions

1. *Can you describe an image or experience from your youth, or ideas from your upbringing, that affected the idea of the "other" in your community?*

2. *This article referred to the heroism following the attack of September 11, 2001. What efforts have you observed in peacemaking or changes in attitude towards the "other" in your community or in your own life in the past few years? How effective were they?*

3. *What do you believe is our greatest challenge in peacemaking as educators and citizens? How might we address that challenge?*

4. *What do you think are the greatest obstacles that limit our hopes for a different kind of future? How might they be overcome?*

5. *This article spoke of the hope that was engendered by the understanding displayed by young people. Can you describe an experience that sustains you in your efforts toward tolerance or peacemaking?*

Bibliography

Bartlett, Anne. "The Power to Name in Darfur." *Peace Review: A Journal of Social Justice* 20.2 (2008): 149–157.

Dorfman, Ariel. "You Want To Free The World From Oppression? Look Inside, Look at the Hidden Language of Violence." *New Statesman* 138.4931 (2009): 54.

Fisher, Mary Pat. *Living Religions*. 6th ed. Upper Saddle River, NJ: Pearson/Prentice Hall, 2005.

Lerner, Michael. *Jewish Renewal: A Path to Healing and Transformation*. New York: Harper Collins, 1994.

Miner, Horace. "Body Ritual among the Nacirema." *The American Anthropologist* 58 (1956): 503–507.

Olson, Kathleen. "Opposing Hate Speech." *Journalism and Mass Communications Quarterly* 84.3 (2007): 648ff.

Prothero, Stephen. "Religious Literacy – What Every American Should Know." Pew Forum Faith Angle Conference. Key West, FL. Dec. 2007.

Schwartzman, R. "Using 'Telogology' to Understand and Respond to the Holocaust." *College Student Journal* 43.3 (2009): 897–909.

Tolson, Jay. "Q & A: Stephen Prothero." *U.S. News & World Report*. Online. April 1, 2007.

Treister, Kenneth. *A Sculpture of Love and Anguish*. New York: Shapolsky, 1993.

Notes

1. Jay Tolson, "Q & A: Stephen Prothero," *U.S. News & World Report*, Online, April 1, 2007, accessed October 23, 2009.
2. Ibid.
3. R. Schwartzman, "Using 'Telogology' to Understand and Respond to the Holocaust," *College Student Journal*, 43.3 (2009): 897-909. EBSCOhost, SUNY Orange Library, Middletown, NY, accessed September 5, 2009.
4. Ibid.
5. Ibid.
6. Anne Bartlett, "The Power to Name in Darfur," *Peace Review: A Journal of Social Justice*, 20.2 (2008): 155. Academic Search Premier, SUNY Orange Library, Middletown, NY, accessed September 5, 2009.
7. Horace Miner, "Body Ritual among the Nacirema," *The American Anthropologist*, 58 (1956): 503-507. Ohio U, Web, accessed December 28, 2009.
8. Kathleen Olson, "Opposing Hate Speech," *Journalism and Mass Communications Quarterly*, 84.3 (Autumn 2007): 648ff. ProQuest, SUNY Orange Library, Middletown, NY, accessed October 16, 2009.
9. Ariel Dorfman, "You Want to Free the World from Oppression? Look Inside, Look at the Hidden Violence of Language," *New Statesman* 138.4931 (Jan. 2009): 54. ProQuest, SUNY Orange Library, Middletown, NY, accessed October 16, 2009.
10. Stephen Prothero, "Religious Illiteracy – What Every American Should Know," Pew Forum Faith Angle Conference, Key West, FL, (Dec. 2007).
11. Ibid.
12. Mary Pat Fisher, *Living Religions* (Upper Saddle River, NJ: Pearson/Prentice Hall, 2008), p. 268.
13. Michael Lerner, *Jewish Renewal: A Path to Healing and Transformation* (New York: Harper Collins, 1994), p. 365.
14. Kenneth Treister, *A Sculpture of Love and Anguish* (New York: Shapolsky, 1993), p. 18.

Auschwitz Carmel:
Introducing Students to the Complexities
of Interreligious Dialogue

■ ■ ■ ■ ■ ■ ■ ■ ■ ■ ■

Linda S. Harrington

Assistant Professor of Theology, Briar Cliff University, Sioux City, IA

Introduction

Communication, despite the ubiquity of Twitter and Facebook, email and cell phones, is always difficult. We may share information with people in all parts of the planet instantaneously, but real communication, real understanding, is difficult to achieve, especially when that information is being passed across national, cultural, or religious boundaries. One reason for that gap is that we do not know each other's stories. Information gains significance only within the stories that shape a people's sense of reality. Different stories can give radically different significance to the same reality and make real communication difficult. As educators, it is important for us to help our students realize that their own story is not the only story, and to help them learn to hear other stories.

Interreligious dialogue, by its very nature, is one of those attempts to communicate across boundaries and to establish some sort of bridge between sometimes radically different visions of reality. Such bridge-building is especially difficult when there is a history of tension and animosity between the groups involved. Studying incidents such as the events surrounding an attempt to build a Carmelite convent at the site of the Auschwitz concentration camp can help students understand how national and religious stories often give very different significance to the same concrete reality and how, without an attempt to understand the other's story, those differing significances inevitably lead to further tension and animosity.

A Tale of Two Camps

The Auschwitz Carmel incident arose out of a collision between two stories of horrendous persecution and heroic endurance. One is the story of Oświęcim, the death camp where the Nazis imprisoned the Polish nation and where tens of thousands perished; the other is the story of Auschwitz, the death camp where the Jewish nation very nearly succumbed to Nazi attempts to obliterate all traces of it.

The latter story is widely known in the West, at least in its general outlines, but not so well known in Eastern Europe. For our purposes, it begins in medieval Europe. The Jewish people, without a country of their own since the end of the first century, led a precarious existence in Christian Europe. Never considered citizens, separated from mainstream society by law and by custom, the Jewish people were the object of prejudice fed by blood libel and the church-sanctioned label "Christ-killer." Ghettos and pogroms, forced migration and confiscation of property are part of the story. In this story, the cross is not a sign of salvation, but a symbol of murder and mayhem. Not even the gradual integration of some sectors of the Jewish nation into European society that came with the Enlightenment could override the prejudice against Jews that permeated European culture. When the Nazis came to power in Germany and instituted their "Final Solution" as a way of purifying the human race, they tapped into a deeply entrenched antisemitism. Jews and other undesirable peoples were systematically arrested and sent to death camps. Over the course of the war, millions of people were killed in these death factories, either outright in the gas chambers or slowly in the labor camps. By the end of the war, two-thirds of Europe's Jews, nearly six million people, were dead.[1]

One camp in particular came to symbolize that catastrophe: Auschwitz. As Allied troops approached the death camps, Nazis force-marched prisoners away from the front and destroyed the camps behind them. However, the Soviet troops approached Auschwitz so quickly that the Nazis did not have time to cover the evidence as they had at many other camps. Auschwitz was not destroyed and there were thousands of prisoners still in the camp when Soviet troops arrived. The gas chambers and the ovens, the barracks and the documentation survived the war relatively intact. As survivors told their stories to the rest of the world, Auschwitz came to symbolize the near extinction of the Jewish nation. As a memorial to those who died and suffered there, it could only be a place of utter, stark desolation, as silent as the world was when Jews suffered at the hands of the Nazis. "When our brothers and sisters met their death in Auschwitz, they were surrounded by a total silence on the part of the world and a very significant silence on the part of the Church. We cannot tolerate that prayers should take place… in this place… from those who could have, at the right time, raised their voice."[2] The appropriate, even necessary, response to the horror of Auschwitz is to maintain "total silence, the silence that was the silence of man and the silence of God."[3]

The other story, hardly known in the West, is the story of the Polish nation. It too begins in medieval Europe when Christianity came to the Poles and Poland came to be called the "bulwark of Christianity," protector of Europe from the Turks and from the Czars. This nation, too, has known its share of persecution and suffering. Partitioned three times by Russia, Austria, and Prussia, decimated under Nazi Germany's attempt to exterminate the Slavic peoples, and then abandoned to Soviet domination by the Allies after World War II, Poles understand themselves as "the Christ of nations, martyred for the sins of the world, resurrected for the world's salvation… a nation whose identity is conserved and guarded by its defender, the Roman Catholic Church,… a nation that has given the world a pope and rid the Western world of Communism."[4] In this story, the cross is not only a powerful religious symbol, but a symbol of Poland and its martyrdom under German and Soviet oppression.

One Nazi death camp in particular came to symbolize the nation's martyrdom; Oświęcim. Built early in the war, the camp was "created for Polish political prisoners: intellectual and professional elites, members of the resistance, priests, and nuns were the main groups imprisoned there until the Final Solution was implemented in 1942."[5] Other camps such as Treblinka, Bełżec, Chełmno and Sobibór were extermination points for Jews from the ghettos of Poland, but Oświęcim is the place where the Nazis attempted to annihilate the Polish nation. The communist government taught generations of Polish schoolchildren that the camp, liberated by the Red Army before it could be destroyed, was a memorial to the victims of Nazi Fascism. Those victims included people of many nations, but the greatest number were Poles.

Prayer and penance, atonement and forgiveness, are constitutive elements of the Catholic response to evil in the world. Thus it seemed quite natural when, in 1984, a few nuns moved into a dilapidated building at the edge of the camp at Oświęcim and established a new Carmelite convent. These women dedicated their lives to an ascetic discipline based on the central commandment of the Carmelite Rule: "to meditate on God's law day and night and to watch in prayer."[6] Their purpose was to offer atonement for the horrendous sins of that place and to make supplication both for the victims and for their persecutors. Their presence would ensure that neither the events nor the victim-heroes of that place would be forgotten.

Two Stories Collide

One would think that the founding of such a convent would go largely unnoticed. Even in a predominantly Catholic nation like Poland, not many concern themselves with those who opt for a secluded life devoted to prayer and penance. Nor do those who choose such a life seek notoriety. However, these women and their monastery became the focus of an international controversy that nearly undid all progress toward mutual understanding achieved in the Catholic-Jewish dialogues since the end of the Second Vatican Council. Why the controversy? Oświęcim and Auschwitz name the same place. In this single concrete reality, this one place where Nazi genocide was carried out most efficiently, two quite different stories of extraordinary suffering and two quite different sensibilities regarding the appropriate response collided.

At first, the convent was largely unnoticed. There were few Jews left in Poland to object; those who remained kept a low profile in the face of rising antisemitism. A few people raised questions about the propriety of altering a building included in the UNESCO World Heritage Site plans for the complex of camps at Auschwitz, but such questions were dismissed.[7] The quiet existence of the Carmelites did not last long, however. In 1985, a Belgian group, Aide à l'Eglise en Détresse, heard of the convent and its need for funds to renovate the building they had rented, the *Theatergebäude,* and launched an international appeal for funds for the convent of Oświęcim. The letter of appeal, composed without consulting either the Carmelites or the Polish hierarchy, caught the eyes of Jewish groups in Europe and the U.S. who voiced objections to this kind of Catholic presence, especially in the building that had been used to store the Zyklon B gas.

Thus began a series of incidents that escalated tensions on both sides. Western ignorance of the reality of Polish victimization was exacerbated by the 1985 Claude Lanzmann film *Shoah*; this nine-and-a-half hour "documentary" of the Holocaust became the best known story of Auschwitz in the West despite its inaccuracies and misrepresentation of the situation in Poland during the war.[8] Poles, taught for three generations that Oświęcim had been built by the Nazis for the purpose of exterminating the best of the Polish nation, were "socialized to the implied 'fact' that they [the Poles] had constituted the majority of prisoners and victims of the camp"[9] and that hundreds of thousands of Poles had died there. Any attempt to change the narrative associated with Auschwitz/Oświęcim into a tale of Jewish suffering seemed to them to be a direct attack on their own identity as a nation. In the end, only direct intervention by John Paul II succeeded in getting the convent moved out of the *Theatergebäude* and into a new convent and prayer center a few kilometers away.

Teaching about Interreligious Dialogue

The collision of national narratives and religious sensibilities that drives the events of the Auschwitz Carmel incident makes it an ideal introduction to the difficulties of interreligious dialogue. Twenty years' hindsight makes the factors that created quite different visions of Auschwitz for Jews and Poles relatively easy to delineate. Similarly, it is easy to see how those differing visions of the same reality made it difficult for either side to really hear the other. Finally, this is a story that captures the imaginations of the students; they do want to find out how things turned out and why so many blunders were made by both sides.

The project described in the assignment below has proven to be a good way to bring this incident into the undergraduate classroom. Because each episode in the decade during which the Sisters lived in the *Theatergebäude* is so charged with national and religious fervor, and because the religious and national symbols involved are not the student's own,[10] it is relatively easy for them to see how differing perspectives cause misunderstanding and hard feelings on all sides. I have found that students take on this project a bit more enthusiastically than they do other research projects because they are charged with finding out not just what people did, but why they acted the way they did. The final task of the project, brainstorming about ways in which things might have been done differently, allows students to internalize the process of noticing when communication is not happening and finding out why.

Thus, the focus of the research project is not just to find information, but to notice the bias from which an author speaks. Requiring both individual and team work in the research and analysis phase of the assignment is a way of honing the skills of students who already have begun to think critically and of coaching those students whose critical thinking skills are less well developed. Classroom discussion is an essential way of helping students process the information that they have found, further honing critical thinking and analytical skills.[11] Finally, the individual reflection papers provide a way of assessing how well each student has understood the ways that different perspectives may give very different significance to the same reality, whether it be a symbol such as a cross, or a place such as Oświęcim, or an event such as the Holocaust.

Research Assignment: The Auschwitz Carmelite Incident

Based on what you have heard in class about this incident, investigate the events that followed the establishment of the Carmelite convent at Auschwitz/Oświęcim. Also look for information about the ways in which Jews and Poles understand the various religious symbols involved in the dispute, as well as the reasons for any differences in understanding.

Part 1: Finding Resources

Each person is to do sections A through D individually. When those steps are complete, work with the others on your team to complete section E. Each person will hand in the results of sections A through D; each team will hand in the results of section E.

Note: Be sure that your lists of resources are not one-sided. Include sources that speak to the Polish as well as to the Jewish understanding of Auschwitz/Oświęcim.[12]

A. Search at least two online library catalogues (Briar Cliff's, the Library of Congress, any major university) for books that deal with Polish and/or Jewish remembrances of Auschwitz/Oświęcim.
    Create a list of at least eight sources that may be useful for your research. Print off that list, noting the library catalogue from which it came and the search parameters that you used to find them.

B. Search the journal databases available in the library for journal articles, essays, and news reports that deal with the Polish and/or Jewish remembrance of Auschwitz/Oświęcim.
    Create a list of at least eight sources that may be useful for your research. Print out that list, noting the database and the search parameters that you used.

C. Select eight sources from these lists. On a separate sheet of paper, provide the following information for each of the sources that you select:
    i.   the name of the resource, along with the author's name and the publication date.
    ii. the library catalogue or database in which you found it.
    iii. identifying information:
        a. for books: the call letters and ISBN or other identifying information.
        b. for articles/essays: the name of the journal (including volume and date) or book in which the source is found and page numbers.
    iv. the reason that you think this source will be helpful in your research.

D. Using Google or some other internet search engine, search for information about the Jewish and/or Polish remembrance of Auschwitz/Oświęcim.
    Select eight websites and for each website:
    i.   Print the first page (this will preserve the url, the date accessed, and give you some indication of what the website includes) and note the search parameters and search engine used to find it.
    ii. note the publishing/sponsoring entity for the website.

E. Together with the other members of your team, compare the results of sections C and D. Decide together on eight books and/or articles that the whole team thinks would be helpful. Also select eight websites that look as if they will be helpful. Divide the research up among the members of the team; each team member should be responsible for at least two library sources and two web pages. Hand in the following information for each of these sixteen sources selected:

i. The name of the resource, the type of resource, the author's name and publication date, and other identifying information.
ii. The team member responsible for reading, summarizing, and reporting on this resource.
iii. Availability of the resource:
   a. if the resource is a book available from our library, request that it be put on reserve.
   b. if the resource is an article or essay available from one of the online databases, print it out and note that it has been printed.
   c. if the resource is not available from our library, request it via inter-library loan, and note that it has been requested.
   d. if the resource is a website, print out the pertinent pages and note that it has been printed.

Part 2: Summarizing and Evaluating Resources
Each student is to obtain, read, summarize, and evaluate the four sources assigned in Part 1, Section E. For each source, provide the following information, which is to be handed in:
A. The bibliographic information for the source.
B. A one- to two-page summary of information in this source regarding the Polish and/or Jewish understanding of Auschwitz/Oświęcim.
C. A one- to two-paragraph evaluation of the information that notes whether it is biased toward one side or the other or it is neutral, and that includes examples that support the evaluation.
D. Each team is to meet and discuss what each student has discovered and to create a synthesis of the research that describes the positions of the Poles and the reasons for their position, and the positions of the Jews and the reasons for that position. This synthesis is to be handed in so that it can be copied and distributed in class.

Part 3: Discovering the Jewish and the Polish Positions regarding Auschwitz/Oświęcim: Class Discussion
A. Each team will present two or three points from their summaries to the whole class.
B. Class discussion (or perhaps small groups consisting of at least two teams each) regarding the situation. The focus of the discussion will be the reasons why Poles and Jews reacted differently to the convent at Auschwitz/Oświęcim and an evaluation of the "anti-Polish" and antisemitic stances of the various participants.

C.   Conclusion – how can such different visions of reality be surmounted in dialogue?

Students will brainstorm about how to recognize when communication is not happening and about strategies for facilitating communication in such situations.

Part 4: Reflecting on What You Have Learned

Each student is to write a three- to four-page reflection paper on the difficulties of dialogue between people who have different world views and who understand religious and/or national symbols differently. This reflection may include a discussion of the dilemma of holding the truth of one's own tradition while at the same time acknowledging the truth of another's, or it may include a discussion of the practical steps that people need to take in order to participate in a dialogue with persons of different religious and/or national traditions.

Student Learning Outcomes

Research skills:

Finding information on the Internet, in the library's databases and in the library catalogue

Evaluating sources

Taking notes

Documentation

Critical thinking skills:

Noting the bias that can be found in both primary and secondary sources

Analysis of the positions of those involved and the reasons for those positions

Writing (and presentation) skills:

Organization of material

Summary and synthesis of information gained during research

Knowledge:

The student will learn basic facts:

About the Holocaust, particularly as it was carried out at Auschwitz

About the Jewish understanding of the *Shoah*

About the Polish experience during and after World War II.

The student will learn about the ways in which world views both enable and limit one's ability to respond to the various situations in which one finds oneself.

The student will learn ways to communicate across the divide created by different world views.

Questions

1. *What are the factors that shaped the Polish understanding of the significance of Oświęcim?*

2. *What are the factors that shaped the Jewish understanding of the significance of Auschwitz?*

3. *Brainstorm about ways in which you could help the Poles understand the significance of Auschwitz for the Jews and ways in which you could help the Jews understand the significance of Oświęcim for the Poles.*

4. *Brainstorm about ways in which you could recognize when two sides in a dispute are speaking from different religious or cultural perspectives about the same reality.*

5. *Brainstorm about what kinds of "standard procedures" could be used to help the two sides in such a dispute at least acknowledge their different visions of reality.*

Bibliography

Banki, Judith Hershcopf. *The Auschwitz Convent Controversy: Historic Memories in Conflict*. New York: The American Jewish Committee, Institute of Human Relations, Oct 1990.

Bartoszewski, Wladyslaw T. *The Convent at Auschwitz*. New York: George Braziller, 1990.

Berger, Alan L., Harry J. Cargas and Susan E. Nowak, eds. *The Continuing Agony: From the Carmelite Convent to the Crosses at Auschwitz*. Academic Studies in the History of Judaism. Binghamton, NY: Global Publications, 2002.

Frymer-Kensky, Tikva, et al, eds. *Christianity in Jewish Terms*. Boulder, CO: Westview Press, 2000.

Garber, Zev and Bruce Zuckerman. "The Furor Over the Auschwitz Convent: The Inside and Outside of the Language of Bias." In *Double Takes: Thinking and Rethinking Issues of Modern Judaism in Ancient Contexts*, Studies in the Shoah XXVI. Lanham: University Press of America, 2004: 57–78.

Glowacka, Dorota. "Forgiving, Witnessing, and 'Polish Shame'." In *Imaginary Neighbors: Mediating Polish-Jewish Relations after the Holocaust*. Eds. Dorota Glowacka and Joanna Zylinska. Lincoln: University of Nebraska Press, 2007: 253–274.

Jewish-Christian Discussion Group of the Central Committee of German
    Catholics. "Convent and Cross in Auschwitz? A Declaration – April 26, 1990."
    In *Coming Together for the Sake of God: Contributions to Jewish-Christian Dialogue
    from Post-Holocaust Germany*, eds. Hanspeter Heinz and Michael A. Signer.
    Collegeville, MN: Liturgical Press / A Michael Glazier Book, 2007: 42–46.
Rittner, Carol and John K. Roth, eds. *Memory Offended: The Auschwitz Convent
    Controversy*. New York: Praeger, 1991.
Sandmel, Samuel. *We Jews and You Christians: An Inquiry into Attitudes, Including a
    Proposed Declaration on the Christians*. Philadelphia: J. B. Lippincott Company, 1967.
Schiffman, Lawrence H. *Who was a Jew? Rabbinic and Halakhic Perspectives on the
    Jewish Christian Schism*. Hoboken, NJ: Ktav Publishing House, 1985.
Suchecky, Bernard. "The Carmelite Convent at Auschwitz: the Nature and Scope
    of a Failure." *Discourses of Jewish Identity in Twentieth Century France*. Yale French
    Studies 85. New Haven: Yale University Press, 1994: 160–173.
Zubrzycki, Geneviève. *The Crosses of Auschwitz: Nationalism and Religion in Post-
    Communist Poland*. Chicago/London: The University of Chicago Press, 2006.

Useful Web Pages

Aerial photos of Auschwitz camps:
    http://www.globalsecurity.org/intell/library/imint/auschwitz.htm
UNESCO site with comments from visitors to Auschwitz:
    http://worldheritagesite.org/sites/auschwitz.html
US Holocaust Museum website:
    http://www.ushmm.org/
YIVO Institute for Jewish Research:
    http//www.yivoinstitute.org/

Some useful sources for Jewish perspectives on Christianity:
Amazon list by Jan Peczkis "Scholar and Thinker" (Chicago IL, USA)
http://www.amazon.com/Auschwitz-Oswiecim-Carmelite-Convent-
    Controversy/lm/R1Y259ZRQFGDDB
Mr. Peczkis shows some bias toward the Polish point of view in his description of
    the books on his list.
Google Books list returned from search on "Oswiecim Carmelite convent" (167 'hits'):
    http://books.google.com/books?q=oswiecim+carmelite+convent&oe=UTF-
    8&um=1&lr=&sa=N&start=10
A Polish website about reconciliation between Jews and Poles (apparently a Jewish
    site): http://www.zydziwpolsce.edu.pl/awprowadzenie.html

Notes

1. There are several resources that one can use for teaching the history of the Jewish people in Europe and the facts of the Holocaust. The most accessible is the website of the United States Holocaust Memorial Museum: www.ushmm.org.
2. Resolution of the European Jewish Congress, May 1986, quoted in Wladyslaw T. Bartoszewski, *The Convent at Auschwitz* (New York: George Braziller, 1990), p. 35.
3. Markus Pardes, quoted in Bartoszewski, p. 36.
4. Geneviève Zubrzycki, *The Crosses of Auschwitz: Nationalism and Religion in Post-Communist Poland* (Chicago/London: The University of Chicago Press, 2006), p. 34. Zubrzycki provides a well-written discussion of the factors that have shaped Polish national identity in the last centuries, especially since World War II, see pp. 34–97. She also provides an analysis of the very different sets of symbolic values that Jews and Poles attached to the camps at Auschwitz/Oświęcim; see pp. 98–140. See also Bartoszewski, pp. 1–30.
5. Zubrzycki, p. 102.
6. The Sacred Congregation for Religious and Secular Institutes, "The Rule of Life, O.C.D.S.", in Carmelite Formation Readings: Formation of the Lay Carmelite, 1990–1993, National Board O.C.D.S., U.S.A. Jurisdictions, John M. Payne, ed., Article 4.
7. Bartoszewski, pp. 137–139.
8. See Bartoszewski, pp. 21–27 for a discussion of Lanzmann's film.
9. Zubrzycki, p. 108.
10. I teach in a small college in northwest Iowa; most students are from the surrounding small towns and cities. Even though there is some diversity on campus, that diversity does not generally include Jews or Poles. The dynamics of discussion would definitely change if the class included Jews or Poles and one would need to manage the discussion carefully to keep it from becoming a heated debate. Even so, such discussion is a good way for students to learn to listen to, and actually hear, what people with different perspectives are saying.
11. A beneficial secondary effect of this project has been that students come to a more nuanced understanding of the wide-ranging devastation caused by the Nazi attempt to "cleanse" the human race.
12. Finding distinctively pro-Polish resources that have been translated into English will be the greatest challenge for students. If you should happen to read Polish, one good source, according to Zubrzycki (p. 4, n. 5), is Peter Raina's book, *Spór o klasztor sióstr karmelitanek bosych w Oświęcimiu* (Olsztyn: Warmińskie Wydawnictwo Diecezjalne, 1991).

Catholicism and Human Rights in Light of the *Shoah*

■ ■ ■ ■ ■ ■ ■ ■ ■ ■ ■

John T. Pawlikowski, O.S.M.

Professor of Social Ethics and Director, Catholic-Jewish Studies Program,
Catholic Theological Union, Chicago, IL

It is not easy to speak of human rights in the Catholic tradition as an isolated topic. From an historical perspective, this concern is rather new to Catholic thinking. This situation is not accidental, but is due to some definite theological perspectives strongly imbedded in the Catholic consciousness for centuries, up to the first part of the twentieth century.

Thomas Aquinas and Catholic Social Thought

Anyone familiar with classical Catholic thought will recognize the dominating influence of Thomas Aquinas on the theology and social outlook of Catholicism, the issue of rights being no exception. In the theological synthesis created by Aquinas, the overriding emphasis was placed on the duties incumbent upon a person as a member of society rather than on the rights individuals could claim within the social fabric in which they lived. As a result of the theory of society and social obligations found in Thomistic thought, the individual person was linked to other persons and to the social institutions of the state by duties which were largely determined by a particular person's place on the social ladder. These duties were not conceived as an integral part of the person, but rather were seen as a consequence of the social function which a given individual fulfilled. Thus, for example, the role of a serf mandated certain obligations to the feudal lord upon anyone who fell into that category. The lord, in turn, bore certain responsibilities toward the serfs in his manor. And only the ruler of a political entity could morally make a judgment about the need to go to war. But once an affirmative judgment was rendered in this regard, all males of age had the obligation to bear arms. A parallel perception of social duties applied to relations among people within the Church.

Social commentators David O'Brien and Thomas Shannon describe the prevailing mindset in the following manner:

> What held the society together was a theory of social obligation that sprang from the very nature of the society and was understood from a theological point of view as related to a hierarchically ordered universe ultimately ruled by God. Consequently, Aquinas and other medieval philosophers and theologians did not have a theory of individual or social rights; they focused on the duties incumbent upon individuals because of their social obligations. This clearly implied that social obligations took priority over individual desires or writs. As a result, claims against society were made in terms of clearly specified social responsibilities that were proper to various roles within the society.[1]

The stress on social duties highlighted by O'Brien and Shannon served as one way of maintaining organic unity within medieval society. Fulfillment of particular responsibilities by each person guaranteed total domestic tranquility. In this perspective, the only condition under which an individual could legitimately claim infringement of human rights would be the state's impeding the person's performance of defined societal duties. Only the breakdown of medieval civilization would eventually force the Catholic Church to take a hard look at the question of human rights as defined in a contemporary sense.

Relationship between Church and State

Another feature of pre-modern Catholic thought that is pertinent to the human rights question is the understanding of the relationship between Church and state that prevailed for centuries, literally up to the period of Vatican II. Church-state unity was viewed as the ideal, with the Church exercising moral dominance in the cultural and political spheres. There was little willingness to acknowledge that the Church itself could be a source of social oppression. This issue, I might say, continues to play itself out in contemporary discussions about the Church's role during the *Shoah*. The late Pope John Paul II showed some awareness of moral failure on the part of institutional Catholicism and its membership during the *Shoah*. But Pope Benedict XVI has been far more reluctant to do so. The 1998 Vatican document on the *Shoah*, *We Remember*, despite its many positive points, contributed to the controversy on this question by arguing that while some wayward Catholics involved themselves in the atrocities, the Church "as such" was blameless.[2] The strongest critique of the Church's actions during the *Shoah* is to be found in a statement from the French Episcopal Conference released in September 1997.[3]

"Error Has No Rights"

A central component of the pre-Vatican II understanding of Church-state relations was the principle that "error had no rights." I think we cannot overestimate the importance of this principle in dealing with the human rights question. In this conception of the ideal society, those outside the Catholic Church were not entitled to political and civil rights because they lacked the true faith. This viewpoint, faith as the determinant of rights, predominated in official Catholic thinking at the highest levels until it was finally buried, with strong support from the American hierarchy and only after the fiercest of struggles, by the Second Vatican Council's Declaration on Religious Liberty.

Catholics in Majority vs. Catholics in Minority

The concept of social duties and the principle that the rights of an individual were based on his/her adherence to Catholic religious truth were the two forces that largely shaped the social ethic of Catholicism for centuries. In this context, when Catholicism found itself to be a minority in a particular geographic area such as the United States, the Church tried to negotiate the best possible deal for itself with respect to religious and political freedom. When Catholics constituted a majority in a given political entity, they tended to push for Church-state union. Non-Catholics in such a society were sometimes tolerated, sometimes persecuted. Certainly there were outstanding exceptions to this pattern on the part of individual bishops, popes and Catholic rulers. But these exceptions should be seen for what they were – the result of personal sensitivity on the part of individuals rather than official Catholic teaching. In some cases where toleration was practiced, the hope of converting people to Catholicism was a major motivation for toleration.

The attitude towards the Jewish community is a good illustration of this latter point. Generally speaking, those moments which saw some reprieve from the regular cycle of persecution and degradation were marked by intensive efforts at the conversion of Jews. These periods were sometimes followed by new bursts of anti-human rights actions against Jews when the proselytizing attempts proved a dismal failure.

Modern Social Encyclicals

Before looking in some depth at the debate over religious liberty at the Council, it would be important to turn for a moment to the scene in Europe at the end of the nineteenth century. In this period, the Catholic Church had to face up to Marxism, in particular its attempt to organize the working class. This challenge led to the issuance of the first modern social encyclical *Rerum Novarum* by Pope Leo XIII in 1891. This was followed forty years later by *Quadragesimo Anno* by Pius XI.[4]

Rerum Novarum

The publication of *Rerum Novarum* was really quite startling given the previous history of Catholicism and the personal background of Leo XIII. There was no historical precedent in the Church for such a decree. The Church's human rights record, while it remained a political reality through control of the papal states, was far from exemplary. Leo himself was part of the conservative, aristocratic faction in the Church, which was doing everything possible to prevent the spirit of the Enlightenment from having an influence on the theology and practice of Catholicism.

So what motivated this strong defense of the rights of the workers and opened the way for participation by Catholics, including clergy, in the unionizing efforts in Europe and North America? Upon close examination of *Rerum Novarum*, one will find that on the theological level it does not represent as much of a breakthrough as is sometimes imagined. A careful reading of the text leaves the distinct impression that the overriding concern is not the human rights of the workers "per se," but the fear that Catholic workers would lose their faith if Marxist unions were the only option available. Thus the encyclical's defense of Catholic workers, though laudatory, was in many ways a byproduct of the historic Catholic concern for preservation of what it believed to be the one true faith. One honestly wonders whether this encyclical would have emerged if Marxism had not proved the threat it did. Thus, while I do not wish to minimize the ultimate impact of *Rerum Novarum*, it must be said that it did not really represent a major theological departure in Catholicism regarding the question of human rights.

Quadragesimo Anno

Quadragesimo Anno by Pius XI does move somewhat closer to the modern discussion of human rights in its defense of Catholic workers. But one senses that even here the preservation of Catholic practice among the workers was the primary motivation. Though the first two social encyclicals contain an appeal to the natural law tradition as a basis for human rights, as well as a strong emphasis on the interrelationship between human personality and property rights in particular, nonetheless the impression remains that the promotion of human rights among workers would never have emerged if Marxism had not posed a strong threat to the traditional Catholic control over the working classes.

Pope Pius XII

The pontificate of Pius XII did not see the issuance of any formal social encyclicals. His well-known Christmas sermons, however, did in part lay the groundwork for the encyclicals associated with John XXIII. Pius XII was, of course, heavily involved with the struggle against Nazism. Hence we can gain some insight into the papal attitude towards human rights questions during this period by examining his stance, especially on the Jewish question.

Historians and popular writers continue to debate at length the morality or immorality of Pius XII's handling of the extermination of the Jews of Europe. I have contributed to this discussion in several essays.[5] Could he have done more? Could he have been more effective in saving Jewish lives if he had gone public in his opposition to the Nazis? We need to continue to pursue these issues, but that is a topic for another essay.

What is crucial in terms of Pius XII's response to the extermination of the Jews for any contemporary investigation of the Catholic tradition on human rights is his ecclesial understanding. The Australian scholar Paul O'Shea, in a recent volume on Pius XII, has correctly argued that ecclesiology is critical in any evaluation of his pontificate.[6] I also have argued this point.[7] There is little doubt that Pius XII's ecclesial vision, molded in the framework of Vatican diplomacy and a non-historical approach to theology which also tended toward a form of Catholic exclusivity in terms of salvation, shaped his response to the challenge of Nazism in general, and to the attack on the Jewish community in particular. Within such an ecclesiological framework, Jews became "unfortunate expendables" in Pius' efforts to protect the Catholic Church. As Holocaust scholar Nora Levin has put it:

> In the years of fateful concern to European Jews this institution (i.e., the Vatican) was entrusted to a man who undoubtedly believed he was being scrupulously neutral in his appraisal of world-shattering events but who, admittedly, believed that National Socialism was a lesser evil than Communism. In this context alone, could Jews be viewed other than as unfortunate expendables? After all, it was the Nazis, not the Bolsheviks, who were destroying them.[8]

For Pius XII the continued existence of the Catholic Church was the highest priority, one that had to be pursued even at the cost of ignoring the lives of others outside the Church. This ecclesiology was not totally indifferent or hostile to non-Catholics, including Jews. Clearly Pius XII undertook some efforts to save Jews. But these efforts remained at the margins of his concern as far as we can determine from a study of the documentation available to us thus far. When hard-nosed decisions had to be made with regard to the very existence of the institutional Church, non-Catholics played no central role in ecclesial self-definition.

Some scholars have rightly observed that our evaluation of Pius XII's pontificate changed after Vatican II and its enhanced emphasis on human rights and the human dignity of all people, particularly those outside the framework of the Catholic community. In terms of the human rights discussion, the most important lesson we must take from a study of Catholicism's response to the Holocaust is the need for a vision of the Church in which the human rights of all people play an indispensable role. Put another way, it is the recognition that Catholicism cannot survive as a meaningful and moral religious perspective if it marginalizes the concern for the rights and dignity of people who stand outside the community of its faith commitment.[9] I would add that this applies to all other religious communities as well. Human rights must become an essential part of religious self-identity. The vision of the Church that must direct post-Holocaust Christian thought is one that sees the survival of all persons as integral to the authentic survival of the Church itself. Jews, Poles, the Roma, gays, and the disabled should not have been viewed as "unfortunate expendables" during the Nazi period – and there is no room for any similar classification today. For Catholics, the late Pope John Paul II made this point in his very first papal encyclical, *Redemptor Hominis*, where he stated that there is no authentic understanding of Christ that does not lead to an affirmation of the human rights of all people.

Vatican II and the Declaration on Religious Liberty

With the coming of Pope John XXIII, the issue of human rights assumed a new priority in his writings and in his personal relationships as he welcomed people to Rome whom the Catholic Church had merely denounced for years (e.g., Protestants, Orthodox Christians, Jews, communist leaders, etc.). In convening the Second Vatican Council, the Pope made the documents on ecumenism, on relations with non-Christians and on religious freedom important priorities. He personally contributed to the discussions at the Council by issuing the encyclical *Pacem in Terris* which included a Charter of Human Rights – unthinkable in prior pontificates – which was influential in the passage of the conciliar document on religious freedom.

In many ways, the most important human rights document that emerged from the Second Vatican Council was in fact the Declaration on Religious Liberty. This Declaration proved to be one of the most contentious of the documents presented to the bishops. It was almost rejected on several occasions because of vociferous protests from the conservative forces at the Council. Clearly, this document was sweeping away nearly one hundred years of papal and Vatican teaching against notions such as religious liberty. Only the strong endorsement of human rights by John XXIII in *Pacem in Terris* and the unqualified support of the American hierarchy, orchestrated by the Jesuit theologian John Courtney Murray who was one of the principal authors of the Declaration, enabled the document to survive the conciliar process.

Murray has described the document as modest in scope, but with implications that go beyond the issue of religious liberty. It committed the Church to the democratic "constitutional" state as the best model for the authentic preservation of religious freedom. In so doing, it moved the Church away from the classical Catholic confessional state model which had the strong allegiance of most Catholic leaders up to, and even during, the Council itself.

The Declaration on Religious Liberty must be seen as an important new dimension in the effort of Roman Catholicism to grapple with the new realities of the modern world. It marks the end of any expectation that government and its socio-political institutions are to serve as defenders of the faith. In the secular, constitutional state the highest value that both state and society are called upon to protect and foster is the personal and social value of the free exercise of religion, which ultimately is rooted in the primacy of individual human dignity and the right to freedom of conscience. The document brought an abrupt end to the longstanding "religious error has no rights," strongly promoted in papal and Vatican statements prior to the Council. Hence, and this must be strongly underscored, the Declaration bears a significance for the issue of human rights far beyond the limited question of religious liberty. Fr. Murray himself wrote of the extended significance:

> Thus the Declaration assumes its primary theological significance: formally, it settles only the minor issue of religious freedom. In effect, it defines the church's basic contemporary view of the world – of human society, of its order of human law and the functions of the all too human powers that govern it. Therefore, the Declaration not only completes the Decree on Ecumenism, it also lays down the premise, and sets the focus, of the church's concern with the secular world....[10]

Murray goes on to add that:

> The foundation of the right is the truth of human dignity. The object of the right – freedom from coercion in religious matters – is the first debt due in justice to the human person. The final motive for respect of the right is a love and appreciation of the personal dignity of man.[11]

Post-Holocaust Christian Theology

The Declaration on Religious Liberty's rootedness in the notion of fundamental and unalterable human dignity is certainly a point of convergence with reflections on ethical directions in light of the *Shoah*. One Holocaust scholar who has strongly emphasized this ethical emphasis is Donald Dietrich. In his volume, *God and Humanity in Auschwitz: Jewish-Christian Relations and Sanctioned Murder*, Dietrich argues that "the Holocaust has reemphasized the need to highlight the person as THE central factor in the social order to counterbalance state power."[12] Put another way, any authentic notion of ecclesiology after the experience of the Holocaust must make human rights a central component. We might note that Pope John Paul II, who championed Catholic-Jewish relations, argued in his first encyclical on human redemption that there is no authentic Christology that does not embrace human rights. The vision of the Church that must direct post-Holocaust Christian thinking is one that sees the survival of all persons as integral to the authentic survival of the Church itself. There is no way for Christianity, or any other religious tradition, to survive meaningfully if it allows the death or suffering of other people to become a byproduct of its efforts at self-preservation, no matter how legitimate that effort at self-preservation might be.

Jews especially were not seen as falling within the range of society's moral concern by most Christians. When we ask why so many people in the Churches remained indifferent to Nazism even if they refrained from active collaboration, the answer is that Jews were not regarded as part of the universe of obligation by the majority. It was not that the majority necessarily hated Jews and other Nazi victims. In fact, some even expressed considerable pity for their plight. But in a situation where expressing any moral concern for the Nazi victims could endanger their own well-being and even self-preservation, they tended to respond: "I'm sorry about what is happening to the Jews and other victims, but my own survival takes precedence."

If there is a moral lesson to be taken from the above analysis, it would be that we need to redefine our identities individually and as members of a religious community in a way that includes the outsider within our universe of moral obligation. As a Christian ethicist, I have insisted on the centrality of human rights for authentic Christian identity, for responsible ecclesial identity. As we examine the history of Christian leadership during the Nazi era, we see a tendency for many in leadership to argue that their fundamental responsibility must be the preservation of their respective religious institution. Paul O'Shea stresses this point quite correctly in his analysis of the pontificate of Pius XII.[13] While supporting human rights was a legitimate goal, in their eyes it had to take a back seat to institutional preservation. My question remains, does such a hierarchy of values in the end sow the seeds of institutional destruction? The German Protestant pastor Martin Niemoeller is famous for his statement that when the Nazis first came for trade unionists, Jews, and some of their other victims, he did not protest because he was not part of the circles of these people. And when the Nazis finally came for him, there was no one left to protest. The point he was making, and it remains a vital point today, is that when the human rights of any group in a society are threatened, the entire society is in fact threatened.

One of the most important conclusions for contemporary ethics to emerge from a study of the Holocaust is the need to recognize the ultimate connection, and even integration, among people, even those who might be legitimately regarded as enemies. I have examined documents from the Nazi extermination camps which report on daily activities at those camps. These reports were totally devoid of any human language, of any indication that what they were recording was the daily destruction of human beings. Such "neutralization" of language can make destruction of people much more palpable to the human conscience. Professor Henry Friedlander, a well-known scholar on the Holocaust, wrote an essay reflecting on the Vietnam War and the Holocaust, in which he compared the language the United States military used in reporting on the deaths of Vietnamese during that war with these reports from Nazi extermination camps.[14] In both, the human dimension was totally absent. And in the current war in Iraq there are virtually no reports on the deaths among the civilian population. Clearly, a legacy of the Nazi era is the neutralization of language regarding casualties in time of war that religious ethics must consistently combat.

The Church in the Modern World

While Vatican II's *Declaration on Religious Liberty* was absolutely crucial for the development of a human rights perspective within global Catholicism, the Council also produced another statement, *The Church in the Modern World*, that also has shaped the Church's outlook on human rights. In this document we see the beginnings of a shift in focus on human rights questions, both with regard to argumentation and content. There is a new emphasis by the Council on cultural rights, something little discussed in prior Catholic teaching. While the document does not enter the complicated discussion about whether food, shelter, and economic sufficiency should be designated as "rights," it clearly argues that there cannot be a full measure of human dignity if we neglect such fundamental issues. *The Church in the Modern World* also moves away from an exclusively natural basis for human rights to an emphasis on their biblical dimension.

The period since the close of the Council has seen some very definite developments in human rights thinking. But almost all of these have followed the path laid out in Vatican II's *The Church in the Modern World* rather than that set forth in the religious liberty document. One has the definite impression that on the human rights question, the latter document, as important as it is and remains, served more to end an era than provide a solid, theological basis for a new one. The one exception here might be a stress in recent years on the importance of religious freedom in Muslim- and Hindu-dominated countries, with the emphasis placed mostly on the rights of the Catholic Church to engage in religious activities, including evangelization. This same argument has been extended to Europe where Catholic leaders, including the present and previous popes, view the continent's rapid secularization as a threat to Catholic religious expression and the Church's moral values.

It was Pope Paul VI who significantly advanced the perspectives originally laid out in *The Church in the Modern World*, particularly in his controversial encyclical *Populorum Progressio*, in which he argued that governments had the right, in certain acute situations, to seize private property and block personal financial assets from leaving the country when the property and fiscal assets were not serving the common good. Despite conservative Catholic efforts to bury *Populorum Progressio*, it was modestly reaffirmed by Pope John Paul II in his social encyclical *Sollicitudo Rei Socialis*, and even more strongly so in Pope Benedict XVI's first social encyclical issued in July 2009, *Caritas in Veritate*. Many regional Church documents have also picked up on these same themes of economic rights, the rights to food and decent lodging, and increasingly, the right to an ecologically sound environment. The emphasis in all these documents is very definitely on political, cultural, and economic rights. There is clearly a shift in stress from individual rights to the rights and needs of the community. There is also a growing emphasis on human solidarity, and even under Pope Benedict XVI, creational solidarity, as well as on the importance of recognizing social duties alongside of legitimate claims to human rights.

Conclusion

The question remains whether an inherent tension exists between the vision of human rights laid out in *The Declaration on Religious Liberty* and that presented in *The Church in the Modern World* and subsequent social encyclicals. I addressed this issue in a paper presented at the Vatican during a conference in March 2005, celebrating the fortieth anniversary of *The Church in the Modern World* conciliar document. My conclusion in that presentation, one that I reaffirm today, is that the more communitarian ethic proposed in *The Church in the Modern World*, and subsequently by Pope John Paul II and Pope Benedict XVI, should serve as the controlling framework for the Catholic approach to human rights. But the vision of *The Declaration on Religious Liberty* must continue to serve as a watchdog lest efforts to evangelize culture lose sight of the primacy of conscience and the profound human dignity of the human person, upon which it rests its argument for religious liberty. There will be a need for a balancing act of sorts on the part of Catholics in some situations. And here the reflections on the centrality of human dignity in light of the Holocaust by Donald Dietrich and others remain absolutely crucial. But restoring these two conciliar documents to a central focus in current discussions about religion and public policy is an absolute requirement if the Catholic Church is to engage society in a significant way.

Questions

1. *Why was the Catholic Church reluctant to embrace the notion of human rights?*

2. *Does an emphasis on human rights clash with Catholicism's traditional emphasis on the common good?*

3. *How does a study of the* Shoah *enhance Catholicism's need to embrace human rights as central to its self-definition?*

4. *How does embracing human rights affect the Catholic Church's self-understanding?*

Bibliography

Banki, Judith H. and John T Pawlikowski, eds. *Ethics in the Shadow of the Holocaust.* Franklin, WI: Chicago: Sheed & Ward, 2001.

Dietrich, Donald J. *God and Humanity in Auschwitz: Jewish-Christian Relations and Sanctioned Murder.* New Brunswick, NJ and London: Transaction, 1995.

Dietrich, Donald J. *Human Rights and the Catholic Tradition.* New Brunswick, NJ and London: Transaction, 2007.

Friedlander, Henry. "The Manipulation of Language." *The Holocaust Ideology, Bureaucracy, and Genocide.* Eds. Henry Friedlander and Sybil Milton. Millwood, NY: Kraus International Publications, 1980.

Gremillion, Joseph, ed. *The Gospel of Peace and Justice.* Maryknoll, NY: Orbis, 1976.

Levin, Nora. *The Holocaust.* New York: Schocken, 1973.

O'Brien, David and Thomas Shannon, eds. *Renewing the Earth.* Garden City, NY: Image Books, 1977: 21–22.

O'Shea, Paul. *A Cross Too Heavy: Eugenio Pacelli. Politics and the Jews of Europe 1917–1943.* Kenthurst, N.S.W, Australia: Rosenberg, 2008: 97ff.

Pawlikowski, John T. "The Legacy of Pius XII: Issues for Further Research." *Catholic International,* 9 (October 1998): 459–462.

Pawlikowski, John T. "The Holocaust: Its Challenges for Understanding Human Responsibility." *Ethics in the Shadow of the Holocaust.* Eds. Judith H. Banki and John T. Pawlikowski. Franklin, WI: Chicago: Sheed & Ward, 2001: 269–280.

Pawlikowski, John T. "The Papacy of Pius XII: The Known and the Unknown." *Pope Pius XII and the Holocaust.* Eds. Carol Rittner and John K. Roth. London and New York: Leicester University Press, 2002: 56–69.

Schreiter, Robert J. "The Church as Sacrament and as Institution: Responsibility and Apology in Ecclesial Documents." *Ethics in the Shadow of the Holocaust: Christian and Jewish Perspectives.* Eds. Judith H. Banki and John T. Pawlikowski. Franklin, WI: Chicago: Sheed & Ward, 2001: 51–60.

Secretariat for Ecumenical and Interreligious Affairs. National Conference of Catholic Bishops. *Catholics Remember the Holocaust.* Washington: United States Conference of Catholic Bishops, 1998.

Stransky, Thomas F., ed. *Declaration on Religious Freedom of Vatican Council II*. New York: Paulist, 1967.

Notes

1. David O'Brien and Thomas Shannon, eds., *Renewing the Earth* (Garden City, NY: Image Books, 1977), pp. 21–22.
2. Cf. Robert J. Schreiter, "The Church as Sacrament and as Institution: Responsibility and Apology in Ecclesial Documents," *Ethics in the Shadow of the Holocaust: Christian and Jewish Perspectives*, eds. Judith H. Banki and John T. Pawlikowski (Franklin, WI and Chicago: Sheed & Ward, 2001), pp. 51–60.
3. The text of the French Bishops, as well as the text of the Vatican statement on the Holocaust, *We Remember*, can be found in the Secretariat for Ecumenical and Interreligious Affairs, National Conference of Catholic Bishops, *Catholics Remember the Holocaust* (Washington: United States Conference of Catholic Bishops, 1998).
4. Cf. Joseph Gremillion, ed., *The Gospel of Peace and Justice* (Maryknoll, NY: Orbis, 1976).
5. Cf. John T. Pawlikowski, "The Legacy of Pius XII: Issues for Further Research," *Catholic International*, 9 (October 1998): 459–462 and "The Papacy of Pius XII: The Known and the Unknown," *Pope Pius XII and the Holocaust*, eds. Carol Rittner and John K. Roth (London and New York: Leicester University Press, 2002), pp. 56–69.
6. Paul O'Shea, *A Cross Too Heavy: Eugenio Pacelli: Politics and the Jews of Europe 1917–1943* (Kenthurst, N.S.W, Australia: Rosenberg, 2008), p. 97ff.
7. Cf. John T. Pawlikowski, "The Holocaust: Its Challenges for Understanding Human Responsibility," *Ethics in the Shadow of the Holocaust*, eds. Judith H. Banki and John T. Pawlikowski (Franklin, WI and Chicago: Sheed & Ward, 2001), pp. 269–280.
8. Nora Levin, *The Holocaust* (New York: Schocken, 1973), p. 693.
9. I develop this point more fully in Pawlikowski, "The Holocaust."
10. Cf. Thomas F. Stransky, ed., *Declaration on Religious Freedom of Vatican Council II* (New York: Paulist Press, 1967), p. 139.
11. Ibid., pp. 147–148.
12. Donald Dietrich, *God and Humanity in Auschwitz: Jewish-Christian Relations and Sanctioned Murder* (New Brunswick, NJ and London: Transaction, 1995), p. 269.
13. Cf. O'Shea, *A Cross Too Heavy*.
14. Henry Friedlander, "The Manipulation of Language," *The Holocaust Ideology, Bureaucracy, and Genocide*, eds. Henry Friedlander and Sybil Milton (Millwood, NY: Kraus International Publications, 1980), pp. 103–113.

BYSTANDERS
RESISTANCE
RESCUE

Passivity of the "Ordinary" German: Factors Leading to the Evolution and Implementation of the Final Solution

. . . .

Michelle Horvath

Recipient of The Ethel LeFrak Outstanding Student Scholar of the Holocaust Award 2009,[1]
Social Studies Teacher, Saucon Valley High School, Springtown, PA

Scholars and students have explored many topics in relation to the Holocaust, including the stages of implementation, the camp system, the experiences of the mosaic of victims, and the role of perpetrators, bystanders, and Righteous Ones. Although there are many questions that arise, one question repeatedly is asked – why? Countless books have been written about why perpetrators, some passionate National Socialists and others "ordinary" men, were willing to implement the Holocaust. Many other books have been written about the 60 million Germans who were neither perpetrators nor Righteous, but simply bystanders. Well-known Holocaust survivor and author Elie Wiesel asked the question for everyone when he stated, "This is the one thing I had wanted to understand ever since the war. Nothing else. How a human being can remain indifferent... For the others, all the others, those who were neither for nor against, those who sprawled in passive patience... those who were permanently and merely spectators – all those were closed to me, incomprehensible."[2] This paper is an attempt to explore this question of why. Nazi racial ideology and antisemitism were the most important factors in the evolution and implementation of the Final Solution for ardent National Socialists, but were only underlying factors for the "ordinary" German.

Before trying to address the statement above, it is important to explore the conditions in Germany in which the National Socialists came to power, as well as their racial ideology. Germany had suffered socially and economically after World War I. High casualties led to high numbers of widows and orphans who were not taken care of by the young, struggling Weimar Republic. Unlike in the case of the victors, England and France, neither the Versailles Treaty nor the war led to the pursuit of pacifism in Germany, but rather to the need for revenge and justice. In addition to high reparation costs, Germany was economically crippled during a bout of hyperinflation in the mid-1920s, which greatly affected the middle class and peasants. Just as the Germans were beginning to recover, the Great Depression hit Germany. By the time Hitler began his pursuit for control of the government, Germans were looking for an answer to their problems.[3]

The Nazis made a special effort to gain power in Germany legally, understanding that a legitimate seizure of power would assure Germans' civic allegiance. In the early years of Nazi power, they claimed to put down the threat of a communist revolution, as well as to return economic stability after the depression. Germans believed that a time of prosperity was returning to Germany.[4] Helga Schmidt was a twelve-year-old student living in Dresden, Germany, at the time of Hitler's appointment in 1933. In an interview, Helga explained the general feeling towards Hitler early on: "He got rid of unemployment. Just about everybody had a job. He helped poor families with lots of children… Security for the population was restored. Crime disappeared completely."[5] Until the start of the war, many Germans were happy with the changes brought by the Nazi Party, although not all were happy with the methods used to accomplish the changes.

National Socialism was based on four principles – race theory, *Lebensraum*, antisemitism, and anti-Bolshevism – in which Hitler was the architect and Nazi minions worked out the details and implemented the policies. The first principle, Hitler's racial policies, was based on Social Darwinism and Eugenics, which were two schools of thought that emerged at the end of the nineteenth century. In her study of perpetrators and bystanders, Irena Steinfeldt summarized Hitler's racial theory: "[T]he history of humanity is the history of an ongoing struggle between races, which pits one race against another, with the strongest ultimately emerging triumphant."[6] Hitler believed he would establish a Germanic-Aryan race that would be served by inferior races.

In keeping with the establishment of a superior Aryan nation, the second principle, *Lebensraum* or living space, outlined what Hitler believed to be Germany's inalienable right to expand into Eastern Europe for resources to support Greater Germany, and to use the inferior races, the Russians and Slavs, for slave labor in specific locations. As the Aryan race expanded, these areas would be used as new living areas for Germans.

The third principle, antisemitism, was the basis of Nazi ideology. The Nazis came to power using pre-existing prejudices to build their policies. Antisemitism was nothing new in Germany, or in Europe as a whole. As Raul Hilberg explains in his extensive research, persecution of Jews had been happening for over 1,200 years, but what was unique to the Nazis was the goal to exterminate European Jews.[7] In an effort to protect Christianity, Jews were subjugated as second-class citizens, limited by laws that would later be resurrected by the Nazis, such as prohibiting intermarriage of Jews and Gentiles, limiting the access of Jews to education or government jobs, and paying additional taxes. The Nazis did not invent the concept of the ghetto. The establishment of the Roman ghetto in the sixteenth century prevented Jews from owning property. They had to seek special permission to rent a home or business space outside the ghetto. In addition, they were required to identify themselves as Jews by the color of their belt.[8]

During the thirteenth to sixteenth centuries, the emphasis became the expulsion of Jews throughout large parts of Western Europe. Jews went from being considered second-class citizens to being a real threat to Christianity, which was espoused in Martin Luther's writings in the mid-sixteenth century, such as in his book *About the Jews and Their Lies*. Luther discussed how Jews had targeted Christians for 1,400 years and described them as "thirsty bloodhounds and murderers of all Christendom," equating them to be "like a plague, pestilence, pure misfortune to our country."[9] He also mentioned that it was a good thing that Jews had been expelled from France, Spain, and Bohemia, believing it should happen elsewhere.

Despite experiencing emancipation during the Enlightenment and the Industrial Revolution, Jews continued to be subjected to a quieter form of antisemitism until the mid-nineteenth century. Three hundred years after the writings of Luther, Jews once again were targeted as scapegoats when a group revealed that they had uncovered a supposed Jewish plot to take over the world, revealed in *The Protocols of the Elders of Zion*. Proven to be a forged document created as machinations on behalf of Czar Nicholas II's regime to prevent the rise of the Bolsheviks after the 1905 revolution, this document allegedly outlined twenty-four protocols that Jews were to follow in the hopes of world domination. This document was a primary weapon used by the Nazi propaganda machine in winning over the German people's support for, or at least apathy towards, their answer to the "Jewish question."

The Protocols were useful in establishing Hitler's fourth principle of a life-and-death struggle against the spread of Bolshevism,[10] which was allegedly one of the protocols. Hitler's crusade to eliminate "Judeo-Bolshevism" would be carried out by Himmler, Heydrich, and his German Army command with the invasion of the Soviet Union in 1941, known as Operation Barbarossa. This principle will be explored later in the text when the motivation of perpetrators is addressed. Many of the perpetrators believed that they were doing their duty to protect Germany from this aggressive ideology created by Jews, according to *The Protocols*.

Some of the hysteria resulting from *The Protocols* document is evident earlier in an 1895 meeting in the German Reichstag. Deputies discussed the need to prohibit immigration of foreign Jews, who were identified now as a race rather than as a religious group. An antisemitic group led the discussion. Deputy Hermann Ahlwardt stated that the "racial qualities of this people are such that in the long run they cannot harmonize with the racial qualities of the Germanic peoples."[11] Other Reichstag members countered the argument with statistics that Jews accounted for a small percentage of the population and were nothing to worry about. In response, Ahlwardt argued that even if a person knew a Jew who had done nothing wrong, they eventually would do so because it was in their "racial qualities." Like Luther, he also went on to equate Jews to "beasts of prey" and people "who operate like parasites."[12] Finally, Ahlwardt stated, "The Jew is no German… Permit me to use a banal analogy… a horse that is born in a cowbarn is still no cow. A Jew who is born in Germany, is still no German; he is still a Jew."[13] These feelings would simmer under the surface of German society, allowing the Nazi Party to easily build upon them during their seizure of power.

Hilberg succinctly summarized the history of antisemitism in Germany by writing, "The missionaries of Christianity had said in effect: You have no right to live among us as Jews. The secular rulers who followed had proclaimed: You have no right to live among us. The Nazis at last decreed: You have no right to live."[14] Forty-five years after the discussion in the Reichstag, the Nazis came to power and built their policies upon pre-existing prejudices. They established a bureaucratic system to carry out their goals towards a "Final Solution to the Jewish Question." The Nazi propaganda machine continued the stereotypical image that Jews were dangerous to German society. Relentless propaganda, such as movies, posters, speeches, and rallies, drummed into German society that Jews were criminals or a dangerous disease responsible for the ills suffered by Germany since the loss of World War I. In a 1940 speech regarding his struggle for power, Hitler talked about his "battle against a satanical power" which held control over the scientific, intellectual, political, and economic aspects of German life. He stated that the "all-powerful Jewry declared war on us."[15] The German people did not react to Hitler's announcement that he planned to remove Jews not only from Germany, but from Europe as well.

Irena Steinfeldt points out that everyone is influenced by prejudices in some manner. The Nazis used these tendencies to successfully change people's views and behaviors, as is seen in the story shared by Ellen Switzer:

> I remember one girl, Ruth… Her most appealing qualities were her total sincerity and her willingness to share whatever she had with a classmate in need… Out of the same generosity that prompted her to share her clothing and her food, she also shared her ideas. Ruth was a dedicated Nazi. Some of us, especially those of us who were called 'non-Aryan' (and therefore, thoroughly evil) in Ruth's booklets, often asked her how

she could possibly have friends who were Jews… when everything she read and distributed seemed to breathe hate against us and our ancestors. 'Of course, they don't mean you,' she would explain earnestly. 'You are a good German. It's those other Jews, pacifists, socialists and liberals who betrayed Germany that Hitler wants to remove from influence.'[16]

After Hitler became Chancellor, laws were passed preventing Jews and non-Jews from socializing any longer. Ellen Switzer continues her story:

Ruth actually came around and apologized to those of us to whom she was no longer able to talk. 'The whole thing may be a misunderstanding,' she explained, 'Maybe it will all be straightened out later. But meanwhile, Hitler must know what he is doing, and I'll follow orders.' Not only did she no longer speak to the suddenly ostracized group of classmates, but carefully noted down anybody who did, and reported them…[17]

The Nazis understood well the need to justify the persecution of the Jews and other groups. Christian Germans had high morals that would need to be dealt with to accept the acts that would take place during the Holocaust. By promoting the stereotypes of antisemitism, the Nazis helped ordinary Germans justify the acts committed by the state by making the victim out to be someone evil who deserved what was happening. German bystanders in some cases saw themselves as doing something right, or at least felt there was nothing wrong with looking the other way.[18] What better time to begin selling this message than to target the youth of Germany, as was seen in the above story?

In his 1935 speech to the Hitler Youth, Gauleiter Julius Streicher told young Germans that the Jews "had ruined the German nation in body and soul." He continued, "Even if they say that the Jews were once the chosen people, do not believe it," citing terrible deeds committed by the Jews, such as taking land from the peasants, making their fathers poor and destitute, torturing and slaughtering animals, and living off the sweat of others. Streicher ended this speech declaring, "For you we… became fighters among the Jewish people, against that organized body of world criminals, against whom already Christ had fought, the greatest antisemite of all times."[19] This indoctrination of Germany's youth helped them justify the persecution of Jews and, in the end, believe that they were doing something morally right in the destruction of European Jewry. Many of these young people would become perpetrators during the war years.

And here, the question of "Why?" is raised once more. Why did perpetrators and bystanders allow the evolution and implementation of the Final Solution? For ardent Nazis, the primary factor was antisemitism. These individuals, such as Himmler,

Heydrich, Eichmann and *Einsatzgruppen* commanders, passionately supported the principles of their party and looked for ways to efficiently achieve the goals set out by Hitler. But what about the "ordinary" Germans investigated by historians like Christopher Browning and Götz Aly? Why did they participate or look the other way? Although antisemitism was an underlying factor, many of these Germans sacrificed their morals out of fear of reprisals by the totalitarian regime, anxiety over being considered cowards by their peers, disassociation with the victim, or pure profit as a result of the removal of Jews from society.

Some perpetrators and bystanders justify their actions by claiming that there would have been reprisals – even death – by the Nazi regime if they had tried to stop the passage of anti-Jewish laws meant to economically and socially segregate Jews. They remained hidden in their homes while their former Jewish friends and neighbors gathered outside for deportation to unknown regions – with again no reaction, for claims of fear. Christopher Browning wrote in *Ordinary Men* that many perpetrators who were part of the Police Battalions serving with the *Einsatzgruppen* still justified their actions by saying they were afraid for their lives. Although there is evidence of reprisals against German civilians, whose dissension needed to be collective to be meaningful, there is no evidence of soldiers or members of Police Battalions ever being punished for refusing to participate. Browning and Bauer have both pointed out in their research that at no time has a defense lawyer for Nazi perpetrators ever been able to produce evidence of reprisals for following one's morals, as is evident in the testimony below:

> Sometimes some of the men refused to participate in shootings. I myself refused a few times. None of my superiors took any action against me and the same applied to other people who refused to carry out orders. We were just assigned different duties. We were not threatened with any kind of punishment, certainly not where the executions were concerned. Statement of Schröder, of Police Battalion 322[20]

Other men revealed that they were not necessarily afraid for their lives, but did not want to be viewed as cowards by their peers. Peer pressure and personal gain were reasons shared by Herbert Jaeger after interviewing an SS participant, "I was afraid that I would be considered a coward… that it would harm me somehow in the future, if I would show myself as being too weak. I did not want L. (my superior) and others to have the impression that I was not as hard as an SS man was supposed to be."[21]

Robert Gellately explored the motivations of bystanders who took a more active role. He examined the expectations for German citizens regarding political involvement in a totalitarian dictatorship. Citizens were expected to have membership in a Nazi organization, to attend locally-staged propaganda events, and to vote in the occasionally held elections where the outcome had already been decided by the Nazi

Party. Gellately mentions that some historians, such as Karl Jaspers, believe that a general indictment of all German citizens should not be made because they had little freedom or choice. Some historians accept that "what they did as citizens amounted to little more than a ritualized, orchestrated, or commanded and coerced performance of duties."[22] Other historians, including Gellately, argue that many Germans had a more active role in supporting the Nazi persecution of Jews and, therefore, did have a choice.

The Nazi regime used propaganda quite successfully to increase antisemitic feelings or apathy, and to justify for Germans why they should not become involved. It is important to note these successes so they can be used as a red flag of awareness for future events that have the potential of becoming genocidal. Victoria J. Barnett explains the environment created by the Nazis:

> Excluding people from the community – defining them as 'outsiders' – profoundly changes the daily relationships between individuals and groups. A gap between the insiders and the outsiders opens; as it is reinforced by law and popular opinion, it widens [as was seen in the above story of Ruth]. Consciously or unconsciously, the insiders reshape their own identities in ways that justify the exclusion of the outsiders. The first step is rationalization... We shape our perceptions to fit the world as it is: somehow, we think, our situation is legitimate and there is a good reason for it. We take steps to secure our own status and position; inevitably, these steps set us more clearly apart from those who do not belong. As the status of 'insider' becomes more secure, that of 'outsider' becomes more precarious. The final, terrible result of this process is that those defined as 'the other' are denied even sympathy...
>
> The tendency to justify the existing order and one's place within it leads many bystanders, as Polish sociologist Stanislaw Ossowski notes, to turn against the victims. The victims are not only blamed for their weakness; those who have benefited from the tragedy – the bystanders – 'convince themselves... that [it] was morally justified.' Victims are not just ignored. Eventually, they 'become repugnant to others' and are perceived as threats to the community and as burdens on society and on the consciences of those who remain silent.[23]

Barnett explains how Germans were able to disassociate themselves from the Jews. The Jews' experiences were not related to the onlookers' lives, so they were not inclined to become involved. In some cases, it had the effect that minor prejudices prior to the Nazi regime grew into strong antisemitic feelings, leading individuals to become more than passive bystanders.

Gellately spent time examining the role of the ordinary citizen in the success of the Gestapo in carrying out its antisemitic policy. He believes that the success of isolating Jews and political dissidents in the early stages of the Holocaust strongly hinged on civilian support for the Gestapo. The establishment of the totalitarian state by gaining control over every aspect of life broadened the possibilities of criminal acts. The Nazis had to deal with the high number of civilian reports turning in individuals for violations against the state. These reports were often not because the person had deep ties to Nazi ideology, but because they were acting in their own interests.[24] The most important information gained from civilians informed the Gestapo about social and sexual relationships, especially after the passage of the Nuremberg Laws in 1935. Neighbors, friends, spouses, and even children reported non-Jewish individuals who kept private relationships with Jews. Gellately cites the Würzburg files as an example where, of the 175 cases reported to the Gestapo to isolate Jews from the rest of society, 57 percent of the cases were turned in by civilian informants.[25] Gellately concludes, "This popular involvement transformed Germany into a kind of auto-surveillance system that drastically limited the social and political spaces in which resistance, opposition, or dissent might have taken place."[26] If there had been less active support of the Gestapo, there may have arisen more opportunities for ordinary Germans to react against Nazi racial policy, rather than allowing it to happen. Active bystanders affected the role of indifferent accomplices as well by having knowledge about what was happening to Jewish neighbors and choosing not only to passively accept the discrimination, but in many cases to openly support it. Non-Jewish Germans wanted to avoid the issue of "race defilement" that was addressed by the Nuremberg Laws so they completely avoided contact with Jews, including many who were friends, colleagues and neighbors. This allowed the Gestapo greater success in isolating the Jews, which was important in achieving the next step of transporting them to ghettos and camps.[27]

Eric Sterling examined the role of bystanders who were indifferent accomplices. Sterling acknowledges that these bystanders do not have the same level of responsibility as the perpetrators, but their indifference allowed the perpetrators to have free rein to commit genocide. Some bystanders believe that they are not guilty of any wrongdoing because they did not physically harm the Jews, or they were simply following the laws of the state. Sterling refutes this belief that social laws should transcend moral laws to help others in need. Any social law created by an evil dictatorship that takes away a person's human rights should not be upheld. He refers to instances where bystanders refused shelter, food, or hiding areas to Jews seeking help. This refusal to help forced Jews further into the open where they were caught or, in some cases, turned in by the very people whom they had asked for help.[28] Raul Hilberg supports Sterling by writing, "Neutrality is a zero quantity which helps the stronger party in an unequal struggle. The Jews needed native help more than the

Germans did."[29] Bystanders' lack of help allowed for the successful harassment and deportation of Jews with little or no resistance.

In answer to bystanders who claim that they did not know what was happening to the Jews inside or outside the camps, Sterling counters, "The people living near the camps exhibited indifference, not ignorance."[30] Although he does not condone this indifference, Sterling recognizes the success of the Nazi dehumanization process by exploring the effect that it may have had on the German bystanders' inability to relate to the Jews. The first concentration camps were built for individuals who were dissidents in need of "political re-education," as is discussed by Falk Pingel in his article, "The Concentration Camps as Part of the National-Socialist System of Domination."[31] These camps were built near population centers to send a message to the general population – unlike the death camps of Poland, which were hidden by a complex plan of secrecy. Germans were constantly barraged with propaganda that accused Jews of being untrustworthy, criminals, subhuman, and contaminants to German life. Along with this propaganda, the Nazis were successful in socially, economically, and politically segregating Jews from civilian life, along with the help of active bystanders, as discussed by Gellately. Many bystanders readily accepted that Jews were to blame for Germany's problems since World War I. Improvements in Germany seemed to coincide with the removal of Jews from society, so maybe Germany would be better off when *Judenfrei* (Jew-free).[32]

Sterling does not accept the excuse from bystanders who claim that they had no choice. He believes that they had a choice, but apathy was easier than risking one's own life or freedom to help another human being. Sterling does not believe that antisemitism was at the root of many bystanders' reactions, but more the existence of egocentricism.[33] To support this belief, Sterling cites an interview conducted by Gordon Horwitz of Frau S., who lived near Mauthausen. Frau S. talked about seeing a starving Jewish prisoner walking, but did nothing to help. She made no mention of her fear of being caught for giving aid to the prisoner, but focused more on her fear of not having enough bread for herself if she gave the prisoner some of her food. She stated, "[I am] happy when I hear nothing and see nothing of it. As far as I am concerned, they aren't interned… It does not interest me at all."[34] After the interview, Horwitz concluded that "Frau S. faces a choice and makes a choice: though she sees, she will look away and ignore what her eyes tell her."[35] Unfortunately, many German bystanders made this same choice. Possibly if more had been willing to speak out against the Nazis, the nation would have been successful collectively in stopping Hitler's Final Solution, rather than allowing it to happen.

Lastly, there is the issue of personal profit experienced by many non-Jewish Germans as a result of the discrimination against and then deportation of Jews. Sterling broaches the topic of the economic gain of bystanders, stating, "[E]ven if bystanders did not participate in or even condone the persecution of Jews, they reaped the benefits of it."[36] Regardless of the excuses explored above, some Germans simply took advantage of the Jews' misfortune through theft of Jewish property, businesses, and valuables. During the mid-1930s, the removal of Jews from government jobs and professions opened positions to non-Jews, who were in some cases unqualified. Also, when Jewish businesses closed, non-Jewish business owners gained customers. Ian Kershaw explains, "'Aryan' businessmen saw in the 'Jewish boycott' a chance to damage or even ruin rivals by reporting their Jewish background to the local Party."[37]

Götz Aly discusses in his book *Hitler's Beneficiaries* that Hitler's regime was popular partly because of the material benefits received by Germans from the government or the military during the war. From the very beginning, Hitler promised that the regime would make the people's welfare a primary goal, and he was able to successfully achieve this by decreasing unemployment, remilitarizing and expanding Germany, hence ending her humiliation from the Versailles Treaty, and providing material benefits that had once belonged to Jews and other groups in Europe considered inferior by the regime. Aly described a family example of such material benefit. His in-laws lived in Bremen, which was heavily bombed by the Allies. After Dutch Jews were deported to the killing centers, hundreds of freight cars were dispatched to Bremen carrying furniture and household goods. These items were given to Germans who had lost personal property in the bombings.[38] Jewish belongings were also sorted at the various camps and sent to Germany to aid civilians affected by losses during the war. This was a very different experience for Germans compared to the experiences of World War I, when citizens suffered greatly as a result of the British naval blockade.

Along with economic gain, there is personal ambition which drove some individuals, rather than their morals. Sterling looks at the specific example of Kurt Waldheim, who was the Austrian presidential candidate in 1986. Waldheim was a translator in the Austrian Army during World War II and claimed ignorance of the genocidal events that surrounded him, although records kept by him during the war proved otherwise.[39] In defense of himself and his generation, Waldheim claimed, "We were not doing anything but our duty as decent soldiers, we were not criminals but decent men who faced a terrible fate."[40] Countering such empty excuses, Robert Herzstein writes, "If history teaches us anything, it is that the Hitlers and Mengeles could never have accomplished their atrocious deeds by themselves. It took hundreds of thousands of ordinary men – well-meaning but ambitious men, like Kurt Waldheim – to make the Third Reich possible."[41]

Elie Wiesel wrote that he wanted to understand the bystanders' choice not to get involved, but unfortunately this understanding may never be achieved. As explored by many Holocaust historians, there are many reasons and motivations – not only antisemitism – driving the decisions of perpetrators and bystanders, including personal or economic gain, fears of reprisals or peer pressure, and indoctrination that led to disassociation with the victims. Time is running out to continue discovering exactly why this generation of Germans chose to do nothing to stop the Holocaust, and in some cases helped to implement it. For lessons to be learned from the Holocaust, there is a need for perpetrators and bystanders to honestly remember why they made their choices. Knowing the answers to the question "Why?" will help society to better understand how to stop such circumstances from existing again, thus preventing future genocidal events.

Questions

1. *In a sermon given during the Montgomery bus boycott (1956), Dr. Martin Luther King, Jr. stated, "The ultimate measure of a man is not where he stands in moments of comfort and convenience, but where he stands at times of challenge and controversy." Reflecting on this quotation and the information in the article, what lessons should be learned to better prepare people to take a stand when it matters most?*

2. *The Chinese refer to their treatment at the hands of the Japanese (1931–1945), particularly during the Nanking Massacre, as their Holocaust. Research the events surrounding the massacre and evaluate the effectiveness of the actions taken by the international bystanders inside the city.*

3. *Investigate the feelings of the general German populace towards the Nazi Party prior to Hitler's appointment as Chancellor, during the 1930s, and during the war years. To what extent does this research support or refute this essay?*

Bibliography

Aly, Götz. *Hitler's Beneficiaries: Plunder, Racial War, and the Nazi Welfare State*. New York: Metropolitan Books, 2005.

Barnett, Victoria J. *Bystanders – Conscience and Complicity during the Holocaust*. New York: Greenwood Press, 1999.

Bartov, O., ed. *The Holocaust – Origins, Implementation, Aftermath*. New York: Routledge, 2000.

Bauer, Yehuda. *Rethinking the Holocaust*. New Haven: Yale University, 2001.

Gellately, Robert. "A Monstrous Uneasiness: Citizen Participation and Persecution of the Jews in Nazi Germany." Mitchell and Mitchell, op.cit.: 174–82.

Hilberg, Raul. "The Destruction of the European Jews: Precedents." Bartov, op.cit.: 21–42.

Horwitz, Gordon J. "Places Far Away, Places Very Near: Mauthausen, the Camps of the Shoah, and the Bystanders." Bartov, op.cit.: 204–18.

Johnson, Eric A. and Karl-Heinz Reuband. *What We Knew: Terror, Mass Murder, and Everyday Life in Nazi Germany – An Oral History*. Cambridge, MA: Basic Books, 2005.

Klee, Ernst, Willi Dressen and Volker Riess. *The Good Old Days – The Holocaust as Seen by its Perpetrators and Bystanders*. New York: Konecky, 1991.

Mitchell, J. R. and H. Mitchell, eds. *The Holocaust – Readings and Interpretations*. United States: McGraw-Hill/Dushkin, 2001.

Pingel, Falk. "The Concentration Camps as a part of the National-Socialist System of Domination." Eds. Yisrael Gutman and Avital Saf. *The Nazi Concentration Camps, Structure and Aims, The Image of the Prisoner, The Jews in the Camps*. Yad Vashem, 1980: 3–17.

Steinfeldt, Irena. *How Was It Humanly Possible? A Study of Perpetrators and Bystanders during the Holocaust*. Yad Vashem, 2002.

Sterling, Eric. "Indifferent Accomplices." Mitchell and Mitchell, op.cit.: 183–92.

Switzer, Ellen. *How Democracy Failed*. New York: Atheneum, 1975.

Notes

1. For further information about The Ethel LeFrak Outstanding Student Scholar of the Holocaust Award, see pp. 319–20.
2. Elie Wiesel, as quoted in J. R. Mitchell and H. Mitchell, eds., *The Holocaust – Readings and Interpretations* (United States: McGraw-Hill/Dushkin, 2001), p. 173.
3. Yehuda Bauer, *Rethinking the Holocaust* (New Haven: Yale University Press), pp. 96–97.
4. Robert Gellately, "A Monstrous Uneasiness," in J. R. Mitchell and H. Mitchell, eds., *The Holocaust – Readings and Interpretations* (United States: McGraw-Hill/Dushkin, 2001), p. 177.
5. Helga Schmidt, as quoted in Eric A. Johnson and Karl-Heinz Reuband, *What We Knew: Terror, Mass Murder, and Everyday Life in Nazi Germany – An Oral History* (Cambridge, MA: Basic Books, 2005), p. 177.
6. Irena Steinfeldt, *How Was It Humanly Possible? A Study of Perpetrators and Bystanders during the Holocaust* (Israel: Yad Vashem, 2002), p. 20.
7. Raul Hilberg, "The Destruction of the European Jews: Precedents," in O. Bartov, ed., *The Holocaust – Origins, Implementation, Aftermath* (New York: Routledge, 2000), p. 21.
8. Ibid., pp. 23–24, 26.
9. Martin Luther, as quoted in Hilberg, pp. 24, 31.
10. Steinfeldt, p. 20.
11. Hermann Ahlwardt, as quoted in Hilberg, p. 32.
12. Hermann Ahlwardt, as quoted in Hilberg, pp. 32–33.
13. Hermann Ahlwardt, as quoted in Hilberg, p. 34.
14. Hilberg, p. 25.
15. Adolf Hitler, as quoted in Hilberg, p. 34.
16. Ellen Switzer, *How Democracy Failed* (New York: Atheneum, 1975), pp. 89–90.
17. Ibid., p. 91.
18. Hilberg, p. 30.
19. Ibid., p. 35.
20. Ernst Klee, Willi Dressen and Volker Riess, *The Good Old Days – The Holocaust as Seen by its Perpetrators and Bystanders* (New York: Konecky, 1991), p. 78.
21. Herbert Jaeger, as quoted in Steinfeldt, op.cit., p. 65.

22. Gellately, p. 175.
23. Victoria J. Barnett, *Bystanders – Conscience and Complicity during the Holocaust* (New York: Greenwood Press, 1999), p. 101.
24. Gellately, pp. 175–76.
25. Ibid., p. 179.
26. Ibid., p. 178.
27. Ibid., p. 181.
28. Eric Sterling, "Indifferent Accomplices," in Mitchell and Mitchell, eds., *The Holocaust – Readings and Interpretations* (United States: McGraw-Hill/Dushkin, 2001), pp. 184, 188–89.
29. Hilberg, p. 188.
30. Sterling, p. 184.
31. Falk Pingel, in Yisrael Gutman and Avital Saf, eds., *The Nazi Concentration Camps, Structure and Aims, The Image of the Prisoner, The Jews in the Camps* (Yad Vashem, 1980), pp. 3–17.
32. Sterling, pp. 186–87.
33. Ibid., pp. 184–85.
34. Frau S., as quoted in Sterling, p. 185.
35. Sterling, p. 185.
36. Ibid., p. 188.
37. Ibid., pp. 187–88.
38. Götz Aly, *Hitler's Beneficiaries: Plunder, Racial War, and the Nazi Welfare State* (New York: Metropolitan Books, 2005), p. 3.
39. Sterling, p. 184.
40. Gordon J. Horwitz, "Places Far Away, Places Very Near: Mauthausen, the Camps of the Shoah, and the Bystanders," in O. Bartov, ed., *The Holocaust – Origins, Implementation, Aftermath* (New York: Routledge, 2000), p. 214.
41. Sterling, p. 184.

The Question Mark/er Project:
A Case Study

■ ■ ■ ■ ■ ■ ■ ■ ■ ■ ■

Carol R. Brode

Assistant Professor of Art, Director of Harlan Gallery,
Seton Hill University, Greensburg, PA

> *"Monuments are history made visible... allowing us*
> *to understand the past in a way that is meaningful*
> *in the present."*[1]

The 1987 opening of the National Catholic Center for Holocaust Education (NCCHE) at Seton Hill University was marked by the planting and dedication of the Peace Tree on the campus, a symbolic presence of the work being done by the Center. As it grew, so too did the work of educating about the Holocaust. However, in 2006 the Peace Tree was severely damaged by lightning, and subsequently removed. This unfortunate incident gave rise to *The Question Mark/er Project*, an ongoing effort at Seton Hill to integrate the arts, history, current events, and the study of genocide in an interdisciplinary manner, and to again symbolize the presence of the NCCHE on Seton Hill's campus.

Initial discussions about creating a new memorial on campus centered on issues such as the following: Should a work of art be commissioned or bought for one site on campus? Where should that site be? Should it be near or in the offices of the NCCHE? Who should be involved? And to the core: What do we want it to do?

Of course it would be a memorial, a way to make history visible, but would there be a way to make something that would promote discussion about history, the present, an individual's role in shaping the present and the future? A way to remember the past and consider the present and future? To involve multiple parts of the university community? As Pati Beachley, Associate Professor of Sculpture at Seton Hill, and Diane Samuels, artist and NCCHE board member, and I discussed these questions, we asked ourselves *What about something that asked questions?*... questions that might encourage discussions about the present in the light (or shadow) of the past. And so *The Question Mark/er Project* was initiated.

An exploration and understanding of the role of art in Holocaust and genocide education can be exemplified by artist Diane Samuels' experience creating a Holocaust memorial in Grafeneck, Germany. Here Ms. Samuels recounts her work on that memorial project:

> In 1996 I was invited to work in the archive of Buttenhausen, Germany, to "respond as an artist." Roland Deigendesch, the chief archivist-historian of the region, wrote to me of his concerns about the dual role of the archive – as a passive document repository and as the official giver-of-meaning to the repository – in post-war Germany. In the invitation letter, Dr. Deigendesch wrote: 'The idea of looking forward is a serious and important purpose. But we historians are – of course – skeptical: What will people learn from Buttenhausen during a time when it is clear that mankind hasn't learned anything at all from (for example) recent German history? On the other hand, it doesn't seem to make much sense to preserve and to look back just for the sake of preserving and just for the sake of looking back. The task of the historian is (in my eyes) to help to position human society in the present. In situations like now, which have no easy solutions, no easy answers, what do we need more than art?'[2]
>
> In accepting the invitation, I had no idea of how archives would change my life and art. On my initial visit to Buttenhausen, Dr. Deigendesch suggested that I might be interested in visiting Grafeneck, about eight kilometers away. I drove up a winding forested road which ended in a huge stone castle. As soon as I parked, my car was surrounded by a group of disabled men who welcomed me to Grafeneck. The only common word we shared was "Hello", which we said to each other and shook hands. The welcoming committee walked with me to a memorial stone with engraved text and a nearby outdoor altar with a crucifix carved on its face. Not reading any German, I took out my German/English dictionary and word-by-word translated the engraved text. It read:
>
> > *For the 10,654 sick and disabled people who were murdered here in*
> > *1940 by the National Socialist Regime.*

There I was, a Jew from America, being helped and guided by a group of disabled people from Germany, standing on German soil in 1996 and reading that text.

Grafeneck, a home for the physically and mentally disabled, was established as "Site A" for the so-called "euthanasia experiments" of the Nazi regime in 1940. 10,654 sick and disabled people were killed there. Today Grafeneck has been re-established as an institution for the disabled run by the Foundation Samariterstiftung, and it maintains a memorial site dedicated to the victims who perished there in 1940. The Grafeneck Memorial Committee, led by historian Thomas Stöckle, is trying to identify all those who perished at Grafeneck and to record their names in a book on permanent display at the memorial site. It had been believed that the victims were all Christian, but in doing the research to identify the victims it was discovered that some of the victims were Jewish.

In May of 1997, I was asked to propose and subsequently was commissioned to build an addition to the existing memorial that would commemorate the Jewish victims as well as the victims whose names will never be found. I proposed an *Alphabet Garden*, based on a Jewish folktale in which the sage Isaac Luria is introduced to a man whose prayers are particularly efficacious and Luria asks him how he prays. The man answers that he cannot read or write but that he can recite the alphabet, so he asks God to take his letters and form them into prayers. The *Alphabet Garden* was built in August 1998 with the assistance of members of the Grafeneck Memorial Committee and other volunteers from the region. *The Alphabet Garden* contains twenty-six small, square granite memorial stones each engraved with a letter of the Roman alphabet, set into a field of 14,000 randomly scattered plants that bloom at different seasons of the year.

In October of 2000, a stone bench was placed in the garden. The stone, part of the Grafeneck castle built in the eighteenth century, is inscribed with the words *"Bitte, nimm meine Buchstaben und forme daraus Gebete."* ("Please, take my letters and form them into prayers.") The garden will remain a work-in-progress for many years as we observe how the plants grow and while the combined efforts of visitors walking through the garden and over the stones spell out the names of the unnamed victims.[3]

In this eloquent description, Samuels captures the very essence of the role of public art and memorials, and was the keynote speaker at a presentation held in February 2009 at Seton Hill, announcing the project to the university and community. We invited the community to initiate conversations about historical and current events relating to genocide, and to submit questions, such as: How could this happen? How can I take responsibility? How can I initiate change? What would I have done? Will I speak out if my voice is in the minority? What can I do right now? Regardless of the student major or faculty discipline, anyone could become involved in the project.

The question submission forms were distributed, and we allowed a month for the questions to be returned to NCCHE. The responses we received (over fifty) were compiled and an advisory board reviewed them, selecting five of the questions, based on their clarity and simplicity, to be considered as the basis for the first markers. These five questions were: Of what are you afraid? Can history teach us love? Why do we love silently, but hate openly? How can our community initiate change in the world? and, What is the role of good people in difficult times?

When initially considering the project parameters, we determined that involving student artists could best exemplify the collaborative and interdisciplinary aspects of the project: it would provide an educational experience for the student artists in creating commissioned public art, as well as initiate dialogue about the Holocaust in the studio and beyond. Sculpture professor Pati Beachley worked with students in her Advanced Three-Dimensional Media class, with Diane Samuels as a visiting artist. Beachley states,

> One of my recent interests is art that has a function, beyond an aesthetic purpose, specifically – the function of public sculpture. When considering a physical presence for the National Catholic Center for Holocaust Education here on campus, many possibilities and questions arose. At the start, we wished to involve both student artists and students of all majors. Second, we desired to engage the community and provoke a contribution or a sense of ownership from the campus community. Additionally, I wanted my students to feel challenged and engaged. With these five questions, I came to my class and challenged them to develop a possible work inspired by one of the questions.[4]

The question chosen by Beachley's class was "What is the role of good people in difficult times?" The students selected *typewriters* as the unifying visual and conceptual element, because it offered the viewer the possibility of interacting with the artist's response to the question. The participating students, Molly Huffman, Ashlan Luft, Desmond McCoy, Joseph Messalle, Tiffany Ramsden, and Rebecca Rentz, each created an individual work by altering and manipulating a typewriter. The use of multiple typewriters allowed for no one single answer or simple solution to the question. Joseph Messalle, one of the student artists and conference panel presenters, discusses the process engaged in by the students:

> The usage of typewriters and the nature of the project allowed us the ability to work largely independently and create our own works with minimal

Photo by Bruce Siskawicz © Seton Hill University

conflict, which was extremely important given the diverse attitudes and working habits of the class. Some of us wished to provide straightforward responses to the question chosen, while others chose to have an interactive semi-functional typewriter that the viewer/user would have to work on and experience a journey of errors to come to an answer, in much the same spirit as the train of catastrophes that man and womankind have taken throughout history to reach this point. Our responses are not perfect. Words are not perfect, nor are our eyes and minds; yet they are the clunky and awkward tools that we have to work with to promote justice, equality, and tolerance. However, they can also be used to build guns, tanks, etc.

Placing a sculpture on a podium is a very traditional idea, and in essence, that is what we did; however, we wished to have stands that complemented our pieces. Although other materials were incorporated, steel was largely the chosen medium, as it is often associated with early to mid-twentieth-century technology, complementary to our typewriters. While being durable and practical, steel also has an aggressive edge, bordering on destruction. Personally, I intended to take advantage of this quality when making my own stand; I wanted something that appeared to be taken out of a locomotive factory. Others chose to be less stark in their design, thinking harder and layering meanings. These look to the future. Thus we covered the spectrum of time.[5]

These six students, along with Beachley, worked on creating individual, altered typewriters on stands over a period of months. Student artist Ashlan Luft describes her decision-making process:

> I decided to cover the typewriter with articles cut from newspapers, since they reminded me of the print and text that could be correlated with a typewriter. I covered the entire typewriter with articles on current events such as war, murders, suicides, and a range of other modern-day tragedies. I also used words in larger text that reminded me of the Holocaust, such as violence, terror, Jews, crisis, murder, etc., and placed these on top of the text. Finally, I used letters to form the question, "What is the role of good people in difficult times?" and placed it right above the keys so it would be one of the first things the viewer reads.
>
> After changing the appearance of the typewriter, I then manipulated it to help the viewer arrive at my answer to the question: love. I ground off the letters from all the keys except for the l, o, v, and e. Finally, I put a continuous roll of paper in the typewriter instead of just a single sheet. I feel it is important for the role of good people to never end. Also, with a continuous paper, the viewer can see how many others have participated in the project, and no one's response will be replaced with a clean sheet.[6]

Photo by Carol Brode © Seton Hill University

While each artist went through the decision-making process individually, they were also cognizant of the fact that this project would also function as a unit, the first *marker* in this ongoing project. When completed, the sculptures were arranged into a cohesive installation in the university's art gallery, which opened during the 2009 Ethel LeFrak Holocaust Education Conference. The work is now on permanent display on campus.

The *Question Mark/er Project* is an example of an initiative that can involve multiple components of the community in Holocaust and genocide education. We envision the project to be ever-expandable: it could occur year after year, accumulating numerous markers that each would ask a different question; the project markers could be literary- or performance-based as well as visual; and the openness of the project can be adapted to function with any community. The resulting memorials/markers could be created by an individual or a group, artists or non-artists, children or adults, and could be permanent or temporary. It involves all of us in creating memorials that make history visible in a way that is meaningful in the present, and we welcome others to create their own Question Mark/er projects.

If a first step in engaging in dialogue about difficult issues is asking a question, perhaps the best aspect of this project is that it does this, rather than giving an answer. And a question that we may all need to ask is, "What can I do?"

Questions

1. *As it was conceived, this project could be adapted to any age group or population. The initial gathering of questions could be generated in a number of ways, for example, after viewing a film, after a study unit, etc. How might you generate a discussion and questions for your specific population?*

2. *Once questions have been collected, a project, or "marker" can be created. In our case, we utilized the talents of college art students, but any group can create a unique "marker," which is not necessarily a sculpture/s. Examples include a mural, a garden, a theatrical interpretation, etc. How can you use the talents and abilities of your students in particular?*

3. *Beyond impacting on the immediate group of those collecting the questions and creating the marker, you might consider involving the broader community. Is there a place to display the project where a large number of viewers might see it? If your project results in a performance – theatrical or musical – can it be presented publicly? How can your project impact on large numbers of people?*

Bibliography

Dupré, Judith. *Monuments: America's History in Art and Memory*. New York: Random House, 2007.

Feinstein, Stephen C., ed. *Witness and Legacy: Contemporary Art about the Holocaust*. Minneapolis: Lerner Publications Company, 1995.

Hornstein, Shelley and Florence Jacobowitz, eds. *Image and Remembrance: Representation and the Holocaust*. Bloomington: Indiana University Press, 2002.

Levitt, Laura, Laurence Silberstein and Shelley Hornstein, eds. *Impossible Images: Contemporary Art after the Holocaust*. New York: NYU Press, 2003.

Young, James E. *The Texture of Memory: Holocaust Memorials and Meaning*. New Haven: Yale University Press, 1994.

Young, James E. *At Memory's Edge: After-Images of the Holocaust in Contemporary Art and Architecture*. New Haven: Yale University Press, 2000.

Zelizer, Barbie, ed. *Visual Culture and the Holocaust*. New Brunswick: Rutgers University Press, 2001.

Notes

1. Judith Dupré, *Monuments: America's History in Art and Memory* (New York: Random House, 2007) p. xxi.
2. Roland Deigendesch, Letter to Diane Samuels, 1996.
3. Diane Samuels, Transcript of presentation, Ethel LeFrak Holocaust Education Conference, Greensburg, PA, October 26, 2009.
4. Pati Beachley, Transcript of presentation, Ethel LeFrak Holocaust Education Conference, Greensburg, PA, October 26, 2009.
5. Joseph Messalle, "Question Marker Statement," email to the author, December 8, 2009.
6. Ashlan Luft, email to the author, January 26, 2010.

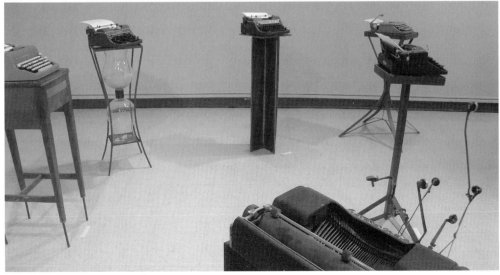

Photo by Carol Brode © Seton Hill University

Refuge, Resistance, and Rescue in Hungary in World War II: Religious and Cultural Interactions

■ ■ ■ ■ ■ ■ ■ ■ ■ ■ ■

Ruth G. Biro

Associate Professor (Retired), Duquesne University, Pittsburgh, PA

> *"Thou shalt not be a perpetrator, thou shalt not be a victim,*
> *and thou shalt never, but never, be a bystander."*
> Yehuda Bauer

This paper celebrates those who offered refuge to Jews, were involved in resistance activities, and accomplished the rescue of Hungarians and those of other nationalities in the Holocaust era. These persons refused to stand by in the face of the Nazi menace. With the admonition of Yehuda Bauer in mind, undergraduate students in an Interdisciplinary Holocaust course and graduate pre-service/in-service teachers enrolled in Multicultural and International Literature at Duquesne University were privileged to hear guest presenter Leslie Banos describe his activities in the resistance, as an aid provider and rescuer in Budapest in World War II. Mr. Banos infiltrated the SS and served as an agent for Allied Intelligence. From 1939–1945, Polish and Slovak Jewish refugees sought sanctuary in Hungary and the activities of Zionist youth, neutral diplomats, and Hungarian Christians in saving Jews are also discussed. Teaching materials relating to the Hungarian Holocaust are included before concluding reflections.

The Hungarian Holocaust occurred late in the war, with Nazi occupation occurring on March 19, 1944. The aftermath of the war involved liberation of the camps, relocation of displaced persons, reuniting families, and reconstructing cities, among other activities, and therefore many details about Hungary did not receive attention until years later. Anticipating that university students may not know relevant details, a summary of refuge, resistance, and rescue in Hungary provides background for the presentation by Banos.

Refugees first started to arrive in Hungary from Germany soon after the passage of the Nuremberg Laws of 1935. Refugees arrived from Austria after the *Anschluss* and the dismemberment of Czechoslovakia in 1938–39. They stayed in Hungary for a few days or weeks while awaiting visas to other locales. Jews arriving from Germany, Austria, or the German-annexed Protectorate often had family or business connections to Hungary, were relatively well off, and required little aid or assistance from Jewish organizations.[1]

In June 1939, the Hungarian Ministry of the Interior organized the transport of 900 Czech, Slovak, Transcarpathian, German, and Austrian Jews to the Danube Delta, where they were met by the ship *Julia Hoemi* for a trip to Palestine, guaranteed by Hungary's Foreign Ministry. In 1939, 20,000 refugees from the northern region of Hungary (the Felvidék) were placed under the care of Hungary's Ministry of the Interior. The social task of refugee assistance was given to the Interior Ministry's Social Work Division IX, and included duties to receive and register each refugee, organize assistance to them and supply food, and find temporary schools for their children. Other assistance was provided by the Hungarian Red Cross, the Committee of Assistance to Hungarian Refugees, the Committee to Help the Transylvanians, and other humanitarian institutions.

Following the Nazi invasion of Poland on September 1, 1939, Polish soldiers and civilians sought safety in Hungary, many Jews among them. At the Hungarian border, guards were instructed by József Antall Sr., head of the Social Service division of the Hungarian Ministry, to register all Polish refugees as Christians. Between 1940–1943, approximately 200,000 refugees received assistance from the government. In 1941, the division was charged with the responsibility of refugees from Bukovina and Hungarians living outside the borders of historic Hungary. Refugees went to Hungary from Transylvania and Yugoslavia in the summer of 1944, fleeing the advance of the Soviet Army. Rudolf Vrba, in his book on his escape from Auschwitz with Alfred Wetzler, mentions that thousands of Jews from Poland and Slovakia sought asylum in Hungary.[2]

The story of the Polish Jews who sought refuge in Hungary during the Holocaust has been little known because much material was written in Hungarian or Polish. Moreover, difficulties with archival resources hampered research on refugee statistics. On March 19, 1944, occupying Germans confiscated the records on Polish refugees and Polish organizations maintained by the Central Office of Alien Control (KEOGH). Records housed in the Interior Ministry and Foreign Ministry were destroyed. Files of the Hungarian Red Cross were partially destroyed at the end of World War II, and again in the decade of the 1950s as a result of a water leak.[3]

Study of Hungary's role in providing refuge to Jewish Poles was inspired by a 2006 exhibit at Duquesne University entitled "A Blessing to One Another: Pope John Paul II and the Jewish People," which mentioned Polish Jews seeking refuge abroad in the Holocaust. Refugees escaping to Hungary were aided by Zionist youth groups, members of Jewish organizations and networks, persons later designated as Righteous Gentiles, and by individuals such as Mr. Banos, honored for his bravery as a rescuer on the Yad Vashem monument at Apor Vilmos Square, dedicated in 2005 in Budapest. These topics were infused into the Interdisciplinary Holocaust course and Multicultural and International Literature course to support the ecumenical mission of the university through teaching the Holocaust.

The Nazi invasion of Poland on September 1, 1939 created a stream of military and civilian refugees, including Jews, into Hungary. Jozsef Antall Sr., head of the Social Service division of the Hungarian Ministry, gave instructions to register all Polish refugees as Christians unless they insisted upon being identified as non-Christians. Polish Jewish intellectual leaders were sheltered in Estergom, the city seat of the Hungarian primate. After the Nazi invasion, several leaders were imprisoned, including Antall, who was in the same prison in Budapest as resister Hannah Senesh. Henryk Slawik, leader of Polish emigration in Hungary who served as president of the Polish Civic Committee for Relief for Refugees, was taken from Hungary to Mauthausen, where he died in August 1944. In the Duquesne University course, resources pertaining to Tsvi Goldfarb and Emanuel Tanay were examined on their experiences as Polish Jewish refugees in Hungary in World War II.

Tsvi Goldfarb, born in Poland in 1921, was a prominent member of the resistance in Hungary. Well acquainted with the horrors of the Holocaust in his own nation, in 1942 he was sent by the "Dror" movement to warn Jews of the Nazi menace and help them prepare for resistance and rescue. After spending a year in Slovakia, he made his way to Hungary, where he operated under various false identities as a refugee from the Carpatho-Ruthenian region or as an Italian tourist, in order to carry out his mission. As a member of the Zionist youth underground in Hungary, he set up bunkers, liberated Jews from forced labor camps, used weapons proficiently, smuggled Jews over the Romanian border, and planned *tiyul* (trip) activities to other locales. In one operation, he and his future wife Neshka (Hungarian-born Agnes Szande) were caught, imprisoned, and tortured. They escaped from the Margit Boulevard military prison in a daring escapade planned by the Zionist youth underground. After the liberation of Budapest in early 1945, Tsvi and Neshka cared for the remaining refugees, organized orphanages, took children to Palestine, and rehabilitated the Dror group – earlier the Hehalutz Hatzair. *Brothers for Resistance and Rescue* is dedicated to his memory.[4]

Emanuel Tanay's memoir, *Passport to Life*,[5] recalls his escape from Poland to Hungary through Slovakia. Tenenwurzel (later Tanay) was born in Wilno, Poland (now Vilnius, Lithuania) in 1928. After the German invasion of Poland in 1939, his family made a failed attempt to flee eastward. In 1943, Tanay, his mother, younger sister, and girlfriend left Krakow by rail, traveled by horse-drawn wagon and on foot, and arrived in Slovakia. They told a false story that Tanay's father was born in Budapest and was now living in Hungary. They stated that they were visiting relatives in Poland when the war broke out, and therefore the fictitious report filed in Slovakia stated that they were Hungarian Jews, not Polish Jews. They were smuggled into Kassa (today Kosice), put on a train bound for Budapest, and instructed about what to expect and how the Jewish community would take care of them there. They were given Christian papers so they would be legal Polish refugees and not identifiable as Polish Jews. At the agency office, a Polish official interrogated Tanay, his mother, sister, and girlfriend, and the official believed or pretended to believe they were Polish Christians.

After a few weeks in Budapest, Tanay, his mother and sister were sent to a camp for Polish Jews near Kolocsa, where they were housed with half a dozen Jewish families pretending to be Christian Poles and ten former Polish soldiers. At the camp, no one admitted to being Jewish, and neither Poles nor Jewish Poles knew the identity of those in the group. Pretending to be Christian, the Tanays went to the Protestant church in Uszod, their first encounter with non-Catholic Christians.

Life in the camp abruptly changed with German occupation of Hungary on March 19, 1944. Because the Kolocsa region was studded with refugee camps for Poles, it would be a target for searches for foreign Jews, so they returned to Budapest where they could be anonymous. Arriving back in Budapest, they learned that the Hashomer Hatzair group run by Slovak Jews was effective in assisting refugees. Tanay contacted Mimis Herbst and later met Rafi Friedel (Benshalom) and Moshe (Alpan) Pil, second in command. The ghettoization of Jews in the provinces of Hungary in April 1944 and systematic deportation in the five regions of Hungary from May 15–July 7, 1944, meant that all areas had been cleared of Jews except Budapest, which held 200,000 Jews. Tanay had continued the ruse of being Christian after his escape into Hungary in 1943. Under Nazi occupation, the Hungarian Jews in Budapest found themselves seeking false documents, when earlier they had thought them unnecessary. The promised land of refuge had become a land of persecution.

Tanay attempted to make his way to Romania, but was arrested at the Hungarian border and sent to the maximum security Csillag Prison in Szeged, where he was incarcerated when he learned of the Allied invasion of Normandy. He was later taken to Tololya concentration camp, then to the Columbus Street camp in Budapest, and to the Fo Street prison, where Hannah Senesh, one of the Jewish parachutists, was interned. In February 1945, he went to Krakow where he learned from two survivors from Plaszow camp that his father (aged 39) had been shot by camp commandant Amon Goeth. In January 1952, Tanay's journey as refugee/displaced person ended when he arrived at New York harbor and later became a professor of psychiatry and forensic psychiatrist in the USA.

Prior to World War I, parts of Slovakia were in Greater Hungary; many Slovaks had Hungarian relatives and spoke some Hungarian. The border between Slovakia and Hungary in the Second World War was established in 1938, when parts of southern Slovakia were turned over to Hungary. When expulsions from Slovakia began in April 1942, Jews fled southward. The Zionist Halutz movements were part of this *tiyul* flight and some members of the Polish resistance were in the group that later reached Hungary.[6] The Slovakian Jewish underground, operating out of Bratislava, was an important source of information. Works pertaining to resistance member and rescuer Rafi Benshalom and Gerta Vrbova, a refugee and courier in Hungary, were explored in our course regarding the presence of Slovaks in Hungary in World War II. Benshalom's book provides extensive details on Zionist youth activities in Budapest and specific accounts of document forging.[7]

Gerta Sidon (later Vrbova), girlfriend of Walter Rosenberg (later Rudolf Vrba), learned from him in summer 1944 details of his internment in Auschwitz and the escape he and Alfred Wetzler had made from Poland to Slovakia in April 1944. Vrbova's volume *Trust and Deceit*[8] details her experiences in Slovakia and Hungary from 1939–1945 when she was aged twelve to eighteen. She and her parents made their way to relatives in Hungary in 1942 to escape deportations taking place in Slovakia. Her boyfriend Walter tried to escape to Hungary in 1942, but was caught by Hungarian militia and returned to Slovakia, where he was sent to Majdanek, then to Auschwitz. Gerta arrived in Budapest, where she obtained documents identifying her as a Catholic from a northern border region which had been part of Czechoslovakia.

In winter 1943–44, Hitler was pressuring the Hungarian government for more troops, supplies, and food. By spring 1944, Nazi "Final Solution" action increased, resulting in Nazi occupation on March 19, 1944, and ghettoization and deportation of Hungarian Jews in April–May 1944. Gerta moved to a new hiding place and obtained another document identifying her as a Catholic from the Slovak-Hungarian border. She practiced Catholic prayers and prepared to return to Slovakia. In Bratislava in April 1944, she adopted the new name Gerta Jurkovic and claimed she was from a village in eastern Slovakia then under Russian control, making verification of her fake documents difficult. Friends produced and distributed forged documents, using her typewriter to prepare fake birth and marriage certificates, medical papers, travel permits, and military exemption papers.

In summer 1944, she met with her childhood sweetheart Walter Rosenberg (Vrba) who had returned to Bratislava after his escape from Auschwitz. She was stunned to see his tattoo 44070 and how he had dramatically changed as the result of camp trauma. He related the horrors of degradation and dehumanization in Auschwitz and his escape with Alfred Wetzler to Slovakia, using information he had memorized from a map he found in "Canada," the camp facility where possessions of the deportees were sorted. In September 1944, Walter Rosenberg left Bratislava, changed his name to Rudolf Vrba, and joined partisans fighting the Germans.

By September–November 1944, most of Gerta's Slovak relatives were in hiding or had been rounded up by the Germans and deported to Auschwitz, Ravensbrück, or Buchenwald. In early November, she and her mother were taken to Gestapo headquarters, where they could hear Allied planes conducting raids overhead, attempting to disable oil refineries. She realized that the only hope was escape because Walter had alerted her to be wary of offers of help or promises of SS men. On the sixth day, she jumped out of a window and ran away while her mother, too afraid to jump, remained behind. Gerta decided to return to relatives and friends in Hungary. Dov, the brother of one of her friends, was preparing forged documents, and he arranged papers for her and gave her a list of his Zionist organization contacts in Budapest, which she memorized. She arrived in Hungary by train but jumped off on the outskirts of Budapest because she possessed Slovak papers, not Hungarian ones. The day was November 28, 1944, her eighteenth birthday.

In Budapest, Gerta saw Jews wearing the yellow Star of David pushing carts laden with household goods, or carrying precious possessions in hand on the way to the Budapest Ghetto, an area near the Dohány Street Synagogue. She realized that the Jews of Budapest were not aware of the contents of Walter Rosenberg's (Rudolph Vrba) and Alfred Wetzler's Auschwitz report warning about the German plan for the fate of Jews. Gerta spent the night under a canoe on the Danube bank because the entire city was in a blackout. The next morning, she set out for her Aunt Manci's apartment near Margit Bridge to ascertain the whereabouts of her father and to obtain food and money. The gate to the residence carried the notice "Protected by the Swedish Government." Gerta later went to the home of Maria, her former French teacher who was hiding three French escapees from a prisoner of war camp. Maria equipped Gerta with a suitcase of clothing and temporary identification as Eva Takacs. Maria's brother, a civil servant in the Ministry of Defense, connected her with the committee that provided refugee support and accommodation.

Gerta was given refugee status documents, an apartment in Buda, and a weekly allowance. After contacting a Jewish name on the Zionist list that Dov had given her in Slovakia, she began service as a courier of forged documents to the Budapest Ghetto. She placed a blue ribbon in her blond hair to enhance her false appearance as an Aryan teenager. In the meantime, her Aunt Manci's Swedish-protected apartment was raided by Hungarian militia and residents were instructed to prepare for a long three-day march to the Austrian border. At the border, Raoul Wallenberg suddenly appeared and directed that Jews under Swedish protection be returned to Budapest. Unfortunately, Manci was sent to the Budapest Ghetto. Armed with a forged birth certificate proclaiming Manci as her mother, Gerta secured her release. By the middle of December, the Russian offensive was in Buda.

When fighting stopped on her street, Gerta and several friends left Budapest on January 15 and journeyed mostly by foot to Szeged. They passed villages where

Russians had confiscated goods and food from abandoned houses. Gerta spoke some Russian so the group hitched rides from Russian soldiers and ate some of their food. In Szeged, they contacted the Zionist Hashomer Hatzair group, which was helping Jews from all parts of Europe to emigrate to Palestine and preparing young people for life in a kibbutz. Gerta served as a Zionist recruiting officer and met survivors from work and concentration camps, those who had been in hiding, or who had been fighting with partisans.

At the end of February 1945, Gerta returned to Budapest to discuss her future plans with her relatives. In May, at war's end, she returned to her hometown of Trnava. Her parents never returned so she sold her family's house in Trnava for a gold watch, a Leica camera, and a typewriter. She, Walter (now Rudolf), and her friend Inge took a summer program in Bratislava to enhance their education and moved to Prague to start their university studies. Gerta and Walter (Rudolf Vrba) married during their student days. She completed studies as a medical doctor, had two daughters, and earned a Ph.D. When the marriage failed, she and her daughters escaped to Copenhagen through Poland and immigrated to England, where she now pursues neuroscience research as Gerta Vrbova.

Examination of the role of youth in the Hungarian resistance was inspired by presentations offered by Yehuda Bauer at Yad Vashem for the Catholic Institute for Holocaust Studies, sponsored by Seton Hill University, which I attended in winter 1998–1999 and in summer 2000. I had already incorporated a discussion of selected Hungarian survivor stories and memoirs in the Multicultural and International Literature course[9] and was anxious to include a presentation by Les Banos on his role in humanitarian activities. His story added important information on refuge, resistance, and rescue in Budapest. Additional Hungarian activists were also included, such as Yoel Palgi (Jewish parachutist) and Sr. Margit Slachta (Christian leader of the Sisters of Social Service), so students could appreciate religious and cultural interactions during the Holocaust era.

Nobel Peace Prize Laureate Elie Wiesel's memoir *All Rivers Run to the Sea* provides information about Polish refugees in Hungary. He observed:

> We knew something of what was happening beyond the borders. The Hungarian and Yiddish newspapers offered vague reports, but we knew things were bad…
>
> From Polish refugees passing throughout town, all bearing bad news, we heard tales of the German army's invincibility and brutality. We were told of arbitrary arrests, systematic humiliation, collective persecutions, and even of pogroms and massacres.[10]

Wiesel's hometown of Sziget (in Romania after World War I) became Maramarossziget again under Hungarian rule, when lost land was returned to Hungary in World War II. He reported that the population joyfully greeted Hungarian troops. He wrote:

> Though no one was yet talking of liquidation or extermination, news of massacres in Poland began to filter through. And it should have been enough to awaken us. In 1941 more than a thousand "foreign Jews"– those unable to document their Hungarian citizenship – were expelled from Hungarian territory to Polish Galicia. I remember going to the station to say goodbye. Everyone was there. We thought we would see them again someday, but only one managed to escape, and that was Moshe the Beadle.[11]

Wiesel reported that the ravages of war seemed far from his city – the fall of Paris, the bombing of Pearl Harbor, Stalingrad – but gradually events came closer when Italian troops passed through Sziget strumming mandolins on the way to the front. Upon returning back through Sziget, the Italians were in silence with heads bowed. He noted that the war brought new challenges to the citizens as they addressed the needs of those who sought refuge in his town: "It had forced its way into our consciousness indirectly when Polish refugees arrived. Assigned by the community to look after them, my father listening to their testimony moved heaven and earth to get them money and false papers and prevent the gendarmes from expelling them."[12] Wiesel commented specifically on how his father helped refugees obtain foreign currency so they could make their way to the underground network in Budapest, rather than being sent back to Poland. He stated:

> When the laws got stricter, my father had a new idea. Having discovered that anyone apprehended with foreign currency would be immediately transferred to the counterespionage bureau in Budapest, he arranged to supply the refugees with a few US dollars, Swiss francs, pounds sterling, which prevented them from being sent back to Poland. In Budapest there was an underground network to help them, and almost all survived.[13]

In order to address the specific elements of resistance in Budapest, students are introduced to categories of resistance in ascending order of involvement, delineated by Vera Laska, a non-Jew in the Czech resistance. In Budapest, she helped the Czech underground spirit away Czechs and some Slovaks to join Allied armed forces in the West. She also was interned in the infamous Csillag Prison in Szeged, Hungary, the same prison in which Tanay from Poland had been interned. After the war, she was a member of the Czechoslovak War Crimes Team. The ten steps of resistance she describes are:

1. Engaging in passive resistance – quietly boycotting;
2. Issuing illegal publications to build moral support or for subversion purposes;
3. Falsifying documents, ration cards, passports, birth certificates, etc.;
4. Acting as messengers and couriers;
5. Hiding the persecuted, Jews, Allied escapees, and evaders;
6. Contacting the Allies, usually by radio;
7. Committing sabotage, acts based on the resister's plan to slow Nazi efforts;
8. Smuggling people through escape routes to freedom;
9. Acting as partisans, conducting paramilitary activities;
10. Carrying out assassinations or revolts.[14]

In Hungary, there were four different and fairly independent Jewish resistance initiatives, with most organized resistance coming from the Jewish youth movements.[15] The groups included:1) The Zionist Association: Otto Komoly, president, which established Department A for Children's Protection as part of the International Red Cross; 2) Moshe Krausz, Secretary of the Palestine Office, who was in close contact with the Swiss consul Carl Lutz and established the extraterritorial status of the Glass House so Jews could be sheltered there; 3) The Rescue and Relief Committee, led by Rezso Kasztner and Joel Brand, which served as the conduit for information about the fate of East European Jewry to Istanbul and the world. Kasztner is known for his efforts to rescue over 1,600 Jews from Hungary and take them to safety in Switzerland; Brand's failed mission was to sell one million Jews for 10,000 trucks; 4) Halutz Youth Movement members, a few hundred men and women who maintained contact with comrades in Slovakia and Poland and worked closely together underground in 1944 with refugees and Hungarian youth.

The Halutz Youth rescued comrades from ghettos in the countryside, warned Jews not to enter deportation trains, and presented false documents to those in ghettos to use in escape in May and June 1944. Another activity was the organization of the *tiyul*, the trip from Hungary to Romania, where at the Transylvanian border a member of the resistance would lead them to a smuggler who would take them onward. More than 2,000 were saved by Halutz action between May and August 1944.[16] As the transport of Hungarian Jews continued in June, three parachutists with the British Royal Air Force, including Hannah Senesh, arrived into Hungary. She was executed in November 1944.

After October 15, 1944, resistance and neutral representatives utilized both genuine and forged protective passes to save Jews. Halutz Youth groups used 7,800 legal Swiss documents to create more than 100,000 additional papers.[17] The Halutz resistance offices also prepared other documents for their members, other Jews, and persecuted non-Jews, including Catholic and Protestant baptismal and marriage certificates, matriculation certificates, residency certificates, military leave passes, ration card validations, etc.[18] After November, when Arrow Cross gangs patrolled the streets, the youth movement rescued Jews from their march to the banks of the Danube, where massacres took place.

Stories of refuge (especially Poles and Slovaks), resistance (Jewish and Christian efforts), and rescue by neutral diplomats (Swedes, Swiss, Portuguese, the Vatican's Papal Nuncio, and others), members of religious orders (e.g. Sisters of Social Service, Monsignor Bela Varga), public officials (Jozsef Antall Sr.), and citizens (the Vanczaks, Banos, and others) are mentioned so that the involvement of people of different religions and cultures can be demonstrated. Hungarian Christians were involved in resistance or rescue, including Dr. Jozsef Antall, Monsignor Bela Varga, Rev. Gabor Sztehlo, Dr. Albert Szent-Gyorgy, and Tibor Baranski. Antall is credited with saving 14,000 lives in World War II. Over 700 Hungarians have been declared "Righteous Among the Nations" by Yad Vashem, including Banos' relatives Margit, Bela, and Zsuzsa Vanczak.[19]

Several representatives of neutral nations and international organizations were also engaged in rescue attempts. These included Swedish delegation members Wallenberg, Carlsson, Anger, and Berg; Swiss representatives Lutz and Feller and Red Cross head Born; and Perlasca, the Italian who masqueraded as the Spanish chargé d'affaires, among others. Papal Nuncio Angelo Rotta was declared a Righteous Gentile, as was Raoul Wallenberg (credited with saving 100,000 Jewish lives); Carl Lutz (who saved 62,000), and Giorgio Perlasca (who rescued between 3,000–6,000 Jews).[20]

Selected materials are used to teach about the Hungarian Holocaust in the Perspectives on the Holocaust course and in the Multicultural and International Literature course. The resources below, not noted in the bibliography for this paper, are easily identified in published materials or on the Internet.

Videos introduce the Hungarian Holocaust: *Fateless* (based on the book by Nobel Laureate Imre Kertesz); *Last Days* (Survivors of the Shoah Visual History Foundation) and *Whatever Happened to Wallenberg?* (History Channel). *Brady's Escape* shows Nazis searching for a downed American airman over Debrecen and Brady's safe passage to partisans in Yugoslavia.

Maps from Martin Gilbert's *Routledge Atlas of the Holocaust*, Yad Vashem's maps on the Holocaust, the USHMM Historical Atlas of the Holocaust, and Braham's *Politics of Genocide* locate places in Hungary.

Jewish Budapest is described in Tim Cole's *Holocaust City* (Budapest Ghetto), Frojimovics et al., *Jewish Budapest*, and Orban, *Guide to Jewish Budapest*. Additional materials relating to Hungary are covered in Patai, *The Jews of Hungary* and Szalai, *In the Land of Hagar*.

Statistics on the Hungarian Holocaust are found in Stark, *Hungarian Jews during the Holocaust and after the Second World War*. Governmental policies are in *I Have Been a Stranger in a Strange Land* by Kinga Frojimovics. Braham with Miller's *The Nazis' Last Victims* details the Hungarian Holocaust. The timeline in *The Holocaust Chronicle* (edited by John Roth et al.) provides dates and comparative Holocaust aspects for other nations.

Eyewitness rescue is found in Fenyvesi's *When Angels Fooled the World*. Anger's *With Raoul Wallenberg in Budapest* and Berg's *The Book that Disappeared* are by Swedish rescuers. Also see *Yad Vashem Studies'* articles by Robert Rozett, Livia Rothkirchen, and Leni Yahil. Rescue by Wallenberg is covered in many works for student and adult audiences, such as those by as Kati Marton, John Bierman, Andrew Handler, Elenore Lester, Harvey Rosenfeld, Werbell and Clarke, and others.

Other resources on resistance and rescue include *Trading in Lives* (Jewish relief and rescue) by Szabolcs Szita; *Operation Hazalah* by Gilles Lambert; Anna Porter's book *Kasztner's Train; Facing the Holocaust in Budapest* by Arieh Ben-Tov (International Red Cross); Cohen, *The Halutz Resistance in Hungary, 1942–1944*, and Cohen and Cochavi, *Zionist Youth Movements during the Shoah*.

The poster set "Traits that Transcend" (Jewish Fund for the Righteous) and excerpts from Paldiel's *Path of the Righteous*, Gilbert's *Righteous*, and Yad Vashem's *Encyclopedia of the Righteous Among the Nations – Europe and Other Countries Pt. I*, provide material on Righteous Gentiles.

Citation to books for school students on the Hungarian Holocaust are provided from Sullivan's *The Holocaust in Literature for Youth*; from *Learning about the Holocaust* by Stephens et al.; and *The Spirit That Moves Us*, Vol. 3 by Stillman. Totten and Feinberg's *Teaching and Studying the Holocaust* demonstrates teaching methodology. Students are also referred to additional resources pertinent to their projects.

Curriculum guides referenced are *Echoes and Reflections* (ADL/ Shoah Foundation Institute/Yad Vashem); *Study of Heroes* (Raoul Wallenberg Association of the US); and Grobman's *Holocaust: A Guide for Pennsylvania Teachers*. Goldberg's *Holocaust Memoir Digest* (3 vols) models survivor memoir study.

A primary source utilized by Biro is Wallenberg's *Letters and Dispatches 1924–1944*. Banos consulted a photocopy of Wallenberg's address and notice book for

1944–45 (in the USHMM). The research of Ervin Staub on the potential role of bystanders to aid those in harm's way in *The Psychology of Good and Evil* reveals an agenda shaped by his experience as a child of six, saved by his Christian maid and Wallenberg.

Students at Duquesne University have been fortunate to hear the personal perspective of Mr. Leslie Banos. As the result of his guest presentation and discussion of his book, *If They Catch You, You Will Die*,[21] several students in the Perspectives on the Holocaust course wrote papers on resistance and two studied Wallenberg's rescue work in Hungary. In the Multicultural and International Literature course, students read several Hungarian Holocaust memoirs. One student developed a literature unit on teenagers interned in Auschwitz, and another student reviewed *The Auschwitz Album*[22] which depicts Hungarian Jews from the Carpathian region arriving in the camp, those who had no refuge or rescue.

The presentation by Mr. Banos regarding his personal experiences serves to remind us that those involved in refuge, resistance, and rescue in Hungary in the Holocaust era did not stand by as their fellow Jewish citizens were persecuted and murdered. Students well understood the moral courage exhibited by Mr. Banos and those who chose to thwart the Nazis to save Jewish lives. May we continue to celebrate the persons who offered refuge to Jews, were involved in resistance activities, and accomplished rescue, realizing the admonition of Yehuda Bauer: "Thou shalt never, but never, be a bystander."

Questions

1. *What specific books, videos, and curriculum guides might be utilized to teach about the Holocaust era in Hungary?*

2. *Why does study of Jewish resistance and Christian rescuers in Hungary illuminate the religious and cultural interactions of refugees, persecuted citizens, and neutral diplomats?*

3. *Explain how refugees from other nations participated in refuge, resistance, and rescue activities in Hungary during World War II.*

4. *How do the memoirs of Holocaust survivors Tanay, Vrbova, and Wiesel serve to connect events, places, situations, and activities in Hungary?*

5. *Do students reveal their understanding of the role of those who did not stand by as Jews were persecuted and murdered through their questions to a guest presenter, class project selections, and course evaluation comments?*

Bibliography

Banos, Leslie. *If They Catch You, You Will Die*. Pittsburgh: Banos Publishing, 2009.

Benshalom, Rafi. *We Struggled for Life: The Hungarian Zionist Youth Resistance during the Nazi Era*. Jerusalem and New York: Gefen, 2001.

Biro, Ruth G. "Representations of Budapest 1944–1945 in Holocaust Literature." *Comparative Central European Holocaust Studies*. Eds. Louise O. Vasvari and Steven Totosy de Zepetnek. West Lafayette, IN: Purdue University Press, 2009: 3–17.

Braham, Randolph L. *The Politics of Genocide: The Holocaust in Hungary*. 2nd ed. 2 vols. New York: Columbia University Press, 1994.

Cohen, Asher. "Resistance and Rescue in Hungary." In David Cesarani, ed. *Genocide and Rescue: The Holocaust in Hungary 1944*. Oxford: Berg, 1997: 123–134.

Gur, David and Eli Netzer, eds. *Brothers for Resistance and Rescue: The Underground Zionist Youth Movement in Hungary during WWII*. Jerusalem: Gefen, 2007.

Gutman, Israel and Bella Gutterman. *The Auschwitz Album: The Story of a Transport*. Auschwitz-Birkenau: Panstwowe Museum and Jerusalem: Yad Vashem, 2002.

Kapronczay, Karoly. *Refugees in Hungary: Shelter from the Storm during World War II*. Trans. Eva Barcza-Bessenyey. Toronto: Matthias Corvinus, 1999.

Laska, Vera. "Non-Jews and Women in the Fight Against Nazism." In *Resisters, Rescuers, and Refugees: Historical and Ethical Issues*. Ed. John J. Michalczyk. Kansas City: Sheed and Ward, 1987: 93–102.

Tanay, Emanuel. *Passport to Life: Autobiographical Reflections on the Holocaust*. Ann Arbor, MI: Forensic, 2004.

Vrba, Rudolph. *I Escaped from Auschwitz*. Fort Lee, NJ: Barricade, 2002.

Vrbova, Gerta. *Trust and Deceit: A Tale of Survival in Slovakia and Hungary, 1939–1945*. London and Portland, OR: Vallentine Mitchell, 2006.

Wiesel, Elie. *All Rivers Run to the Sea*. New York: Knopf, 1995.

Notes

1. See further, Randolph L. Braham, *The Politics of Genocide: The Holocaust in Hungary*, 2 vols. (New York: Columbia University Press, 1994).
2. Rudolf Vrba, *I Escaped from Auschwitz* (Fort Lee: Barricade, 2002), p. 305.
3. See further, Karoly Kapronczay, *Refugees in Hungary: Shelter from the Storm during World War II*, trans. Eva Barcza-Bessenyey (Toronto and Buffalo: Matthias Corvinus, 1999), pp. 71–72.
4. See further David Gur and Eli Netzer, eds., *Brothers for Resistance and Rescue: The Underground Zionist Youth Movement in Hungary during WWII* (Jerusalem: Gefen, 2007). Goldfarb's book, *On the Verge of the End*, was published in Hebrew in 1980 by the Ghetto Fighters' Museum in Israel.
5. Emanuel Tanay, *Passport to Life: Autobiographical Reflections on the Holocaust* (Ann Arbor, MI: Forensic Press, 2004).
6. Asher Cohen, "Resistance and Rescue in Hungary," in David Cesarani, ed., *Genocide and Rescue: The Holocaust in Hungary, 1944* (Oxford: Berg, 1997), p. 125.

7. See further, Rafi Benshalom, *We Struggled for Life: The Hungarian Zionist Youth Resistance during the Nazi Era* (Jerusalem and New York: Gefen, 2001), pp. 151–153.
8. Gerta Vrbova, *Trust and Deceit: A Tale of Survival in Slovakia and Hungary, 1939–1945* (London and Portand OR: Vallentine Mitchell, 2006).
9. Ruth G. Biro, "Representations of Budapest 1944–1945 in Holocaust Literature," in Louise O. Vasvari and Steven Totosy de Zepetnek, eds., *Comparative Central European Holocaust Studies* (West Lafayette, IN: Purdue University Press, 2009), pp. 3–17.
10. Elie Wiesel, *All Rivers Run to the Sea: Memoirs* (New York: Alfred Knopf, 1995), p. 27.
11. Ibid., p. 28.
12. Ibid., pp. 30–31.
13. Ibid., p. 31.
14. Vera Laska, "Non-Jews and Women in the Fight Against Nazism," in John J. Michalczyk, ed., *Resisters, Rescuers, and Refugees: Historical and Ethical Issues* (Kansas City: Sheed and Ward, 1987), pp. 93–102.
15. Cohen in Cesarani, op.cit., p. 124.
16. Ibid., pp. 127–129.
17. Ibid., p. 130.
18. See further, Benshalom, *We Struggled for Life*.
19. http://www1.yadvashem.org/yv/en/righteous/stories/pdf/virtial_wall/hungary.pdf.
20. See further, Braham, *Politics of Genocide*.
21. Leslie Banos, *If They Catch You, You Will Die* (Pittsburgh: Banos Publishing, 2009).
22. Israel Gutman and Bella Gutterman, *The Auschwitz Album: The Story of a Transport* (Auschwitz-Birkenau: Panstwowe Museum and Jerusalem: Yad Vashem, 2002).

My Role in the Hungarian Resistance and as Aid Provider and Rescuer in Budapest: A Personal Perspective

■ ■ ■ ■ ■ ■ ■ ■ ■ ■ ■

Leslie Banos

Retired Video Coordinator for Sports, Department of Athletics, University of Pittsburgh, Pittsburgh, PA

I am frequently called upon to tell the story of my humanitarian actions during World War II to university students, school pupils, community organizations, professional and military audiences. When addressing groups as a guest presenter, I offer my perspective regarding my role in the Hungarian resistance and as an aid provider and rescuer in Budapest. At age sixteen, I became an agent of Allied Intelligence by joining the resistance. When Hungary was occupied by the Germans on March 19, 1944, I infiltrated the Hungarian SS division, interacted with Nazi officers, and provided information about plans against the Jews to my resistance contact. During this time, I falsified orders on military stationery, created safe conduct papers, and changed orders to reroute many who were destined for deportation. On Allied assignment in 1944, I transported American and British airmen in my SS military car to Csepel Island, where awaiting partisans would take them to safety. I also joined with the Vanczak family – my maternal Aunt Margit, her husband Bela, and their daughter Zsusza (Zsuzsanna) – to hide Jews, exiles, and persecuted persons at their Csányi Street furniture factory in Budapest. Almost 300 lives were saved. I also interacted with the Swedish diplomat Raoul Wallenberg during the first days of the Soviet liberation of Pest, just before Wallenberg disappeared into the Soviet gulag, never to be seen again in the West. The Vanczaks have been honored as Righteous Gentiles by

Yad Vashem. Over fifty relatives on my father's Jewish side of the family perished in the Hungarian Holocaust, including my father and younger step-brother, Pál.

Some aspects of my life and background in Hungary will serve to introduce the story of rescue in which I and the Vanczak family were engaged during the period of turmoil in Europe and in Hungary under German occupation. These facts set the stage for the situation I faced in the early period of World War II, the years before the occupation of Hungary on March 19, 1944, the eleven months of occupation, the aftermath of the Holocaust, and my emigration from Hungary in 1947.

I was born in 1923 in Nyirbátor, a city in northeastern Hungary near Romania. My father, Maurice (Moritz), was Jewish and my mother, Bertha (Berta), was Christian. My mother died when I was not yet one year of age. I was sent to Budapest to live with my maternal grandmother, aunt Margit (my mother's sister), and her family (husband Bela and cousin Zsusza). The Vanczak family owned a factory that made furniture and other goods from steel on Csányi Street and Király Street, located not far from the Dohány Street Synagogue in Budapest. I remained in Budapest until the age of six, when I returned to Nyirbátor to live with my father, stepmother and baby stepbrother Pál (Pali). In 1937, at age fourteen, I returned to Budapest to continue my education in the capital city. I worked half the day in the Vanczak steel fabricating firm and spent the other half attending technical school.

My mother's Vanczak family in Budapest was prominent in the Social Democrats. My great-uncle Janos Vanczak was the head of the Steel Workers' Union, editor of the Social Democrats' newspaper *Népszava*, and member of Parliament representing the city of Győr. The family was anti-fascist and anti-Nazi. When the Nazis annexed Czechoslovakia in 1938, officers fled to Poland, then to Hungary after Hitler invaded Poland in 1939. The Vanczak family hired Czech refugees to work in the factory and sheltered them until they could be smuggled to safety. Many refugees were Jewish leaders and professionals who were persecuted by the Nazis. This situation was responsible for inaugurating my resistance and rescue activities in the capital city.

In 1939, when I was aged sixteen, I became an agent for Allied Intelligence (as Laszlo Banos) by joining the resistance. The German invasion of Poland in September 1939 prompted the calling of meetings where I represented the Vanczak family. Plans were made to hinder Hitler's actions, minimize his support, and implement strategies against Nazi ideologies. Hungarian resistance members infiltrated factories and sabotaged operations. They frustrated German transportation efforts by misrouting materials. For example, shipping labels were switched so that heavy clothing and cold-weather oil were shipped to Italy instead of to Russia, and the light clothing was sent to Russia. Perishables and ammunition were also rerouted to wrong destinations.

In 1941, when I was eighteen, the underground resistance placed me in a government-owned factory (Manfred Weiss on Csepel Island) on assignment for Allied Intelligence. My sole contact with the Allies was Julius Schweiger, an engineer in residence on 64 Rákóczi Street, not far from the Dohány Street Synagogue and the Vanczak factory on the edge of the Jewish section. Mr. Schweiger had connections with the Yugoslav partisans, the British Secret Service, and the American Office of Strategic Services (OSS, today's CIA). Allied Intelligence needed information about the activities and production of the Manfred Weiss factory – which provided materials to the German war effort – so that the Allied bombers could target air raids and assess the damages inflicted. The Weiss factory employed 35,000 people and manufactured diverse products such as dive bombers, tanks, ammunition, weapons, and textiles. Because my uncle owned a steel-fabricating facility, I was able to acquire a workbook as a master welder, which allowed me free movement into different departments as a maintenance troubleshooter in the Weiss factory. I was given a tiny camera disguised as a welder's lighter so I could report on activities there.

A break came for the resistance in 1944 when the Waffen-SS was recruiting in Budapest. The resistance requested that I meet with Mr. Schweiger in his office, where it was explained that papers had been obtained from a dead university student of German descent from eastern Hungary near Romania, and I was to assume his identity. As a result, at age twenty, I was recruited by the underground to join the SS under the assumed identity of George (György) Nemeth. I was assigned to the SS Headquarters in Budapest as a liaison between the Hungarian Army and the SS operations in Budapest. Although this was a dangerous assignment, I spoke German, set about learning all facets of the background of George Nemeth and volunteered for the *SS Jagdverband*, a special SS unit. The *SS Jagdverband Sudost Einsatzgruppe Ungarn* (SS Task Force, South East, assigned to Hungary) under Adolf Eichmann was the division in which I served. I was accepted by the SS and the company commander sent me to the officers' orientation at Ludovika Military Academy (the Hungarian West Point), based on Nemeth's educational background.

With this cover, therefore, after the German Army occupied Hungary on March 19, 1944 in "Operation Margarethe," I infiltrated the Hungarian Nazi SS division, interacted with high-ranking Nazi officers, and provided my resistance contact with information about Nazi plans against the Jews of Budapest. I falsified orders on German military stationery, created safe conduct papers for those in danger, and changed orders within the SS subcommand to reroute many people destined for deportation back to the Budapest ghetto. As part of my assignment from Allied Intelligence in 1944, I transported American and English airmen in my SS military car to Csepel Island, where waiting partisans secured their return to safety.

My daily assignments began in the SS offices with a short recap of the previous day. After reviewing the assignments of the day, I carried out routine orders, checking with the Arrow Cross command and relaying orders to the Hungarian SS group stationed at Ludovika. I had been given a car with a license plate that indicated it was an SS Headquarters vehicle. When these activities were completed, I was able to move about and take advantage of the fact that most assignments were verbal, not written. As this was the case, without written orders it was possible for me to lie without the fear of getting caught. For additional safety, I prepared two false documents identifying me as George Nemeth, a member of the Headquarters staff. On one, I signed the signature of SS General August Schmidthuber, SS military chief of Budapest, and on another, I penned the fraudulent signature of Edmund Veesenmayer, head of the German legation in Budapest. I also had access to the official rubber stamp of SS Headquarters.

During this time, I was able to accomplish many tasks for Mr. Schweiger. I also joined with my maternal Aunt Margit and her husband Bela, who owned the Vanczak furniture factory on Csányi Street near the Budapest ghetto, to hide Jews, political exiles, and others subject to persecution in a secret space in the sewer system of the factory. I smuggled food to feed the refugees. Aunt Margit provided those in hiding with one hot meal each day. In 1975, Hungarian television filmed a documentary on the hiding place in the Vanczak factory, showing Aunt Margit and her daughter Zsuzsa at the location of the hole where Jews were given safety.

I personally met Raoul Wallenberg, the Swedish diplomat sent to Budapest under the auspices of the U.S. War Refugee Board of the Roosevelt administration, who is credited with saving the lives of 100,000 Jews between July 1944 and January 1945. Mr. Schweiger's son, George, was sent to my Aunt Margit with a message which directed me to go to Mr. Schweiger's office, where Mr. Wallenberg and two others were waiting. Because Wallenberg's car, driven by Mr. Langerfeld, was known to the authorities, it could not be used to take people to safety on Csepel Island. This was the beginning of my cooperation with Wallenberg, whose requests were relayed through Mr. Schweiger to my Aunt Margit, and on to me. Most of the people I transported to Csepel Island were at the request of Wallenberg.

I next saw Wallenberg at Liberation on January 17, 1945. He came to the Vanczak factory and explained that he had left his car with his chauffeur, Langerfeld, in front of Russian Headquarters at the Hotel Royal. I accompanied him there because he wanted to testify on my behalf. Before we got far from the factory, we were stopped on Király Street by a Russian soldier with a machine gun, who demanded our documents – which he proceeded to tear up and throw into a snow bank. We were directed to a courtyard, where Russians were rounding up Hungarian men aged fourteen to sixty for transport to the railroad station for forced labor in Siberia. Wallenberg said that he had diplomatic immunity and spoke Russian, and remained behind. He promised to look for me when things simmered down. The building's concierge, Mr. Toth, whom I knew, urged me to try to escape. I jumped over the high wall, cut my hand, and made my escape in another direction when the Russians were not looking. When I arrived back at the factory, I explained to my aunt that it was imperative I escape because I was still wearing German underwear and shoes from my SS wardrobe. This was at the end of the day, on January 17, 1945. Wallenberg disappeared shortly after I had interacted with him earlier in the day and he was never seen, or heard from, again in the West.

The Soviet liberation of the Pest side of Budapest was completed on January 17, 1945, but the Buda Hills were not liberated until February 13, 1945. The western portion of Hungary was finally liberated in April 1945. During the Hungarian Holocaust period, I witnessed the mass executions of the Budapest Jews on the banks of the Danube. When and wherever possible, I used my SS status to rescue people from certain death. While I was assigned to the SS Headquarters as a driver and liaison interpreter, I became a clandestine confidant of many Nazi officers, while at the same time I was hiding and saving people within the Vanczak family factory. Also, I was on the Margit Bridge in Budapest when German explosives prematurely detonated. I survived, but the two Nazis in my car perished in the waters of the Danube. I watched Budapest residents armed with axes, hacksaws, and butchers' knives attack dead horses in the street for meat during the bitterly cold winter of 1944–45. The siege of Budapest caused additional food and safety problems for the citizens. Occupation by the Russian Army was characterized by drinking, looting, and rape. Watches and valuables were confiscated. Budapest was in ruins.

Over 437,000 Hungarians perished in the Holocaust, most of them in Auschwitz, including my father and stepbrother Pál. Their names are listed in the Yad Vashem Central Database of Shoah Victims' Names, which attempts to document those who perished in the Holocaust. The information on them was provided to Yad Vashem by my cousin, Moshe Jakab, and can be accessed by the surname Banos or by the locale – Nyirbátor.[1] Approximately 300 men, women, and children were saved by their humanitarian actions. My aunt, uncle, and cousin Zsuzsa were declared Righteous Gentiles by Yad Vashem – Bela in 1998, and his wife Margit and daughter Zsuzsa in 2001. In 1999, the family received the Bravery Award from Hungary. The factory building was declared an historical landmark by the Hungarian government in 2004.

For courageous action in the Holocaust, the name of Laszlo Banos (Leslie Banos) appears on the Award of Bravery monument at Apor Vilmos tér in Budapest, which was dedicated on October 6, 2005. Most of my Jewish relatives on my father's side of the family perished at Auschwitz in 1944, as did my father (Maurice/Moritz) and stepbrother (Pál), who were deported from our hometown of Nyirbátor in northeastern Hungary. Of the 899 Jews who lived in Nyirbátor, only twenty returned to an unfriendly welcome. My Jewish classmate, Josef Farago, had tears in his eyes when we met in 2005, as he remembered the old days before the Holocaust when the whole town lived and worked together as a close-knit Hungarian community. In Budapest that same year, I met with Mrs. Gabor Molnar, whose mother and brother I saved in 1944. When she thanked me profusely, I felt her thanks represented others who were saved and that her gratitude extended to all those who rescued Jews in World War II.

After the war's end, I went to school briefly and managed three movie theaters in Budapest for the MAFIRT film organization. With the increasing communist presence, my life was in danger. One day, I heard a remark from someone walking near the Vanczak factory. "Did I see this young man during the war in an SS uniform?" I knew I must leave the area immediately since all my documents and ID papers had been confiscated by the Russian patrol when Raoul Wallenberg and I were captured. Mr. Schweiger was nowhere to be found to testify to my involvement during the war. Since I also possessed a permit for work in a small movie theater in Sopron, a city a few miles from the Austrian border, I made my way there despite nationwide travel restrictions in place at the time. In Sopron, the caretaker of the movie theater gave me Austrian money for food and a rail ticket when I explained that I was going to Vienna to obtain medicines – my ruse. Thus, I illegally emigrated from Hungary on December 7, 1947 to avoid communist questioning about me or my family. I arrived in the Russian section of Vienna and needed a passport to enter the American zone in Salzburg. I was given a passport in German, English, French, and Russian with a woman's picture on it. I balked. I was instructed to show the document accompanied by a bottle of vodka, which would insure that the woman's image would be ignored. This worked, and I finally arrived in Salzburg and spent the night in a refugee shelter.

From the American zone in Vienna, I went to Munich and then became a Hungarian refugee in Bamberg, Germany, where I worked with the American Army Labor Service. Later, I worked with the United Nations (UNESCO in Germany), reuniting children with their families. In Germany, I met and married my wife, Georgine. I immigrated to the United States in 1951 with my wife and one child. In my newly adopted city of Pittsburgh, Pennsylvania, I first worked in a junkyard cutting up cars, trained as a locksmith working at Sears, then secured a job at the William Penn Hotel. In 1955, I studied at the University of Pittsburgh under the Lawrence Frank scholarship, specializing in television production and direction. I interned at WQED (Pittsburgh PBS) with noted television personality Fred Rogers. After working at local television station WTAE-TV as motion picture film editor and news and sports cinematographer covering local and national sports, I became the head photographer for the Pittsburgh Steelers and the Pittsburgh Pirates between 1969 and 1976. Now retired from my position as video coordinator for sports in the Department of Athletics at the University of Pittsburgh, I volunteer my time aiding community organizations and assisting elderly residents in their homes. I also serve as a docent for the collection of my photographs of the late humanitarian baseball player Roberto Clemente at the Clemente Museum in Lawrenceville. My photographs of Clemente have also been on display at the Heinz History Center of Pittsburgh, and I spoke on a PBS American Experience program devoted to the life and accomplishments of Clemente.

My wife and I raised our five children in Pittsburgh, where she and I continue to reside today. I often address university, school, community, professional, and military audiences, in the local area and elsewhere in the nation, on my experiences as a young Hungarian infiltrating the SS, and my mission to save the lives of the persecuted while serving Allied Intelligence to defeat the Nazis. I continue to reflect on how learning and teaching about the Holocaust can help create a better future for all. I can never forget what I have seen. Those memories will remain with me for the rest of my life.

In the intervening years since the end of the Holocaust and World War II, I have tried to keep the memories of my involvement free from information other than that which I personally experienced. Hence, I do not research topics in historical accounts or read survivor memoirs; rather, I try to recall my personal activities so I may tell my story from my perspective, not from the writings of others. I traveled to Hungary to explore documents relating to my activities and to consult with scholars about relevant materials. For those seeking citations regarding facets of the Hungarian Holocaust, I recommend three bibliographies compiled by Holocaust scholar Randolph L. Braham,[2] and his magisterial two-volume work entitled *The Politics of Genocide: The Holocaust in Hungary*.[3] The bibliography for this paper contains citations to resources such as *Echoes and Reflections*, three hours of testimony for the Shoah Foundation, the University of Southern California Visual History Biographic Profile,[4] and the WQED (Pittsburgh PBS) book and video presentation that note my participation in the Hungarian resistance and my role as an aid provider and rescuer in Budapest in World War II.[5]

In presentations, articles, and interviews I have described what motivated me to volunteer for resistance and rescue work at the terrible time of man's inhumanity to his fellow citizens. I also have encouraged those I address to learn more about those who worked diligently to preserve Jewish lives in the Hungarian Holocaust era. During and after my presentations, audience members are invited to provide comments, observations, and questions. Most have inquired about why I volunteered to conduct the actions I undertook during the Holocaust, and why they have not heard stories such as mine before this time. I credit my survival to my youthful boldness and my service to Allied Intelligence. The effectiveness of my presentations, and those of other guest speakers who experienced the Holocaust in other countries, has been confirmed by positive comments written by students in university course assessments. In my conclusion to each presentation, I offer additional reflections regarding my life experiences and relate the study of past events to the creation of a better future.

I have written a 40,000-word book with photographs about my experiences during World War II in Hungary. The book, entitled *If They Catch You, You Will Die*,[6] published in 2009, provides an inside look into the Hungarian SS and the Nazi menace in Budapest, and my undercover activities at the time. The title comes from the admonition of my aunt concerning my bold escapades: that if I were caught, I would surely die. The book details my childhood years, my experiences as a rescuer and aid provider, and as a survivor of the Holocaust era in Budapest. It includes maps, photographs, documents, a chronology of events pertaining to the Hungarian Holocaust, a glossary of terms, people and places, and a bibliography for further reading. It also describes my immigration to the United States in 1951 and the years thereafter.

To future generations, I offer the thought that we must learn from the past and respect all human beings. I was there in the midst of the Holocaust and participated in an undercover resistance movement to save as many lives as possible. In my youth, my mission was to save as many lives as possible and to serve Allied Intelligence to defeat Hitler. In today's world, we must continue to prevent man's inhumanity to man.

Questions

1. *How do the humanitarian actions of sanctuary to refugees, resistance activities against the Nazis, and rescue of the persecuted in Hungary reflect reactions to events occurring in other countries at the time?*

2. *What elements distinguish a personal testimony from historical accounts of the Holocaust era?*

3. *Explain how the actions of the Vanczak family (Margit, Bela, and Zsuzsa) from 1938–1945 exemplified Yehuda Bauer's admonition, "Thou shalt never, but never, be a bystander."*

4. *Why should Raoul Wallenberg's rescue of upwards of 100,000 Jews in Budapest in July 1944–January 1945 be studied by future generations as an example of moral courage against man's inhumanity to man?*

5. *Do students hearing a personal testimony concerning refuge, resistance, and rescue ask questions that demonstrate they connect and relate to the individual's motivation and actions, and recognize the dangers and courage present in efforts to thwart the Nazi menace?*

Bibliography

Banos, Leslie, with Martha McCully. *If They Catch You, You Will Die*. Pittsburgh: Banos Publishing, 2009.

Banos, Les. "If They Catch You, You Will Die, Les Banos, Penn Hills." In Cherry Amanda Nikeson, ed. *Pittsburgh WW II Stories: Preserving Our Legacy*. Pittsburgh: WQED, 2008. 183.

Banos, Leslie. Testimony to the Shoah Foundation Institute. Interview conducted by Merle Goldberg, July 12, 1995. http://tc.usc.edu/vhiechoes/video.aspx?testimonyid+4003.

Banos, Leslie. "Visual History Biographic Profile of Leslie Banos." USC Shoah Foundation Institute for Visual History and Education, 2007. http://tc.usc.edu/vhiechoes/bios/Banos.Leslie.pdf.

Banos, Leslie. WQED (PBS). "Les Banos, The Good Spy." Video to accompany Ken Burns War series, 2008. http://www.wqed.org/tv/war/pittsburgh.php?cat+6&id=262.

Braham, Randolph L. *The Politics of Genocide: The Holocaust in Hungary*. 2nd ed. 2 vols. New York: Columbia University Press, 1994.

Braham, Randolph L. *The Holocaust in Hungary: A Selected and Annotated Bibliography, 1984–2000*. New York: Columbia University Press, 2001.

Braham, Randolph L. and Julia Bock, comps. and eds. *The Holocaust in Hungary: A Selected and Compiled Bibliography*. New York: Columbia University Press, 2008.

University of Southern California. *Echoes and Reflections: A Multimedia Curriculum on the Holocaust*. Los Angeles: University of Southern California, ADL/Shoah Foundation Institute/Yad Vashem, 2005.

Yad Vashem. Central Database of Shoah Victims' Names. Jerusalem: Yad Vashem. http://namesyadvashem.org/wps/portal/IY__Hon_Welcome.

Notes

1. See further Randolph L. Braham, *The Politics of Genocide: The Holocaust in Hungary*, 2nd ed. 2 vols. (New York: Columbia University Press, 1994) for information and statistics on the Holocaust in Hungary. See Central Database of Shoah Victims' Names, Yad Vashem, Jerusalem: Banos, Moritz, and Banos, Pali from Nyirbátor, submitted by Moshe Jakab, nephew of Moritz and cousin of Pali, http://namesyadvashem.org/wps/portal/IY__Hon_Welcome, accessed October 10, 2009.

2. See further Randolph L. Braham, *The Holocaust in Hungary: A Selected and Annotated Bibliography, 1984-2000* (New York: Columbia University Press, 2001); Randolph L. Braham, *The Hungarian Jewish Catastrophe: A Selected and Annotated Bibliography*, 2nd ed. (New York: Columbia University Press, 1984); and Randolph L. Braham and Julia Bock, eds., *The Holocaust in Hungary: A Selected and Compiled Bibliography* (New York: Columbia University Press, 2008) for citations pertaining to the Hungarian Holocaust by topic, geographic area, or name of author of memoir, for example.

3. See Randolph L. Braham, *The Politics of Genocide*, for citations within an historical context, for example, Treatment of Jewish Refugees in Hungary, pp. 105–112, Rescue and Resistance, pp. 1058–1169, Rescue Activities of Hehelutz Youth, pp. 1135–1148, Neutral Countries, pp. 1225–1246.

4. See *Echoes and Reflections: A Multimedia Curriculum on the Holocaust*, (Los Angeles: University of Southern California): ADL/Shoah Foundation Institute/Yad Vashem, 2005. See Ch. 7 – Rescue information, questions for students, two video clips on CD pertaining to Leslie Banos; and the websites http://tc.usc.edu/vhiechoes/video.aspx?testimonyid=4003, Leslie Banos' testimony to the Shoah Foundation Institute (three hours on video from interview conducted by Merle Goldberg, July 12, 1995, accessed March 16, 2010); and http://www.echoesandreflections.org/pdfs/bios/Banos.Leslie.pdf, "Visual History Biographic Profile of Leslie Banos," USC Shoah Foundation Institute for Visual History and Education, 2007, accessed March 16, 2010.

5. See also Les Banos, "If They Catch You, You Will Die, Les Banos, Penn Hills" in Amanda Nickeson Cherry, ed. *Pittsburgh WW II Stories: Preserving Our Legacy* (Pittsburgh: WQED, 2008), p. 183; and websites pertaining to WQED (PBS in Pittsburgh) http://www.wqed.org/ondemand/onq.php?cat=6&id=262, "Memories of WW II," accessed March 16, 2010); and http://www.wqed.org/tv/war/pittsburgh.php, WQED (PBS), "Les Banos, The Good Spy," video to accompany Ken Burns War Series, 2008, accessed March 16, 2010.

6. Leslie Banos, with Martha McCully, *If They Catch You, You Will Die* (Pittsburgh: Banos Publishing, 2009).

HOLOCAUST EDUCATION

Challenges to Teaching the Holocaust in Teacher Preparation Programs

■ ■ ■ ■ ■ ■ ■ ■ ■ ■ ■

Leah G. Stambler

Professor, Education and Educational Psychology Department,
Western Connecticut State University, Danbury, CT

Introduction

Some events in world history provide valuable lessons about moral choices. The Holocaust is a prime example of such an event. It is the responsibility of teacher education programs to prepare the K-12 classroom practitioner for his/her role in the curriculum movement that envisions Holocaust education as a conduit to producing critically thinking citizens of high moral and civic character. Multiple research studies referred to in the article "Teacher Preparation Makes a Difference" validate the importance of teacher preparation programs in producing effective classroom teachers who influence their students' learning achievements.[1]

Supporters of character, moral, and civics education in the curricula have turned to Holocaust education as a means of analyzing the principles of goodness of behavior and implementation of moral decisions. Author Thomas D. Fallace has chronicled the history of those developments in American public schools as being propelled by classroom teachers.[2] Holocaust education lies within the parameters of society's concerns for a revival in character, moral, and civics education in American schools, but inclusion of the former depends on connecting its moral and intellectual aims with the function of the latter.

Holocaust education in the United States has a history of more than two decades of being in existence in the nation's K-12 grade level schools, mostly as a result of mandated curriculum policies and laws passed by various states' legislatures. The website of the United States Holocaust Memorial Museum (USHMM) provides an interactive, clickable map of the United States that offers profiles about the condition of Holocaust education in the fifty states: "Text of state legislation about the teaching of the Holocaust, and Holocaust-explicit History/Social Studies and English/Language Arts state content standards," as well as contact information for state departments of education.[3] Federal legislation that mandates the inclusion of Holocaust education into K-12 grade level curriculum does not exist because of the decentralized nature of public education in the United States of America.

An educational imperative for teaching Holocaust curricula in the nation's schools was visible in the 1990s with the building of the USHMM. Curriculum developments in the writer's state of Connecticut are a case in point. The Connecticut State Department of Education (CSDE), in line with the 1990s' national trend of incorporating Holocaust education in the curricula, developed a Holocaust Resource Guide in 1997. Bill No. 126, Public Act 95–101, An Act Concerning Holocaust Education states that "The State Board of Education, within available appropriations and utilizing available resource materials, shall assist and encourage local and regional boards of education to include Holocaust education and awareness as part of the program of instruction offered pursuant to subsection (a) of this section."[4]

The contextual framework for change in American education is based on: demographic projections about modifications in the nation's population; a time of great ferment in American education; an imperative to infuse Holocaust education into the curricula of the nation's teacher preparation programs in colleges and universities in order to enhance pre-service teacher candidates' and practitioners' knowledge, skills, and dispositions, which would lead them to become "culturally skilled educators."[5]

What do we mean by that terminology? Culturally skilled educators require an education to expand their cognitive domain in order to gain extensive knowledge, awareness, and acknowledgment of their personal assumptions, values, and biases. They are familiar with strategies and techniques for use in their K-12 classrooms that necessitate the application of critical thinking skills during the teaching/learning process, encourage moral and good character skills, and model the processes of civic engagement.[6]

One and a half million Jewish children were murdered during the Holocaust. Thousands of other Jewish children survived the catastrophe because they were hidden in various parts of Nazi-occupied Europe until the end of World War II (e.g. in Le Chambon, France), while others simultaneously were given sanctuary in countries not controlled by Nazi Germany (e.g. the United Kingdom). What benefits may accrue for American adolescents to study the Holocaust and to learn about applying aspects of moral, character, and civics education? Can analysis of individual case studies about the experiences of Jewish children who were sent to safe locations through the *Kindertransport* program heighten American adolescents' willingness to engage in civic responsibility in their local communities and nation? Further research and a longitudinal study would be needed to answer this question. Could knowledge of character and civics education, as well as techniques of teaching critical thinking, facilitate secondary-level teachers to assist their students in making meaning of the story of the *Kindertransport* during the Holocaust? This, too, would require other research and a longitudinal study to secure an answer.

How can the events surrounding the Holocaust and its perpetrators, victims, bystanders, and rescuers be introduced into Teacher Education Programs that prepare pre-service teacher candidates and practitioners for their instructional roles with the K-12 curriculum, when university departments in schools of Arts and Sciences are the hosts for Holocaust courses? Procedures for the introduction and acceptance of a curriculum in higher education institutions often are long and complicated processes, raising the specter of programmatic and departmental "turf wars" over students' and faculties' credit loads. Frequently, obstacles arise in the system of governance which can challenge and stymie acceptance of new course proposals.

Multiple challenges generally are present in academia for teacher educators when they proceed to implement their mission of preparing their pre-service candidates and practitioners to teach "their" K-12 students with the knowledge, skills, and dispositions that are necessary to meet the accountability demands for high quality teachers by the stakeholders in American public education (i.e. accreditation agencies, federal/state/local legislatures and governments, the courts, national professional organizations, taxpayers, religious institutions, and the business sector).

Major systemic obstacles are present for K-12 classroom teachers when it comes to teaching about the Holocaust: (1) states' mandated teaching standards encourage teachers to "cover the material," engaging in the study of facts instead of taking the time for critical thinking that an in-depth study of the Holocaust requires; (2) limited funding in local education districts' budgets precludes professional development opportunities for teachers to receive instruction about teaching the Holocaust to their students; (3) additional high stakes assessment responsibilities interfere with instructional time allotments; (4) increased high school graduation requirements take away from the possibilities of elective Holocaust courses; (5) permission for Social Studies teachers to gain certification without having a strong background in history limits them from having adequate education to teach about the Holocaust; and, (6) inconsistent discipline-based rationales for teaching about the Holocaust compromise the quality of instruction provided to students.[7] Teacher educators and practitioners are confronted with these specific challenges, as well as others, when a Holocaust curriculum is the question of the day. These challenges have been formatted into questions that will be answered during the course of this paper.

Method and Questions

The method used to conduct the research for this study was a qualitative one. Qualitative research is a method that seeks insights through verbal and written, rather than statistical and measurable data. Qualitative research is used when there is an exploratory study that seeks to identify the dimensions of a problem, draw assumptions based on collected data from documents and a variety of primary and secondary sources, and attempt to understand the motivations of the stakeholders involved with the problem. Multiple preliminary research questions were formulated by the writer about the central issue in this study, Challenges to Teaching the Holocaust in Teacher Preparation Programs. Three major challenges will be addressed: Infusing the Holocaust in Teacher Preparation Courses; Coping in Higher Education with Holocaust Deniers; and, Effectively Teaching about How to Teach the Holocaust.

Extensive review of the literature pertinent to the problem resulted in the formulation of multiple research questions which eventually were used to guide the collection of qualitative data for this study: What is worth teaching to prepare K-12 students for the twenty-first century? Why teach about the Holocaust in the twenty-first-century curriculum? What is the etiology of Holocaust denial? How did the Holocaust denial movement develop? How do Holocaust deniers operate? What are the responses to Holocaust denial claims? What is the appropriate methodology for teaching about the Holocaust? How can teacher educators and practitioners make meaning of the Holocaust for students living in a democracy? How does analysis of photographs demonstrate the use of critical thinking skills when teaching about the Holocaust? How can critical literacy and ethical decision-making be applied when studying the Holocaust and issues related to the *Kindertransport* effort?

Challenge Number 1: Infusing the Holocaust in Teacher Preparation Courses

What is worth teaching to prepare K-12 students for the twenty-first century?

The Partnership for 21st Century Skills, a foremost advocacy organization composed of business people, educators, and policymakers, contributed its vision for change to the conversation about what should be included in the curriculum of twenty-first-century American schools at the June 12, 2009 meeting of the National Education Summit on 21st Century Skills in Washington, D.C.[8] Critical thinking and problem solving, communication and collaboration, life and career skills are major student outcomes that are anticipated with the application of the 21st Century Skills curriculum; and those skills are based on students' mastery of multiple disciplines: (1) English, reading or language arts; (2) World Languages; (3) Arts; (4) Mathematics; (5) Economics; (6) Science; (7) Geography; (8) History; and, (9) Government and Civics.

Certain themes in these subjects stand out as major components for American students to learn and become versed in over their educational lifetimes: (1) global awareness to address global issues; (2) financial, economic, business, and entrepreneurial literacy to prepare to make personal and societal choices; (3) health literacy to come to grips with national and international public health and safety issues; (4) environmental literacy to meet the challenges of, and participate in, the various national and global environmental issues that may arise; and, (5) civic literacy to analyze the implications of, and engage in, adult decision-making, public practices, and responsibilities of American citizenship on all governmental levels; "The attributes of civic character and civics education are significant tools to arm citizens against future genocides."[9] George Santayana, the great philosopher, cautioned the world that "Those who cannot remember the past are condemned to repeat it."[10] These words are significant when the subject of investigation into the past is the Holocaust, and when the need for education about it rests on the shoulders of teacher educators and practitioners:

> [I]t was a systematic persecution and annihilation of a target population (6 million Jews); contemporary high school students and their parents have limited to no knowledge about this massive event of genocide; and school age students must be alerted that vigilance is necessary in order to prevent a like event from occurring.[11]

Why teach about the Holocaust in the twenty-first-century curriculum?

Six major rationales for teaching the Holocaust in American schools include: (1) It was a watershed event in human history; (2) It allows students the opportunity to learn about the consequences of prejudice, racism, and stereotyping, and to appreciate the value of pluralism and acceptance in a diverse society; (3) It demonstrates the implications of silence, apathy, and indifference toward the oppressed; (4) It exposes a government's use of high levels of technology and bureaucratic organization to execute destructive policies of social engineering and genocide; (5) It provides a context for students to consider the parameters of power, and think about how individuals, organizations, and nations respond to impingement on people's civil rights or governmental use of genocide policies; and, (6) It exemplifies the variables that operated to destroy democratic values during the event known as the Holocaust, and teaches students that as citizens in a democratic nation they must be vigilant to protect its existence.[12]

The joining of humiliation of the Jewish victims and the application of German technological inventiveness to the act of killing made the Holocaust unique. Avishai Margalit and Gabriel Motzkin have defended the uniqueness of the Holocaust: "… it was a unique event in history, and therefore merited study."[13] The Nazis favored death for all Jews; there is dignity in death for the individual; the Nazis wanted to deny the Jews that dignity; and they combined humiliation of the target group prior to its industrial-styled process of extermination.

… It was the only time in recorded history that a state tried to destroy an entire people, regardless of an individual's age, sex, location, profession, or belief. And it is the only instance in which the perpetrators conducted this genocide for no ostensible material, territorial, or political gain.[14]

Challenge Number 2: Coping in Higher Education with Holocaust Deniers

What is the etiology of Holocaust denial?

Early origins of Holocaust denial were embodied in the Nazis' use of the term "the Final Solution to the Jewish Question." Post-World War II evidence of Nazi atrocities, exposed at the Nuremberg trials, was dismissed by Nazi apologists as not having occurred. Trotskyist and anarchist French followers of Paul Rassinier also ignored Holocaust evidence as "Stalinist atrocity propaganda."[15]

How did the Holocaust denial movement develop?

Holocaust denial became "Holocaust Revisionism" in 1979 in America. Willis Carto, founder of the Liberty Lobby, was responsible for this transition. It was he who incorporated the Institute for Holocaust Review (IHR) to accomplish his propaganda in the United States.[16] The Anti-Defamation League reported that the IHR was "a pseudo-academic enterprise" made up of "professors with no credentials in history," "writers without formal academic certification," and "career anti-Semites."[17] Examples of Holocaust deniers affiliated with IHR and Willis Carto have been Bradley Smith (USA), Ernst Zündel (Canada), Carlo Mattogno (Italy), David Irving (England), and Mark Weber (USA).[18]

How do Holocaust deniers operate?

Examples of how Holocaust deniers package their ideas include three major techniques: (1) Denial of science and science of denial exemplified by "scientific" arguments to "prove" that the Nazi regime could not have used gas chambers to carry out an extermination program against Jews and Gypsies; (2) Misrepresentation demonstrated in the comic book story "Death Camp," which was written by J. M. DeMatteis; and, (3) Outright fabrication as occurred with the deniers' attempt to discredit Thomas Keneally's story of Oskar Schindler's "List."[19]

Holocaust deniers engage in multiple claims, such as, there was no single "Master Plan" to annihilate the Jewish people of Europe; gas chambers were not used for the supposed mass murders at Auschwitz and other Nazi death camps; the lack of objective documents to prove that the Nazis engaged in genocide is covered by reliance on survivors' testimony; there was no net loss of Jewish lives for the years between 1941 and 1945; and that the Nuremberg trials were a staged farce.[20]

Two conferences were held to push Holocaust denial claims, and demonstrated their motivation to use Holocaust denial as a tool to delegitimize Israel, thereby exhibiting what has been called the "new antisemitism." The International Conference on Review of the Holocaust: Global Vision, held on December 11–12, 2006 espoused the false claim that the Holocaust never occurred during World War II, and that Israel was not a legitimate international entity.[21] Three years later, Durban II or the United Nations World Conference Against Racism, reiterated the 2001 Tehran Declaration that Israel was committing "genocide," "crimes against humanity," and "a new kind of apartheid."[22] This conference exemplified how Holocaust denial was being twisted to fuel the deniers' assertion that Israel was established for Holocaust survivors as a tool of the imperialistic powers of western Christendom against Islam.

What are the responses to Holocaust denial claims?

Multiple responses to Holocaust deniers' claims have been made by prestigious universities, academic organizations, and scholars. These statements were published on the 2001 Online Guide to Exposing and Combating Anti-Semitic Propaganda by the Anti-Defamation League.[23]

The History Department at Duke University adopted a statement that historians did not doubt the "actuality" of the Holocaust or the systematic murder of "Jews, Gypsies, political radicals, and other people" by Hitler's Nazi Germany. Professors Oshinksy and Curtis of Rutgers University issued a statement that "If the Holocaust is not a fact, then nothing is a fact." More than 300 members of the American Historical Association issued two statements at the 1991 and 1994 annual conferences of the organization that "No serious historian questions that the Holocaust took place."

The Emory University internet website, "Holocaust Denial on Trial: Using History to Confront Distortions" is the repository of an extensive defense of the Holocaust's actuality. Myth/Fact sheets issued by the University analyze Holocaust deniers' claims and "refute them with high quality scholarship." Trial documents from Professor Deborah Lipstadt's legal action against the Holocaust denier David Irving support the website's reliability and are included in an online archive.[24]

The most powerful recent response to Holocaust deniers is located in the archives of Yad Vashem in Jerusalem, Israel. It is an exhibit entitled "The Architecture of Murder: The Auschwitz-Birkenau Blueprints." Deniers' claims that gas chambers were not present at Auschwitz have been torpedoed by the existence of these documents.[25]

Challenge Number 3: Effectively Teaching About How to Teach the Holocaust

What is the appropriate methodology for teaching about the Holocaust?

Teacher educators need to be informed not only about the substance of the Holocaust, but how to instruct their pre-service teaching candidates and practitioners about the methodological nuances for teaching the subject. Fourteen recommendations for teaching about the Holocaust with sensitivity and thoughtfulness are found in the USHMM Teacher's Guide. They are valuable caveats for beginning and experienced educators who teach any and all aspects of the Holocaust: (1) Define the term "Holocaust"; (2) Avoid comparisons of pain; (3) Avoid simple answers to complex history; (4) The event was not necessarily inevitable; (5) Strive for precision of language; (6) Make careful distinctions about sources of information; (7) Avoid stereotypical descriptions; (8) Engage students' interest by striking a balance in the history; (9) Place the event in its historical European context; (10) Provide memoirs and first-person accounts to emphasize the human element of the historical statistics; (11) Approach horrific images and written content with sensitivity for students' individual differences and thresholds for violence; (12) Use balance in establishing whose perspective informs the study; (13) Select appropriate thought-provoking learning activities that support the rationale for which the Holocaust is being taught, and minimize the attempt to have students engage in simulations and role play; and, (14) Reinforce the lessons' objectives during their initiations and closures by dispelling misinformation and encouraging students to reflect on what they learned for their own purposes and as citizens in a democracy.[26] Number ten especially will be difficult to implement as Holocaust survivors pass away. However, collections of interviews on DVDs and written testimonies exist for posterity. Children of Holocaust survivors possibly may be drafted to continue their parents' practice of visiting classrooms to share their Holocaust narratives.

How can teacher educators and practitioners make meaning of the Holocaust for students living in a democracy?

Critical thinking skills, the principles of character and civics education, and models of civic engagement are appropriate auxiliaries when teaching about the Holocaust to secondary students. They are provided with the opportunity to hone their civic literacy skills in the context of a major historical event.

> The Holocaust is 'one of the most effective, and most extensively documented subjects for a pedagogical examination of basic moral issues… it yields critical lessons for an investigation of human behaviour through structured inquiry… it addresses one of the central tenets of education in the United States, which is to examine what it means to be a responsible citizen…'[27]

General findings, from "a review of 56 documents" about whether or not academic achievement was enhanced by instructing students how to engage in thinking skills, indicated that "nearly all of the thinking skills programs and practices investigated were found to make a positive difference in the achievement levels of participating students."[28]

Critical thinking may be understood as "the active intellectual process of conceptualizing, applying, analyzing, synthesizing, and/or evaluating data collected during an individual's observation, experience, reflection, reasoning, or communication."[29] A major problem facing the nation is that critical thinking ability among students has not been widespread in the recent past.[30]

Implementation of civic knowledge, skills, and dispositions during the study of the Holocaust allows students to reflect on personal and collective applications of the lessons that they learn. Students can learn several civics concepts and character traits in studying the Holocaust: "responsible citizenship; appreciation for democracy; silence and indifference can perpetuate problems; and history just doesn't happen. It occurs because individuals, organizations and government made choices."[31]

Civic education's knowledge, skills, and dispositions clear the path for civic engagement by individuals and groups. Two components of civic engagement are "Working to make a difference in the civic life of our communities and developing the combination of knowledge, skills, values, and motivation to make that difference"; as well as "promoting the quality of life in a community through both political and non-political processes."[32]

Teacher educators can infuse their instruction with Holocaust modules and resources in their courses when teaching about Character and Civic Education, Integrated Language, Moral Development, and Comparative Education Systems. Samples of how the writer has done so in her courses at Western Connecticut State University include:

1) **Foundations of American Education**, e.g., application of the principles of character education programs to ethical questions about equal access to education and racial theories relevant to Germany's Nuremberg Laws and American States' Segregation Laws; comparison of government control or lack thereof for the teaching profession in Nazi Germany and the U.S.A;

2) **Adolescent Development**, e.g., comparison of aspects of character and moral development among the *Hitler Jugend* (Hitler Youth) and American teens; investigation of the effects of separation of *Kindertransport* children from their parents; applying the principles of Josephson's, Kagan's, and Lickona's character education programs to the analysis of rescuers' and Righteous Among the Nations' motivations for resisting

Nazi warnings against their lives if they helped, hid, or saved Jewish men, women, and children from capture;

3) **Curriculum of the Secondary School**, e.g., sample lesson plans about "upstanders" from Facing History and Ourselves; comparison of pre-World War II Jewish life in the ghettos from the USHMM and Yad Vashem websites; and analysis of Hidden Children's life stories from the Museum of Tolerance, Yad Vashem, and USHMM;

4) **Methods of Teaching Social Studies in the Elementary School**, e.g., introduction to children's art and poetry resources from Terezin (Theresienstadt), such as the play *Brundibar* and the poem "The Butterfly";

5) **Secondary Methods of Teaching**, e.g., sample lessons from the multimedia curriculum on the Holocaust entitled *Echoes and Reflections*;[33] introduction to valid and reliable internet websites about the Holocaust;

6) **Integrating Language in the Secondary School**, e.g., students select and apply various genres of literature about children and teens during the Holocaust in their Webquests and curriculum modules for middle or upper secondary grade levels.

How does analysis of photographs demonstrate the use of critical thinking skills when teaching about the Holocaust?

Analysis of photographs is an excellent application of critical thinking skills. The photograph archives on the websites of the United States Holocaust Memorial Museum, Yad Vashem, Museum of Tolerance, Nizkor Project, Holocaust Museum of Southern Florida, Aisch, and the Australian Memories of the Holocaust represent some of the websites that provide teacher educators and classroom teachers with a plethora of materials for students to apply their critical thinking skills about the moral and civic issues inherent in the study of the Holocaust.

Four steps in the analysis of photographs include: (1) Observation: What do you see in this photograph? (people, objects, activities) List separately; (2) Inference: Make some reasonable guesses about the photograph (when, where, what are people doing? why was it taken?; (3) Inquiry: Write a question that is unanswered by this photograph; and, (4) Research and answer questions asked by the teacher.[34]

How can critical literacy and ethical decision-making be applied when studying the Holocaust and issues related to the *Kindertransports*?

Character, moral, and civics education and engagement are served for elementary, middle, and high school students when they are exposed to age-appropriate study of questions about the Holocaust and the *Kindertransport*. "Who were the *Kinder*? Why were the *Kindertransports* put into operation? Who stepped forward to assist the *Kinder*?

How were they housed, fed, educated, and socially integrated into a new society? How did the adult *Kinder* remember and assess their experiences? What emotional baggage did the *Kindertransport* survivors carry as adults?"[35] Students' research into the actions of perpetrators, victims, bystanders, resisters, and rescuers during the Holocaust is enhanced by the use of critical literacy and ethical decision-making techniques.

Comparisons of primary and secondary sources from multiple viewpoints about the *Kindertransport* enable students to further their critical literacy by focusing on issues of power, recognizing complexities in problems, and not accepting one-dimensional responses to problems. In essence, students (1) learn to appreciate diverse perspectives; (2) take an active, critical stance when reading and thinking; (3) expand their abilities to reason; and, (4) set in motion the prospect of relieving inequity and injustice in society.[36] The nature of the *Kindertransport* and the people connected with it give cause to raise the question of how to employ ethical decision-making: "What prompts some individuals and groups to help others in a time of crisis while others turn away?[37] There are specific ethical decision-making steps that may be followed by students when working with Holocaust education resources, such as the materials that tell the story of the *Kindertransport*: (1) Identify the problem; (2) Determine the nature and dimensions of the dilemma; (3) Generate potential courses of action; (4) Consider the potential consequences of all options, choosing a course of action; (5) Evaluate the selected course of action; and, (6) Implement the course of action.[38]

Concluding Comments

The introductory paragraphs to this paper placed responsibility on teacher educators to instruct pre-service teacher candidates and practitioners about the Holocaust as a substantive base for producing critically thinking citizens of high moral and civic character. Unfortunately, examples of genocide in Cambodia, Darfur, and Rwanda have taken place since the Holocaust of World War II, and demonstrate the continuation of mankind's inhumanity to mankind. The writer encourages teacher educators to infuse aspects of the Holocaust into their courses, and trusts that the challenges discussed herein would not mitigate that objective. Research tells us that teacher preparation programs can make a difference in the effectiveness of practitioners' influence on their students' achievements. Therefore, it is important to reiterate the moral and civic benefits of including the study of the Holocaust in the twenty-first-century curriculum, as previously cited for American students in USHMM sources: (1) to learn about the consequences of prejudice, racism, and stereotyping; (2) to value pluralism and diversity; (3) to rebuff silence, apathy, and indifference directed toward the oppressed in society; (4) to disallow social engineering and genocide policies from being instituted by government officials; (5) to analyze the parameters of power before people's civil rights are infringed upon by government's genocide policies; and, (6) to comprehend that citizens' vigilance is necessary to protect the existence of democracy in a nation.

Questions

1. *Thomas Lickona, Michael Josephson, and Spencer Kagan are known for their character education programs that are applied in K-12 schools. Think about how you would apply the character traits of caring, citizenship, cooperation, courage, fairness, honesty, integrity, leadership, respect, responsibility, and trustworthiness during instruction about Jewish children and families who were hidden and/or saved by people known as the "Righteous of the Nations."*

2. *Discuss with your colleagues how to apply Thomas Lickona's "Eleven Principles of Character Education," after teaching about the Holocaust, with respect to his suggested school-wide strategies to develop moral students: caring beyond the classroom, creating a positive moral culture in the school, and making schools, parents, and communities into partners.*

3. *How can the infusion of the character and civic education lessons of the Holocaust in teacher preparation programs for pre-service teacher candidates and practitioners be extended to include case studies of twentieth-century genocides?*

Bibliography

Anti-Defamation League (2001). *Holocaust Denial: An Online Guide to Exposing and Combating Anti-Semitic Propaganda*: "Historians Respond: Denial Denounced as Academic Fraud." http://www.adl.org/Holocaust/academic.asp.

Anti-Defamation League (October 30, 2007). Press Release. "Echoes and Reflections Holocaust Curriculum Recognized by Peers with National Media Award." adl.org/PresRele/Education_01/5158_01.htm.

Fallace, Thomas D. *The Emergence of Holocaust Education in American Schools.* Secondary Education in a Changing World. Palgrave Macmillan, 2008.

Figuedo, Juliet H. 21st Century Skills. December 2, 2009. http://embedr.com/playlist/21st-century-skills

Florida Center for Instructional Technology, College of Education, University of South Florida, 2005. "Marietta Drücker tells her story of rescue from Vienna on a Kindertransport." http://fcit.coedu.usf.edu/holocaust/resource/MOVIES/DRUCKERM/INDEX.HTM.

Friedmann, Pavel. *Poetry of the Holocaust: The Butterfly.* June 14, 1942. http://www.edu.gov.mb.ca/k12/cur/socstud/foundation_gr6/blms/6-2-4b.pdf

Harris, Mark Jonathan, dir. *Into the Arms of Strangers: Stories of the Kindertransport*, 2000. Documentary film produced with the United States Holocaust Museum http://www2.warnerbros.com/intothearmsofstrangers/.

KTA Kindertransport Association (no date). "Kindertransport History: Introduction, 1933–1938." In "The Reich, Rising to the Moment, Life in Britain, Detour to Normandy, Kaddish in London." http://www.kindertransport.org/history.htm.

Kushner, Tony & Maurice Sendak, Illustrator. *Brundibar*. Hyperion Book CH. 1st Edition, 2003.

Mináč, Matej. *Nicholas Winton – The Power of Good*. Video clip of the DVD. http://www.powerofgood.net/.

Stambler, Leah G. "Infusing Holocaust Studies in Pre-Service and Graduate Level Teacher Education Courses to Assist Educators in Becoming Culturally Skilled." Paper delivered at the Eighth International Conference on Holocaust Studies. Hebrew University. Jerusalem, Israel. December 27, 1999–January 2, 2000.

Stambler, Leah G. "Teaching Character Education and Citizenship Through Holocaust Literature." 34th Northeast Regional Conference on the Social Studies, The Boston Park Plaza Hotel and Towers, Boston, MA, March 11, 2003.

Stambler, Leah G. "Civic Engagement Through Civic Education." In *Democracy & Civic Education: Implications for Teacher Preparation and a National Agenda for Inquiry*. American Association for State Colleges and Universities (AASCU), June 2007: 34–38.

Stambler, Leah G. "Civics Education as a Stepping Stone to Civic Engagement." Paper and Powerpoint presentation at the Annual National Meeting of the American Democracy Project-AASCU, June 6–9, 2007, Philadelphia, Pennsylvania.

Sue, Derald Wing. *Multicultural Counseling Competencies*. Multicultural Aspects of Counseling and Psychotherapy, vol. 11. Sage Publications, Inc., 1998.

United States Holocaust Memorial Museum (no date). "Life in the Shadows: Hidden Children of the Holocaust."
http://www.ushmm.org/museum/exhibit/online/hiddenchildren/index/

Notes

1. American Association of Colleges of Teacher Education, retrieved December 16, 2009, http://www.aacte.org/index.php?/Traditional-Media/Resources/teacher-preparation-makes-a-difference.html.
2. Thomas D. Fallace, "The Origins of Holocaust Education in American Public Schools," *Holocaust and Genocide Studies*, Volume 20, Number 1 (2006): 80–102.
3. United States Holocaust Memorial Museum, State Profiles on Holocaust Education, Beyond Our Walls, http://www.ushmm.org/education/foreducators/states/.
4. Ibid., State Profiles on Holocaust Education, Beyond Our Walls: Connecticut Legislation.

5. All course syllabi created by the author include a framework for a position statement of "How to Become a Culturally Skilled Educator," based on the work of Derald Wing Sue and David Sue, as found in *Counseling the Culturally Different: Theory & Practice* (John Wiley & Sons Inc, 1990), 2nd edition, chapter 8.

6. The term "culturally skilled educator," as used by the author, is based on the 1992 statement "Culturally Skilled Counselors," issued by the Association of Multicultural Counseling and Development (AMCD). See also Leah G. Stambler, "Infusing Holocaust Studies in Pre-Service and Graduate Level Teacher Education Courses to Assist Educators in Becoming Culturally Skilled," paper delivered at the Eighth International Conference on Holocaust Studies, Hebrew University, Jerusalem, Israel, December 27, 1999–January 2, 2000.

7. International Task Force for Holocaust Education, Remembrance, and Research, United States Holocaust Education Report, 2010.

8. The Partnership for 21st Century Skills, June 12, 2009.

9. Margaret Lincoln, "The Holocaust Education Project: A media specialist's story in online resource use, staff collaboration, and community outreach," *Multimedia Schools*, Sept 2003, 10 (4): 32–36.

10. George Santayana, "Reason in Common Sense," in *The Life of Reason*, vol. 1 (1905), accessed at http://www.gutenberg.org/files/15000/15000-h/15000-h.htm.

11. Margaret Lincoln, op.cit.

12. "Guidelines for Teaching about the Holocaust," USHMM, 2001.

13. Avishai Margalit and Gabriel Motzkin, "The Uniqueness of the Holocaust," *Philosophy and Public Affairs* (Winter 1996), retrieved October 12, 2007 from http://www.codoh.com/reference/uniqofholo.html.

14. Deborah Lipstadt, Quotation in *The Complete Idiot's Guide to Jewish History and Culture* (1999), retrieved September 18, 2007 from http://www.aish.com/ho/i/48951916.html.

15. Anti-Defamation League, Holocaust Denial: An Online Guide to Exposing and Combating Anti-Semitic Propaganda: "Origins of the Denial Movement," 2001, retrieved September 30, 2000, at http://www.adl.org/Holocaust/origins.asp.

16. Anti-Defamation League, ibid.

17. Anti-Defamation League, ibid.

18. Anti-Defamation League, ibid.

19. The Nizkor Project, Deceit and Misrepresentation: The Techniques of Holocaust Denial, (1991–2009), retrieved October 15, 2009 at http://www.nizkor.org/features/denial-of-science/.

20. Anti-Defamation League, op.cit.

21. Holocaust Denial as a Tool of Iranian Policy, http://www.iranholocaustdenial.com/views/holocaust-denial-as-a-tool-of-iranian-policy-2.htm, (n.d.), retrieved October 1, 2010.

22. "Durban II revives the hateful rhetoric of the 2001 Tehran Declaration," (n.d.), http://www.iranholocaustdenial.com/, retrieved October 1, 2009.

23. Anti-Defamation League, Holocaust Denial: An Online Guide to Exposing and Combating Anti-Semitic Propaganda: "Historians Respond: Denial Denounced as Academic Fraud," 2001, http://www.adl.org/Holocaust/academic.asp, retrieved September 30, 2010.

24. Emory University, Holocaust Denial on Trial: Using History to Confront Distortions, http://www.hdot.org/en/denial, retrieved October 2, 2010.

25. Yad Vashem, The Holocaust Martyrs' and Heroes' Remembrance Authority (2010), Architecture of Murder: The Auschwitz-Birkenau Blueprints, http://www1.yadvashem.org/yv/en/exhibitions/auschwitz_architecture/index.asp, retrieved January 28, 2010.

26. United States Holocaust Memorial Museum, "Guidelines for Teaching about the Holocaust," (2001), pp. 3–8, from http://www.ushmm.org/education/foreducators/guideline, retrieved September 27, 2007.

27. United States Holocaust Memorial Museum, *Teaching about the Holocaust: A Resource Book for Educators*, (2001), p. 1.

28. Kathleen Cotton, "Teaching Thinking Skills," Close-Up #11, (1991), from Northwest Regional Educational Laboratory's School Improvement Research Series website: nwrel.org/scpd/sirs/6/cu11.html, retrieved November 3, 2007.

29. Richard Paul and Linda Elder, *The Miniature Guide to Critical Thinking Concepts and Tools*, 4th edition (The Foundation for Critical Thinking, 2006).

30. R. Beyth-Marom, R. Novik, and M. Sloan, "Enhancing Children's Thinking Skills: An Instructional Model for Decision-Making Under Certainty," *Instructional Science* 16 (3) (1987): 215–231.

31. Judy Bartel, "Guidelines for Teaching Holocaust," mandelproject.us/Bartel.ppt, retrieved September 20, 2007.

32. Thomas Ehrlich, ed., "Service Learning for Civic Engagement," excerpts from *Civic Responsibility and Higher Education* (Oryx Press, 2000), Preface, p. vi.

33. *Echoes and Reflections: A Multimedia Curriculum on the Holocaust*, Anti-Defamation League, (2005–2007), echoesandreflections.org/default.asp, retrieved November 12, 2007.

34. National Council for the Social Studies, "Analyzing Images," *MLL Middle Level Learning* #35, (May/June 2009).

35. Leah G. Stambler, "Character and Civics Education as Scaffolds for Teaching Holocaust Studies," *Paths to Teaching the Holocaust*, edited by Dr. Tibbi DuBoys (Sense Publishers: 2008).

36. M. McLaughlin & G. DeVoogd, "Critical literacy as comprehension: Expanding reader response," *Journal of Adolescent & Adult Literacy*, 48 (1) (2004): 52–62.

37. Margot Stern Strom, "A Study Guide for The Children of Willesden Lane," Facing History and Ourselves, with the Milken Foundation, (2003), www.facinghistory.org/campus/reslib.nsf/studyguides/Children +of+Willesden+Lane,+The?OpenDocument, retrieved November 1, 2007.

38. Manuel Velasquez, Dennis Moberg, Michael J. Meyer, Thomas Shanks, Margaret R. McLean, David DeCosse, Claire André, and Kirk O. Hanson, "A Framework for Thinking Ethically," (2009), originally found in *Issues in Ethics*, 1, no. 2 (Winter 1988), http://www.scu.edu/ethics/practicing/decision/framework.html, retrieved October 6, 2009.

The Historian and the Holocaust: A New Holocaust Curriculum

■ ■ ■ ■ ■ ■ ■ ■ ■ ■ ■

Irene Ann Resenly

*Ph.D Candidate, Department of Curriculum and Instruction,
University of Wisconsin, Madison, WI*

Introduction to my Work

As a life-long learner and burgeoning Holocaust educator, I have found myself captivated by Holocaust history. On the one hand, I have been overwhelmed – on many levels – by the enormity of the Holocaust. To begin to understand this dark period in history is to unravel layers upon layers of stories and experiences, triumphs and tragedies. On the other hand, I have been inspired and motivated by the historians who were able to expose those layers in a captivating, meaningful way.

When I considered writing this curriculum, I pondered how I could channel an admiration of the work of historians and a passion and need for this subject for a high school audience. As I began to review existing Holocaust curricula, I asked myself, "Why hasn't any curriculum given *the students* the opportunity to be their own Holocaust historians?"

This unique Holocaust curriculum, *The Historian and the Holocaust*, is my response. Designed for a twelfth-grade, public school elective course, *The Historian and the Holocaust* takes students on a journey to become Holocaust historians. The first unit, "Understanding History and the Historian," orients students to key ideas and themes in historical theory. They learn the importance and use of primary sources, while reflecting on the function of history, historical perspectives, and fact versus viewpoint.

The second unit, "Understanding Holocaust Histories," allows students to experience and analyze two different Holocaust narratives. While neither attempts to give a complete picture of the tragedies of the Holocaust, both model how primary sources drive Holocaust history. The final unit, "Creating an Informed Holocaust Narrative," guides students in the creation and crafting of a Holocaust history from a perspective they choose and develop. Whether it be a historical essay or a mini-exhibition, students will use primary sources to enhance their understanding of a focused aspect of Holocaust history.

A New Approach

In the more than thirty years since its introduction to the classroom, Holocaust education needs to take a different approach. Over sixty years since the events of the Holocaust took place, teachers and scholars have an unprecedented amount of resources available to them. Though faced with time constraints, teachers can have students explore the rich, moving, and varied histories encapsulated in Holocaust history through these resources. It is time for students to take ownership of that learning, and for teachers to step back and be facilitators as opposed to lecturers. Curricula should not rely on fiction, like *Schindler's List* or *The Boy in the Striped Pajamas*, but on the wealth of primary sources available to them. We need curricula that can be taken into the next thirty years, a time when survivor testimony will have to resonate through video testimony, diary entries, or memoirs – curricula that will have the flexibility and creativity to help connect people, events, ideas, and themes that *students* find meaningful.

The Theory Driving My Curriculum

After exploring the literature of the field, I believe what will set my curriculum apart from the existing curricula is the way in which the Holocaust will be taught. My curriculum will be interdisciplinary, appeal to students with multiple intelligences, and treat the students as actual historians. While other curricula are rich in content, my curriculum will be rich in content and pedagogy. I have relied on Grant Wiggins' and Jay McTighe's *Understanding by Design* to create my innovative work.

An educator can teach students to think critically and incorporate their life experiences in the classroom by creating curricula through "backward design." In moving from theory to design, *Understanding by Design* helps educators shift the focus of the curriculum from teaching to learning. Their three-stage theory details how the curriculum should reflect teaching for understanding. Stage One, "Identify Desired Results," has educators identifying the outcomes of the curriculum by making the desired understanding transparent. It aims to answer the questions, "What should students know, understand, and be able to do? What content is worthy of understanding? What *enduring* understandings are desired?"[1] Stage Two, "Determine Acceptable Evidence," offers educators an opportunity to determine how they will establish proof that the students have achieved the level of understanding they desired. By emphasizing assessment as the second stage in the design process, Wiggins and McTighe are forcing educators to place understanding before instruction. Stage Three, "Plan Learning Experiences and Instruction," is where educators identify the methods and knowledge needed in order for students to reach their performance goals.

Wiggins and McTighe assert that "backward design" will prevent educators from falling into the two traps of traditional design. First, in their best efforts to establish student-centered classes, educators often create activities that are "hands-on" but not "minds-on." Though the activities might be new and enjoyable, they often do not have a connection to an enduring understanding. "Backward design" emphasizes the importance of the outcomes and not the activities. Also, traditional design often places too much importance on covering pages and pages of material. Here, "backward design" emphasizes the performance of the understanding of the material, as opposed to the regurgitation of the content.[2]

Therefore, according to Wiggins and McTighe, good design needs to channel big ideas into specific facts and skills. This is achieved through essential questions. Essential questions place understanding at the forefront of education by focusing on how one *comes to* an answer, as opposed to focusing on just the answer itself. They facilitate connections between ideas within and across disciplines; they engage the learner. The authors characterize these essential questions in four distinct ways. First, they could stir up issues that occur in people's lives and get at "big ideas." Another way to view essential questions is by examining main ideas within a specific discipline. They could be historically relevant and/or seek to understand the essence of a particular subject. Third, essential questions could help students make sense of difficult ideas through exploration. Finally, essential questions must be able to simultaneously engage specific and diverse learners. So while the term "essential" is ambiguous, any of these connotations of the word are meant to reflect a sense of meaning and purpose attached to students' learning.[3]

Through the use of essential questions, the best designs must be both engaging and effective.[4] Performance goals should be clear and challenging. Activities must not only be "hands-on" but "minds-on." Students must be immersed in the experience of learning for understanding, and teachers must be prepared to be facilitators as opposed to lecturers. Lessons should include a variety of tasks and employ multiple methods, while never losing sight of establishing meaning for the students. Finally, a system of feedback and room for "trial and error" should offer both students and teachers the opportunity to constantly improve, reflect, and grow.[5]

Meaning and purpose must extend through every teaching strategy and through every aspect of design. Wiggins' and McTighe's *Understanding by Design* can be used as a support and model for David Kobrin's application of his "student historian theory."

The driving question in his book *Beyond the Textbook: Teaching History Using Documents and Primary Sources* asks what methods must be employed so that students can learn history through the use of primary sources.[6] Kobrin advocates "'constructing' history as a way of learning history."[7] Defining history is not just an academic question; it is a method of learning and teaching. A "best story" that every teacher, parent, student, and historian can agree upon does not exist. All histories are based on inclusions and exclusions, politics, and the perspectives of the writers themselves.

As a result, Kobrin proposes that teachers place the construction of history in the students' hands. His "student historian theory" allows learners to establish meaningful connections to history by enabling them to grapple with the same historical choices and dilemmas that adult historians face. Kobrin starts by articulating the importance of exposing students to the idea that history is always controlled by someone. The very question of who controls the writing of history is the first question that students need to consider when examining primary sources. After students understand that history is constructed, they should begin to grapple with the challenges of actually constructing history. In order to engage the students in this process, teachers need to assist students in finding personal and meaningful connections to the history. Students need to remain involved and active in the learning of history through meaningful texts.[8]

Kobrin's work, combined with that of Wiggins and McTighe, shifts one's thinking of curriculum from content to comprehension. By emphasizing how students will understand, analyze, and criticize, as opposed to how they can memorize and regurgitate, the curriculum becomes more of a roadmap for understanding and reflection instead of a sequence or organization of events.

Based upon my research, no published Holocaust curriculum exists in which "backward design" and "student historian theory" have been applied to a Holocaust curriculum. As a result, my curriculum will fill a niche in the field by providing students with the tools to construct their own narratives, thus providing them with the skills to obtain enduring understandings.

My Curriculum

Rooted in three overarching, enduring understandings – the meaning of history and the role of the historian, the analyzing of specific Holocaust narratives, and the creation of an informed Holocaust narrative through a structured process involving creating, revising, reflecting, and presenting – *The Historian and the Holocaust: A Holocaust Curriculum* is outlined as follows:

Unit/Lesson	Topic
1.1	**Introductions** Aim: What do you bring to the course?
1.2	**Defining History and the Historian** Aim: Why study history? What do people mean when they use the word "history" or "historian"?
1.3	**Perspectives on History** Aim: How do competing perspectives on history and the historian enrich one's understanding of them?
1.4	**Historical Truth** Aim: How do historians tell a story?
1.5	**Historical Perspective** Aim: Through whose eyes do we view history?
1.6	**Demystifying Primary Sources** Aim: Why do historians use primary sources?
1.7	**Unraveling Primary Sources** Aim: How do historians use primary sources?
2.1	**Defining the Holocaust** Aim: What was the Holocaust?
2.2	**The Nazi Party** Aim: Under what circumstances did the Nazis gain and maintain momentum?
2.3	**A Changing Germany** Aim: To stay or leave? The question of the November pogroms.
2.4	**World War II** Aim: From what perspective(s) has the Holocaust been told thus far in the curriculum? How did World War II affect the course of the Holocaust?
2.5	**Ghettoization** Aim: What can these "unexpected historians" teach us about life in the ghettos?
2.6	**Destruction of Life** Aim: How can we begin to understand the "Final Solution"?
2.7	**Response** Aim: How did Jews and non-Jews respond during the Holocaust?

2.8	**Exploring "Other" Genocides** Aim: Never again?
2.9	**Remembrance** Aim: How do we remember?
3.1	**Embarking on the Journey** Aim: How can a library's resources help me construct a Holocaust narrative?
3.2	**The Research Begins** Aim: How do primary source documents enable the writing of a Holocaust narrative?
3.3	**Assessing Our Progress** Aim: How is the project progressing?
3.4	**Peer Review** Aim: How can historians assist and inspire each other?
3.5	**The Halfway Point** Aim: Where are we now?
3.6	**Presentations** Aim: What can we learn from each other's Holocaust narratives?
3.7	**The Historian and the Holocaust** Aim: What have you brought to this course?

Below is an example lesson from each unit:

In unit 1, "Understanding History and the Historian," lesson five on "Historical Perspective" helps students understand the different viewpoints historians bring to their work. As part of the lesson, students decide on a current event or topic that everyone in the class is able to discuss. Next, the students are divided into groups and asked to write dialogues based on the current event. After presenting these dialogues to the class, the teacher facilitates a conversation on how each group told history differently. Why did that occur? What factors contributed to each group telling the same story? How does this connect to the work you will be doing as historians?

In unit 2, "Understanding Holocaust Histories," lesson five allows students to explore the topic of ghettoization during the Holocaust through two perspectives: that of a Nazi official through the movie *A Day in the Warsaw Ghetto: A Birthday Trip in Hell*[9] and that of a young boy being held captive in the Lodz Ghetto through the book *The Diary of Dawid Sierakowiak: Five Notebooks from the Lodz Ghetto*.[10] Combining the documentary and diary, these varying and competing perspectives of bystander and victim give the students a richer and more complete understanding of life in the ghettos.

Finally, in unit 3, "Creating an Informed Holocaust Narrative," lesson two, "The Research Begins," the teacher gives the students the tools they need to be self-motivated learners. The teacher distributes a list of sources that serve as a starting point for the students' research and offers a daily log that allows students to assess their progress each day they are conducting research. The questions include:

1. What did I accomplish today? How did I meet my goals from the previous day (if applicable)?
2. What roadblocks did I encounter? How can I attempt to overcome them?
3. What are my goals for the next day? How do I plan to achieve them?

By guiding the students to work independently, the teacher is helping them develop lifelong learning skills, while also helping them foster an interest in a subject about which they feel invested in learning more.

Final Thoughts

While this curriculum, in part or in whole, has never been implemented, I believe that in crafting it through the use of essential questions and desired enduring understandings, students will be able to use primary sources in a more active manner. Beyond the questions of who, what, where, why, and how, students will be able to extract the historical nuances from these documents to create an accurate and creative narrative.

My work will add an innovative and captivating Holocaust curriculum to the field that places students at the center of their own learning. Instead of only studying a predetermined outline of the history of the Holocaust, my work equips students with the skills to work as historians and construct their own Holocaust narratives. They are trained to make choices based on the perspective from which the history is told, as well as on what to include in their histories, and how to justify the reasons for their choices. Unlike existing Holocaust curricula, students become their own teachers.

Additionally, by using this unique, student-centered approach to Holocaust education, I believe that the process of working as student historians will not only enrich the students' understanding of the Holocaust, but it will empower students to think critically in their lives as well. My curriculum will strive to inspire students to make learning an active, interesting, rewarding and dynamic experience.

Ultimately, by encouraging an emotional investment and a creative outlet, educators will nurture a personal, lasting connection to history. As students review firsthand the very voices of the Holocaust, they will have time to ponder not only the greater historical whole, but also the ability to make a conscious effort to process and share the personal impact it has on them.

Questions

1. *What are the benefits of having students research and develop their own Holocaust narrative? What are the challenges?*

2. *As educators, how can we ensure that students work diligently as young historians and still maintain an emotional connection to the history?*

Bibliography

Bower, Bert, Jim Lobdell and Lee Swenson. *History Alive! Engaging All Learners in a Diverse Classroom*. United States: Teacher's Curriculum Institution, 1999.

Brenner, Rachel Feldhay. "Teaching the Holocaust in Academia: Educational Mission(s) and Pedagogical Approaches." *The Journal of Holocaust Education* 8 (2) (Autumn 1999): 1–26.

A Day in the Warsaw Ghetto: A Birthday Trip in Hell. Dir. Jack Kuper. Gold Apple, National Education and Video Film Festival, 1992.

Engel, David. *The Holocaust: The Third Reich and the Jews*. Seminar Studies in History. Harlow, England; New York: Longman, 2000.

Fallace, Thomas. "The Origins of Holocaust Education in American Public Schools." *Holocaust and Genocide Studies*. 20(1) (2006): 1–22.

Gallant, Mary J. and Harriet Hartman. "Holocaust Education for a New Millennium: Assessing our Progress." *The Journal of Holocaust Education*. 10(2) (Autumn 2001): 1–28.

Haynes, Stephen. "Reflections on a Decade of Teaching the Holocaust." Teaching *About the Holocaust: Essays by College and University Teachers*. Eds. Samuel Totten, Paul R. Bartrop and Steven L. Jacobs. Westport: Praeger, 2004: 105–121.

Kobrin, David. *Beyond the Textbook: Teaching History Using Primary Documents and Primary Sources*. Portsmouth: Heinemann, 1996.

Lenga, Ruth-Anne. "Holocaust Education: The Search for a Suitable Pedagogy." *The Journal of Holocaust Education*. 7(3) (Winter 1998): 53–60.

Levstik, Lisa. "Articulating the Silences." *Knowing, Teaching, and Learning History: National and International Perspectives*. Eds. Peter N. Stearns, Peter C. Seixas and Samuel S. Wineburg. New York: New York University Press, 2000: 284–305.

McTighe, Jay and Grant Wiggins. *Understanding by Design*. Columbia: Pearsons Publishing, 2005.

Schweber, Simone. *Making Sense of the Holocaust: Lessons from Classroom Practice*. New York: Teachers College Press, 2004.

Sierakowiak, Dawid, Alan Adelson and Kamil Turowski. *The Diary of Dawid*

Sierakowiak: Five Notebooks from the Lodz Ghetto. New York: Oxford University Press, 1996.

Totten, Samuel. "Teaching the Holocaust in the United States." *Teaching the Holocaust: Educational Dimensions, Principles and Practice*. Ed. Ian Davies. London: Continuum, 2000: 93–105.

Notes

1. Jay McTighe and Grant Wiggins, *Understanding by Design* (Columbia: Pearsons Publishing, 2005), p. 17.
2. Ibid., p. 17.
3. Ibid., pp. 107–111.
4. Ibid., p. 195.
5. Ibid., pp. 196–197.
6. David Kobrin, *Beyond the Textbook: Teaching History Using Primary Documents and Primary Sources* (Portsmouth: Heinemann, 1996), p. 1.
7. Ibid., p. 5.
8. Ibid., pp. 21–22.
9. Dir. Jack Kuper, Gold Apple, National Education and Video Film Festival, 1992.
10. Dawid Sierakowiak, Alan Adelson, and Kamil Turowski, *The Diary of Dawid Sierakowiak: Five Notebooks from the Lodz Ghetto* (New York: Oxford University Press, 1996).

Shotgun Approach to Holocaust Education:
Firing it out, Hoping it Hits and Sticks

■ ■ ■ ■ ■ ■ ■ ■ ■ ■ ■

Mary E. Haas

Professor of Curriculum and Instruction/Literacy Studies,
College of Human Resources and Education, West Virginia University, Morgantown, WV

Robert A. Waterson

Assistant Professor of Curriculum and Instruction/Literacy Studies,
College of Human Resources and Education, West Virginia University, Morgantown, WV

During the summer of 2009, we conducted a week-long teacher institute on teaching the Holocaust. To be eligible for the institute, participants had to have had experience of teaching the Holocaust and also to indicate that in the next year they would be teaching about the Holocaust. Teachers arrived with a wide range of years and experiences as teachers. While everyone anticipated an interesting program, all knew that it would be emotionally stressful, especially the visit to the United States Holocaust Memorial Museum (USHMM).

One of the workshop participants suggested that we try to add some humor to the study of the serious and tragic events associated with the Holocaust. Hence, the origin of the title of this paper, that at first may seem a bit odd. Although the title often gets slight chuckles, the sad and ironic truth is that many attempts at teaching the Holocaust actually result in an enactment of this statement. Making the lessons of the Holocaust stick in the minds of learners so these lessons are acted upon in both the classroom and daily life is the real goal. Even the very best speakers and films that provide accurate and new information require assistance in preparing the listener and guiding intentions to appropriate action.

As veteran civic educators in a democracy, we advocate the need to transfer what is learned in a lesson into actions that support the principles of an enlightened democracy. Educational goals serve to build the nation and to encourage participation in community and national life. Hitler understood this important idea and used both the schools and the media to educate and encourage participation, but his philosophy was never that of supporting an enlightened and just democracy. In retrospect this is quite clear, but it was not so clear to the world in the 1930s and 1940s, whose citizens and leaders were caught up in other endeavors and subject to organized propaganda campaigns.

In our paper, we seek to apply learning theory to knowledge about the Holocaust and advocate that others do this as they work with teachers or students. We cannot guarantee that this procedure will work every time, but we have responses illustrating that learning and understanding do increase with the application of appropriate learning theory procedures. We provide data from our institute experience and then offer several short activities that help make learning experiences more meaningful. These learning activities also focus on the need to personally act in ways that illustrate support for democratic ideals and values.

At our teacher institute, we engaged in a number of activities designed to add depth to the knowledge of the participants, following the standard guidelines provided for the study of the Holocaust by the United States Holocaust Memorial Museum and by Yad Vashem. We also worked with participants on the ways to assist their students in multiple methods of processing information about these key ideas. The instructional procedures used allowed the participants to provide guidance to us, as we studied and gathered data on the impact or success of the ideas and issues of Holocaust education we were pursuing.

Our participants arrived having taught about the Holocaust and genocide because they were basically good people and wanted their students to become good people. Most did not realize that their own knowledge about the Holocaust was not just missing newly discovered information, but was void of significant and meaningful information. Most did not understand the philosophy behind the actions of the Nazis, and the ways in which the Nuremberg Laws were used to control people and take away the rights of some citizens for the benefit of other groups.

We worked on helping participants fill in gaps in their factual knowledge, but most importantly in their understanding of the major concepts that propelled the issues and events. We also worked with them on ways to assist their students through using multiple instructional methods of processing information about these key ideas. The focus on the instructional strategies provided some relief from the intensity of the content and allowed for personal and group reflections. Participants were provided time to seek their own paths to resources and lessons to complete the course requirements, and to prepare for teaching their own students through a new and more goal-directed approach.

It is important to note because of the growing scarcity of survivors, complicated by the even fewer with the motivation and physical abilities to travel and speak, that technology is not a substitute for flesh-and-blood presences. Beyond meeting and talking with a survivor, our successful activities included:

1. Art
2. Museum visit
3. Readers' Theater
4. Discussions
5. Free time.

Three textbooks, each presenting the content of the Holocaust in a different way, were required reading:

1. *The Holocaust in Perspective* by Edith Rechter Levy is a textbook designed for the beginner to learn about the events related to the Holocaust and is personalized with examples from the author's experiences of survival. It also contains thinking questions designed to promote critical thinking about motives, events, and the beliefs and rights of all people.

2. *No Way Out: A Reader's Theatre* by Susan Prinz Shear is the story of an extended family and its successes and failures to flee Germany after *Kristallnacht*. It has a slide presentation and written speaking parts for narration. The book is a way to involve students in the interpretation of events and has the possibility of students using these materials as a formal presentation to others. Thereby, it extends the teaching beyond a single classroom or course, and provides students with the opportunity to help inform others of the emotions and struggle many Jews often experienced in vain to flee the increasing pressures of the Nuremberg Laws.

3. *The World Must Know* by Michael Berenbaum served our participants as both an introduction and review of the permanent exhibit at the USHMM. In the debriefing session, participants told us that this was the most difficult book. Through probing, it was learned that the difficulty was the vividness of the account, and particularly a number of pictures that provided graphic encounters for the reader.

At the close of our workshop, participants were challenged to reflect on and evaluate the importance of what they had experienced during the conference. This strategy was a way to make the objectives of the message "stick," and to prepare the students for the process of writing their lessons with more meaningful content. In the final discussion, the group listed what they considered the important ideas they had learned about the Holocaust throughout the entire institute. They were then challenged to narrow the list to the five most important, and then to the two most important ideas. The five conclusions were:

1. Chronological content
2. Propaganda (truth/reality)
3. Antisemitism
4. Geography
5. Genocide.

Because participants believed that the five ideas were closely related and could subsume each other, their two summary conclusions were the importance of:

1. Chronological content
2. Propaganda.

A qualitative analysis of the two-week-delayed reflection essays revealed three major experiences that participants believed the teacher institute provided them. Students described that they would now:

1. focus their thinking on important ideas that they would use to improve their teaching;
2. select more meaningful content for their lesson;
3. introduce students to human issues and commitments: personal rationales and responsibilities as important lessons to be gained, along with the need to individually stand up for human rights.

While the specific procedures selected for use in the lesson plans varied, the participants' lesson plans tended to include content focused on:

1. Propaganda
2. Antisemitism
3. Standing up for others
4. Why the Jews did not leave Germany and German-controlled territory.

The activities we suggest that others might want to use are samples of activities that we believe assist teachers and youth in focusing on the various concepts that our participants identified as important to improving their teaching of the Holocaust and genocide. We recognize that most who teach the Holocaust have very little time to devote to teaching the Holocaust. English teachers using one of the biographically-based novels or chapter books are most likely to devote the greatest amount of time to teaching the Holocaust. Social studies teachers face the problem of including instruction related to the Holocaust in courses with many content objectives, only some of which directly address the Holocaust and genocide. The short activities presented here are designed to begin consideration of the following questions:

1. What does it mean to be a citizen?
2. What was the role of the years between Hitler's becoming Chancellor and the instrumentation of the "Final Solution"?
3. How do teachers learn students' misconceptions or specific missing information so they can help youth gain more accurate and meaningful lessons from studying the Holocaust or genocide?
4. How can lessons be designed to solidify the learning into meaningful behaviors and dispositions that students will practice as citizens of today's world?

We detail several examples of exploratory introduction activities that must be followed by longer, more traditional engagements with content related to the Holocaust. Each activity provides a stimulus to open the study and combine it with prior knowledge, to identify the need to examine more and greater detailed sources of information in order to become more knowledgeable about important issues and concepts. Speculation on reasons and attempted explanations by the students are welcomed, but strong conclusions or "correct" answers are not expected from these short activities. Recognizing that you personally do not know the answers, and therefore the need for more information and study to clarify your thinking is the ultimate goal of an exploratory introduction. Building motivation in students for meaningful study linked to ideas or experiences that they understand is the major reason a teacher would teach any of these short lessons.

Exploratory Introduction Activities
1. For a lesson that considers the importance of citizenship and its loss to what happened during the Holocaust, ask students to write a short journal entry on what it means to be an American citizen. Follow the writing by a sharing of ideas and discussion on the benefits of being an American citizen that ends with a conclusion that citizenship is important in providing basic rights and services to people. Those who are not citizens can be denied privileges that may lead to denial of even the basic needs, such as food, clothing, and shelter. International laws changed as a result of

World War II. The following important documents that established human rights for all people should be examined in the lesson's development by discussion and identifying examples of actions that each supports: The U.N. Declaration of Human Rights (http://www.un.org/en/documents/udhr/) and the (1948) Convention on the Prevention and Punishment of the Crime of Genocide (http://www.preventgenocide. org/law/convention/text.htm).

Alternatively, a teacher might focus the journal entry and discussion on the importance of a passport, and the obligations of the person who has a passport and of the nation that issues the passport. This content and its related discussion can lead to examining the difficulty of leaving a nation and gaining entry into other nations – something that many sought to do, but relatively few succeeded in doing during the Holocaust, and something that currently is at issue considering the problems linked to terrorism.

2. The importance of geographic location to variations among nations is approached by using a world map with national boundaries. Distribute world maps to students, along with some star stickers. Tell the students that the Jewish population of the world was not nearly as large as the world's population of Christians or Muslims. Assign students to do one of two possible quick tasks, depending on the specific information you want to pre-measure and discuss. One choice is to locate where the Jews lived in the pre-World War II world by placing one star on the map in the approximate locations where students believe a few Jews lived, and two or three stars close together where they believe there were large populations of Jews living before World War II. An alternative task is to tell students that some Jews were able to survive by getting out of Germany and German-controlled territory before the war began. Ask the students to place a star on the locations to which they believe the Jews fled. After students have committed to their choices by marking the map, ask them to share their maps in small groups or by holding them up in front of their body and standing around the room. Look for the commonalities and the differences in selected locations. Use these as the basis to probe and discuss: How do students know this was where the Jews lived or went? End this discussion with a statement similar to, "We seem to think that this is where the Jews were or went," and asking, "Where can we find out if we are correct?" The door is now opened for research using statistics or anecdotal accounts in a region of the world with its unique answer to the original question.

Alternatively, the class might examine the plight of children and families in England where the *Kindertransport* took Jewish children, and investigate how this worked compared to the experiences of children who went to France that were quite different. There are many stories of youth who went to both of these areas that might be read and examined in detail, or monuments that commemorate aid given to Jews that might be studied to make students aware of attempts by individuals or groups to help children to survive. Many films or video accounts are available concerning survival through immigration, providing details about the physical difficulty and sacrifices parents made to assure the survival of a portion of their family during the Holocaust. In our workshop, we expanded participants' knowledge by learning about South America and Shanghai as places of refuge.

An outline of a world map showing the nations prior to World War II can be downloaded from http://www.eduplace.com/ss/maps/world.html.

3. If, however, your objective is to focus on the great loss of life and Jewish culture in Europe during the Holocaust, have students compare the 1930 map and the 1950 map showing the distribution of European Jews in the world. Ask the students to identify those nations with the largest Jewish populations before and after the war. Discuss and predict answers to questions such as: What conclusion can they make about the numbers? Why might some nations have had larger or smaller percentages of the Jews who died or survived? What does this suggest about the fighting and/or occupation in these nations? Can the students offer other additional factors that might have contributed to the differences in the percentages of survivors? Do the students think that the survivors wanted to return and remain in their former homes after the war?

Resources for this lesson include:

- European Jewish Population Distribution circa 1930 from the USHMM *Holocaust Encyclopedia* provides information on where Jews lived before and after World War II: http://www.ushmm.org/wlc/media_nm. php?lang=en&ModuleId=10005143&MediaId=358
- European Jewish Population Distribution circa 1950 from the USHMM *Holocaust Encyclopedia*: http://www.ushmm.org/wlc/media_nm.php?lang =en&ModuleId=10005143&MediaId=360

4. To measure the extent of knowledge about the "general story" of the Holocaust, give each student a picture. Tell students to examine the picture and identify the event illustrated in the picture. Have students share their pictures and explanations. Next, have the students arrange themselves with their pictures in chronological order to illustrate what happened during the Holocaust. If there are pictures that the students cannot explain, tell them to make their best guesses about the event and where it might belong. Alternatively, these pictures can be lined up on a bulletin board with the "unknowns" in a designated place. As the study proceeds and concludes, re-examine the pictures adding and moving pictures along the timeline.

Alternatively, students might be asked to count the number of pictures they are confident in placing on the timeline at the beginning of the study and again at the end, noting their progress in learning about the events in the larger story. Record and save these numbers. At the end of your study, repeat the task and see how many more pictures can be confidently placed in order as a review of what has been learned through studying. Are there still events that you do not recognize? Ask students to reflect on what this might indicate about their knowledge and understanding of the Holocaust, and the reason why research on the Holocaust is a major task of the USHMM and other interested individuals and groups. Consider with your students how in the future they might learn more about the Holocaust.

Just as we illustrated for the last activity its use as both a beginning and ending activity, so might each of the other activities, or something similar, be repeated as a review of what has been learned. Additional pictures, tasks, or questions that incorporate newly learned information can also be added to the activity. Having the class interact in a final conclusion or closure helps to make learning stick, while also allowing the teacher to use probing questions to reinforce important points and lesson objectives that students may have neglected to recognize as important. Individual summaries or projects can follow the class review for grading purposes.

Between the exploratory introduction and the final review, teachers help students to develop greater knowledge about the Holocaust through the use of one or more of the many available sources of information. These activities need to have clear objectives related to the larger questions of the Holocaust. Particularly important to examine are the causes, events, and value lessons important to citizens and leaders in today's world. It is not possible or even desirable that all students become experts on the Holocaust, but it is necessary that all students are familiar with the events and lessons in human rights that can be drawn from this tragic event. That is why it is important to devote the time, to focus on illustrative information, and to recall what is presented rather than fire out a rapid series of bits and pieces of information.

Questions

1. *Given that the Holocaust is a complex topic, what do you think will be the level of knowledge of the Holocaust that the teachers attending your workshop will have?*

2. *How can you best focus the attention of workshop participants on learning important information that will be both interesting to them and meaningful to the students they will be teaching?*

3. *How might you modify one of the activities outlined in the paper so that it would fit well near the end of your workshop and help to make important ideas from the workshop "stick" in the minds of your participants?*

4. *What do you think are the most important ideas about the Holocaust to teach to students in the middle school (grades 5–8), that will lay the groundwork for studying more about the Holocaust during the high school years?*

5. *What are the major differences in the approaches of English, Art, and Social Studies teachers to the study of the Holocaust? Which of these perspectives does a science teacher share?*

Bibliography

Berenbaum, Michael. *The World Must Know*. Washington, D.C.: United States Holocaust Memorial Museum, 2005.

Haas, Mary E. "NCSS Notable Trade Book Lesson Plan: Hana's Suitcase." *Social Studies Research and Practice* 2(1). Spring 2007. http://www.socstrp.org/issues/viewarticle.cfm?volID=2&IssueID=4&ArticleID=50.

Haas, Mary E. "Examining the Important Civic Values with Elementary Students using Trade Books about the Holocaust: A 5-6 Day Unit." *Social Studies Research and Practice* 3(2), 2008. Summerhttp://www.socstrp.org/issues/viewarticle.cfm?volID=3&IssueID=8&ArticleID=120

Levine, Karen. *Hana's Suitcase*. Morton Grove, IL: Albert Whitman and Company, 2003.

Levy, Edith Rechter. *The Holocaust in Perspective*. Morgantown, WV: West Virginia Commission on Holocaust Education, 2001.

Shear, Susan Prinz. *No Way Out: A Reader's Theatre*. No Way Out Project, 2000.

Totten, Samuel. *Teaching Holocaust Literature*. Boston: Allyn & Bacon, 2001.

Totten, Samuel & Stephen Feinberg. *Teaching and Studying the Holocaust*. Charlotte, NC: Information Age Publishing, 2009.

Wiesel, Elie. *After the Darkness: Reflections on the Holocaust*. New York: Random House, Inc., 2002.

I'm Still Here: Real Diaries of Young People Who Lived During the Holocaust. (DVD 48 minutes). New York: MTV Networks, 2008.

The Wonder of their Voices: Using the Voices of the Survivors in the Twenty-First-Century Classroom

Lisa Muller

United States Holocaust Memorial Museum Teacher Fellow,
English and Language Arts Teacher, Castle High School, Newburgh, IN

We have all had those moments that seem insignificant at the time, but they turn out to be the experiences that change our view of the world. In my career as a teacher and Holocaust educator, I have had two of those experiences, precipitated by hearing the voice and seeing the face of a Holocaust survivor. The first was in 1996, and it was the first time I had ever heard a survivor speak. The second was an innocuous-sounding email from the Shoah Visual History Foundation at the University of Southern California (USC) last winter, asking me if I would be interested in piloting a lesson using testimonies from their collection in my classroom. Thinking about the impact of these two events makes clear the value and importance of using the actual voices of the survivors, along with those of the liberators and rescuers, as we teach the history, the literature, and the lessons of the Holocaust. The facts and statistics are the backbone of our lessons, but it is the survivors and the wonder of their voices that bring the lessons to life and make a lasting impression on our students.

Hearing a survivor for the first time was a life-changing experience for me. In 1996, at a conference sponsored by the National Council of Teachers of English, I heard Gerda Weissman Klein tell her story. By the time I reached the room in which she was scheduled to speak, the room had filled and people were being turned away from the door. I must have looked quite stricken because the person at the door allowed me in, although I was required to sit on the floor. I sat right in front of Mrs. Klein as she spoke, and I felt as if she was talking just to me. I think that every person in the room felt the same way.

As she told her story on that cold November day, we teachers heard a heartbreaking story of horror and cruelty. What happened to Gerda Klein and millions of others should not have happened to any of our fellow human beings. She was fourteen years old when World War II broke out in 1939. She was just the age of the students I see every day in our high school when she went through the horrors of losing everything, as she went first to a ghetto, then to a series of labor camps, and finally on an unimaginable death march in the winter of 1945.

As she continued her story, telling of her rescue and her life since the Holocaust, I began to see her as one of the most amazing human beings I had ever encountered. She loved life with a passion, and her sense of gratitude and kindness towards her fellow human beings was an inspiration to everyone in the room. She had rebuilt her life and learned how to love again. She had learned what was truly important in life, and she forever changed all of us who heard her message. I became a passionate Holocaust educator that day, and I immediately began to wonder what I could do to see that others could hear her message.

As we all know, the opportunities to see and hear the survivors firsthand are dwindling with each year that passes. We also know the power of these encounters and their importance in keeping the story alive. A few years ago, I was part of a study group at Seton Hill University. Eight Holocaust educators from around the country met to talk about our experiences with Holocaust education as a transformative, life-changing experience for both students and teachers. We were asked what ignited our passion as Holocaust educators. What had transformed us from interested, competent instructors to those who were passionate about the subject? In all eight cases, it was actually hearing the voice and seeing the face of a survivor that transformed us. The next question became: "How could we provide that experience for others, especially as time moves on?"

The second experience, that email that I received from the Shoah Visual History Foundation last winter, helped provide the answer. We live in an area in which there are virtually no survivors. We have had a few survivors come, one of whom was Gerda Klein, but it has always been difficult to raise the funds and secure the support of administrators. Teachers in my area have always had to rely on alternate ways to provide firsthand experiences for our students. Using the unedited testimonies of the Shoah Visual History Foundation, some of which are several hours in length, is an amazing but also daunting and impractical option for many educators. The new program from the Foundation, called *Living Histories: Seven Voices from the Holocaust*, has recognized and solved those difficulties for teachers.

Living Histories: Seven Voices from the Holocaust, which is available for streaming or downloading on the USC Shoah Foundation Institute's website at http://college.usc.edu

/vhi/education/livinghistories/, contains the testimonies of a rescuer, a liberator, a political prisoner, a participant in the Nuremberg trials, a Jehovah's Witness, and two concentration camp survivors. Educators can easily preview the testimonies and have a wide variety of experiences to choose from. The testimonies are supported by well-researched historical background, as well as carefully developed lesson plans and suggestions for using them. On the opening page for each survivor, the Foundation has provided easy links to the United States Holocaust Memorial Museum's website, with instant access to relevant articles and maps from the museum's online encyclopedia. The website also provides guidelines for using visual testimony and a technophobe's guide to using technology in the classroom. The Institute has done everything to make using these histories a valuable and stress-free experience for both students and teachers.

In my classes, I piloted one of the series of seven testimonies, that of a woman, Johtje Vos, who had rescued thirty-two Jewish people by hiding them in her home. This, along with the other testimonies in the collection, is appropriate for students in grades 9–12. They would also be appropriate for introductory courses in the college setting. The heart of the lesson was the testimony itself. Students watched the thirty-minute abridged version of the original full-length testimony. We had assigned readings before viewing the testimony, a small group activity after watching, and a large group discussion after that. All of these were based on the materials provided by the Shoah Foundation. The students then wrote a reflective journal entry about the experience. Because we were trying out the lesson for the Shoah Foundation, we also had a voluntary after-school focus group, which was professionally videotaped for the Foundation.

The students loved the whole experience. They were very much inspired by the testimony, and they appreciated the chance to see the rescuer's face and hear her voice as she told her story. They connected to the material in the unit in an extraordinary way. More than one student wrote in their journal entries that seeing her [Johtje Vos's] face as she told her story really changed how they felt about the material. The story of the Holocaust became more real to them. Many remarked that the history became more believable. In a world where denial is an increasing phenomenon, this is crucial.

Both the United States Holocaust Memorial Museum in Washington, D.C. and Yad Vashem in Israel emphasize the central role of the individual story in understanding Holocaust history. As Shulamit Imber, Pedagogical Director at Yad Vashem, has stated:

> The International School's educational philosophy places the human being, the individual, at the center of our understanding of history. Facing the Holocaust means probing not only… the statistics of death and the chain of historical, political, and military events. It also involves an attempt to understand human beings and the manner in which they contended with extreme situations and profound ethical dilemmas. The story of the

Holocaust is first and foremost a human story. Any discussion of its victims, its perpetrators, or those who stood by and watched must attempt to understand the human being involved. The encounter between students and the "ordinary" people who were present in the events of the Holocaust – their daily lives and reality – must serve as the foundation for meaningful educational work.[1]

In its *Resource Guide for Educators*, the United States Holocaust Memorial Museum has the following advice for teachers considering the use of first person testimony:

In any study of the Holocaust, the sheer number of victims challenges easy comprehension. Show that individual people... are behind the statistics, and emphasize that within the larger historical narrative is a diversity of personal experience. Precisely because they portray people in the fullness of their lives and not just as victims, first-person accounts and memoir literature provide students with a way of making meaning out of collective numbers and add individual voices to a collective experience.[2]

Teachers considering the use of video testimonies in their classrooms now have a wealth of materials and support in using them. Along with the sources previously cited, educators can also consult the *Voices Project* at the Illinois Institute of Technology, which is the project to restore and make available the earliest recordings of survivor testimony.[3] This website tells the fascinating history of Dr. David Boder and the first attempt to collect the testimonies of the survivors as early as the summer of 1946. The story of Dr. Boder and his unique collection of early testimonies went largely unrecognized in his own time, but he was the first to understand "the wonder of their [the survivors'] voices."[4] The ongoing project at Yale University[5] is another exceptional storehouse of materials. Additionally, educational resources developed by Yad Vashem provide many opportunities for educators to use, and for students to experience, video testimony.[6]

After this experience, I look forward to making video testimony an even greater part of Holocaust education in our area. As we study this history, seeing the faces and hearing the voices of those who lived through it, while remembering all those who did not survive, continues to touch all who see and hear them. For many of us, hearing and meeting a survivor turned an interest into a passion. This can happen again for our students when we utilize these voices in our classroom as we teach not only the history, but also the lessons of the Holocaust.

Questions

1. *What is the role of video testimony in Holocaust education? What are its strengths and limitations? What steps should the teacher take before showing the testimony?*

2. *What activities and materials can the teacher use to contextualize the testimony? How can the teacher use maps, timelines, and other teaching tools to fit it into the "big picture"?*

3. *What follow-up activities would best give each student a chance to express how the testimony affected his learning and his perceptions of the Holocaust?*

4. *What poetry, music, or other forms of expression could be used to enhance the impact of the testimonies? What creative writing or research assignments could be generated from the testimonies?*

5. *How can teachers assess student learning?*

Bibliography

Anti-Defamation League. "Using Testimonies for Teaching and Learning about the Holocaust." *Dimensions Online* 17:1 (Spring 2003). www.adl.org/education/dimensions 17/default.asp.

Browning, Christopher. *Collected Memories: Holocaust History and Postwar Testimony.* Madison: The University of Wisconsin Press, 2003.

Niewyk, Donald L. *Fresh Wounds: Early Narratives of Holocaust Survival.* Chapel Hill: The University of North Carolina Press, 1998.

Rosen, Alan. "Early Postwar Voices: David Boder's Life and Work." Illinois Institute of Technology, 2009. http://voices.iit.edu/david_boder.

United States Holocaust Memorial Museum. *Teaching about the Holocaust: A Resource Guide for Educators.* Washington, D.C.: United States Holocaust Memorial Museum, 2001. http://www.ushmm.org/education/foreducators.

USC Shoah Foundation Institute for Visual History and Education. "Considerations and Guidelines for the Use of Visual Testimony in Education." USC Shoah Foundation Institute, 2009. http://college.usc.edu/vhi.

Yale University Library: Fortunoff Video Archive of Holocaust Testimonies. New Haven, CN. http://www.library.yale.edu/testimonies.

Notes

1. Shulamit Imber, "How Do We Approach Teaching about the Shoah?" *Emerging Issues in Holocaust Education: Selected Conference Proceedings, Seventh Holocaust Education Conference, November 5–7, 2006*, p. 35.
2. *Resource Guide for Educators*, United States Holocaust Memorial Museum website, accessed January 15, 2010, http://www.ushmm.org/education/foreducators.
3. http://voices.iit.edu.
4. Alan Rosen, Lecture at the Evansville, Indiana, public library, October 20, 2010.
5. http://www.library.yale.edu/testimonies.
6. http://www.yadvashem.org.

The Children of the Holocaust: An Important Focus for the Twenty-First Century

■ ■ ■ ■ ■ ■ ■ ■ ■ ■ ■ ■

Judith A. Vogel

Associate Professor of Mathematics and Associated Faculty in Holocaust & Genocide Studies, The Richard Stockton College of New Jersey, Pomona, NJ

As the study of the Holocaust becomes more removed from the actual events of the Holocaust, it is now more important than ever for teachers to develop new approaches to Holocaust education. The study of the children of the Holocaust is a subject close to my heart, and it is at the center of how I teach the Holocaust in the classroom. There is great motivation for teaching the events of the Holocaust by concentrating on the experiences of the children, and this is a timely and important focus for the twenty-first century.

I currently teach a course entitled "Children of the Holocaust" at a liberal arts college with a strong Holocaust and Genocide program. I began teaching the course over five years ago, with the belief that the child victims of the Holocaust had a heightened experience of both persecution and aid, and therefore their experiences served as an important model for study. As the course has developed and changed, I have come to believe that there are other tangible reasons why it is vital for this generation to study the Holocaust through the plight of the children.

In focusing on the children, it is important not to lose sight of all the victims. It should never be purported that the children are a special class of victims, or that the children suffered more than any other group. In fact, the categorization of people into levels of victimization is disrespectful to that which was endured by all. However, the children's experiences during the Holocaust can be used as an important educational tool for studying the events as a whole. The children's experiences add a depth to the academic approach and a richness to class discussions, and as such, this focus honors the experiences of all those who suffered under the Nazi regime.

The study of the Holocaust should be both an academic and an emotional experience. It is important that our students are given an intellectual and factual perspective of this time in history. They need to know the logistical progression of Hitler's ascent to power. They need to know the timeline and events of the Holocaust. They need to know that 6 million Jews were murdered. However, no study of the Holocaust is complete if students are only presented with the facts. It is equally essential that students make a very real emotional connection to the material. In essence, they need to see the *one* in the midst of the 6 million. By concentrating the study on the children's experience, it is possible to provide a deeper level of study for both the academic and the emotional and thereby, give a more profound model for studying the Holocaust as a whole.

Children are the continuation of a race, the hope of the future, and the strength of a nation. As such, the young were often specific targets of atrocities. Whether by design or just by nature of the young not having any real worth to the Nazi mechanism, the children were often disproportionately affected by the restriction of rights and the focus of atrocities. Consider the ban on education, the lack of nutritious foods, the lack of proper medical care, the confiscation of pets, etc.[1] In all of these examples, the children's future was attacked physically, intellectually, and emotionally.[2] These examples also illustrate the focus that was put on children by the Nazis. From the onset of the deterioration of rights employed by the Nazi rule, there was a conscientiousness to deny a future for the Jewish population. This objective was equivalent to ensuring that Jewish children would never attain a viable, vibrant, educated adulthood. Even in death, the children were disproportionately the focus. The numbers of the Holocaust are well known. Six million Jews were murdered, which represents a staggering two-thirds of all European Jewry. The numbers for the children are, if possible, even more staggering. Out of 1.6 million Jewish children, as many as 1.5 million children may have been murdered in the Holocaust. This is close to 94 percent of all Jewish children murdered.[3]

These incomprehensible numbers display the unimaginable odds of survival for a Jewish child, but they also display a double threat to the life of the children, that is, the threat of losing their own life and the threat of losing their caregiver.[4] In assignments where students are asked to compare the basic needs of adults and children, there is one main difference that is always listed.[5] While all people require food, water, and shelter to survive, children need someone to administer these basic necessities. They need a caregiver. The effect of losing a caregiver during the events of the Holocaust was, in most cases, tantamount to losing their life. The plight of orphans in ghettos is testament to this fact.[6] Without a caregiver, a child's life was under an even greater threat. Orphanages were among the first victims of ghetto *Aktions*.[7] Street urchins were rounded up for deportation in much the same way that dog catchers chase down stray pets.[8] These same unfortunate children lived in such a deplorable state of hunger and filth, leaving one witness to observe: "Their bodies are horribly emaciated; …Some of these children have lost their toes; they toss around and groan… They no longer beg for bread, but for death."[9]

The children also had a heightened experience of aid during the Holocaust. They were the focus of many relief efforts, large and small. They were hidden in convents and orphanages; they were smuggled out of camps and ghettos; they were educated in secret; and nutritious food and clean water was reserved for their consumption.[10] The aid given to children became one of the greatest achievements of the Jewish community.[11] There are many reasons why the children were the direct recipients of relief efforts. The children were at the heart of the Jewish support structure because children mean there will be a future. As such, any energies directed at saving the children constituted a direct protest against the powers that were trying to deny that very same future.[12] Within the Warsaw Ghetto, organizations like CENTOS (The National Society for the Care of Orphans) focused exclusively on the needs of children, "on whom, as one CENTOS official put it, 'all our hopes rest, our future, our survival.'"[13] Children were often the easiest to hide. The identity of a child is more easily changed than that of an adult. Infants can be raised as adopted children or "twins" of a mother's own infant. The resilience and adaptability of youth make them malleable vessels for learning new names, languages, and customs.[14] Many hidden children learned their new life so well that they did not recognize that there was a life before the hiding.[15] Relief focused on children also touches a community more profoundly than any other form of refugee assistance. The *Kindertransport* was successful chiefly because it only provided refuge for the children. They were not a threat to England's workforce; there was a greater likelihood for emigration out of England at the conclusion of the war, and there were families willing to support a child rather than an adult.[16] These same children were also of no worth to the Nazi mechanism, thus making it easy for the Nazi regime to let the children leave.

In relief efforts, the focus on saving the life of a child often superseded any efforts to save the life of an adult. When a plan to smuggle prominent Jews out of the Warsaw Ghetto was conceived, it was never implemented because the Jewish Underground insisted that it was the children who should be considered for rescue first.[17] Within ghettos and camps, the relief efforts for children did more than support their physical survival. They nurtured the children intellectually, emotionally, and culturally. Teachers risked their own lives to educate the young.[18] Cultural communities grew in the bleakest of conditions: children's plays and programs were enacted, libraries were created, and bombed ruins were turned into green spaces for the children to play.[19]

The slogan for Children's Day in the Warsaw Ghetto pays tribute to the intrinsic needs of children: "Give the children a little joy in their lives."[20] Because of the heightened effects of atrocities and aid, the children's experiences do more than mirror the experiences of all the victims. They provide a deeper insight into all that was suffered.

Focusing on the children also provides a deeper impact into all that was suffered. Students are touched on a more emotional level when the topic concerns children. As a population, we are often more affected by the suffering of children. Consider the natural response we have towards a hurt child. It is often easy to turn from the suffering of an adult, but not from the suffering of a young child. Even among the most hardened criminals, crimes against children are considered the most heinous of all. The intensity of feeling that we have toward children cannot be denied. As such, by focusing on the children, we can infuse a more tangible emotional connection with the events of the Holocaust. As time passes, there is a sincere risk of losing much of the emotion surrounding the Holocaust and seeing it as a purely historical event. More and more, programs concerning the Holocaust brace the discussion in terms of a wartime catastrophe, thereby lessening the inhumanity of the event. Hitler is often studied for his strategic abilities and not for his monstrous acts.[21] Additionally, there is the dangerous trend of the Holocaust being used for humor in our entertainment and advertisements. Indeed, the Holocaust is becoming the punch line of a joke. Consider how sitcoms are now using references to Hitler to get a quick laugh or how often you have heard someone sarcastically called a "Nazi" for following the rules too stringently. We are at the precipice of turning the Holocaust into a footnote of history that can be used for humor in this way. By focusing on the children, we can successfully maintain the emotional impact in the study of the Holocaust, and we guard against this frightening eventuality.

The children's Holocaust is also a significantly timely topic for the twenty-first century because the child victims are our only living survivors. They are our witnesses to this history, and it is now more important than ever that their story is told and studied. As such, it is our responsibility that they should be given every opportunity and encouragement to share their stories with today's students. By approaching the study of the Holocaust through the children's experiences, we open up the discussion and provide the venue for more survivor memoirs to be written, read, and appreciated. For too long, the children's voices were not heard in the academic pursuit of the Holocaust. There are several myths concerning children's memories that devalued their experiences. These myths include that children's memories are inaccurate, children do not put their memories into a historical context, and children's memories are based on their senses and not on fact. Children's memories were also discounted because the children were often considered second-generation survivors, not victims themselves. Rosette Goldstein expresses her inability to classify herself as a victim: "I never thought I was a Holocaust survivor. I went to a meeting in the city, and they asked Holocaust survivors to stand up. What am I? Am I a survivor, or am I second-generation?"[22] Because of these myths, children often did not share their stories until recently.

With the passing of time, child survivors are now recording their experiences in memoirs. They are recognizing their own mortality and want to document the events that happened to them. They are also being encouraged to share their stories by their grandchildren, which can be a very powerful appeal.[23] With the new influx of child survivor memoirs, we are now able to recognize the value and purity of the children's memories. Children's memories have no political agenda. They are not couched in the historical events surrounding the experience. They simply record what happened to them. Their memories are not altered to "fit" what people record as fact. They are the facts that they, and perhaps no one else, experienced. In addition, as children describe their memories using details of sight, smell, sound, etc., today's students gain a more vivid picture and appreciation of the victims' experiences. Each Holocaust experience needs to be valued as contributing significant depth and breadth to the body of knowledge making up the study of this topic. The memories and memoirs of each survivor need to be respected for their worth as documentation of the experiences of the Holocaust. The testimonies of children in hiding, children of the *Kindertransport*, children of the *Lebensborn* program etc., all serve to build a record of the events of the Holocaust and are thus a necessary and important part of the academic literature on the Holocaust.

While many people talk about the importance of the last generation of Holocaust survivors, it is equally important to recognize that today's students are the last generation to meet a Holocaust survivor. As such, they have a great responsibility to be the voice for the next generation. In order to be a voice, there needs to be a connection to a survivor's story and a passion for keeping that story alive. As teachers of the Holocaust, we have accepted the awesome responsibility of instilling this passion in our students. It ought to be a priority that each class meets a Holocaust survivor, and the importance of that meeting should not be minimized. Students need to be taught that they are the educational bridge to the continuation of this study. If they are never given a passion for this topic, the study will not continue to the generation to come. It is in the words of the victims that students gain this passion and make a connection to the material, and that is why it is of paramount importance that the teaching of the topic revolves around memoirs and testimonials.

During the first semester of teaching my "Children of the Holocaust" course, I used a single memoir as a text, with the rest being academic tomes and scholarly articles. Although this approach worked well, it was not as effective as I would have liked. I believe that a course should be dynamic, and as I changed and adapted the approach each semester, I realized the importance of studying the Holocaust through the experiences of the eyewitnesses. The texts for the course now contain eight or nine different survivor memoirs, which change each semester, and one academic text detailing the history. With this approach, I have seen firsthand the intensified response that students now have to the subject matter. My lectures can fill in the historical details of the topic, but they cannot replace the connection that students make with the words of the victims. I believe that each Holocaust scholar who has a passion for the topic does so because of a single meeting with a Holocaust survivor, either in person or remotely by reading their words. There is always one story that touches you more deeply or builds in you a more reverent respect for all that occurred. By giving students a multitude of opportunities to make such a connection, we can inspire them to have that same passion for this study.

Finally, setting the focus on the children allows students to reflect on the loss of life experienced even by the survivors. In a course where memoirs are the primary source of information, it is easy to focus only on the survival and to forget the great loss of life. Reading memoirs about those who survived against incredible odds can sometimes minimize the effect of those victims who lost their all. Even when memoirs report on the loss of life around them, the author of the memoir is always a survivor. By focusing on the child survivors, the students do see a real and significant loss experienced by the children. They lost their innocence, they lost their childhood, and in many cases they lost their Jewishness.[24] In essence, they lost the life that they should have had. In the memoir, *I Have Lived a Thousand Years*, the author describes an encounter with a stranger following Liberation: "A middle-aged German woman approaches me. 'We had no idea. You must believe me. Did you have to work hard also? ... At your age, it must have been difficult.' At my age. What does she mean? ... 'How old do you think I am?' She looks at me uncertainly. 'Sixty? Sixty-two?' ... 'I am fourteen.'... I am fourteen years old, and I have lived a thousand years."[25] Although the author survived the events of the Holocaust, the tragedies she endured robbed her of the life she was meant to have and changed forever whom she would be.

In our discussion of *why* we should study the children of the Holocaust, it is also important to discuss *how* we should study the children of the Holocaust. When the focus is on the children, it is helpful to pay particular attention to how the experiences of the children differed from those of the adults. In so doing, it helps to cement the experiences of both. For example, I spend a great deal of time discussing the different responses that children and adults have to acts of prejudice. This response is documented nicely in the Brown-Eyed/Blue-Eyed experiment performed by Jane Elliot in *A Class Divided*.[26] While adults lash out, become angry, and organize revolt, children internalize, become sad, and feel alone. One group is not affected more or less than the other, but they are certainly affected differently.

In the course of studying the children, I also ask my students to create two lists detailing what adults need to be happy and what children need to be happy. Without fail, the lists for adults contain more materialistic and monetarily-based needs, while the lists for children include needs which are fundamental to growth and development. Even when there are comparable needs detailed on both lists, the tone associated with the children is more intrinsic. For example, adults need good food and nice clothing, while children need nutritious food and warm clothing. We use these lists throughout the semester while studying the deterioration of rights experienced by the Jewish community and the effect that it had on child development.

Another way that I approach the course is in my choice of memoirs. I specifically choose memoirs that are easily read, memoirs that are written in "the voice of a child." I want my students to hear the child of the Holocaust talking, not the adult looking back. This reinforces my intention of having them actually meet the survivor, not just hearing their story retold. When teaching about the children, the classroom needs to be an extremely interactive environment. The lessons should allow plenty of opportunity for discussion and questions, and there should be a lively activity-based component. When the topic is children, students tend to have plenty of their own life experiences to share. After all, they have all completed this special time of life called "childhood," and most have a strong opinion about every facet of our discussions. It is a disservice to discount this valuable input, and it is sometimes necessary as an instructor to let go of the reins and let the class lead. Students should be encouraged to examine their own prejudices, judgments, and values. They should engage in individual introspection and group awareness of the values of others. In essence, the classroom should be an energetic environment where students are given freedom to express their views and debate their ideas.

As we study the children of the Holocaust, it is important to remember the children of today. It is their education that will reduce prejudice and guard against additional genocides in their lifetime.[27] Every study of the Holocaust should, by necessity, have an educational component. Our students will one day bear the responsibility of passing on their knowledge to the next generation. They will be teachers, parents, aunts, and uncles, and it is in their hands that we are passing the banner for continuing Holocaust education. I encourage my students to make this a very personal experience. Each semester, my students complete a project in which they "adopt" a child of the Holocaust. Throughout the semester, they follow their child's experiences based on the timeline of what we are studying, and they put together a portfolio and presentation based on their child's life. In this way, the students become the voice of their child for the semester, and at the conclusion of the course, I challenge them to become the voice of their child for their lifetime. If each student continues to tell the experiences of just one child, the message of Holocaust education will never be lost. I want my students to recognize the necessity of teaching the Holocaust to the generations to follow; I also want to prepare my students to teach the Holocaust effectively. As such, we complete projects using children's literature to teach different age groups about prejudice and where it can lead. Students leave my classroom knowing that they are not just students of the Holocaust; they are tomorrow's teachers.

The experiences of the children of the Holocaust are not the whole story, and I would never contend that this is the only valid approach for teaching the Holocaust. However, teaching the events of the Holocaust by focusing on the children can be a powerful and effective means of teaching the twenty-first-century student and reaching them on an emotional level. As the children of today learn from the children of this time, we build a connection to a past which is strengthened by this emotional tie. The voices of the victims cry out to be heard as the students become their voice for the future.

Questions

1. *Why is it important to study the events of the Holocaust by focusing on the children's experiences?*

2. *In what ways do the children's experiences enhance the academic and emotional connection to the material?*

3. *Does studying the children of the Holocaust provide us with a deeper insight into the experiences of all Holocaust victims?*

4. *What are the key points that children of today can learn from the children who suffered during the Holocaust?*

5. *What tools and strategies are effective for teaching the Holocaust through the children's experiences?*

Bibliography

Bartoszewski, Wladyslaw. *The Warsaw Ghetto*. Trans. Stephen Cappellari. Boston: Beacon Press, 1987.

Bauer, Yehuda. *A History of the Holocaust*. New York: Franklin Watts, 1982.

Berg, Mary. *Warsaw Ghetto*. New York: L.B. Fisher, 1945.

Bitton-Jackson, Livia. *I Have Lived A Thousand Years*. New York: Simon Pulse, 1999.

Chow, Marilyn P. *Handbook for Pediatric Primary Care*. New York: John Wiley and Sons, 1979.

Dwork, Deborah. *Children with a Star*. New Haven: Yale University Press, 1991.

Eisenberg, Azriel. *The Lost Generation*. New York: The Pilgrim Press, 1982.

Fogarty, Shana. *Of a Comb, a Prayer Book, Sugar Cubes, & Lice*. Margate: ComteQ Publishing, 2006.

Fox, Anne and Eva Abraham-Podietz. *Ten Thousand Children*. Springfield: Behrman House, 1999.

Greenfeld, Howard. *The Hidden Children*. Boston: Houghton Mifflin Company, 1993.

Harris, Mark Jonathan and Deborah Oppenheimer, eds. *Into the Arms of Strangers*. New York: Bloomsbury Publishing, 2000.

Marks, Jane. *The Hidden Children: The Secret Survivors of the Holocaust*. New York: Ballantine Books, 1993.

Rittner, Carol, John K. Roth, and James M. Smith, eds. *Will Genocide Ever End?* Saint Paul: Paragon House Publishing, 2002.

Sakowska, Ruta. *The Warsaw Ghetto*. Warsaw: DRUKPOL, 2006.

Sax, Boria. *Animals in the Third Reich: Pets, Scapegoats, and the Holocaust*. New York: Continuum International Publishing Group, 2002.

Notes

1. See, for example, Yehuda Bauer, *A History of the Holocaust* (New York: Franklin Watts, 1982), pp. 100, 170, 179; Leon Poliakov, *Harvest of Hate* (New York: Holocaust Publications, 1979); and Boria Sax, *Animals in the Third Reich: Pets, Scapegoats, and the Holocaust* (New York: Continuum International Publishing Group, 2002), p. 182.
2. For further reading on the needs of children, see, for example, Marilyn P. Chow, *Handbook for Pediatric Primary Care* (New York: John Wiley and Sons, 1979).
3. Statistics taken from the online exhibit, "Life in Shadows: Plight of Children," United States Holocaust Memorial Museum: http://www.ushmm.org/museum/exhibit/online/hiddenchildren/plight_of_children.
4. See, for example, Wladyslaw Bartoszewski, *The Warsaw Ghetto*, trans. Stephen Cappellari (Boston: Beacon Press, 1987), p. 9.
5. Information taken from in-class activity, "Children of the Holocaust" course, Richard Stockton College, Dr. Judith Vogel.
6. See, for example, Bauer, p. 171, and Yisrael Gutman, Livia Rothkirchen, eds., *The Catastrophe of European Jewry* (Jerusalem: Yad Vashem, 1976), p. 403.
7. See Gutman, pp. 408, 417.
8. Gutman, pp. 418–419.
9. Mary Berg, *Warsaw Ghetto* (New York: L.B. Fisher, 1945), p. 87.
10. See, for example, Lucy S. Dawidowicz, *The War Against the Jews* (New York: Bantam Books, 1986), pp. 197–222.
11. Paraphrased from Gutman, p. 403.
12. See, for example, Deborah Dwork, *Children with a Star* (New Haven: Yale University Press, 1991), pp. 178, 180.
13. Dawidowicz, p. 245.
14. See further Howard Greenfeld, *The Hidden Children* (Boston: Houghton Mifflin Company, 1993), pp. 23, 36; and Jane Marks, *The Hidden Children: The Secret Survivors of the Holocaust* (New York: Ballantine Books, 1993).
15. See, for example, the testimony of Jana Levi reported in Michael Berenbaum, *The World Must Know* (Baltimore: The Johns Hopkins University Press, 2005), p. 198.
16. See further Mark Jonathan Harris and Deborah Oppenheimer, eds., *Into the Arms of Strangers* (New York: Bloomsbury Publishing, 2000), pp. 10–12; and Anne Fox and Eva Abraham-Podietz, *Ten Thousand Children* (Springfield: Behrman House, 1999), p. 44.

17. Bartoszewski, pp. 65–66.
18. Azriel Eisenberg, *The Lost Generation* (New York: The Pilgrim Press, 1982), p. 65.
19. See further Gutman, pp. 402–405 and Ruta Sakowska, *The Warsaw Ghetto* (Warsaw: DRUKPOL, 2006), p. 9.
20. Gutman, p. 407.
21. See, for example, the documentary, *How Hitler Lost the War*, The Hoffman Collection, (Platinum Disc Studios, 1989).
22. Greenfeld, p. 111.
23. As in the case of Shana Fogarty, *Of a Comb, a Prayer Book, Sugar Cubes, & Lice* (Margate: ComteQ Publishing, 2006).
24. See, for example, Berenbaum, p. 197.
25. Livia Bitton-Jackson, *I Have Lived a Thousand Years* (New York: Simon Pulse, 1999), p. 205.
26. To view the video, *A Class Divided*, see http://www.pbs.org/wgbh/pages/frontline/shows/divided/etc/view.html.
27. See further Carol Rittner, John K. Roth, and James M. Smith, *Will Genocide Ever End?* (Saint Paul: Paragon House Publishing, 2002).

Children and the Holocaust: Universal Aspects

■ ■ ■ ■ ■ ■ ■ ■ ■ ■ ■

Jennifer L. Goss

*Recipient of The Ethel LeFrak Outstanding Student Scholar of the Holocaust Award 2010,[1]
Fleetwood Area High School, Fleetwood, PA
Pennsylvania Holocaust Education Council, USHMM Museum Teacher Fellow*

Children survived the Holocaust in a variety of ways. Some children managed to procure the necessary immigration papers to leave Europe with their families while others were sent on the *Kindertransport*, alone or with siblings. Other children survived in hiding; some in hiding and "hidden," while others were hiding in the open under false pretenses. Miraculously, some children even managed to survive the horrors of the ghettos, concentration camps, and death camps. The experiences of children during the Holocaust often varied according to their pre-war location, social status, level of religious observance, and many other factors; however, one thing is certain, all Jewish children were at risk of extermination during one of the most horrific tragedies of the twentieth century. Only approximately 6–11 percent of the 1.7 million Jewish children who lived in Europe prior to 1933 would survive beyond May 1945.[2] Despite the fact that major differences occurred within the experiences of those who survived, many universalities can be noted.

The first universality that exists in the experience of children during the Holocaust is that these children suffered a loss of formal schooling. This loss occurred in a variety of ways. For some children, their removal from school was part of a gradual legislative process. A few German Jewish children had to leave their school after the passage of the 1933 "Law against the Overcrowding of German Schools," which limited the Jewish population in schools to 1.5 percent of the total population; however, this initial law did not have a mass effect. Even the passage of the Nuremberg Laws in 1935 did not affect the children on a daily basis. It was not until *Kristallnacht* (November 9–10, 1938), and the subsequent measure on November 15 barring German Jewish children from public schools, that many children in Nazi-occupied Europe felt extremely distressed about the situation. As the Nazis began to occupy various areas of Europe, this legislation spread to other countries.

For other children, the loss of schooling was an overnight action. In some areas of Eastern Europe, as children were forced into the ghettos, formal schooling ended overnight. Though formal schooling was ended by these actions, many children who ended up in ghettos continued to be educated by older individuals within the ghetto, despite the illegal nature of this educational system. In Western Europe, children continued to be educated by their parents until they, too, found themselves in the system of ghettos and camps that existed throughout Nazi-occupied Europe. Children who were in hiding had varied situations when it came to continuing their schooling. Some children who were "in hiding" and in the "open" could continue to attend school with their false papers, yet for other children "in hiding" and in the "open," this was too risky. Children who were "in hiding" and "hidden" could not continue formal schooling and only some rescuers chose to continue the hidden child's education within their hiding place. In the case of Philip Maas, he was fortunate that his rescuers valued education. He states, "They were members of two libraries and they very cleverly sometimes only took one or two books from one library while at the same time taking many books from the other."[3] Sara Spier was not as lucky. Sara and her distant cousin were hidden with a farmer and his wife during the war. She relates, "We could sit with our knitting work and chat, but we were not allowed to read, because to read all those books and novels was sin. The only thing we were allowed to read was the Bible."[4]

A second universality for children during the Holocaust was the loss of many friendships with Gentile children. Many testimonies relate an extended story about the loss of a particular Gentile friend during the Holocaust, or the loyalty of another. Lydia Hasman-Csato, a Romanian Jew, was thrown out of school at the age of fifteen. She mentions that one of her Gentile friends stuck by her, but that a second close friend wouldn't remain friends with her because she was "from a cursed race." Csato goes on to say, "I suffered in one thing, and that is as bad as dying. Humiliation."[5] Regardless of their fate during the Holocaust, this was the experience of so many children during this period, and it is evident from its prevalence in survivor testimony that it was a very impacting experience.

Not only was a hunger for education and friendship a universality during the Holocaust, but so was physical hunger. Maria Ezner was placed in the Kunhegyes Ghetto (Hungary) at the age of thirteen. She relays their situation by stating, "We had a hunger you cannot imagine. We had nothing to eat in the ghetto. We had nothing to eat."[6] This was a theme that was rampant throughout Deborah Dwork's chapter, "Ghettos," in *Children with a Star*, and also in Martin Gray's *For Those I Loved*. Gray paints a vivid picture of this dilemma throughout his text. He states, "... I saw groups of ragged children huddled together, holding out their hands. The whole ghetto was swarming with famished orphans, begging."[7] Food was scarce in the ghettos; daily rations often totaled only 300 calories, certainly nowhere near the 1,500 calories a human is said to need to maintain physical condition. In some situations, it was even worse for children. Richard Rozen relays his experience in the Lublin Ghetto. He states, "Food was very, very scarce, and children, who were not even classified as people, got nothing to eat. My parents had to share their meager rations with me."[8] Rations were the same in the camps and it did not take long for those children who managed to survive as forced laborers to resemble the *Muselmänner* so eloquently described by Elie Wiesel in *Night*. Those who managed to be selected for experimentation, such as the twins chosen by Josef Mengele, received better rations, but still suffered terribly from hunger.

Children in hiding also suffered from hunger. Kim Fendrick spoke of the experience of her family in *The Hidden Children*. The family was on the run and hiding in the forest at one point. She said, "In the forest we had nothing to eat and no means of survival except for dew on the leaves and raw potatoes, which my mother would cut with a knife into paper-thin slices."[9] Later, the family hid in a cave. Fendrick says about that time, "Our main focus was on getting enough to eat, because there was never quite enough. Every other day we got a bucket of soup, a loaf or two of bread, and baked potatoes. By then, there were fourteen of us in the cave. My father devised a method of portion control so that whatever we had would be divided up fairly."[10]

Lola Kaufman was hidden away from her family with three other Jews in a hole in a Ukrainian peasant's barn. She was grateful for the woman's assistance, but the situation was made more difficult by the fact that the rescuer's son did not want his mother hiding Jews. Kaufman relates how this caused hunger. "Mrs. Zacharczak wasn't able to feed us if her son came home unexpectedly. Sometimes we had to go for two days with nothing to eat... I dreamed about food constantly. I felt the hunger pains sharply in my chest, and I would literally tremble with anticipation when Mrs. Zacharczak brought us something."[11]

Even some of the children on the *Kindertransport* complained of hunger during their experience. Hedy Epstein relays a story of her treatment by the Rose family. They incorrectly believed that she was starving in Germany and that she needed to be fed slowly-increasing rations. Hedy suffered from hunger for many weeks until a woman serving as a social worker for the *Kinder* interceded and found her a new home. Fortunately, her new family provided Hedy with a more than adequate diet.[12] Sadly, she was not the only one of the *Kinder* to endure this type of deprivation.

Identity issues are another factor that can be identified as a universal experience for children during the Holocaust. These issues began, for some, shortly after Hitler's rise to power. In *Into the Arms of Strangers*, Hedy Epstein tells the story of her teacher identifying her as Jewish. Hedy was very upset by this and went home to complain to her mother. "I came home and said, 'I don't like the teacher.' My mother wanted to know why and I told her. She said, 'But you are Jewish.'" It took Hedy a few moments to actualize this and she concluded, "When Hitler came to power, I began to realize what it meant to be Jewish."[13] Thus, Hedy had to reform her sense of identity. For others, it was the loss of identity that upset their inner balance. Rosa Sirota indicated a feeling shared by many hidden children. She mentioned that it was difficult for her to feel a sense of belonging due to the loss of her roots.[14] This seems to be one of the most prominent feelings mentioned by hidden children during their testimonies. Joseph Steiner also said that he found it difficult to belong.[15] Other children, such as Richard Rozen, had to deal with even larger identity crises. In order to safely pass while hiding "in the open," Rozen had to adopt a female identity for a period of time.[16]

Another layer of this identity issue can be examined in light of the experience of the children who served as Mengele twins. Some of these twins lost their "other half" as a result of the experimentation that occurred. Judith Yagudah was haunted by the death of her sister, Ruthie, as was her mother. Yagudah explains her mother's post-war anguish, which had a tremendous effect on Yagudah's life. "She had been a doting mother of twins. She came back with only one child: It broke her heart."[17] Moshe Offer watched the slow and torturous decline of his brother at the hands of Dr. Mengele. This would cause Offer mental anguish for many years after the war. He states, "I became so depressed. I find myself thinking I would have been better off if I had died along with my brother at Auschwitz."[18] Treatment would help Offer manage his emotional pain but it would never completely disappear.

The necessity of growing up before one's time was also a universal aspect of children's experiences during the Holocaust. For example, many ghetto children had a responsibility such as they had never known. Some of these responsibilities were fairly simple. Yitskhok Rudashevski describes his changing role in the ghetto: "My parents work and I have become the 'mistress' in the house. I have learned to cook, to wash floors…"[19] In some cases, children were responsible for their family's survival. Mietek Eichel relates his tale in *Children with a Star*. His mother, father, and sister were suffering from typhus and no medicine was available in the ghetto. He and his brother sneaked out of the ghetto and procured medicine on the Aryan side. This was just the first in many times that they crossed the wall to obtain items to help their family survive. He was nine years old.[20] Martin Gray's life changes from that of a carefree young boy to the provider, not only for his own family but for so many other families throughout the Warsaw Ghetto. Historian and archivist Emmanuel Ringelblum wrote of the peril that mothers allowed their children to be put in: "Emaciated three-

or-four-year-old children crawl through the culverts to fetch merchandise from the Other Side. Imagine what a mother must go through when her child is in momentary danger of death."[21] Elie Wiesel soon finds himself being the parent to his own father, as the latter suffers greatly during their internment experience and, in the end, can no longer look after himself. Rosa Sirota said that remaining a child was not an option. "The point was you couldn't be a child. You had to grow up overnight and to think as a responsible adult…"[22]

Ultimately, the most tragic and universal aspect of the experience of children during the Holocaust was their loss of innocence. All of the items were contributors to this effect of the Holocaust, but other factors can also be taken into account. Children saw things during the Holocaust that most adults never have to view in the course of their lifetime. They were exposed to death and violence, in some cases on a daily basis. A particularly haunting passage in *For Those I Loved* describes Martin Gray's encounter with a dead child while he is escaping capture and on the run in the ghetto. "In the room was a little girl, dressed in white, thin, with taut yellow skin, motionless, cuddling a doll. Dead. Starved."[23] Gray also brings forth the concept of daily exposure to the horror. "Every day, people who'd starved to death were picked up on the streets; every day there were killings. Raid followed raid; people no longer dared go out but took to their cellars. I saw corpses stripped of their clothes, lying in the streets....."[24]

In *Children with a Star*, Deborah Dwork comments on the deprivations and suffering of those who entered the camp system. "Young people who entered the slave labor network, whether through the selection at Auschwitz/Birkenau or because they were sent directly to a forced labor camp, shed their childhood with their names. They were robbed of their youth just as they were stripped of their packages, clothes, and hair. From the moment they joined the slave ranks they had no choice but to act as the adult laborers they were taken to be."[25] Wiesel illustrates again and again throughout *Night* the various horrors that he endured. In one of the most pivotal sections of the book he speaks of one of his initial experiences at Birkenau. "Not far from us, flames, huge flames, were rising from a ditch. Something was being burned there. A truck drew close and unloaded its hold: small children. Babies! Yes, I did see this, with my own eyes… children thrown into the flames. (Is it any wonder that ever since then, sleep tends to elude me?)"[26]

In the end, survivors of the Holocaust, including child survivors, would have to go through the process of rebuilding their lives. Few decided to return to their pre-war homes; most decided to emigrate to the United States, Canada, or present-day Israel. Regardless of where they chose to live, the memories of the past would remain with them. Some child survivors sought to deal with those memories on their own, while others had the assistance of others who had also endured the suffering. Many of the male Mengele twins continued to keep in contact with "Twins Father"/Zvi

Speigel. Speigel helped many of these twins journey back to their hometowns to start the process of rebuilding.[27] Many of the twins corresponded with "Twins Father" throughout the years. Peter Somogyi related a story of having the opportunity to visit with "Twins Father" when the latter traveled from his home in Israel to the United States to visit his daughter. Peter simply dropped everything and rushed to Massachusetts, perhaps as children would do for their own true parents if they had not seen them in many years. "Twins Father" will do the same and drop everything if the twins ever contact him, which many of them still do, a testament to his vital importance in helping these twins rebuild their lives.[28]

Memories of life during the Holocaust will never go away and child survivors needed to face these memories during the rebuilding process, finding a new sense of "normal." In her preface to *Children of the Flames*, author Sheila Cohn Dekel states, "For the survivors, all is always Auschwitz."[29] While this was not the case for those who were, for example, members of the *Kindertransport* or those who were hidden children, the experiences of the Holocaust will remain with the survivors and their families forever. Inge Sadan, a child survivor from the *Kindertransport*, relays, "I notice that my children have suffered from the five years I spent as a refugee in England. There are all sorts of feelings and reactions peculiar to the children of the *Kindertransport*: anxiety if you don't meet the person you're supposed to meet at that time or at that place, a general feeling of having been abandoned, of having to fight for everything."[30] Annette Baslaw-Finger, Ph.D, survived on the run in southern Europe. Her post-war life can be viewed as successful. She married, had a family and earned an advanced degree. Yet Baslaw-Finger struggles to deal with the aftereffects of the Holocaust. "As for my moods, those are also intense: When I'm happy, I'm very, very happy – the way a child is happy. Of course when I'm unhappy, I'm beyond consolation."[31] Others have a more optimistic approach. Charlotte Levy, also a survivor from the *Kindertransport*, states, "All those I know who have escaped the Holocaust and started a new life have done well. The deeply shaking and uprooting experience had ploughed us and brought more strength to the surface than we had attributed to ourselves. This has been the Jewish fate and experience all through history."[32]

It is important to avoid comparisons of pain while studying the Holocaust; however, it is important for scholars to identify these universalities to better study the events that children endured during this horrific period. By studying the experience of children during the Holocaust, others can learn about the long-term effects of genocide on a population. Unfortunately, genocide continues to occur today and children continue to suffer. The experiences that were universal to children during the Holocaust are also universal to many child victims of genocide today. These lessons can be utilized to help child survivors of other modern genocides rebuild their lives, to find *Shleimut*, wholeness. Hopefully, with increased education and outreach our worldwide community will recognize and implement these lessons to truly realize the concept of "Never Again."

Questions

1. *What are the "universalities" of children's experiences during the Holocaust?*

2. *How have the experiences of some child survivors of the Holocaust affected them as adults? How do you think they manage to cope?*

3. *What does it mean to say that "the most tragic and universal aspect of the experience of children during the Holocaust was their loss of innocence"? How do you think such an experience might affect a survivor as an adult?*

Bibliography

Dwork, Deborah. *Children with a Star: Jewish Youth in Nazi Europe*. New Haven: Yale University Press, 1991.

Gray, Martin. *For Those I Loved*. Charlottesville, VA: Hampton Roads Publishing Company, 2006.

Harris, Mark Jonathan and Deborah Oppenheimer. *Into the Arms of Strangers: Stories of the Kindertransport*. New York: Bloomsbury, 2000.

Marks, Jane. *The Hidden Children: The Secret Survivors of the Holocaust*. New York: Fawcett Columbine, 1993.

Lagnado, Lucette Matalon and Sheila Cohn Dekel. *Children of the Flames: Dr. Josef Mengele and the Untold Story of the Twins of Auschwitz*. New York: Penguin Books, 1992.

USHMM, Initials. (2010). "Plight of Jewish Children." *Holocaust Encyclopedia*. Retrieved April 23, 2010, from http://www.ushmm.org/wlc/en/article.php?ModuleId=10006124

Wiesel, Elie. *Night*. New York: Hill and Wang, 2006.

Notes

1. For further information about The Ethel LeFrak Outstanding Student Scholar of the Holocaust Award, see pp. 319–20.
2. USHMM, Initials (2010). "Plight of Jewish Children," *Holocaust Encyclopedia*. Retrieved April 23, 2010 from http://www.ushmm.org/wlc/en/article.php?ModuleId=10006124.
3. Deborah Dwork, *Children with a Star: Jewish Youth in Nazi Europe* (New Haven: Yale University Press, 1991), p. 72.
4. Dwork, p. 77.
5. Dwork, p. 21.
6. Dwork, p. 166.
7. Martin Gray, *For Those I Loved* (Charlottesville, VA: Hampton Roads Publishing Company, 2006), p. 45.

8. Jane Marks, *The Hidden Children: The Secret Survivors of the Holocaust* (New York: Fawcett Columbine, 1993), p. 45.
9. Marks, p. 59.
10. Marks, p. 62.
11. Marks, p. 85.
12. Mark Jonathan Harris and Deborah Oppenheimer, *Into the Arms of Strangers: Stories of the Kindertransport* (New York: Bloomsbury, 2000), p. 133.
13. Harris and Oppenheimer, p. 37.
14. Marks, p. 24.
15. Marks, p. 136.
16. Marks, p. 46.
17. Lucette Matalon Lagnado and Sheila Cohn Dekel, *Children of the Flames: Dr. Josef Mengele and the Untold Story of the Twins of Auschwitz* (New York: Penguin Books, 1992), p. 110.
18. Lagnado and Dekel, p. 222.
19. Dwork, p. 191.
20. Dwork, p. 199.
21. Dwork, p. 200.
22. Marks, p. 20.
23. Gray, p. 87.
24. Gray, p. 76.
25. Dwork, p. 228.
26. Elie Wiesel, *Night* (New York: Hill and Wang, 2006), p. 32.
27. Lagnado and Dekel, p. 92.
28. Lagnado and Dekel, p. 259.
29. Lagnado and Dekel, p. 13.
30. Harris and Oppenheimer, p. 250.
31. Marks, p. 213.
32. Harris and Oppenheimer, p. 253.

A Team-Taught, Introductory, Interdisciplinary Holocaust Course: The Advantages and Challenges

■ ■ ■ ■ ■ ■ ■ ■ ■ ■ ■

Mark Frisch

Associate Professor
Department of Modern Languages and Literatures, Duquesne University, Pittsburgh, PA

In this paper, I will chronicle our journey toward the creation of a team-taught, interdisciplinary, university-level Holocaust course, and will highlight the value and the challenges of such an endeavor. At Duquesne University, we created such a course, successfully taught it for a semester and are teaching it again this semester, Spring 2010. I will highlight how we have proceeded, share our progress and successes, and explain some of the difficulties we have encountered. My hope is that our experiences may encourage others to develop a similar course and help them avoid or overcome some of the problems we encountered.

In considering a course like this, one of the first questions that arises is: Why do a team-taught, interdisciplinary course on this topic? The Holocaust is, arguably, the most important defining event and the most widely studied single event of the twentieth century for the Western World. It has influenced the thinking and writing of twentieth- and twenty-first-century artists and scholars in a way that no other single historical experience has. One cannot talk about the first half of the twentieth century without taking into account the way in which the thinking and actions of the times culminated in World War II and the Holocaust. One cannot seriously discuss post-World War II Western culture without considering the role of the Holocaust in the crisis in thought and the shift in culture. Whether the intellectual exchange centers on existentialism, modernism, postmodernism, deconstruction, pluralism/diversity, the existence of God, man's/woman's relationship to God, the role and place of science and technology in our lives, the nature of truth, or a myriad of other issues, the Holocaust hovers over us as we contemplate it. With denials of the Holocaust on the rise, the material begs to be studied, taught, and analyzed.

The Holocaust is a subject that naturally lends itself to multiple, interdisciplinary approaches. It is an incomprehensible event that no one will ever grasp in its totality. Its complexity approaches that of woman/man and of existence itself. It underscores the best and worst of Western civilization. We will never understand fully why it happened, how it could have taken place, what actually occurred in all the gory details, who showed courage, and who did not. Literature, psychology, history, sociology, political science, education, theology, philosophy, film: all offer valuable and different perspectives, and underscore its incomprehensible complexity. Anyone trying to understand what happened and why it happened realizes the limitations and shortcomings of any one point of view in grasping the totality of the intricate, multi-faceted, horrific events that that word represents, let alone the problems involved in editing, filtering, and re-presenting it to students. The victims, the eyewitnesses, the poets, the artists, the novelists, the photographers, the sociologists, the psychologists, the historians, the biologists, the film directors, the philosophers, the economists and the political scientists will all give us different and sometimes conflicting accounts and responses to those questions. Those who lived through it will visit its horrors and comprehend its commentary on the human condition and our times in a different way from those of us who were born in the generation after it occurred. With this in mind, a group of us at Duquesne University decided to try to organize such an interdisciplinary course.

The decision to start up such a course actually arose from a controversy on campus relating to abortion. Although outside political organizations are generally not permitted to demonstrate or distribute materials on the Duquesne campus, an administrator gave a pro-life group permission to pass out leaflets. The group brought in huge posters with graphic photos of aborted fetuses and displayed them on sticks. The incident created an uproar, and the administrator, when queried by the *Duquesne Duke*, the student newspaper, compared abortion to the Holocaust. This offended both Jewish and non-Jewish professors with a pro-choice inclination and/or with an interest in the Holocaust, who felt that such an analogy diminished the unprecedented nature of the Holocaust. Members of an Ad-Hoc Social-Action Committee, which deals with political and social issues relating to the University, formed a delegation and addressed the issue with the Provost. The Provost expressed his disagreement with the comparison and eventually, I believe, the President, in an interview, also underscored the special status of the Holocaust.

Dan Burston, a psychology professor and a member of the delegation, decided to try to organize a group to deal with Jewish-related issues on campus. Duquesne has no Jewish Studies program or department at present. A group of professors from different religious denominations and different departments came together to talk about the possibility. Among our goals was to offer an interdisciplinary, team-taught course on the Holocaust.

Six of us from the Departments of Psychology, Sociology, Education, Modern Languages, Theology, and Social Policy began work on the course, preparing a statement of purpose and a syllabus. As we outlined themes, topics, and readings, we saw an exciting, stimulating, and challenging course take shape. However, what we had initially – somewhat unwittingly – created was a course for a graduate student or an advanced undergraduate.

When we talked about whom we actually wanted to reach, we decided that our most desirable audience was young undergraduates. The Dean of the College at the time, Dr. Cesareo, said that we would need ten students for every professor teaching the course in order to have the course approved. Thirty to forty students was a very high bar, especially for a first-time course, and almost impossible for a graduate-level course. With these two pieces of information in mind, we redirected our course at freshmen and sophomores who, we assumed, knew little or nothing about the Holocaust. We wanted a course that would attract as broad a range of students as possible. We also realized that the subject matter was so vast and encompassing that it easily lent itself to more than one course. We decided to offer two courses: one on the history of antisemitism, and a second course specifically on the Holocaust.

We pursued several different tracks to help bring our ideas for these courses to fruition. First, we sought a grant to help develop them. The University offers NEH (National Endowment for the Humanities) grants to help develop, among other things, new interdisciplinary or team-taught courses. We divided up into two groups of three. At that point, another colleague from the School of Education, Wayne Brinda, joined the three of us, Ruth Biro, Daniel Lieberfeld, and myself, Mark Frisch, to put together this Holocaust course. One group would focus on the antisemitism course, the other on the Holocaust. We wrote up and submitted tentative syllabi and grant applications. Both courses were granted $2,000 to help in their development. At the same time, we looked into the possibility of including the courses in the University's core curriculum. It just so happened that the University was reworking its core. We discussed the possibility with the Chair of the committee responsible for re-working the core and received permission to include it in one of the categories where students have a large number of courses from which to choose, the section on Social Justice. For those developing such a course, I would recommend both taking advantage of in-house grants and linking such a course into any college or university core requirements where possible. That not only helps enrollment, but assists in giving the new course credibility.

We had other problems to work out as well. One concerned a competing course. A professor in the History Department has taught a History course on the Holocaust for a number of years. The NEH Grant Committee, (which is composed of departmental chairs who must ultimately approve this course), was concerned that our course would overlap and conflict with his. We approached Dr. Weiss and invited him to join the Jewish Faculty Forum. He respectfully declined. However, he saw no problem with offering our course. "The more the merrier," he quipped. He acknowledged that the course is difficult to teach because of the depressing nature of the subject matter. We believe that what distinguishes our course from the traditional History course is our team-taught, interdisciplinary approach. The subject matter with all its implications is so vast that it lends itself to many different perspectives and points of view. Our approach can most effectively take advantage of that. We have continued to offer Dr. Weiss the opportunity to join us in the class. He recently stated that he would like to join us the next time we offer the class.

Another problem we faced concerned where to house the course. Every course in the McAnulty College of Liberal Arts must have a home, a department in which the course is listed as part of its, and the University's, curriculum. It seemed to make most sense to cross-list the course in the departments of the professors who were teaching it. However, two of my colleagues in the first semester taught in the School of Education. We agreed that the course more appropriately belonged in the McAnulty College of Liberal Arts, since most of our students would probably come from that area. Another of my colleagues, Dr. Lieberman, teaches in the program in the Institute for Social and Public Policy. That is a graduate program, but our course is an undergraduate course. As he is affiliated with the Political Science Department as well, he approached them and asked them to house the course. His proposal was met with skepticism about whether Political Science is an appropriate place, and questions about how much Political Science would actually be taught. He decided not to pursue that further.

That left my department, the Department of Modern Languages and Literatures. When I proposed the course, I met similar questions and skepticism. There were objections to housing the course in our department because we are a language and literature department. There were questions about how much "literature" would actually be taught in the course. I argued that the Department of Modern Languages and Literatures is a very appropriate place for the course. I emphasized that we are a Catholic university and that Pope John Paul II issued a statement, *We Remember*, calling for the teaching of the Holocaust. I stressed that the United States Catholic Conference recognized the importance of this theme and has called on Catholic schools at all levels to teach the Holocaust.[1] I and others who supported the housing of this course emphasized that similar courses are taught in Modern Languages departments around the country. I emphasized that by its nature, the Modern Languages and Literatures Department is an interdisciplinary department. We teach not only language and literature, but also culture, and this course is about European culture.

One cannot teach literature and culture without at some level also introducing the other arts, as well as history, political science, sociology, psychology, and philosophy, among other things. I stressed that one of the central themes and lessons of such a course is the importance of pluralism and diversity, understanding of others, respect and tolerance for other cultures and religions. I underscored that diversity, pluralism, and respect for others was a central mission of our department as we had defined it, more than almost any other department in the University. Once it saw the syllabus, my department ultimately approved housing it in the department as a pilot course for one year.

We offered the first class during the Spring 2008 semester. One of the people scheduled to teach it received a sabbatical, so we found someone else to fill in. One of the things we discovered was that because people have different schedules, it is very helpful to have a group of different people who can do this class if it is to be offered on a regular basis. We were pleasantly surprised by the enrollment. We had about forty-three students who registered for the class. Two things helped support this registration. As I mentioned before, we got the course approved as a University core curriculum course. We also had it approved as an Honors course. I would recommend that anyone attempting to create a Holocaust class try to link the course with as many learning communities and college and university requirements as possible.

Overall, the course was a success, although there were things that could have gone better, and things that we needed to change. The written part of the student evaluation captures some of this. This evaluation had two questions on the written part: 1) What aspects of the instructor's teaching were most effective? 2) How could this instructor improve his/her teaching effectiveness? Here are some of the written responses we received:

Question 1: What aspects of the instructor's teaching were most effective?

- "Guest speakers who were Holocaust survivors were extremely interesting!"
- "X very good at speaking/teaching, very knowledgeable and interesting. I looked forward to his lectures. X well learned & interesting. More Powerpoints are helpful!"
- "The depth of knowledge the instructors had made for better understanding of the material for all the students."
- "Enthusiasm and knowledge. Teacher's background on the subject. Visuals like movies."
- "Examples, photos, videos, in class discussion."
- "X very passionate about the subject. X: good teaching method. X prepared. X: good use of books/teaching."
- "Guest lecturers. Videos. Class discussion."

- "Dr. X was very enthusiastic and knew what he was talking about. He made class interesting. Dr. X also knew what she was talking about. Dr. X was always seeing if we had questions, which was good. Dr. X always seemed informed on what is going on in today's world that is relevant. I loved when they brought in survivors and survivors' children because it really brought the Holocaust alive in my eyes."

Question 2. How could this instructor improve his/her teaching effectiveness?

- "All in all the teachers needed to communicate more."
- "Make the class more interactive instead of solely lecturing the majority of the time."
- "Work together more! There's a lot of confusion most of the time. Maybe break the semester into four chunks instead of alternating teachers every day – better flow."
- "Better organization with assignments, lectures, etc."
- "Organization, timeliness of return of assignments."

From these evaluations, while we did some things right, we had to make some changes. We needed to coordinate the lectures of the faculty more effectively. The students had difficulty seeing the unifying structure at times. We have taken the advice of several students who suggested that each person teach a segment of several weeks together, as opposed to interweaving back and forth throughout the semester. On the syllabus itself, some readings were listed to accompany lectures, but because of technical and logistics problems, they did not appear on Blackboard, the university online coordination program. We plan to use Duquesne Library's Electronic Reserves in the future to avoid that. We are also looking for techniques to encourage more student participation, as that is a little more difficult in a larger class.

One of the things we discovered, and these evaluations bear it out, was that the students appreciated the firsthand accounts and outside lecturers. We brought in Moshe Baran, a Holocaust survivor; Les Banos, a Hungarian SS officer, interpreter, and driver who served in German headquarters and worked undercover for the Allied forces during the war, saving the lives of Jews and American soldiers; Mikael Kimelman, the son of two Holocaust survivors; Dr. Marie Baird, a theology professor; and Dr. Edith Krause, a German professor and Chair of the Department of Modern Languages who spoke on the Weimar Republic. I would encourage others to also bring in outside survivors or witnesses, where available. We found it helpful to scatter these visits throughout the semester to provide a change of pace.

One unforeseen advantage of the team-taught approach was that it allowed us to cover for each other in emergencies. We had one in particular, where Dan Burston had a death in the family and had to be absent for about ten days. We were able to fill in for him and read one of his lectures, while adjusting the syllabus for the other classes.

While there are many advantages to the team-taught approach, I do not want to diminish its challenges. One of the principal difficulties was coordination. With four different main lecturers teaching, as well as some guest lecturers, making sure that everyone had the opportunity to cover what she/he was supposed to and was hoping to was not always easy. Transitions from one person to another also presented problems. The fact that this was our first time through made those transitions more difficult. Also, covering the historical aspects did create certain challenges as none of us was a history professor. However, we basically supported each other and handled it reasonably well. I do see a definite advantage to having a historian in the team, but if that is not possible, it is not essential as long as those teaching are well versed in the history.

As we will teach this course every other year, we are teaching it again this semester, Spring of 2010. In preparing for that, I had to go to my department again and ask for their approval to house the course there, as last time that was only given on a trial basis for one year. Once again, it was controversial and the debate was emotional. The motion to house the course in our department passed by one vote. However, I had to agree to teach it as an overload as we are short on full-time faculty to teach our regular courses.

One of the reservations of those who opposed housing the course in our department was again that someone in History is teaching a course. I realized that that would be an issue, so before I brought the issue to my department, I approached Dr. Weiss again to ask him to join us. He informed me that he was officially retiring as of this fall, so it was not his issue. He said that we were welcome to teach it if we wanted. Later, I found out from Dr. Weiss that his retirement is a partial retirement. He will teach one course a semester. While he is not able to teach with us in 2010, he left the door open to future years. I learned that patience, persistence, and openness are important in these situations.

I have included below our Spring 2010 syllabus. We have numerous goals. Although we have restructured the course this time, our goals are very similar to the last time we taught the course. We want to provide the students with an appreciation of the complexity of the Holocaust and of what happened. We realize that that means offering them numerous perspectives – historical, literary, social, psychological, philosophical, theological, economic, political, etc.

We begin with a discussion of the chronology. We created a Powerpoint timeline and devote the first week to fleshing out that history. We then divide the course into three sections, the Literature, the Psychology, and the Theology sections, each four weeks long. The Literature section, which is the section that I teach, is subdivided into three parts: 1) Jewish Life Before the Holocaust – Who are the Jews? / Literary Modernism; 2) The Holocaust; and 3) Responses to the Holocaust: The Postmodern Turn. We require the students to write a paper for each part. Last time through, we gave them the option of doing an oral presentation at the end of the semester to buttress their class participation grade. Those reports were good, but there were time restraints because of the size of our class. We are not doing that this semester. Initially, we used Yehuda Bauer's *A History of the Holocaust* to provide historical background, *Out of the Whirlwind* as an anthology for the literature of the Holocaust that offers various perspectives, along with stories from Tadeusz Borowski's *This Way for the Gas, Ladies and Gentlemen*, and we are doing so again. All three texts served us well and I would recommend them. I also incorporate films to support my discussions and lectures. One film that proved quite effective in capturing the inexplicable nature of the Holocaust, as well as its horrors, was the French film *Night and Fog*. Two of my colleagues in the Modern Languages Department and I coordinate a Human Rights Film Festival yearly. I am asking the students to attend either *Sand and Sorrow* or *War Child* from that Festival, which are films on the genocide in Darfur and the Sudan. I believe this is an effective way to link the course to other genocides.

The Psychology section is taught by my colleague in Psychology, Dr. Daniel Burston. He will do an in-depth discussion of salient aspects of *Mein Kampf*, raising the question: How could it happen? He will underscore what Psychology can (and cannot) teach about the Holocaust. He will also refer to other mass murderers – Charles Manson, Jim Jones. He will delve into theories of Hitler's personality and motivation, and explore the motivations of the SS, the career army officers, and the rank and file as well.

The Theology section is taught by my colleague in Theology, Dr. Marie Baird. She will discuss the development of Christian anti-Judaism and its transformation into religiously-motivated antisemitism. She will also discuss the resistance movements, the rescuers, and the witnesses/ survivors.

There are several other professors from other departments who are interested in teaching in this course and are qualified to do so. In the future, if they do participate, they will teach their particular perspective and discipline. I mention this to emphasize that it is possible to create this type of course in other colleges and universities, using professors from a variety of different backgrounds.

Also, we were able to take advantage of one incredible opportunity that proved very worthwhile and could be very valuable to anyone creating a similar course, or anyone who has a Holocaust course up and running. The Agency for Jewish Learning in Pittsburgh and Duquesne University provided funding for four of us to travel to Israel for ten days to participate in an intense seminar on the Holocaust at Yad Vashem. We spent eight to nine days in classrooms at Yad Vashem, listening to lectures from some of the world's most prominent scholars on various aspects of the *Shoah* and on pedagogical methods for teaching the Holocaust. It was very informative and helpful, and the material was quite useful. Yad Vashem offers such seminars on a regular basis, I believe, to groups from all over the world. I would strongly encourage anyone who can make such arrangements to take advantage of it. We are presently entering into discussions with the Provost, the Dean and the Director of Mission to link Yad Vashem's online courses and programs to Duquesne, and to use them to support a Jewish Studies minor.

I have attempted to outline some of the challenges and hurdles that we have overcome, or are still encountering, in realizing this course. The importance of this memory is clear in our political environment today, where Holocaust deniers are becoming more vocal and numerous, or at least receiving more media attention. While memory by itself will not prevent another Holocaust or genocide, or antisemitism or racism, without it, those ugly monsters will almost certainly arise again. This is one of our most effective weapons to combat them.

Questions

1. *In which department(s)/ division/ school should an interdisciplinary course on the Holocaust be lodged?*

2. *How do you structure a class to fulfill as many different college and/or university requirements as possible and thus attract the most students?*

3. *If a course on the Holocaust is team-taught, who should be part of the team? From which disciplines? How many classes should each person teach to maintain continuity in the course? What is the best way to organize the different segments?*

Bibliography

Bauer, Yehuda. *A History of the Holocaust*: Revised Edition. New York: Franklin Watts, 2001.

Borowski, Tadeusz. *This Way to the Gas, Ladies and Gentlemen*. New York: Penguin Books, 1976.

Catholic Teaching on the Shoah: Implementing the Holy See's We Remember, Bishops' Committee for Ecumenical and Interreligious Affairs, 2001. USCCB Publication no. 5–406.

Friedlander, Albert H., ed. *Out of the Whirlwind: A Reader of Holocaust Literature – Revised and Expanded Edition*. New York: UAHC Press, 1999.

Notes

1. Publication 5-406, "Catholic Teaching on the Shoah: Implementing the Holy See's *We Remember*."

Syllabus
Perspectives on the Holocaust:
A Team-Taught Interdisciplinary Course

Spanish, French, German, Italian 270; Psychology 270; Theology 272

Professors

Dr. Marie Baird, Department of Theology.

Dr. Daniel Burston, Department of Psychology.

Dr. Mark Frisch, Department of Modern Languages and Literatures.

Goals/Objectives: This course provides students with:

- An understanding of the historical and cultural origins of the Holocaust, including the effects of European anti-Semitism, nationalism, the Weimar Republic, and World Wars I and II. A realization that the Holocaust was not an accident in history – it occurred because of choices made by individuals, organizations, and governments.
- A detailed understanding of specific events during the Holocaust, particularly from primary sources. An understanding of the numerous aspects of this history and its connection with World War II.
- An understanding of the range of responses to the Holocaust on the part of Jewish communities, Christian Europeans and their institutions, and by countries such as the United States.
- An exploration of perspectives and explanations of the Holocaust, including political science and social psychology.
- A comparative perspective on genocide, with reference to other genocides of the twentieth century.
- An understanding of some of the prominent artistic, cultural, philosophical, and theological responses to the Holocaust.
- An understanding of the after-effects of the Holocaust for world politics, including the Arab-Israeli conflict, and for international human-rights law.
- Engagement with the moral issues raised by the Holocaust. Experience through in-depth research, writing, and presentation on various aspects of the Holocaust.

Methodology: Various methods will be employed in the classroom to facilitate learning: lectures, Socratic question and answer methods, class discussion, among others. Readings will be discussed in some detail. Students are expected to complete the assigned readings and prepare the lessons before each class, and come to class ready to participate. During the course of the semester, students will write three short research papers (to be handed in at the end of weeks 5, 9, and 13). There will be a final exam during finals week, with the questions distributed ahead of time. Students will also be asked to view some movies outside of class.

Grading: As noted above, each student will be required to submit three short research papers (3–5 pages each, double-spaced) and a final exam. Each student will be expected to come to class prepared and to participate actively.

> **Three Research Papers 60%**
> **Final Exam 20%**
> **Attendance and Participation 20%**

Academic Integrity: (Normal statement)

Class Participation / Attendance: Your class participation grade is composed of three parts, oral quality, oral quantity, and attendance. All three parts are interrelated. If you are not attending, you are not participating orally. However, more is required than just attending. All students are expected to participate constructively in class and to contribute to an environment that fosters mutual learning.

Students are responsible for finding out from classmates about material covered or assignments given. If you miss more than three classes during the semester, your overall course grade may be affected. Numerical grades for class participation range from 0 to 100, with most grades between 50 and 95.

As a courtesy to the professor and the other students, all cell phones are to be turned off and left off during class time. Playing with cell phones, doing homework or other things not related to the class are not permitted and will affect your class participation grade.

Learning Outcomes: Upon completion of the course, students will come away with a detailed understanding of what the Holocaust was and will appreciate how respect, understanding, and social justice for all races, religions, and cultures must be a common concern for all.

1. After surveying the long history and the causes of anti-Semitism, the students will be able to weigh whether the Holocaust was an isolated aberration, as some claim, or a product of the prejudices and stereotypes passed from generation to generation and affecting attitudes and behavior toward Jews.

2. The students will be able to examine, scrutinize, analyze, and interpret diverse written, oral, and visual statements about this and similar events. They will determine for themselves whether the claims of the Holocaust deniers are correct or not.

3. Students will be able to analyze the various responses to the Holocaust on the part of the Jewish and the Christian European communities, and determine whether everything that could have been done was done. They will judge who showed courage and who failed in their moral obligations.

4. Students will compare the Holocaust to other genocides and formulate an opinion about factors leading to historical events like the Holocaust. They will weigh and assess strategies for how future genocides may be avoided.

Perspectives on the Holocaust Syllabus

Texts: Required
Beckett, S. *Waiting for Godot*. Grove Press, 1982.
Friedlander, A. *Out of the Whirlwind: A Reader of Holocaust Literature*. New York: UAHC Press. 1999.
Fromm, E. *Escape From Freedom*. New York: Avon Books, 1965.
Hitler, A. *Mein Kampf*. Trans. Ralph Manheim. New York: Houghton Mifflin, 2006.
Kafka, F. *The Metamorphosis*. Bantam.
Scholl, Inge. *The White Rose: Munich 1942–1943*. Trans. Arthur R. Schultz. Hanover, NH: Wesleyan University Press, 1983.
Spiegelman, A. *Maus I, My Father Bleeds History*. New York: Pantheon Books, 1991.
The Holocaust Chronicle – Reference
Selections from various works, available at Gumberg Library's Electronic Reserve
Texts: Recommended
Bauer, Y. *A History of the Holocaust*. Revised Edition. New York: Franklin Watts, 2001.

Week One
1.Introduction to the course
2. Overview of Holocaust chronology
3. Reading – first few class periods: Sholom Aleichem, "The Town of the Little People," "Modern Children," "Hodel," "Chava," "On Account of a Hat"

(Electronic Reserve ER); Yehuda Bauer, *A History of the Holocaust* – Ch. 9, "The Final Solution" (Electronic Reserve ER).

Literature Section: Perspectives on the Holocaust
Jewish Life before the Holocaust in Europe: Who are the Jews? Modernism

Week Two
1. Auden, "Refugee Blues;" Sholom Aleichem, "The Town of the Little People," "Modern Children," "Hodel," "Chava" (Electronic Reserve ER). Begin reading Kafka.
2. Sholom Aleichem, "On Account of a Hat" (Electronic Reserve ER); Kafka *The Metamorphosis*.
3. Kafka, *The Metamorphosis*.

Holocaust

Week Three
1. The Weimar Republic. Dr. Edith Krause. Read Wiesel, "An Evening Guest" in *Whirlwind*, pp. 3–9.
2. Andre Schwarz-Bart, "The Last of the Just" in *Whirlwind*, pp. 84–103; Tadeusz Borowski, *This Way for the Gas, Ladies and Gentlemen*, pp. 29–49 (Electronic Reserve ER); Primo Levi "The Drowned and the Saved" in *Whirlwind*, pp. 208–226, or Wiesel, *Night* in *Whirlwind*, pp. 400–411.
3. Art Spiegelman, *Maus I*, "Night of the Mist," in *Whirlwind*, pp. 192–207. Poetry: Dan Pagis, "Written in Pencil in the Sealed Freight Car," (ER); Abraham Sutzkever, "The Leaden Plates of Romm's Printing Works" (ER)

Responses to the Holocaust: The Postmodern Turn

Week Four
1. *Maus; Night and Fog* – Film; Jorge Luis Borges short story
2. *Maus*; Jorge Luis Borges, "The Library of Babel" (ER)
3. Borges; Primo Levi "Shema" (ER); Begin reading Beckett, *Waiting for Godot*.

Week Five
1. *Godot*
2. *Godot*
3. Abraham Joshua Heschel, "No Religion is an Island" (Link to article on Blackboard)

First research paper due

Film Series: Injustice and Indifference
Films and Dates:

Tuesday, January 19	*Jonny Gammage*, 7:00 pm Power Center
Monday, January 25	*Sand & Sorrow*, 7:00 pm 105 College Hall
Tuesday, February 2	*War Child*, 7:00 pm 105 College Hall
Wednesday, February 10	*Flow*, 7:00 pm 105 College Hall
Tuesday, February 16	*Mardi Gras*, 7:00 pm College Hall
Wednesday, February 24	*Dishonored*, 7:00 pm 105 College Hall

Psychology Section: Perspectives on the Holocaust

Week Six
1. Overview of the section, followed by an in-depth discussion of salient aspects of *Mein Kampf*; How Could It Happen? What Psychology Can (and Cannot) Teach About the Holocaust: other mass murderers – Charles Manson, Jim Jones.
2. Required Reading: *Mein Kampf*, book 1.
    1. Hitler as orator and author
    2. His childhood, adolescence, education
    3. Ideas about Jews and Aryans
    4. Attitude toward liberals, capitalists and Marxists
    5. Approach to Social Psychology and Propaganda

Week Seven
1. Theories of Hitler's Personality and Motivation, including but not limited to "The Authoritarian Personality," Erich Fromm and Erik Erikson's portraits, more recent ones, etc.
2. Required Readings: Fromm, E., *Escape from Freedom*; Burston, D., "The Authoritarian Personality," in *The Encyclopedia of Psychology and Religion*, ed., Leeming, D., Springer, 2009, vol 1.
3. Recommended Readings: Erikson, E., "The Myth of Hitler's Childhood," in *Childhood and Society*. New York: W.W. Norton, 1950; Zillmer, Harrower et al., "The Quest for the Nazi Personality."

Week Eight
1. This week will be spent exploring the motivations of the SS, the career Army officers and the rank and file. We will also explore officer training and military culture, and the role of psychiatry in officer training/selection.
2. Required Readings: Stern, K., "Stauffenberg," in *Love and Success*. New York:

Farrar Straus and Giroux; chapter on Nazi Psychiatry and officer selection.
3. Recommended Reading: Zillmer, Harrower et al. on Eichmann, Donnitz, pink chameleons; Baum R.

Week Nine

1. This week focuses on Nazism as a political religion:
    a. its repudiation of Enlightenment ideals of equality, democracy, and progress
    b. reflections on the way it subverted/attacked the Protestant and Catholic Churches
    c. the weird syncretism of neo-pagan and pseudo-messianic beliefs and attitudes in the symbology of its civic religion.
2. Required Readings: Berman, M., "The Twisted Cross," in *Coming to Our Senses*; Burston, D., "Anti-Semitism" in *The Encyclopedia of Psychology and Religion*; Burston, D., "Nazism" in *The Encyclopedia of Psychology and Religion*.
3. Recommended Reading: TBA

Second Research Paper Due

Theology Section: Perspectives on the Holocaust

Week Ten

The Development of Christian Anti-Judaism and its Transformation into Religiously Motivated Anti-Semitism
1. Cardinal Michael Faulhaber as an exemplary case from the Nazi era
2. How did Christianity develop its hostility to Judaism and how did such hostility become hardened into religiously motivated anti-Semitism?
3. Required Readings: Tyson, J., "The Death of Jesus," in *Seeing Judaism Anew: Christianity's Sacred Obligation*. ed. Mary C. Boys. New York: Rowman and Littlefield, 2005; O'Hare, P., "Anti-Judaism, Antisemitism: History, Roots, and Cures" in O'Hare, P., *The Enduring Covenant: The Education of Christians and the End of Antisemitism*. Valley Forge, PA: Trinity Press International, 1997. (ER)

Week Eleven

Eric Voegelin on the Failure of the Christian Churches; Resistance as Exemplified by The White Rose
1. The Ecclesiastical Abyss: The Roman Catholic Church
2. The Ecclesiastical Abyss: The Protestant denominations
3. Resistance to the Abyss: The White Rose
4. Required Readings: Voegelin, E., "The Ecclesiastical Abyss: The Roman Catholic Church" and "The Ecclesiastical Abyss: The Protestant Churches" in Voegelin,

E., *Hitler and the Germans*. eds. Detlev Clemens and Brendan Purcell. Columbia MO: University of Missouri Press, 1999 (ER); Scholl, I., *The White Rose*.

Week Twelve

The Rescuer/Victim

1. A Levinasian interpretation of Holocaust rescue
2. Lorenzo Perrone and Etty Hillesum: rescuer/victims
3. Required Readings: Levi, P., "Lorenzo's Return" in *Moments of Reprieve*. tr. Ruth Feldman. New York: Penguin, 1986; Hillesum's letter as a witness to deportation and Jopie Vleeschhower's letter about Hillesum's deportation in *Letters from Westerbork*. tr. Arnold J Pomerans. New York: Henry Holt, 1996. (ER)

Week Thirteen

The Witness/Survivor

1. Primo Levi
2. Required Readings: Levi, P., "The Grey Zone" in *The Drowned and The Saved*. tr. Raymond Rosenthal. New York: Vintage International, 1988; Levi, P., "The Story of 10 Days" in *Survival in Auschwitz*. tr. Stuart Woolf. New York: Macmillan, 1960; Levi, P., *The Reawakening*. tr. Stuart Woolf. New York: Simon & Schuster, 1965, pp. 15–34. (ER)

Third Research Paper Due

Week Fourteen

1. Closing Considerations and Distribution of Final Exam Questions

Final Examination on Thursday, April 29, 8:30 – 10:30 am

Team-Teaching the Holocaust at a Jesuit University

■ ■ ■ ■ ■ ■ ■ ■ ■ ■

Carl Schaffer

Professor of English, University of Scranton, Scranton, PA

About fifteen years ago, I received a call from a doctoral candidate at the University of Delaware. She was making a study of various courses on the Holocaust offered by colleges and universities across the country, and ours, she said, was of particular interest to her. It seems that our multidisciplinary approach, where the Holocaust is taught from five (sometimes six) different academic areas – History, Philosophy, Sociology, Art, and Literature (with an occasional segment in Theology) was, according to her study, unique in the United States. That fact came as somewhat of a surprise to me, since, as everyone at the Seton Hill conference who has gone through the Yad Vashem seminar series knows, it is similar to what all of us have experienced. And in fact, it was that seminar which induced me to try to create one at our own school. The purpose of this paper, then, is to outline both the process and result of constructing a team-taught course on the Holocaust at the University of Scranton.

Creating and coordinating such a course would be difficult enough at any institution; it was even more problematic at a school such as ours, which is not only small, with limited academic resources, but is also Catholic and Jesuit, with a student body not likely to be drawn to Jewish Studies. Moreover, unlike Yad Vashem, which is able to bring in an array of top scholars in their respective fields, we needed to approach faculty within our own academic community – faculty who, even when interested in the prospect of creating the course, had for the most part different areas of expertise than the Holocaust, and would need time away from their own areas to prepare for it. To that end, we drew on funds from our then limited Judaic Studies Program to provide financial inducements for them to work on their preparations. We also went through the usual bureaucratic gauntlet of finding a department willing to "house" the course; gaining approval for it from those faculty members' individual departments (some of which found the course in direct competition with some of their own); bringing the approved course through various administrative Arts and Sciences committees for their approval as well; and getting the final nod from the university administration. All of this entailed a great deal of time, and it was about two years before all could fit into place. As a last step, we had to find a common time when all of us could teach the course – we started it at first as a January Intersession course, but it has now moved into the regular school semester – and had to find an appropriate payroll compensation. The five of us agreed to share equally a double stipend for the extra course.

The Course Itself

By the time we began the class, every faculty member had prepared his and her particular segment for several months. As has already been said, the faculty began with different areas of expertise. Our historian's specialty was twentieth-century European history; our philosopher's, modern and contemporary philosophy; our sociologist's, the "crimes of the powerful" (particularly white-collar and state abuses); our art historian's, the Renaissance, and particularly Italian, Art History; and finally, my own, modern literature and creative writing. Each instructor worked independently; each created his and her own reading syllabus. Our historian at first elected to use Michael Berenbaum's *The World Must Know* as a lead-in to our trip to the Holocaust Museum in Washington; after several changes over the years, he now uses Doris Bergen's *War & Genocide*. The rest of us created our own anthologies of texts, which we decided that first year to compile into a self-made textbook, which later had to be abandoned because of copyright problems. The result was an unwieldy compilation of reading material – a problem endemic to many team-taught courses – but which we have learned to pare down in time.

Appended to this paper, the reader will find a selection of five syllabi taken from either Intersession or regular semesters (see appendices A-E). In summary, the largest segment of the course is quite naturally History, which takes up about three weeks or a quarter of the semester, followed by two and a half weeks each of Sociology/Criminal Justice and Philosophy, and finally, about a week and a half apiece designated to Art and Literature. Our evaluation process is relatively simple: there are quizzes on the reading material, a midterm and a final, and a long term paper on any one of the course's areas, overseen by the appropriate faculty member. I should add, too, that one day is set aside for a trip to the Holocaust Museum in Washington, paid for by a fee attached to the tuition, followed afterward by two or three days set aside for survivor testimony, drawn from members of our local community. They have included an American liberator, Abe Plotkin, who photographed his experience (some of his pictures are in the Veterans' Museum in Washington), survivors of various camps and ghettos, a Hungarian man who escaped from a detention camp and later returned as an American Army private, and a man who managed to survive the war but whose new family was killed a year later in the pogrom at Kielce. Needless to say, this testimony by survivors who literally live in the same community as our students gives tangible evidence of the otherwise abstract academic materials we offer to our class. It is a resource which is, of course, fading over the years; and no amount of tapes or videos will ever be able to replace it.

Each faculty member has his and her own approach to the course. Our historian, Frank Homer, whose segment is equivalent to about three or four weeks of a regular semester (see Appendix A), focuses on the "Nazi racist ideology," beginning with the treatment of the Jews before 1939. Professor Homer also presents a psychological profile of Hitler. Especially relevant to our student population is his emphasis on Nazi ideology's bias against Catholics in general.

When we do have a theology component, it follows the historical one and is taught by Marc Shapiro. He approaches the history of antisemitism, bringing in materials that show depictions of Jews from the medieval period on. These kinds of images, which can readily be found in publications such as Joshua Trachtenberg's *The Devil and the Jews* or the *Encyclopedia Judaica*, include illustrations of stereotypical images of Jews, hook-nosed and predatory, carrying moneybags, preying on young Gentile women, eating pig carcasses, and even slaughtering and serving Gentile children. It is, for many of our students, an eye-opening lecture.

William Rowe, our philosophy professor, divides his roughly two-week segment into seven parts. As you can see by the attached syllabus (Appendix B), he begins with a class called "The Philosophical Element in Holocaust Study," focusing on Didier Pollefeyt's "The Kafkaesque World of the Holocaust"; moves on to "The 'Death of God' and the Philosophy of Nietzsche," using readings from *The Gay Science* and *The Genealogy of Morals*; then to "The Ideology of National Socialism," with selections from *Mein Kampf* ("Nation and Race") and Alfred Rosenberg's *The Myth of the Twentieth Century*; then to a class on "Describing the Camps," using a chapter from Primo Levi's *Survival in Auschwitz* titled "The Drowned and the Saved," as well as a chapter titled "Total Domination" from Hannah Arendt's *The Origins of Totalitarianism*; afterward to "Interpreting the Camps," with one reading from Inga Clendinnen's *Reading the Holocaust* called "The Auschwitz SS," and another reading from Giorgio Agamben's *Homo Sacer* titled "The Camps as the 'Nomos' of the Modern"; and finally, two classes on the aftermath which he addresses as "Ethical Responses" – the first, called "Witness," with a reading by Edith Wyschogrod, titled "Concentration Camps and the End of the Life-World," and then another class called "Forgiveness," discussing Jacques Derrida's essay by that name. Along with these readings, he also shows excerpts from two films: *The Triumph of the Will* and *The Wannsee Conference*.

David Friedrichs, our sociologist, approaches his own segment with a series of readings, which have included Peter Hare's "The Abuse of Holocaust Studies," Ronald Aronson's "Why? Towards a Theory of the Holocaust," excerpts from Hoess's autobiography, Ingo Müller's "Punishing Nazi Criminals," and excerpts from Hannah Arendt's *Eichmann in Jerusalem* (see Appendix C.) He also shows the film *Night and Fog* and encourages a group discussion on it. Professor Friedrichs's wide expertise in jurisprudence has been especially useful in connecting with other state crimes in history. This is a controversial subject, but one which Yehuda Bauer has approached in our seminar at Yad Vashem. I should add, too, that Professor Friedrichs has created a poll through which he tests our classes' knowledge of the Holocaust before and after the course; the results have been consistently illuminating (see Appendix F).

Josephine Dunn and Darlene Miller-Lanning, our art historians, have over the years created an interesting collection of Holocaust art – art made by professional artists as well as by survivors and even by inmates themselves, especially those in Theresienstadt. Professor Dunn finishes by showing artistic renderings from other periods of mass brutality, such as some of the works by Goya (see Appendix D). Professor Miller-Lanning addresses, in her words, "the various ways visual imagery has been used to express and embody ideas and identities in relation to the Holocaust. Topics include Nazi art and propaganda, including Hitler's interest in art and the 'Entartete Kunst' exhibition; German Expressionism and its challenge to Nazi ideals; camp art, including sanctioned and clandestine pieces, the use of art as personal and cultural resistance; and finally themes and symbols of the Holocaust in art of the late twentieth- and early twenty-first centuries, including Cain, Job, Ezekiel, and the Dry Bones, the Pietà, and the Crucifixion." Professor Miller-Lanning adds that she tries whenever possible to integrate the class's museum experience into her segment; and, as the director of our Hope Horn Gallery, she has had special exhibitions at our gallery of the photographs by Abe Plotkin, mentioned before; sculptures by Frank Root; paintings by Samuel Bak; and illuminations and political cartoons by Arthur Szyk. Indeed, she has since published a paper with the Arthur Szyk Society.

My own approach to my segment on literature has been to introduce the students to various genres of Holocaust literature: straightforward accounts, creative non-fiction, fiction, and poetry (see Appendix E). This is also tied in with some of the materials taught in the other segments (see Appendix G). My readings begin with the account written by Yankiel Wiernik on his year in Treblinka and the spectacular uprising that occurred there; Rachel Patron's "I Remember the Smell," which purports to be about her experience after a long forced train ride east where she and her mother were given soap that she learned was made of "real Jewish fat" – a widespread but disproved belief; creative personal accounts, such as Elie Wiesel's *Night* and a chapter from Primo Levi's memoir *Survival in Auschwitz* – "The Canto of Ulysses." Fiction readings have included excerpts from André Schwarz-Bart, Edmond Jabès, and Elie Wiesel as well as some short stories, such as Ida Fink's "The Key Game," Cynthia Ozick's "The Shawl," and James Skibell's "From the Mayseh Book"; and finally, some examples of Holocaust poets, such as Abba Kovner, Nelly Sachs, Dan Pagis, Paul Celan, and Primo Levi, among others. Many of these selections have been chosen from our Yad Vashem segment on literature.

The result has been a five- or, in some instances, six-segment comprehensive course which we have learned to integrate over the years. This is, perhaps, the greatest challenge in presenting such a course. We consider seriously our post-op evaluations in order to reconfigure our course and to create better cohesion with the various segments. Whenever possible, we sit in on our colleague's sessions and try to include in our own lectures the material presented by those who have preceded us. And we have learned how to present to our classes the relevance of the Holocaust, not just to Jewish history, but to the common history of humanity.

Aftermath

Our course on the Holocaust has proven to produce lasting effects on our university curriculum. When it first began, there were very few courses at all in Judaic Studies; presently, we have a full-fledged program, including courses in Philosophy and Judaism, Biblical Hebrew, Jewish Approaches to Ethics, and even a new course on Levinas taught by our own William Rowe. Indeed, our Judaic Studies Program has even sponsored a trip to Europe for our Holocaust faculty, where we visited various historic sites discussed in our lectures. Even more important, our faculty has gone on to further their work in what was for them once a new field: Professor Friedrichs, for example, has read papers on his area at various conferences here and overseas, and his syllabus reflects his publications as well. Professor Dunn was awarded a place in the NEH (National Endowment for the Humanities) summer seminar at Oxford for teachers in Judaic Studies, her subject entitled "Representations of the Jew in Medieval Culture," a subject inspired, she says, by our faculty's European trip; she is now developing a new course on antisemitism in Christian art. Darlene Miller-Lanning, our art historian as well as the director of our university gallery, has created several exhibits in Judaica and has published on the subject; Frank Homer, our historian, was awarded a summer grant at Washington's Holocaust Museum. As for myself, I teach a separate course in Jewish literature and have published on the work of Edmond Jabès, Nelly Sachs, H. Leivick, and other Jewish writers.

To sum up, our Holocaust course has not only served to present a subject which had previously been mostly ignored; it has served as springboard to develop our entire Judaic Studies program: in new classes, in publications, in presentations, in community outreach. And it has been a model for interdisciplinary courses which unite faculty members who otherwise would have been utterly separated by department and discipline. Indeed, in a questionnaire geared to address the Seton Hill meeting, I asked my colleagues what spurred them at first to participate in our course. It seems they were motivated, first of all, to develop a course in this new area; but they were specially motivated by the idea of teaching a team-taught course. Professor Rowe responded that his decision was rooted in two things: first, a "strong need I felt to understand the event of the *Shoah*, and the chance to join a teaching team in this unusual course." Josephine Dunn, one of our two art specialists, emphasized that she was intrigued to "participate in an interdisciplinary course," and that she has since "made interdisciplinary teaching a hallmark of [her] career." Frank Homer, our historian, was intrigued to explore an area he had not gone into very deeply before. David Friedrichs, whose family is from Germany, was motivated not only by his scholarship in sociology and criminal jurisprudence, but by personal history: his parents were refugees from Nazi Germany. Professor Friedrichs tells our class about his father, a Christian, "who left Germany because he was deeply disturbed by the Nazi regime and of course could not marry his Jewish fiancée in Germany. The letter he sent resigning his professorship was ignored, and he received a document from Berchtesgaden signed by Adolf Hitler dismissing him from this position." He shares a copy of that document with our Holocaust class. In short, it is this wide range of experiences that has not only brought our faculty together; it has enabled us to create an evolving course in the spirit of the integrated academic universe that Cardinal Newman called the "Idea of the University."

Questions

1. *The process of creating a team-taught course is considerably more complicated than creating a new class in our own respective fields. What are those steps? How can we make the process less complicated, and less time-consuming?*

2. *How is it possible, first, to select faculty from various departments to teach a course such as this, and second, to provide conditions by which they are able to prepare effectively for its instruction?*

3. *How does one go about creating a reading list from several different fields that is not only manageable, but which creates an integral pedagogical bloc?*

4. *How can faculty themselves work to make the classroom experience not just a series of pedagogical segments, but a truly integrated course which creates a lasting and unified understanding of such a cataclysmic event as the Holocaust?*

> 5. *How can this specialized course be used to further other courses and projects throughout one's own university?*

Bibliography

Arendt, Hannah. *The Origins of Totalitarianism*. New York: Harcourt, 1973.

Bergen, Doris L. *War & Genocide: A Concise History of the Holocaust*. Lanham: Rowman & Littlefield, 2003.

Clendinnen, Inga. *Reading the Holocaust*. New York: Cambridge UP, 2002.

Friedrichs, David O. "The Crime of the Century? The Case for the Holocaust." *Crime, Law, and Social Change* 34: 21–41.

Langer, Lawrence L. *The Holocaust and the Literary Imagination*. New Haven: Yale UP, 1975.

Langer, Lawrence L. *Art from the Ashes: A Holocaust Anthology*. New York: Oxford UP, 1995.

Levi, Primo. *Survival in Auschwitz: The Nazi Assault on Humanity*. New York: Collier, 1971.

Muller, Ingo. "Punishing Nazi Criminals." In *Hitler's Justice*. Cambridge: Harvard UP, 1971: 241–60.

Roth, John K., ed. *Ethics after the Holocaust: Perspectives, Critiques, and Responses*. St. Paul, MN: Paragon, 1999.

Schaffer, Carl. "The Fantastic in Holocaust Poetry: Abba Kovner's Ahoti Ktana." In *The Poetic Fantastic*. Eds. Patrick Murphy and Vernon Hyles. Westwood, CT: Greenwood, 1989: 79–88.

APPENDIX A: HISTORY

INTD 209: THE HOLOCAUST
SPRING SEMESTER 2010

SYLLABUS FOR DR. HOMER'S CLASSES

Textbook: Bergen, Doris L. *War & Genocide: A Concise History of the Holocaust.* Second Edition. Rowman & Littlefield. 2009.

Outline & Reading Assignments:

Monday, February 1st   Course Introduction - Background to the Holocaust

Wednesday, February 3rd   Anti-Semitism in European and German History
                                            Assignment: Bergen, Preface and Chapter 1

Friday, February 5th   The Nazi Rise to Power in Germany
                                            Assignment: Bergen, Chapter 2

Monday, February 8th   Germans and Jews Under Nazism, 1933–1939
                                            Assignment: Bergen, Chapters 3 and 4

Wednesday, February 10th   Polish Ghettos and Euthanasia Programs in Germany
                                            Assignment: Bergen, Chapter 5

Friday, February 12th   The Final Solution
                                            Assignment: Bergen, Chapters 6 and 7 (pp. 167–203)

Monday, February 15th   Film: *Conspiracy* (Will conclude on Wednesday)

Wednesday, February 17th   Jewish Resistance
                                            Assignment: Bergen, Chapter 7 (pp. 203–214)

Friday, February 19th   End of the Holocaust and Its Legacy
                                            Assignment: Bergen, Chapter 8 and Conclusion
                                            Quiz: A short quiz will be given on Tuesday, February 19th.

Mid-Term Exam: 50% of the Mid-Term exam on Wednesday, March 10th will be devoted to questions relating to Dr. Homer's segment of the course.

Papers: Approximately 20% of the students in the class will be permitted to do their paper on historical topics to be graded by Dr. Homer. Topics should be as precisely focused as possible upon either a specific episode, event or individual related directly to the Holocaust. Papers are expected to be approximately 12–15 pages in length, with documented source references. **Those wishing to do papers under Dr. Homer must submit their topics for approval by Dr. Homer no later than Friday, March 12th.**

Research should be done primarily using published books and articles. While some material accessed throughout the internet can be used, **any internet web sites that lack identifiable authors are NOT acceptable sources**. Papers must include documentation in the form of both individual reference notes and bibliography using the format in the History department's style sheet, copies of which will be provided by Dr. Homer. **Papers for Dr. Homer must be submitted no later than Friday, May 7th.**

Classroom Etiquette:

1. **Students should arrive for class on time.** Dr. Homer will **usually** not begin class until a minute or so after its scheduled start and students arriving before the taking of attendance is completed will not be considered late. However, it is quite inconsiderate for students to appear 5 or more minutes late, and two late arrivals will count as one absence under the course attendance policy.

2. **Students arriving late should make sure to see Dr. Homer <u>after</u> the class to ensure that they are not charged with a cut.** Attendance will be taken at the beginning of each class and it is the responsibility of latecomers to inform the instructor of their presence.

3. **Students are expected to remain in the classroom for the entire class period.** Dr. Homer will make every effort to avoid going beyond

the scheduled end of each class. Students should make use of restrooms and water fountains **BEFORE, NOT DURING** class. Students walking in and out of class disrupt both classmates and the instructor.

4. **TURN OFF ALL CELL PHONES, PAGERS, ETC. BEFORE CLASS AND KEEP THEM TURNED OFF UNTIL THE CLASS IS OVER.** If you are awaiting an emergency call of some sort, please inform Dr. Homer before class. Students wishing to use tape recorders or lap top computers to facilitate note taking may do so as long as their use does not disturb others in the class.

5. **Make every effort to avoid scheduling anything that conflicts with your class meeting time.** University personnel, including Deans, other faculty, advisors, counselors, Student Life officials, athletic coaches, etc. understand that classes take priority in most cases, and students making appointments should take the initiative in informing others of their class schedules.

APPENDIX B: PHILOSOPHY

The Philosophy Portion of the Holocaust Course

William Rowe: St Thomas Hall, Room 566, x6319

READING ASSIGNMENTS

We will discuss our Philosophy readings (totaling 153 pages) beginning Monday, February 22nd and ending Monday, March 8th. Please complete all readings before the scheduled discussion.

Readings for Monday, February 22: *The Philosophical Element in Holocaust Study*:
• Didier Pollefeyt, "The Kafkaesque World of the Holocaust: Paradigmatic Shifts in the Ethical Interpretation of the Nazi Genocide" from *Ethics After the Holocaust* (30 pages).

Readings for Wednesday, February 24: *The 'Death of God' and the Philosophy of Nietzsche*:
• Nietzsche, § 25 from *The Gay Science* and § 10–13 from *The Genealogy of Morals* (11 pages).

Readings for Tuesday, Friday 26: ***The Ideology of National Socialism***:
- Adolf Hitler, "Nation and Race" from *Mein Kampf* (24 pages).
- Alfred Rosenberg, Chapters I and V from *The Myth of the Twentieth Century* (5 pages).

Readings for Monday, March 1: ***Describing the Camps***:
- Primo Levi, "The Drowned and the Saved" from *Survival in Auschwitz* (11 pages).
- Hannah Arendt, "Total Domination" from *The Origins of Totalitarianism* (13 pages).

Readings for Wednesday, March 3: ***Interpreting the Camps***:
- Inga Clendinnen, "The Auschwitz SS" from *Reading the Holocaust* (20 pages).
- Giorgio Agamben, "The Camps as the 'Nomos' of the Modern" from *Homo Sacer*. (15 pages).

Readings for Friday, March 5: ***Ethical Response: Witness***:
- Edith Wyschogrod, "Concentration Camps and the End of the Life-World" (11 pages).

Readings for Monday, March 8: ***Ethical Response: Forgiveness***:
- Jacques Derrida, "Forgiveness" (13 pages).

MIDTERM EXAM – Wednesday, March 10, 2010

On Wednesday, March 10th we will have an in-class mid-term exam covering the History and Philosophy sections of the course. The Philosophy section will include true-and-false and short essay questions.

AN ASSIGNMENT AT THE HOLOCAUST MUSEUM

As a follow-up to our Philosophy discussions in class, please reflect on two things during your visit to the Holocaust Museum in Washington, D.C. First, consider the series of exhibits near the beginning of the tour, illustrating the spiritual mood in Germany in the 1920s and 30s. Using clues from our early readings look for signs of the spirit of the times. Second, reflect on the exhibit devoted to the camp at Auschwitz. Consider the question, what kind of *reality* is the death camp?

A TERM PAPER IN PHILOSOPHY

Please consider writing your term paper for this course on a *philosophical* topic.

Philosophy is part of this course because philosophy considers *meaning*. You and I are *bystanders* of the Holocaust – neither perpetrators nor survivors, but simply witnesses. But witnessing is not simple: it involves responsibilities. Among the bystander's responsibilities is the need to consider whether the Holocaust has a *meaning*.

The first signs of this question, perhaps, are emotional. Bystanders encounter the Holocaust with feelings of compassion (for victims), outrage (at perpetrators), and horror (in the face of our own responsibility). But unless we also *think* about our encounter, our response will be sentimental and not a form of responsibility. Outrage can inspire reflection and questions like: What is morality and the force that opposes it? Why did our civilization's morality *withdraw* from public life, permitting the Nazi tyranny and genocide? Is that morality *still* in retreat? Is the Holocaust actually a legacy of our morality and religious tradition? Is it the result of the decay of this tradition? Do we need a new moral sense of vocation? You should at least consider writing a paper on a question like this.

APPENDIX C: SOCIOLOGY

SPRING, 2010
THE HOLOCAUST: SYLLABUS/COURSE CALENDAR
FOR SECTIONS CONDUCTED BY
Professor David O. Friedrichs
Dept. of Sociology/Criminal Justice

Friday, March 12

FUNDAMENTAL ASSUMPTIONS UNDERLYING OUR APPROACH TO THE HOLOCAUST

Reading: The following article, on reserve in the Weinberg Memorial Library, Alan Rosenberg, "The Crisis in Knowing and Understanding the Holocaust," pp. 379–395. In Alan Rosenberg and Gerald E. Myers, Editors, *Echoes from the Holocaust: Philosophical Reflections on Dark Times*. Philadelphia: Temple University Press. 1988.

Film: "Night & Fog"

SPRING BREAK: March 15–19

Monday, March 22

CONCLUDING OBSERVATIONS ON BASIC ASSUMPTIONS; THE RISE OF NAZISM AND CONDITIONS CONTRIBUTING TO THE HOLOCAUST: SOCIOLOGICAL & PSYCHOLOGICAL DIMENSIONS

Among the issues to be considered:

Social conditions leading to the rise of Nazism.

Cultural values and Nazi Ideology.

The socialization process in Germany, 1865–1945.

Reading: The following article on reserve in the Library:

Ronald Aronson, "Why? Towards a Theory of the Holocaust," pp. 25–45 [From R. S. Gottlieb, *Thinking the Unthinkable: Meanings of the Holocaust*, New York: Paulist Press. 1990.]

Wednesday, March 24

SOCIAL CONDITIONS IN NAZI GERMANY

Mechanisms of social control adopted by the Nazis ... Status and role-playing in Nazi Germany, and in the Concentration Camps ... Social class and socio-economic dimensions of the Holocaust ... Inter-group conflict, racism and anti-Semitism ... Movements, collective behavior and the rise of Nazism ...Modern mass society and the Holocaust: The role of the Bureaucracy and mass communication ... Anomie, alienation and principles of social change as factors in the rise of the Nazis

Film: "Cabaret" {Brief excerpt}

Film: "Triumph of the Will" Part I

Friday, March 26

THE HOLOCAUST AND THE DEATH CAMPS: SOCIOLOGICAL AND BEHAVIORAL DIMENSIONS

Among the issues to be considered:

The crime of obedience... the banality of evil ...the authoritarian personality ... patterns of adaptation to extreme circumstances ..

Reading: "Excerpts from *The Autobiography of Rudolph Hoess*, pp. 289–304 [From J. E. Dimsdale, *Survivors, Victims and Perpetrators: Essays on the Nazi Holocaust*. Washington, D.C. Hemisphere.]

Monday, March 29

THE HOLOCAUST: THE HOLOCAUST AS CRIME; NAZI GERMANY AS A CRIMINAL STATE; THE HOLOCAUST AND CORPORATE CRIME

Reading: David O. Friedrichs, "The Crime of the Century? The Case for the Holocaust," *Crime, Law & Social Change* 34 (2000): 21–41.

Wednesday, March 31

LAW & THE HOLOCAUST
JURISPRUDENTIAL DIMENSIONS: JUSTICE IN THE WAKE OF THE HOLOCAUST; THE ISSUE OF ANALOGY, UNIQUENESS & CONTEMPORARY RELEVANCE

The Aftermath: The Nuremberg Trial; the Eichmann Trial; the Barbie Trial; the Demjanjuk Trial ... Implications of the Holocaust for our understanding of crime, law and justice today ... The prospects for an authentic International Legal Order and System of Justice, and contemporary War Crimes trials.

Reading: The following articles on reserve in the Library: Michael Marrus, "The Nuremberg Trial: Fifty Years After," *The American Scholar*, 1997, pp. 563–570; Ingo Müller, "Punishing Nazi Criminals," pp. 241–260 [From *Hitler's Justice*. Harvard University Press. Cambridge, MA. 1991].
Film: "The Legacy of Nuremberg"

EASTER BREAK, April 2–5

Wednesday, April 7

CONCLUDING OBSERVATIONS ON LAW AND THE HOLOCAUST; THE QUESTION OF THE UNIQUENESS OF THE HOLOCAUST

The role of America and the contemporary relevance of the Holocaust ... Parallels and differences between the Holocaust and other cases of oppression and genocide ... Can it happen again? Can it happen here? The question of the uniqueness of the Holocaust, historical analogies, and the relevance of the Holocaust for understanding contemporary developments in the world.

Reading: The following article is on reserve in the library: Avishai Margalit and Gabriel Motzkin, "The Uniqueness of the Holocaust," *Philosophy and Public Affairs*, Vol. 25, No. 1, Winter, 1996, pp. 65–81.

Optional Recommended Background Reading:

Social and Behavioral Dimensions of the Holocaust:

C. R. Browning, "Bureaucracy and Mass Murder: The German Administrator's Comprehension of the Final Solution," pp. 125–144, in *The Path to Genocide – Essays on the Launching of the Final Solution*. New York: Cambridge University Press. 1992; Robert J. Lifton and Eric Markusen, "Professionals," pp. 99–155, in *The Genocidal Mentality – Nazi Holocaust and Nuclear Threat*. New York: Basic. 1990; A. G. Miller, "Genocide from the Perspective of the Obedience Experiments: A Case Study of Controversy in Social Science." *The Obedience Experiments*. New York: Praeger, 1986; A. Z. Bar-on, "Measuring Responsibility," pp. 255–272, in L. May and S. Hoffman, *Collective Responsibility*. New York: Rowman & Littlefield, 1991; David S. Wyman, "Responsibility," pp. 311–340, in David S. Wyman, *The Abandonment of the Jews: America and the Holocaust, 1941–1945*. New York: Pantheon Books. 1984; Henri Zukier, "The Twisted Road to Genocide: On the Psychological Development of Evil During the Holocaust," *Social Research*, Volume 61, No. 2, Summer, 1994, pp. 423–455; Nora Levin, *The Holocaust: The Destruction of European Jewry 1933–1945*. Schocken. 1968; 1973.

Criminological and Jurisprudential Dimensions of the Holocaust:

Richard Grunberger, Ch. 8, "Justice", in *The 12-Year Reich – A Social History of Nazi Germany 1933–1945*. New York: Ballantine. 1971. Ingo Müller, *Hitler's Justice: The Courts of the Third Reich*. Cambridge, MA: Harvard University Press, 1991, especially: Introduction by Detlev Vagts; Ch. 9, Nazi Jurisprudence; Ch. 17, The People's Court; Ch. 27, Punishing Nazi Criminals; Ch. 29, Jurists on Trial; and Ch. 32, An Attempt at Explanation. Lon Fuller, "The Problem of the Grudge Informer" from *The Morality of Law*. New Haven: Yale University Press, 1964. Joseph Borkin, *The Crime and Punishment of I. G. Farben*. New York: The Free Press. 1978, especially Ch. 8, I. G. at Nuremberg. David Luban, "The Legacies of Nuremberg," *Social Research*, Winter, 1987, pp. 779–830. Hannah Arendt, *Eichmann in Jerusalem*, especially: Ch 4, The First Solution: Expulsion; Ch. 5, The Second Solution: Concentration; Ch. 6, The Final Solution: Killing; Ch. 7, The Wannsee Conference, or Pontius Pilate; Ch. 8, Duties of a Law-Abiding Citizen; Ch. 14, Evidence and Witnesses; Ch. 15, Judgment, Appeal, and Execution; [Epilogue; Postscript].

APPENDIX D: ART

THE HOLOCAUST
Intersession 2002
J. M. Dunn, Ph.D.
January 3, 2002

ART AND THE HOLOCAUST
"To Purge; To Witness; To Remember"

The history of art, generally speaking, is the history of people, ideas, events, beliefs and technologies.

Although it may seem incredible to pair the words "Art" and "Holocaust" (as epitomes of beauty and atrocity), we must not lose sight of the fact that art is a form of communication, not simply a tool for describing/defining beauty or giving pleasure. Art communicates. The Nazi Party knew the power of images, some of which were employed with great verve and others which were destroyed with impunity. When you view in class the film *Triumph of Will* by the German woman director Leni Riefenstahl, you will see, firsthand, how important images were to Hitler's image of state and self.

There are a number of ways I can approach teaching on the general topic of Art and the Holocaust. When I first taught this course almost five years or so ago, I limited myself to discussion of art produced by trained artists and self-taught artists in the concentration camps. Now, I would like to expand my discussion to include new topics related to broader issues that comprise our subject: censorship; the power of symbolic images; the art of atrocity; is art capable of describing the immensity of the Holocaust?; the artist as social critic; and, art in the service of social justice.

In the two days of lecture time allotted to me as a member of the teaching team, I will cover the following topics:

Art and Propaganda in the 20th Century
Purging Art and Artists in 1930s Germany
An Art That Witnesses (in the concentration camps)
The Arts at Theresienstadt (Terezin)
Modern Art and Artists after the Holocaust
Art and Remembrance: Holocaust Memorials

I regret to say that there is no single text for this part of the course. Reading materials will be placed on electronic reserve for access from your computer; or, placed on reserve in the library. [A reading list will be handed out on January 7, in class.]

Topics for RESEARCH PAPERS

The Research Paper will be 10 pp. in length; double-spaced, with endnotes and bibliography; 1" margins on all sides of paper. Students are expected to discuss their thesis with Dr. Dunn before research and writing.

- A specific artist and his/her point of view
- A theme depicted often in Holocaust art
- The role played by photography for artists who did not experience the Holocaust
- Holocaust Memorials
- Christian themes in Holocaust art
- Women as depicted in Holocaust art
- Common symbols in Holocaust art and literature

FINAL EXAM

I. Short answer questions

1. Explain three obstacles that inmates faced in the creation of their images.

2. Cite three subject matters found among the images made by inmate artists. Regarding each subject matter, what point of view is generally taken by the artist?

3. Explain three reasons why those interred in the concentration camp were compelled to create images of the Holocaust.

4. What role did photographs play in the creation of Holocaust images?

5. Discuss the meaning of three symbols used by non-inmate artists of the Holocaust to depict the event.

II. Slide Essay

You will be shown one image for 8 minutes. Assume that you have come upon this image while moving through a museum in Europe, and you have an opportunity to **<u>explain what it means</u>** to your traveling pal (me). Enlighten me. You may assume that I know little of the Holocaust and even less of art!

APPENDIX E: LITERATURE

(N.B. Because of constraints of space, this is the syllabus for one of our Intersession courses, where each day (1-4:20) was the equivalent of about a week or so of the regular school year.)

Literature segment:
The purpose of this segment is to provide literary representations of the Holocaust, drawing on the lessons the class has already learned thus far from the historical, philosophical, sociological, theological and artistic segments. The readings will be drawn from a) actual accounts of events (Wiernik, Ringelblum); b) creative non-fiction (Levi, Wiesel, Patron); c) fiction (Ozick, Skibell, Fink, Jabès); and d) poetry (Celan, Pagis, Levi, Sachs, Kovner).

<u>Contents of Packet</u>

Wed., Jan. 26 Lecturer: Schaffer
 Fink, Ida. "The Key"
 Jabès, Edmond. Selections from *The Book of Questions*
 Levi, Primo. "The Canto of Ulysses"
 Ozick, Cynthia. "The Shawl"
 Patron, Rachel. "I Remembered Its Smell"
 Ringelblum, Emmanuel. Selection from *Notes from the Warsaw Ghetto*
 Skibell, Joseph. "From the Mayseh Book"
 Wiesel, Elie. Selection from *Night*
 Wiernik, Yankiel. "One Year in Treblinka"
 Reading quiz

Thursday, Jan. 27 Lecturer: Schaffer
 Read all poetry handouts.
 Celan, Paul. "Death Fugue."
 Pagis, Dan. "Europe Late."
  "Instructions for Crossing the Border."
  "The Roll Call."
  "Testimony."
  "Written in Pencil in the Sealed Railway Car"
 Kovner, Abba. Selections from *My Little Sister*
 Levi, Primo. "If This Is a Man"
  "Reveille"
  "Shema"
  "Singing"

Sachs, Nelly. "Golem Death"
"Hands"
"O the Night of the Weeping Children"
"Someone Blew the Shofar"

Suggested readings, esp. for those writing Literature papers:

Glatstein, Jacob, ed. *Anthology of Holocaust Literature*. New York: Atheneum, 1982.
Langer, Lawrence. *The Holocaust and the Literary Imagination*. New Haven: Yale UP, 1975.
Schaffer, Carl. "The Fantastic in Holocaust Poetry." *The Poetic Fantastic*. Ed. Vernon Hyles. Westport, CT: Greenwood, 1991.

APPENDIX F

THE HOLOCAUST: SOME FUNDAMENTAL QUESTIONS AND ASSUMPTIONS
[Prof. David O. Friedrichs]

Why Devote a Course to the Holocaust?
[Why have you enrolled in this course?]

	'95	'96	'97	'98	'99	'00	'02
Personally curious	47%	87%	72%	70%	66%	54%	86%
Historical importance	20%	4%	14%	6%	19%	13%	0%
Interdisciplinary format	23%	4%	3%	6%	0%	4%	0%
Need credit/convenient time	7%	4%	8%	6%	13%	25%	9%

A/ Holocaust as "cataclysmic event" in Jewish history:
• Of direct concern to Jews;
• To non-Jews concerned with understanding the Jewish experience;
• Holocaust as a pivotal event in 20th-century history, and history generally;
• Should concern all humans, whether directly affected or not.
[This latter claim has been contested.]

B/ Potential lessons of the Holocaust for the present, and the future
[Basic paradox: If unique, what lessons? If incomprehensible, how can we learn from it?]

- Brings fundamental questions - e.g., re human nature, social behavior, law, and crime - into sharp focus.

C/ The fascination of evil;

D/ Other considerations:

- In relation to family history;
- Interdisciplinary format.

[Which aspect of the Holocaust do you believe you need to know more about?]

	'95	'96	'97	'98	'99	'00	'02
Historical	40%	40%	28%	27%	47%	42%	41%
Philosophy/Theology	17%	13%	19%	18%	16%	17%	18%
Literary/Art	13%	11%	11%	6%	3%	17%	9%
Social/Jurisprudence	30%	29%	42%	37%	34%	25%	27%
Other		4%		3%			5%

- Pragmatic factors;

One basic issue: Should we better focus on current manifestations of evil and suffering?

II. The Epistemological & Metaphysical Challenge

A/ How can we know anything, or that anything is real?

B/ Do we know for sure that the Holocaust occurred?

	'95	'96	'97	'98	'99	'00	'02
Yes	100%	100%	97%	97%	100%	100%	100%
No	0%	0%	3%	0%	0%	0%	0%

How should we respond to those who deny it occurred?

C/ If we know it occurred, what is the specific basis of our knowledge?

What do we know with certainty; what is contestable?

D/ Can we have the hope of fully knowing and understanding –

- i.e., comprehending – the Holocaust, and the experience of the victims?

	'95	'96	'97	'98	'99	'00	'02
Yes	3%	7%	14%	12%	3%	17%	5%
No	37%	91%	86%	85%	97%	83%	95%

E/ What – if anything – does the Holocaust have to tell us about "human nature"? Which, if any, historical view of human nature does the Holocaust confirm?

	'95	'96	'97	'98	'99	'00	'02
Humans/selfish, predatory, and aggressive	23%	31%	36%	45%	38%	29%	23%
Humans/altruistic, passive, and cooperative	43%	44%	31%	27%	31%	46%	41%
Humans/wholly malleable, and no innate tendencies	27%	22%	33%	24%	31%	25%	27%

F/ Did those who carried out the Holocaust willfully choose to do so? Is human behavior voluntaristic, determined, or some mixture?

	'95	'96	'97	'98	'99	'00	'02
Human beings/free will	23%	40%	21%	33%	22%	50%	45%
Human behavior/determined	13%	22%	17%	21%	31%	39%	18%
Human behavior/mix	63%	38%	42%	42%	47%	21%	36%

III. The Question of Responsibility

A/ Who, if anyone, can finally be held responsible for the Holocaust, and what does it mean to say we hold people "responsible"?

Re: **Primary** responsibility

	'95	'96	'97	'98	'99	'00	'02
Hitler	37%	18%	53%	21%	28%	50%	27%
The Nazis	23%	22%	14%	12%	9%	8%	23%
Germans	7%	0%	0%	3%	0%	4%	5%
People of many nationalities who cooperated with Nazis/didn't stop them	20%	36%	31%	56%	53%	29%	36%
Human nature/other	13%	20%	3%	6%	9%	8%	9%

[What "other": God?...]

B/ Do you believe that the idea of "collective responsibility" is valid?

	'95	'96	'97	'98	'99	'00	'02
Yes	83%	87%	81%	88%	94%	75%	86%
No	17%	13%	19%	6%	6%	21%	14%

IV. The Question of Uniqueness, and Analogy

A/ Do you believe that the Holocaust was fundamentally unique, or principally one extreme case of historical genocide?

	'95	'96	'97	'98	'99	'00	'02
Fundamentally unique	37%	42%	33%	33%	25%	33%	50%
A case of historical genocide	63%	58%	67%	64%	75%	67%	50%

B/ Do you believe that it is appropriate or useful to invoke the notion of a "holocaust" with reference to such contemporary phenomena as Bosnia, the threat of nuclear war, and abortion or euthanasia?

	'95	'96	'97	'98	'99	'00	'02
Appropriate	23%	62%	53%	42%	41%	54%	41%
Inappropriate	73%	36%	47%	55%	59%	46%	59%

APPENDIX G: CONNECTING THE DISCIPLINES

DEATH MARCHES
Michael Berenbaum

In the winter of 1944/45, the Nazis knew the war was lost. As the Allied armies closed in on the Nazi concentration camps — the Soviets from the east, and the British and Americans from the west — desperate SS officials tried frantically to evacuate the camps. They wanted no eye-witnesses remaining when the camps were overrun. A concerted effort was made to conceal the crimes that had been committed. The concentration camps were destroyed and buried. But Germany still needed slave labor and more time to complete the Final Solution. The inmates of the camps were moved westward in the dead of winter, forced to march toward the heartland of Germany, where their presence would be less incriminating.

In January 1945, just hours before the Red Army arrived at Auschwitz, sixty-six thousand prisoners were marched to Wodzislaw, where they were put on freight trains to the Gross-Rosen, Buchenwald, Dachau, and Mauthausen concentration camps. Almost one in four died en route. On January 20, seven thousand Jews, six thousand of them women, were marched from Stutthof's satellite camps in the Danzig region. In the course of a ten-day march, seven hundred were murdered. Those who remained alive when the marchers reached the shores of the Baltic Sea were driven into the sea and shot. There were only thirteen known survivors.

History

WHO IS RESPONSIBLE?
Ronald Aronson

Sociology/ Criminal Justice

How far can we now generalize beyond Hitler, his circle, and the SS troops involved—beyond even the Nazi movement and its supporters—in attributing the Final Solution to German *society* or *Germany*? It is true that no matter how hard we look beyond Hitler we never see more than a relative handful of k actors. But this tells us more about our century's machinery of destruction than about the man Hitler and the German nation-state. Those who co win control over the machinery and organize society around it, needed in the end a relative handful of obedient servants to operate it. Hitler, we may say, got all th cooperation that was needed.

Camp Art: Va

Central image © Archive/Ghetto Fighters' Museum/Israel

THE SHAWL
Cynthia Ozick

Stella, cold, cold, the coldness of hell. How they walked on the roads together, Rosa with Magda curled up between sore breasts, Magda wound up in the shawl. Sometimes Stella carried Magda. But she was jealous of Magda. A thin girl of fourteen, too small, with thin breasts of her own, Stella wanted to be wrapped in a shawl, hidden away, asleep, rocked by the march, a baby, a round infant in arms. Magda took Rosa's nipple, and Rosa never stopped walking, a walking cradle. There was not enough milk; sometime Magda sucked air; then she screamed. Stella was

Literature

ravenous. Her knees were tumors on sticks, her elbows chicken bones.

Philosophy

Friedrich Wilhelm Nietzsche

Every elevation of the type 'man' has hitherto been the work of an aristocratic society — and so it will always be: a society which believes in a long scale of orders of rank and differences of worthy between man and man and needs slavery in some sense or other.

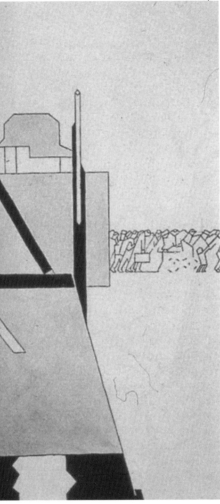

lass Deportation. 1944.

USING NEW TECHNOLOGIES

Using New Technologies to Study and Teach the Holocaust in the Twenty-First Century

. . . .

Ephraim Kaye

Director, International Seminars for Educators,
The International School for Holocaust Studies, Yad Vashem, Israel

From the beginning, Yad Vashem, the institution I represent in Jerusalem, Israel, was entrusted with the work of documenting the history of the Jewish people during the Holocaust, preserving the memory and story of each of the 6 million, and imparting the legacy of the *Shoah* for generations to come through its archives, library, school, museums, and special departments. This work began officially with the ratification of the Yad Vashem Law on August 19, 1953. Fifty-seven years later, we can say that we have come a long way. And this is especially true when we look at the area of education.

The early years were the days of books, blackboards, chalk, mimeograph, maybe an overhead projector. Technology was simple and classes and classrooms were small. The teacher was the ultimate authority and educator. Imagination and memorization were skills to be encouraged and honed. The *mind* was the ultimate computer, and the focus of education was the skill base of the students. Since we began in 1953, and especially in the last fifteen years, we have undergone a radical change, especially with technology.

In fact, as we fast-forward to the present, the twenty-first century, technology is all the rage. Look at what we have: I-pod, I-phone, computer classrooms with smartboards and personal computers. Here we need to assess our situation. Are we any better? The simple answer is yes, and yet there are some negative aspects to this technological revolution. First, there is the loss of the personal dimension, especially felt through what I identify as the displacement of the teacher. This person no longer is the "ultimate authority." So while the teacher has not disappeared, she or he must acquire new skills, techniques, and openness to a constant flow of new information. Second, easy access to information by students may require some supervision and watchful direction. Why do I say this?

I think first of all that the Internet is replete with information on the Holocaust which includes so many denial sites, and many disguised as such. Reliable sites must be the ones that are presented for classroom use. Along with these sites, careful instructions should be given on how to use them, so that written work and projects are original, not just the result of Google research with Wikipedia.

But with the new technology we have a tremendous advantage, too. We need to capitalize on these tools to bring the latest information and techniques in Holocaust education to our students. We can connect our students to teachers and scholars all over the world by arranging video conferences. We can expose students, especially at college and university levels, to online courses at other institutions. At other levels, we can show them programs that can enhance their knowledge and experience. There is the teacher-student relationship that grows by written online communication; sometimes this is as important as the personal encounter, and at the least it can enhance the ongoing dialogue that is so important in the art of education. One other area where the new technology has played a major role is in the preservation of survival testimony, now and for the time when the survivors may be gone from our midst.

Our website at Yad Vashem (http://www1.yadvashem.org/yv/en/education/educational_materials/index.asp) is one of those unique websites that I would like to use to illustrate some of the points I have just made. There, under the heading "Educational Materials," you will find a wonderful interactive program on the ghetto. This program is designed for middle and high school, but even college students will be enriched. It is user-friendly in that once the student enters, she or he will find much material that they will want to share on life in the ghetto. Such topics as "Children at Work," "Schools in the Ghetto," and "Hunger" become a technological experience that adds depth to students' human understanding of this dire situation during the *Shoah*.

Another program on this same site that could be used both in high school or college is the "Educational Journey beyond the Image: *And Despite It All, I Am Alive*." Here the story of the experience after the war has a certain sadness that is conveyed both with text and picture. But the instructions allow the teacher great freedom to use what is suitable for the class. The four topics presented are: General, Family, Children, and the DP Camp.

In the same section, under "Educational Materials," teachers and students can experience the most up-to-date testimonies by survivors. There is one that I recommend,

May Your Memory Be Love, the story of Ovadia Baruch, a survivor who was deported with his family from Salonika in Greece to Auschwitz-Birkenau. This segment is part of a DVD (45–50 minutes in length) that is the joint project of Yad Vashem and the Hebrew University. This project consists of eight DVDs of survivors who were followed on their journey back to where they were born before the Holocaust, during the Holocaust, and afterwards, their return to life. Each of these fits into a classroom period. Needless to say, nothing replaces the living survivor, but as we move into the second decade of the twenty-first century, we will have to develop ways to present their stories, to make them come alive for our students without their physical presence. We are beginning to prepare for this time through this project, and we hope and encourage others to do all that they can to preserve the testimonies of their local survivors.

As we make use of all the technology, we need always to keep in mind these powerful words of Haim Ginott from *Teacher and Child*:

> I am a survivor of a concentration camp. My eyes saw what no man should witness. Gas chambers built by learned engineers. Children poisoned by educated physicians, infants killed by trained nurses, women and babies shot and burned by high school and college graduates. So, I am suspicious of education. My request is: help your students become more human. Your efforts must never produce learned monsters, skilled psychopaths, educated Eichmanns. Reading, writing, and arithmetic [and we can add computer and other technologies] are only important if they serve to make our children more humane.[1]

This is our goal with Holocaust education: that we help to make our students, and ourselves as teachers, more humane, more sensitive to the needs and suffering of others, inspired by the survivors to engage in *"tikkun olam,"* the mending, the healing of our world.

Questions

1. *How can we make use of the latest in educational technology to educate teachers and students about the Holocaust?*

2. *What is the most effective way to incorporate the voices of Holocaust survivors in the twenty-first-century classroom?*

3. *What are the challenges we face as we try to "help to make our students, and ourselves as teachers, more humane, more sensitive to the needs and sufferings of others"?*

Bibliography

Davies, Ian ed. *Teaching the Holocaust: Educational Dimensions, Principles and Practice*. New York: Continuum, 2000.

Greenbaum, Beth Aviv. *Bearing Witness: Teaching about the Holocaust*. Portsmouth, NH: Boynton/Cook Publishers, 2001.

Lauckner, Nancy A. and Miriam Jokiniemi, eds. *Shedding Light on the Darkness: A Guide to Teaching the Holocaust*. New York: Berghahn Books, 2000.

Totten, Samuel. *Holocaust Education: Issues and Approaches*. Boston: Allyn and Bacon, 2002.

Totten, Samuel and Stephen Feinberg, eds. *Teaching and Studying the Holocaust*. Boston: Allyn and Bacon, 2001.

Notes

1. Haim G. Ginott, *Teacher and Child: A Book for Parents and Teachers* (New York: Macmillan, 1972), p. 72.

Going Beyond the Cognitive Domain: Twenty-First-Century Students Make Discoveries about the Holocaust

Wayne Brinda

Assistant Professor, University of Pittsburgh, Bradford, PA

A stated goal of those of us who designed and taught a new Holocaust course for twenty-first-century students at Duquesne University was to do more than to teach this history. We were committed to engaging undergraduate students who will become our future leaders by stimulating their personal responses and encouraging them to pose questions about the Holocaust and its implications for today. The rationale came from our observations of freshmen and undergraduates who tend to follow a model of thinking which many developed in high school of relying on right-or-wrong, black-or-white answers to questions. Research conducted by Perry found that freshmen and undergraduates tend to be at a learning stage where they believe that the "right answer exists somewhere for every problem, and authorities know them. Right answers are to be memorized by hard work."[1]

In his book, *Emotional Intelligence: Why it can matter more than IQ*, Goleman warned that "higher education has focused for too long on inculcating and assessing those cognitive skills that are relatively easy to acquire – remembering, understanding, and applying – rather than the arguably more important skills of analyzing, evaluating, and creating."[2] Lombardi found that: "Educators have largely ignored the other major learning domains, particularly the conative."[3] To help our students see the Holocaust as more than a collection of facts, we created learning experiences that went beyond textbooks, lectures, and static PowerPoint presentations with a blend of the cognitive and aspects of the conative learning domain "which determines how we have to (out of necessity) apply our mental energies and influence the way we make decisions and even solve problems [which] is more related to our mental DNA... But the real value of understanding our innate talents that stems from this Conative domain is that we can then focus more of our day to day actions towards that which is more natural to us."[4]

While preparing the course, we found significant parallels between the conative domain, the United States Holocaust Memorial Museum rationale for teaching the Holocaust, and strategies for creating authentic learning experiences. Noteworthy was the idea of confronting students with knowledge and perspectives to help them make reflective judgments by gaining awareness of problems that may not have concrete right or wrong answers. The Holocaust Museum states that studies and lessons of the Holocaust should be designed to help students learn and consider the uses and abuses of power, as well as how individuals, organizations, and nations responded when confronted with violations of their civil and human rights. Our approach to this course of blending the cognitive and conative domains inspired us as a team to find ways to create truthful, thought-provoking, potentially life-changing learning experiences in which students were intrinsically driven to connect intellectually, spiritually, and emotionally with the content through guest speakers, survivors, and the use of technologies.

Reeves, in *Technology and the Conative Learning Domain in Undergraduate Education*, pointed out: "Teaching is about asking the right questions but learners must care... Teaching with technology works when learning tasks are authentic."[5] Charlotte Briggs, Director of Curriculum Development at the University of Illinois at Chicago, wrote on the positive results of authentic learning: "By confronting students with uncertainty, ambiguity, and conflicting perspectives, instructors help them develop more mature mental models that coincide with the problem-solving approaches... where there may not be a right or a wrong answer per se. Such a nuanced understanding involves considerable reflective judgment, a valuable lifelong skill that goes well beyond the memorization of content."[6] Real-world, complex problems and their solutions, which are a hallmark of authentic learning, enabled students to go beyond the cognitive domain into the conative domain. This was achieved by incorporating interactive technology which met the multi-level learning interests and needs of our students. Students "cared" about learning the history by being able to confront truths of the history with a Holocaust survivor who not only shared her experiences, but posed moral and ethical questions. Our students discovered that more than right answers existed for every problem. Answers were no longer memorized.

However, with Holocaust survivors growing older and many unable to travel, students may miss the life-changing learning experience of meeting a survivor in person. How could students learn from survivors to overcome challenges, make decisions, and even solve problems? The answer was Skype, a twenty-first-century audio and video conferencing technology that engaged students. This software program, developed by a global internet communications company, enabled us to make a free, international, video and voice interactive conference with a Skype user. Students watched, listened, and interacted with a Holocaust survivor who was thousands of miles away in Israel.

Successes with technology inspired me to adapt this learning experience for another group of students. These undergraduate pre-service teachers were in a rural community in north central Pennsylvania. The city had a small Jewish population, a high school where a majority of students were disinterested in learning, and a university that is seeking ways to expand the knowledge and motivation of young people to learn. The Holocaust is briefly introduced in history classes. I saw the need and opportunity to challenge the thinking, insights, and knowledge of these students through the study of a non-fiction work of Holocaust literature. The choice was *I Have Lived a Thousand Years: Growing up in the Holocaust* by Livia Bitton-Jackson. My goal was to incorporate what I had learned from the Holocaust course at Duquesne University and present an experience where the Holocaust would become more than a literature or an academic unit.

Bringing a Holocaust survivor to the class was the initial thought. But wouldn't it be more effective for students to speak not only with a survivor, but with the author of the book they were reading? Following the ideas of Goleman, Lombardi, Briggs, and Reeves, an authentic learning experience was designed. Because Dr. Bitton-Jackson lives in Israel and was unable to visit our campus personally, I worked with the IT Department of the University of Pittsburgh Bradford, which recommended the use of Skype to create an international, interactive, video conference with Ms. Bitton-Jackson, students in the class, and members of the university, as well as the community.

For many of those who attended this event, it was their first time to meet and encounter a Holocaust survivor. It was also the first time for many students to encounter an author, particularly one of her international status and experience. This event became not only an opportunity for students to meet, but also to speak with, and learn from, a person who shared her experiences in ways that speak to and connect with young adult audiences. Advances in twenty-first-century technology made this happen. Using Skype, this experience was created for over thirty-five people, including the President and Academic Dean of the University.

In preparation for the conference, I asked my students to write questions that I emailed to Dr. Bitton-Jackson prior to the conference. The questions showed a level of curiosity that transcended book learning: "My biggest question as of right now is what prompted Mrs. Jackson to write this book? To live what she went through would have been very hard, let alone to have to relive it while writing it. Did she use it as a way to push past those feelings?" Another student asked: "What do you think of the people who claim that the Holocaust never happened?" and "What was the most terrifying moment for you in the Holocaust?"

During the conference, Livia not only addressed each question. Since she could also see the audience, Livia invited the students who wrote the questions to introduce themselves so she could answer each student directly. In addition to Livia sharing her experiences of before, during, and after the Holocaust, she posed questions to members of the audience. Her first question created an interesting response as the presenter/survivor became the teacher: "You know about how I and other Jews had to wear badges or yellow stars on our clothing. How would you feel about having to wear a badge identifying your culture and religion so others know who you are?" At first, the audience was reticent because their initial expectations were based on past experiences of typically only passively listening to a presenter at events.

After encouragement by Dr. Bitton-Jackson and me, members of the audience shared responses with her, such as this one from a college student: "I would be ashamed to wear it because it would make me different from others." To this, Livia responded: "Good. You have to understand there was at first an unspoken hatred of Jews. The very idea that you had to wear a badge was not as a show of honor, but because you were to be humiliated. We had to wear that as a sign of humiliation. That was what was so very painful to me as a young girl. Do you see the point?" To this, the student responded: "I've read about this in school, but I never felt that emotion behind having to wear that before."

This higher level of learning was spellbinding for everyone. The experience of interacting with a survivor who was thousands of miles away, but was also close enough to reach out and communicate firsthand with each person, strengthened each individual's desire to learn. Students and adults saw the Holocaust not through texts in books, or from the words of historians. They learned truths and saw the deeply personal, emotional results of those truths through her personal anecdotes not found in books, nor even in her literature. With her, we all felt the pain and anguish of those experiences, albeit now memories. The technology made the learning life-changing for several future teachers as Ms. Bitton-Jackson reached out and connected with students and adults beyond the miles.

Through this international, interactive video conference, everyone saw that there were more than "right-or-wrong or black-and-white answers" to this history. This experience modeled how to transcend the cognitive domain and reach the conative learning domain. We were able to watch Livia's face, hear the tone and tremble of her voice, and share moments when she collected her emotions. Everyone felt a personal drive to reconcile her loss, confusions, questions, anger, and frustrations. We questioned things with her as she took us on her personal journey – dreaming of ambitions as a young girl, being terrified in the camps, feeling confusion after the Liberation, and rebuilding her life as a survivor, wife, mother, and grandmother. Through this experience that went beyond reading textbooks, listening to lectures, or watching a video or YouTube presentation, a learning environment was created that accomplished what Goleman and Reeves, along with Lombardi, defined as attainable with technology: "Learners are able to gain a deeper sense of a discipline as a special 'culture' shaped by specific ways of seeing and interpreting the world."[7]

The live conversation with Dr. Bitton-Jackson attained the conative level of learning for each person by increasing his and her personal commitment, drive, or passion for improving, transforming, setting and achieving goals, taking risks, and meeting challenges. A student who reflected on the experience wrote: "I have a hard time that my generation is blind to global politics and to human rights violations that occur at an alarming rate. By sharing the truths and reality of what hate can do to others, we can prevent another Holocaust for future generations." Another future teacher stated: "The spirit of Ms. Bitton-Jackson as a Holocaust survivor made me feel her faith. I would use this literature for more than the Holocaust. It could teach that people can overcome anything."

The courses and the technological experiences provoked students into thinking, feeling, and building their personal beliefs about the Holocaust based on truth. Students connected with, observed, and learned more than history from this Holocaust survivor and author. The words in her books, and the words of others who have written about the Holocaust, became more than black ink spots on white pages, or knowledge-based details. Her words, face, and the challenges she gave to us became sources of inspiration that will last a lifetime for those of us who met and spoke with Ms. Bitton-Jackson.

In conclusion, even though we may not always see it, our students inherently want to be intellectually, emotionally, and personally challenged. Students in the Duquesne Holocaust course and in the small town showed us that they want to do more than ask questions and seek immediate right or wrong answers. They want to intellectually challenge their teachers, as well as experts. They want to go beyond hearing research and personally experience the events. Twenty-first-century technology, such as Skype and other video conferencing programs, can answer their needs and interests. Technology will and must be used to create learning experiences that address learning in the conative domain, which is vital in education, and especially higher education. As shared by a student who was studying to be a teacher: "Participating in this video conference with a Holocaust survivor from Israel made me reflect on my own life. Dr. Bitton-Jackson is now my personal role model and is a role model for younger generations for years to come. Thank you." How can we teachers achieve that level of learning? Use twenty-first-century video conferencing technology to create life-changing connections across thousands of miles.

Questions

1. As teachers of freshmen or undergraduate students, what challenges do you see in students being interested in learning more than facts and basic information?

2. How do you challenge your students to see beyond the idea that the "right answer exists somewhere for every problem, and authorities know them. Right answers are to be memorized by hard work" (Perry 1981)?

3. What learning experiences have you successfully created that encourage students to go beyond the cognitive learning domain to reach objectives in the affective and conative domains?

4. Have you, or could you use long-distance, interactive video conferencing with a survivor to engage your students in seeing the truths and addressing provocative questions about the Holocaust?

5. With advances in technology and the interests of twenty-first-century students, how have you created learning environments that address all the learning domains of our students?

Bibliography

Goleman, Daniel. *Emotional Intelligence: Why it can matter more than IQ*. London: Bloomsbury, 1996.

Lombardi, Marilyn M. "Authentic Learning for the 21st Century: An Overview." Ed. Diane G. Oblinger. http://net.educause.edu/ir/library/pdf/ELI3009.pdf (2007).

Perry, Jr., William G. "Cognitive and Ethical Growth: The Making of Meaning." *The Modern American College: Responding to the New Realities of Diverse Students and a Changing Society*. Eds. Arthur Chickering and Associates. San Francisco: Jossey-Bass, 1981.

Reeves, Thomas C. *Technology and the Conative Learning Domain in Undergraduate Education. ELI Podcast*. January 30, 2008. http://www.educause.edu/Resources/TechnologyandtheConativeLearni/162527.

Notes

1. William G. Perry, Jr., "Cognitive and Ethical Growth: The Making of Meaning," *The Modern American College: Responding to the New Realities of Diverse Students and a Changing Society*, edited by Arthur Chickering and Associates (San Francisco: Jossey-Bass, 1981) p. 79.

2. Daniel Goleman, *Emotional Intelligence: Why it can matter more than IQ* (London: Bloomsbury, 1996), quoted in Marilyn M. Lombardi, "Authentic Learning for the 21st Century: An Overview," Diane G. Oblinger, ed., http://net.educause.edu/ir/library/pdf/ELI3009.pdf (2007), p. 8.

3. Marilyn M. Lombardi, "Authentic Learning for the 21st Century: An Overview," Diane G. Oblinger, ed., http://net.educause.edu/ir/library/pdf/ELI3009.pdf (2007), p. 8.

4. Stephen Booy, "Supporting the Learning Journey of Individuals towards Personnel Fulfilment," (2003), http://www.mbf-international.com/pdfs/supportlearning.pdf.

5. Thomas C. Reeves, *Technology and the Conative Learning Domain in Undergraduate Education. ELI Podcast*, (January 30, 2008) http://www.educause.edu/Resources/TechnologyandtheConativeLearni/162527.

6. Charlotte Briggs, quoted in "Authentic Learning for the 21st Century: An Overview," Diane. G. Oblinger, ed., http://net.educause.edu/ir/library/pdf/ELI3009.pdf (2007), p. 10.

7. Marilyn M. Lombardi, "Authentic Learning for the 21st Century: An Overview," Diane. G. Oblinger, ed., http://net.educause.edu/ir/library/pdf/ELI3009.pdf (2007), p. 1.

Recommendations for Teaching the Holocaust through Film at the Secondary Level

Jennifer L. Goss

Fleetwood Area High School, Fleetwood, PA
Pennsylvania Holocaust Education Council, USHMM Museum Teacher Fellow

Sean D. Gaston

Fleetwood Area High School, Fleetwood, PA
Pennsylvania Holocaust Education Council

Film is a medium that is synonymous with life. Most individuals can quickly name their favorite movie, or even tell you where they were the first time they saw a particular film. Today's youth are part of a culture that is saturated with films on every subject imaginable, including an extensive collection of films related to one of the most horrific events of the twentieth century, the Holocaust.

It is understandable, therefore, that educators gravitate toward using film in their classrooms. The students of today are part of a generation that expects to be entertained while they are educated. They are a product of a society where entertainment and information is available "on demand," and this availability is literally at their fingertips. Education is often challenging cell phones, other handheld devices, the Internet and the television for a student's attention. Educators often turn to film as a way of gaining an edge in this competition.

Properly utilized, film can be a wonderful tool in the classroom. Teaching the Holocaust using film can add an additional dimension to the lecture and photographs that are the norm in many classrooms. Unfortunately, there are many pitfalls that educators must avoid in order to effectively use film to educate about the Holocaust. In this paper, we will examine some of these pitfalls and also recommend effective strategies for the use of film in the classroom.

Categorizing Holocaust Films

In order to effectively utilize Holocaust films in one's classroom, it is important to have a general understanding of the structure of this genre. Within this genre of film, we would like to establish three categories: raw footage, documentaries, and dramatizations. Raw footage is the film taken of actual events while they were occurring. This type of footage has typically been seen as part of newsreels, but was also gathered by the Nazis and the Allied Powers for documentation purposes. Some of the earliest broadcast footage of the Holocaust occurred when major television stations worldwide included a story on the Nazi book burnings in May of 1933.

Documentaries are films that attempt to share factual information with the viewer from the standpoint of the filmmaker. Various styles of documentaries exist and one could write an entire paper on simply that topic alone. For the purposes of the Holocaust film genre, we are considering documentaries to be films made after the period of time in which the events occurred that contain period footage, interviews, and/or site visits in an attempt to educate the viewer about the Holocaust. Examples of documentaries in the Holocaust genre include *Night and Fog*, Claude Lanzmann's *Shoah*, and *The Last Days*.

The third category, dramatizations, is the most difficult to succinctly define. In order to bring some clarity to this widespread category, we would like to propose two sub-categories. The first sub-category we have established is "docudrama." Docudramas attempt to portray events based on reality but the director will often take some creative license with the subject. Famous examples of Holocaust docudramas include *Schindler's List* and *The Pianist*. The second sub-category we have established is the "art film." Art films are loosely based on reality (i.e., events that are shown in the film are similar to events that did occur during the period), but the director takes creative license with the main characters and plot. Examples of art films based on the Holocaust include famous films such as *Life is Beautiful*, *The Boy in the Striped Pajamas* and *The Reader*. We also place into this category many short films that have been made featuring the Holocaust as the main subject such as *Chaim*, *Forgotten Souls* and *The Witness*.

Guidelines for Showing Film in the Classroom

When choosing films to show in the classroom, educators must first decide how a film fits into their rationale. Every Holocaust educator should know exactly what they hope to accomplish by educating their students about the Holocaust. There is no set rationale for every classroom, but it is important to know your own so that you can select a film that will fit within this rationale and help you accomplish the desired result. In order to develop your rationale, the United States Holocaust Memorial Museum (USHMM) poses three key questions:

- Why should students learn this history?
- What are the most significant lessons students should learn from a study of the Holocaust?
- Why is a particular reading, image, document, or film an appropriate medium for conveying the topics that you wish to teach?[1]

By answering these questions within the context of your own classroom, you are now ready to choose a film that will fit within your overall purpose and therefore be most effective for your students.

An unfortunate practice that occurs too often in classrooms is when educators select films related to the Holocaust based on their "shock" value. The "shock and awe" technique of showing Holocaust films is not effective pedagogy and should be avoided at all costs. Films should be selected for their educational value, not to scare students into believing the horrors of the Holocaust. If an educator has a strongly established rationale, this practice is more likely to be avoided. Leaders in the field of Holocaust education often caution that it is the educator's job to lead the students safely through this material. This should be done so that students recognize the horrors, but also so that they do not suffer lifelong scars related to the material.

Once one has selected a potential film for the classroom, it is important to pre-screen the film. Many educators can probably think of a time when a film was shown in their classroom without first being screened. Normally this does not backfire; however, Holocaust films are part of a very sensitive subject and it is important to be prepared for what is being shown. Additionally, it is wise to obtain permission from one's administration and parents prior to allowing students to view the film. Some districts have a very liberal policy when it comes to film viewing, but most do not allow "R"-rated films. Due to the subject matter of Holocaust films, many are rated "R" and the educator should proceed with caution. "R"-rated films are not appropriate at the middle-school level, but when showing any Holocaust film, it is still a good idea to keep administrators and parents informed that their students will be viewing a film that may raise questions about the atrocities of this period in history.

After carefully selecting the film(s) to be shown in the classroom and getting the proper permission, educators should be certain to give students proper background to the film they will be viewing. Most educators can probably think of a teacher who throws a DVD in the DVD player and hits "play" without properly introducing the film. This not only is a disservice to the students but to the subject matter as well. It gives students the message that the educator is not showing the film because of its merits, but simply as an activity to fill space. It is important to provide proper historical background prior to showing the film. It is also recommended that students be given a brief insight into the filmmaking process as well, such as why this particular film was created and if it is a dramatization, and why the director felt that this particular subject was important to portray. The latter information can make students feel like insiders. This can bond them to the movie more tightly and make the viewing experience that much more memorable. Information about the film's genesis is not difficult to locate in this information age and can readily be obtained from sources such as the Internet Movie Database (www.imdb.com). Additionally, there are several informative works on the Holocaust in film that have been published in the last decade. Many are cited in the attached bibliography.

While proper background and preparation to the film are important, proper follow-up to the viewing is also essential. In our course, "The History of the Holocaust through Film and Literature," students view films from all of the categories outlined earlier in this paper. With each film we show, we are sure to stop the movie at least three-five minutes prior to the end of the period in order to take questions and comments. A good practice when showing any film in the classroom, this is particularly important when showing films related to the Holocaust. The nature of these films often generates questions from students. If one allows the students to watch the film until the bell rings, the educator often loses that "teachable moment" that is triggered by the film. By the time the educator sees the student in the following class period, the question has been buried in their mind and will most likely go unanswered. This time is also necessary for students to debrief regarding some of the difficult material they have just seen. It is not a good idea to send students to their next class period without giving them time to decompress from the viewing as this can cause further difficulty in processing the material.

At the conclusion of the films shown in our classroom, we often have students journal their thoughts regarding the film. Prompts vary from the simple, "What are your thoughts on this film?" to more complex questions regarding specific features of the cinematic experience, such as the score, setting, camera angles etc. Appendix A contains some suggestions for journaling activities. The journals serve as an excellent vehicle for students to lay out their thoughts about a certain film and the content portrayed in it. We often ask students to tie in previously viewed material as a way of connecting the various films that are shown during this course. This can also be an important part of a classroom discussion as students often learn by the practice of comparing and contrasting.

If one is short on time and does not have the luxury of showing a feature film or lengthy documentary, there are still plenty of ways to incorporate excerpts into your curriculum. The USC Shoah Foundation Institute is one of several sites that make testimony clips available for classroom use. This site also includes lesson plans with suggestions on how to incorporate the clips into a curriculum. Most documentaries offer a multitude of options for short clips that can be tailored for specific lessons on the Holocaust. There are also several shorter documentaries available that can be shown in less than twenty minutes. One of our personal favorites is *The Camera of My Family*, which features photographs and voiceover to give the viewer a look into a family who were affected by the Holocaust. This particular film features mainly pre-war Jewish life and is an excellent way of showing students that pre-war Jewish families lived lives similar to their own. This film helps to translate statistics into people, one of the guidelines offered by USHMM in teaching about the Holocaust.

Excerpts from feature-length docudramas can also play a useful role in the classroom. Some controversial docudramas, such as *The Boy in the Striped Pajamas*, work better as excerpts than as full-length films. Information on other strategies based on film excerpts is included in the next section.

Strategies for Using Film in the Classroom

"The History of the Holocaust through Film and Literature" is a quarter-long, elective course. The course runs for forty-three days. This length of time allows us to utilize many different strategies when showing film in our classroom. In this segment of the paper, we would like to share a few of those strategies.

An exercise that can be utilized in nearly any setting, the Roundtable Alphabet provides an introduction to the topic of the Holocaust in film. Students receive the worksheet (Appendix B) that contains all of the letters of the alphabet and are asked to list associations they have with each letter for the topic of the Holocaust in film. It is common for us to receive responses such as "Auschwitz" for "A" and "*Schindler's List*" for "S." Most students that take this elective course have a background in the subject area and are able to fill many of the letters. This is best done as a timed activity and can work well as a "set" for any topic. It can also be used as a follow-up activity to determine how much students have retained from viewing.

Story maps are another strategy that can be utilized to engage students while viewing a film. This exercise is best done with a feature-length docudrama. Students "map" key points in the story, building to the climax and then documenting the falling action. They also identify the key turning point of the story. Adopted from a literature exercise, this activity may require periodically pressing the "pause" button the first time it is used to allow students to develop the technique of story-mapping. The exercise can also lend itself to discussion regarding the intent of the director and screenwriter in regards to how the story is structured. A copy of the story-mapping worksheet is included in Appendix C.

Another powerful activity that can be utilized in Holocaust instruction is the "Scene Activity." This particular exercise may involve background research on the part of the educator the first time it is implemented. The exercise involves asking the viewer questions prior to and after viewing a particular scene of a film. The exercise can be taken a step further by sharing additional information with the viewer and then asking them to incorporate this information into their previously existing schema. During the portion of our course where we discuss filmmakers manipulating reality to sell movies, we do this activity with a scene from *Schindler's List*. The majority of our students have viewed *Schindler's List* during their American History course and are familiar with the story of Oskar Schindler. We begin by asking them to answer the basic question, "What do you know about Oskar Schindler?" We then survey students for their responses and inevitably hear that he saved Jews during the Holocaust, that he was a Nazi, a drunk and a womanizer. Following this discussion, we show the scene from the film where Stern presents Schindler with the ring that the workers have made for him from the crowns in their teeth. It is a very emotional scene where Schindler breaks down and proclaims that he did not do enough, and it ends with a shot of him leaving the factory to escape the incoming Russian troops. After students have viewed the scene, we ask them, "What result does this particular scene have on your perception of Schindler?" Students reply that he was a good man, that he tried hard, that he was sad that he couldn't do more etc. We then tell them that this scene did not happen in reality, that Spielberg added it to the film to enhance the viewing experience.[2] Students conclude by jotting down their thoughts about this deception and many recognize that you cannot always trust what you see in the movies, even when it is based on a true story.

Another activity that works well in a classroom setting is to write/re-write the ending. This activity can be used with a full-length film or even an excerpt from a particular film. Though *The Boy in the Striped Pajamas* has its faults, there are several scenes in this film that can work well for this activity. During one scene, Shmuel is brought into the house to polish the glasses because he possesses small hands. Bruno encounters Shmuel working at this project and offers him a cookie from the platter in the room. Shmuel accepts hesitatingly and is then caught eating the cookie by the SS man stationed at the house. Bruno is asked whether or not he gave the cookie to Shmuel and, scared of the consequences, he says that he did not. At this point in the film, we press "stop" and ask the students to write what they think Shmuel's fate will be, based on events that transpired earlier in the film and on their own personal knowledge of the Holocaust.

Educators looking to utilize various learning styles can implement a scriptwriting activity in their classrooms. A free and easy-to-use service can be found at www.celtx.com. This site includes a tutorial to utilize the Celtx software, which the user downloads onto his or her own computer. Within a short period of time, students can become scriptwriters. Since our course is a combined study of film and literature, we make the scriptwriting activity our culminating project. Students select a piece of literature that they have read throughout the quarter and create a script to accompany either the entire piece or a specific portion of it.

These are just a few of many strategies that exist for educators who wish to include Holocaust films in their curriculum. We hope that these ideas have inspired you to try some new things in your classroom. We also hope that the guidelines provided earlier in the article will give you some assistance in developing your rationale for teaching the Holocaust and incorporating films within that rationale. Film is a large part of our students' lives and by incorporating this medium in the classroom, we can help to elevate their interest in a subject that is of great importance to us all.

Questions

1. *What is your purpose for using film within your curriculum?*

2. *How do you know what films to show in your classroom?*

3. *What type of preparation should you complete before showing a film in your classroom?*

4. *What types of follow-up activities can you do with the films that you show?*

Bibliography

Baron, Lawrence. *Projecting the Holocaust into the Present: The Changing Focus of Contemporary Holocaust Cinema.* New York: Rowman and Littlefield Publishers, Inc., 2005.

Bartov, Omer. *The "Jew" in Cinema: From The Golem to Don't Touch My Holocaust.* Indianapolis: Bloomington University Press, 2005.

Doneson, Judith E. *The Holocaust in American Film: Second Edition.* Syracuse, NY: Syracuse University Press, 2002.

Eaglestone, Robert and Barry Langford, eds. *Teaching Holocaust Literature and Film.* New York: Palgrave Macmillan, 2008.

Flanzbaum Hilene, ed. *The Americanization of the Holocaust.* Baltimore: The Johns Hopkins University Press, 1999.

Haggith, Toby and Joanna Newman, eds. *Holocaust and the Moving Image: Representations in Film and Television since 1933.* New York: Wallflower Press, 2005.

Hirsch, Joshua. *After Image: Film Trauma, and the Holocaust.* Philadelphia: Temple University Press, 2004.

Insdorf, Annette. *Indelible Shadows: Film and the Holocaust*. Third Edition. New York: Cambridge University Press, 2003.

Klein Kassenoff, Miriam and Anita Meyer Meinbach. *Studying the Holocaust through Film and Literature: Human Rights and Social Responsibility*. Norwood, MA: Christopher-Gordon Publishers, Inc., 2004.

Loshitzky, Yosefa. *Spielberg's Holocaust: Critical Perspectives on Schindler's List*. Indianapolis: Indiana University Press, 1997.

Mintz, Alan. *Popular Culture and the Shaping of Holocaust Memory in America*. Seattle: University of Washington Press, 2001.

Palowski, Franciszek. *The Making of Schindler's List: Behind the Scenes of an Epic Film*. Seacaucus, NJ: Carol Publishing Group, 1998.

Saxton, Libby. *Haunted Images: Film, Ethics, Testimony and the Holocaust*. New York: Wallflower Press, 2008.

United States Holocaust Memorial Museum. *Guidelines for Teaching about the Holocaust*. www.ushmm.org.

Notes

1. United States Holocaust Memorial Museum, *Guidelines for Teaching about the Holocaust*, accessed Jan.10, 2010, http://www.ushmm.org/education/foreducators/guideline/.
2. Omer Bartov, "Spielberg's Oskar: Hollywood Tries Evil," *Spielberg's Holocaust: Critical Perspectives on Schindler's List*, Yosefa Loshitzky, ed. (Indianapolis: Indiana University Press, 1997), pp. 41–60.

APPENDIX A

USING JOURNALING WITH HOLOCAUST FILMS

Journaling can be a powerful tool in the classroom. We use journaling to help students reflect upon the movies they have just watched or the literature they have just read.

We use the following grading tool when reviewing the journals:

0 = No Effort
1 = Poor Effort
2 = Average Effort
3 = Above Average Effort

Student addressed prompt. _____/3
Student provided reasoning within the journal entry. _____/3
Student followed content directions (length, style etc.) _____/3
Journal was turned in on time _____/1

Below are some sample questions that can be used when viewing Holocaust films. We tell students that these questions are sometimes meant to complicate their thinking on an already complicated subject.

1. Is it history or is it art?
2. What are the moral responsibilities of the filmmaker?
3. How are the complexities of the Holocaust communicated?
4. Is there a suitable cinematic language for this subject?
5. The U.S. vs. Europe in portrayal? Is there a U.S. "spin" on it?
6. Does Hollywood have the right to use dramatic interpretation?
7. Black comedies about the Holocaust....do they have a place in Holocaust education?
8. In what ways does editing shape your perception of what happened?
9. Can a filmmaker truly manipulate the viewer? Do they show both sides?
10. Is it reality or perceived reality?
11. Does the Holocaust "belong" to any group?
12. Is the Holocaust exploited for financial gain? Is this right? Wrong? Indifferent?
13. Is the portrayal of Jews as passive victims or active opponents accurate?
14. Do artistic films about the Holocaust have a place in Holocaust education?

APPENDIX B

The Sequential Roundtable Alphabet

A	B	C	D	E	F	G	
H	I	J	K	L	M	N	
O	P	Q	R	S	T	U	
V	W	X	Y	Z			

(Ricci & Wahlgren, 1998)

Classroom Strategies for Interactive Learning, 2nd Ed., by Doug Buehl ©2001. Newark, DE: International Reading Association. May be copied for classroom use.

With kind permission of the author

APPENDIX C

Story Map

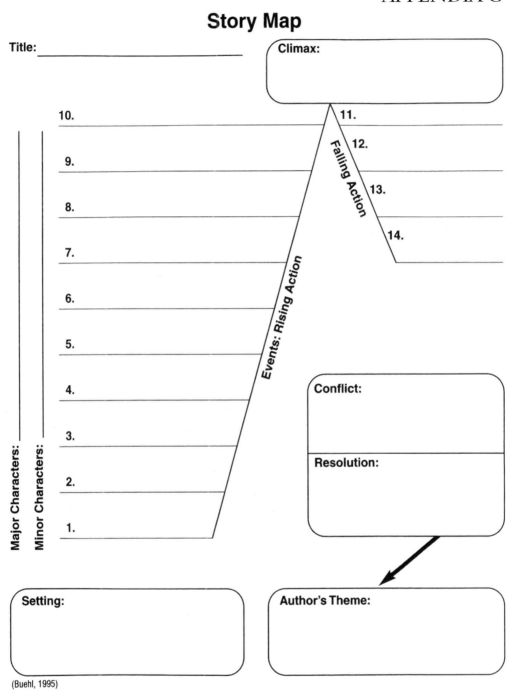

Title: _____

Climax:

10. _____

11.

12.

Falling Action

9. _____

13.

8. _____

14.

7. _____

Events: Rising Action

6. _____

5. _____

4. _____

Conflict:

3. _____

2. _____

Resolution:

1. _____

Major Characters:

Minor Characters:

Setting:

Author's Theme:

(Buehl, 1995)

With kind permission of the author

The Resistance of the White Rose: Using Film to Promote Holocaust Education

■ ■ ■ ■ ■ ■ ■ ■ ■ ■ ■

Vicky Knickerbocker

Human Services and Sociology Instructor,
Inver Hills Community College, Inver Grove Heights, MN

The Holocaust is a historical event that many educators agree should be remembered so that it will never happen again. In many schools across the nation, high school and college students are being taught about the historical significance of the Holocaust to help them become more informed, socially conscious, culturally competent, and ethical decision-makers. To help promote these important life lessons, the following study guide was authored. It highlights the instructional value of using the film *Sophie Scholl: The Final Days* in the classroom and validates the crucial role students have played, and can continue to play, in promoting a more civil and just society. Pre-viewing, viewing, and post-viewing activities are featured.

Part 1: Pre-Viewing Activities

This film's primary focus is on the last six days of Sophie's life. Thus, this film does not provide a great deal of historical narrative about events that took place before Thursday, February 18, 1943. To increase students' understanding of what motivated these students to act in such a defiant manner, it is important for teachers to provide some additional information about the social, political, legal, and economic conditions that fostered the rise of the Nazi Party and subsequently prompted German resistance. Here are three instructional tasks that teachers can complete to achieve these educational objectives:

1. Share information about the rise of the Nazi Party and Nazification. I would recommend using the timelines provided by the Florida Center for Instructional Technology at: http://fcit.coedu.usf.edu/holocaust/timeline/timeline.htm.

2. Encourage students to visit an interactive learning site entitled, "Mapping the Holocaust" created by the United States Holocaust Memorial Museum to further strengthen their understanding of the historical events that took place during the Nazi era and their diverse impacts on people's lives: http://www.ushmm.org/wlc/media_nm.php?lang=en&ModuleId=10005143&MediaId=3372.

3. Share the following historical narrative with your students to enhance their awareness of how Hans and Sophie Scholl first got involved in the resistance movement and why other students supported them in resisting the Nazi regime. The information used to construct this historical narrative was obtained from four primary sources:

a. The book *Sophie Scholl and the White Rose* written by Annette Dumbach and Jud Newborn

b. http://www.historyplace.com/pointsofview/white-rose1.htm

c. http://www.holocaustresearchproject.org/revolt/whiterose.html

d. "The White Rose," (pamphlet) Franz J. Muller, et al., White Rose Foundation, Munich, 1991.

A Brief Historical Narrative

Between 1939 and 1943, the German students who came to make up the White Rose, Sophie Scholl, Christoph Probst, Hans Scholl, Alexander Schmorell, Jürgen Wittenstein and Willi Graf attended the University of Munich.

This close-knit group of friends shared many common interests in music, art, medicine, and theology. Together, they listened to music, went to the theatre, hiked through the mountains, enjoyed skiing, drank wine, and conversed about controversial authors and banned books. They also attended scholarly lectures given by Professor Huber, Professor of Philosophy, Psychology, and Musicology at the University of Munich, and discussed with him their anti-Nazi views.

As Nazi terror and brutality escalated in Germany and other parts of Europe, these students decided to take more action. After reading a copy of Bishop Galen's sermon condemning the killing of inmates in hospitals, gas chambers, and asylums in what the Nazis called the "T-4"program (sometimes erroneously called euthanasia), Hans Scholl stated, "Finally someone has the courage to speak."

The Catholic bishop of Münster, Clemens August (Count von) Galen, was an outspoken critic of the Nazis. In July 1941, he stood up in his church and expressed spiritual outrage about the Nazis' T-4 killing program, which resulted in the murder of many handicapped people. According to Nazi ideology, the handicapped and those with genetic disorders from birth were "degenerates" and "life unworthy of life." More than 100,000 people were killed within Germany itself – Germans who were "Aryans" but who did not fit the ideal biological description of an Aryan. Bishop Galen declared that this selective breeding "was against God's commandments, against the law of nature, and against the system of jurisprudence in Germany." Bishop Galen's sermons were transcribed, reproduced, and circulated widely throughout the country of Germany.[1]

Galen's protest encouraged Hans Scholl and Alexander Schmorell to publish their own anti-Nazi literature. In June and July of 1942, Alexander Schmorell and Hans Scholl wrote the first four leaflets of the White Rose. Christoph Probst helped to draft the texts.

These illegal documents were distributed throughout central Germany. They were left in telephone books in public phone booths, mailed to professors and students, and taken by courier to other universities for distribution. This social activism was extremely difficult and dangerous to carry out as stationery and stamps were severely rationed at the time. If one bought any of these items in large quantities, one would have become instantly suspect.

Transporting these leaflets to other cities was also very risky because trains were constantly patrolled by military police, who demanded the identification papers of any male of military service age. Anyone traveling without official marching papers was taken into custody immediately and faced dire consequences.

The leaflets bore the title: "Leaves [leaflets] of the White Rose." All four leaflets carried the same message; they mentioned the mass extermination of Jews and Polish nobility, as well as other atrocities committed by the Nazis and the SS. However, it is important to note that their main focus was <u>not</u> on the Holocaust, but rather the resistance to Nazi dictatorship.

The leaflets were mailed from various cities, to confuse Nazi authorities. These messages were written to undermine a belief in Hitler and to provoke feelings of doubt and shame. They called for "self-criticism," "liberating German science," "freeing the spirit from the evil," a "rebirth of German student life to make the university again a living community devoted to the truth."[2]

In May of 1942, Sophie enrolled at the University of Munich to study biology and philosophy. When she discovered the secret activities of her brother, she confronted him about the serious risks he was taking. In spite of these dangers, she realized there was no turning back when she told Hans and his friends to "be performers of the word" and "not just listeners." She would now join them as an active co-conspirator.[3]

After serving as medics on the Russian front, several members of the White Rose published the fifth leaflet titled, "A Call to all Germans!" The fifth and sixth leaflets have the same main title, "Leaflets of the Resistance in Germany," but different subtitles: "A Call to Action" and "Fellow Students." In November 1942, Kurt Huber became involved when he was shown a draft of the fifth leaflet by Hans Scholl, which he helped edit. He drafted the sixth leaflet by himself.

In addition to publishing these leaflets, Hans Scholl, Alex Schmorell, and Willi Graf engaged in another type of civil disobedience. On three separate evenings in February of 1943, they painted slogans on the walls of Munich University and neighboring buildings. They wrote "Down with Hitler," "Hitler Mass Murderer," "Freedom," and drew crossed-out swastikas.

The most celebrated members of the White Rose were:

★ Hans Scholl   ★ Willi Graf
★ Sophie Scholl   ★ Kurt Huber
★ Christoph Probst   ★ Alexander Schmorell

To find out more about these individuals, visit the following website: http://www.spartacus.schoolnet.co.uk/GERschollH.htm. Why did these group members resist when others did not? To answer this question, I would encourage teachers to share with their students the following excerpt from a reflective essay written by George J.Wittenstein, M. D., a former member of the White Rose.[4]

George J. Wittenstein's Testimony

We were students, and students, throughout history, have been idealistic, rebellious, and willing to take chances: rebellious against existing order, against old and empty conventions (the United States and Europe experienced their share of it in the Sixties). Most of our group had been members of the *"Bündische Jugend."* These were youth organizations (somewhat similar to the Boy Scouts), which had come into being around 1908 in Europe and were particularly strong in Germany. In essence they grew out of a disillusionment of young people with the old established order, and with schools, which had failed them badly, as well as rebellion against overbearing parents. They were infused with typically German romanticism. Their ideals and stated goals were: personal freedom, self-imposed discipline, and strict adherence to highest moral and ethical principles.

These students came from bourgeois families. Their parents were opposed to Hitler, which must have influenced them to a large degree.

Most of us were medical students, except for Sophie Scholl, who majored in biology and philosophy. We shared a common interest in and a deep love for the arts, music, literature, and philosophy. Most of us had Jewish friends or classmates, who were evicted or deported or who had suffered in the "Crystal Night" pogrom [November 9–10, 1938 in Germany and Austria].

It all began, if you will, in the winter of 1938/39. Those who served their compulsory two year army service and planned to enter medical school were consigned to a "*Sanitätskompanie*," a training school for medics, for their final six months. This is where I met Alexander Schmorell: he was multi-talented, a gifted sculptor, deeply interested in literature and music; he was born in Russia, to a German father, a physician, and a Russian mother. We soon discovered our similar political leanings, and became close friends. Some of you may have read in one of the books about the White Rose, what Alex Schmorell said to me, pointing to the door of our room in the barracks: "Maybe ten years from now there will be a plaque on this door which will read: 'This is where the revolution began.'"

By the following spring (1939) most of us enrolled at the University of Munich. There were two days of required political indoctrination, which no one took seriously. Although fraternities had been dissolved and incorporated into the National Socialist Student Organization, we felt exhilarated by the degree of freedom one enjoyed as a student, compared to what lay behind us: namely six months of "*Arbeitsdienst*" (a compulsory paramilitary work service in uniform), followed by two years of military service. Yet, most kept their opinions to themselves in view of the palpable sense of oppression, of being watched, and the ever looming threat of concentration camps.

Still, student unrest was smoldering. For example, at the end of the summer semester, the leader of the Nazi student organization (for the state of Bavaria) ordered a convocation, in which he informed us that we were ordered to spend our summer vacation bringing in the harvest, otherwise we would not be permitted to re-enroll for the fall semester. There were demonstrations, students at the chemistry department set off stink bombs, and the Gestapo (secret police) was brought in.

Shortly after World War Two was unleashed by Germany's invasion of Poland... [on September 1, 1939] most medical students were drafted, housed in barracks, and required to attend classes in uniform. In the beginning, this was carried out in typically Prussian manner: students were crowded into barracks, up to ten to a room, which made studying extremely difficult; marching to class in columns in the morning, returning the same way in the evenings. Eventually the absurdity and impracticality of this became obvious, and more freedom was permitted; we were allowed to live in private quarters, and to even wear civilian clothes during our senior year. Only Saturday morning roll call and drill remained mandatory. Many of us would not show up, and friends would respond for those missing during roll call, shouting "here" when their names were called.

In this student company I introduced Alex Schmorell and Hans Scholl to each other.

To find out more about how these young people met and why their social activism grew, teachers might want to review Chapters 1–6 of the book *Sophie Scholl and the White Rose*.

Part 2: Viewing Activities

Listed below are several important scenes with time code references and supplemental educational activities that could be used by teachers to address crucial questions raised by this film.

Question 1: What type of resistance activities did the members of the White Rose initiate?
Pause the film at 03:43, just as copies of the sixth leaflet are being reproduced and stuffed into envelopes. Ask the students where this illegal activity is occurring and why only a few people are involved in it. Read aloud the finished product of the leaflet. A copy of it can be found in *Sophie Scholl and the White Rose*.[5]

Ask students what the main message of this leaflet was, and who was its primary audience. Also, ask students what these group members decided to do with the copies they had made. Did they agree about what should be done with these copies or any extras? Why did they need to be so careful and cautious?

Question 2: Why did the resistance activities of the White Rose terminate?
Pause the film at 13:40, just as Jakob Schmidt, a middle-aged custodian, is yelling, "You're under arrest!"

Ask students who this custodian was and what gave him the right to arrest Hans and Sophie. Where did he ultimately take them, and why did they go with him without much fuss? Was the custodian a loyal citizen following the law? Why was he so fanatical about stopping Hans and Sophie?

Pause the film at 14:25, as Robert Mohr is ordering them to be taken to the Gestapo headquarters and Hans pulls out a piece of paper, rips it up, and attempts to stuff it in his mouth. At this point, ask your students why Hans did this.

Provide them with copies of this document, which was the draft of the seventh leaflet, and read it out loud. Explore with them when it was written, by whom, and for what purpose. A copy of it can be found in *Sophie Scholl and the White Rose*.[6] Ask students to note how additional evidence is obtained against the members of the White Rose.

Question 3: Who were considered "enemies of the state" in Nazi Germany?
Pause the film at 29:45, just as Sophie is being strip-searched and advised by her future
cell mate, Else Gebel, to destroy any incriminating evidence she may have on her
person right away.

Ask your students to do some additional research about Else Gebel to find out
who she was, why she was imprisoned, and what prompted her to befriend Sophie.
Explore with your students why Else and Sophie were both considered "enemies of
the state" in Nazi Germany.

Who else did the Nazis consider to be an "enemy of the state"?

To acquaint students with other Germans who opposed Nazi tyranny, teachers can
download an educational document called "Resistance during the Holocaust," which
is published by the National Holocaust Memorial Museum in Washington D.C. Pages
40–44 of this document specifically address the topic of resistance in Nazi Germany.

An educational website offering additional information about German resisters is:
http://www.spartacus.schoolnet.co.uk/GERresistance.htm.

Note that National Socialism had political enemies, racial enemies, religious enemies,
artistic enemies, and sexual enemies. Differentiate how dangerous each group might be.

Question 4: What was the Nazi response to this student movement?
The Nazis' response to this student protest was swift and brutal. Following their arrest
at the University of Munich on Thursday February 18, 1943, Hans and Sophie were
taken to Gestapo headquarters, where they were questioned and interrogated incessantly
for four days. There are several scenes featured in the film which depict Sophie being
subjected to this harsh and brutal interrogation.

Although both Hans and Sophie denied any initial involvement, they both
confessed after they were shown incriminating evidence that the Gestapo had found
– including a large bunch of eight-pfennig stamps and a letter to Hans which matched
the handwriting on the sheet of paper Hans had attempted to destroy earlier.
However, neither Hans nor Sophie implicated anyone else.

While viewing these scenes, students could be asked to explore in greater detail how
these confessions were obtained by Nazi officials, and whether they were obtained
legally. Some of the following questions may be used to prompt this class discussion.

1. What types of questions was Sophie asked?
2. Was she threatened, intimidated, or harmed by her interrogators?
3. Was she coerced into signing a confession?
4. Was the interrogation a form of mental torture?
5. Where and when did these interrogations take place?
6. Who was present when these interrogations took place?
7. Did she have a lawyer?

8. Were these interrogations recorded?

9. Was she deprived of any of her basic human needs while these interrogations took place?

10. Did she have any choice to participate in these interrogations?

Students will also gain some valuable insights about Sophie from watching this part of the film, as she remains extremely composed during the course of these lengthy and intense interrogations. The following scene can be used to highlight Sophie's calm yet defiant personality.

In this interrogation scene, Robert Mohr tries to save her life by persuading her to claim that she was not personally responsible for her actions. Sophie responds to this offer of leniency by assertively stating that she was not led by her brother, and that she indeed knew the consequences of her actions. She rejects Mohr's "National Socialist" worldview that Hitler is a noble leader who should be respected and admired for the great things he has accomplished when she replies, "You're wrong. I would do it again – because I am not wrong. You have the wrong world view."[7]

On Monday February 22, 1943, all three of these student protestors were taken to the "People's Court," where they faced charges of high treason. The People's Court (*Volksgerichtshof*), a creation of the Nazi Party, was feared for its denial of justice and cruelty. The trial lasted only three hours. The trial proceedings were presided over by Roland Freisler, President of the People's Court, who is reported to have ranted and raved, screamed, and jumped to his feet numerous times, acting more like a prosecutor than a judge. Throughout these demoralizing trial proceedings, the court-appointed defense counselors did not make any effort to speak up for or defend the accused. This was not a trial that most Americans would recognize as legitimate.

Pause during these court scenes and ask your students whether these students received a fair trial. Point out to them that the judge had unlimited powers; he shrieked, he screamed, made wild accusations, and lashed out at the defendants. The only witnesses called were for the prosecution, but none for the defense.

Prosecution witnesses included Gestapo interrogators, Mohr and Mahler, and the custodian, Jakob Schmidt, who had already received a 3,000 Reichsmark reward and a promotion in the university system. The judge pronounced the verdict himself, which was a death sentence within a matter of four hours.[8]

Consider the following:

* Is there any trial procedure like this in American history?
* Talk about historic problems of rights of African-Americans and Native Americans in American courts, as well as problems with lynchings and internment of Japanese-Americans.
* Talk about the issue of the legitimacy of the death penalty.

Sophie Scholl was the only one who refused to remain silent while this bogus trial was being conducted. During these court proceedings, she courageously interrupted and contradicted the President of the People's Court, Roland Freisler (known for his perversion of justice), by saying, "You know as well as we do that the war is lost. Why are you so cowardly that you won't admit it?" She also boldly defended this group's deviant actions by proclaiming that "what we have said and what we have written is what so many people believe only they don't dare to speak up." Ask your students what prompted her to speak up when so many others chose not to.

At 1.30 p.m., Freisler ordered that Hans, Sophie, and Christoph be given death sentences. Three hours after their trial ended, all three were executed by guillotine at the Munich Stadelheim prison. Hans and Sophie were buried in Perlach Cemetery in south Munich on February 24, 1943.

- ★ What is a guillotine?
- ★ When was it invented?
- ★ Is its use considered cruel and unusual punishment?

Ask your students why the Nazis tried and executed these three student protestors so quickly. Following their deaths, four additional trials were held between April and October of 1944. Several other collaborators of the White Rose were executed, including Kurt Huber, Alexander Schmorell, Willi Graf, and Hans Leipelt. Others were imprisoned for aiding and abetting the activities of the White Rose. In one case, Marie-Luise Jahn was sentenced to a twelve-year term in a maximum-security penitentiary for reproducing and distributing copies of the sixth leaflet, and for collecting monies to support the destitute widow of Professor Huber.

Part 3: Post-Viewing Activities

After viewing this film, teachers are encouraged to discuss with their students a number of key issues:

1. Why it is important to remember this story, and how the memory of the White Rose can be kept alive today.
2. In this follow-up discussion, teachers can further examine why it was necessary for these students to protest, and what happens when a government restricts the freedom of speech and other civil liberties.
3. Students can be asked to compare the social activism of these students to other groups of protestors who dared to oppose repressive governmental policies/structures. This comparison exercise will increase students' awareness that social activism occurs in diverse ways and is carried out by a wide variety of people, including many determined and committed

college students. It will also identify the social and cultural context that prompted some to resist while others remained passive.

4. To begin a class discussion of this type, use the following statements made by Professor Kurt Huber, Hans Scholl, and Sophie Scholl.

"A state that suppresses all freedom of speech, and which by imposing the most terrible punishments, treats each and every attempt at criticism, however morally justified, and every suggestion for improvement as plotting to high treason, is a state that breaks an unwritten law."
Kurt Huber

"There is a point at which the law becomes immoral and unethical. That point is reached when it becomes a cloak for the cowardice that dares not stand up against blatant violations of justice."
Kurt Huber

"Long live the Freedom!"
Hans Scholl

"We will not be silent. We are your bad conscience. The White Rose will not leave you in Peace."
Leaflet four, authored by Hans Scholl and Alexander Schmorell

"What we have said and what we have written is what so many people believe only they don't dare to speak up."
Sophie Scholl

Questions

1. *How can the film* Sophie Scholl: The Final Days *be used to promote students' knowledge of the Holocaust and the role that young people played in Holocaust resistance?*

2. *What role have college students historically played in addressing issues of genocide, and what can they do now to make a positive difference?*

3. *What are the positive and negative consequences of student activism?*

4. *How can students keep the memory of the White Rose alive today?*

5. *What is social deviance and is it necessarily a bad thing?*

Bibliography

Axelrod, Toby. *Hans and Sophie Scholl: German Resisters of the White Rose*. New York: Rosen Publishing, 2001.

Dumbach, Annette and Jud Newborn. *Sophie Scholl and the White Rose*. Oxford: Oneworld Publication, 2006.

Rothemund, Marc, film producer. *Sophie: The Final Days*. Zeitgeist Video, 2005. Supplemental history: http://www.zeitgeistfilms.com/scholl_html/flash.html.

United States Holocaust Memorial Museum. "Resistance during the Holocaust." http://www.ushmm.org/education/foreducators/resource/pdf/resistance.pdf.

White Rose, The (pamphlet). Franz J. Muller et al., White Rose Foundation, Munich 1991.

Wittenstein, George. "Memories of the White Rose." http://www.historyplace.com/pointsofview/white-rose1.htm.

Notes

1. Annette Dumbach and Jud Newborn, *Sophie Scholl and the White Rose* (Oxford: Oneworld Publications, 2006), pp. 67–68.
2. http://www.historyplace.com/pointsofview/white-rose1.htm.
3. Dumbach and Newborn, p. 60.
4. http://www.historyplace.com/pointsofview/white-rose1.htm. Quoted by kind permission of the author.
5. Dumbach and Newborn, p. 201.
6. Dumbach and Newborn, p. 204.
7. Dumbach and Newborn, p. 151.
8. Dumbach and Newborn, p. 157.

HOLOCAUST
AND
GENOCIDE

"Holocaust and Genocide: What's in a Name?"

. . . .

Steven Leonard Jacobs

Aaron Aronov Endowed Chair of Judaic Studies,
Associate Professor of Religious Studies, The University of Alabama, Tuscaloosa, AL

"The wrongs which we seek to condemn have been so calculated, so malignant and so devastating, that civilization cannot tolerate their being ignored, because it cannot survive their being repeated."
Robert H. Jackson (1882–1954), United States Supreme Court Justice and Chief Prosecutor, International Military Tribunal (IMT), Nuremberg, Germany (November 21, 1945–January 10, 1946)

Introduction

In 1989, Professor Zev Garber, Los Angeles Valley College, now retired, and Professor Bruce Zuckerman, University of Southern California, co-authored an essay entitled "Why Do We Call the Holocaust 'The Holocaust?' An Inquiry into the Psychology of Labels."[1] In that essay, they made a number of trenchant and astute observations. Without taking you through the entire piece, let me outline for you, however briefly, what I believe are their most important observations. (It should be further noted that each of their trenchant comments is itself worthy of further exploration and conversation.)

1. The power latent in words and phrases must be taken seriously, especially when they come to bear as much cultural weight as "The Holocaust" has been made to bear in the modern world. (p. 198)

2. Only in the post-war period has "holocaust" become largely divorced from its heretofore most common sense: "religious sacrifice." (p. 199)
3. The modern Hebrew term for the Jews' genocide, "*Shoah*," has no religious or sacrificial overtones. This term, which comes into modern Hebrew from biblical Hebrew, simply means "destruction, ruin." (p. 200)
4. Whether intended or not, when one adopts the "holocaust" label, one also implies a particular religious correspondence between the Jews and the Nazis. If the former are the holocaust sacrifice, then it implicitly follows that the latter are the sacrificers, the officiants who offer up the sacrifice. In effect, one casts the Nazis into a quasi-"priestly" role. Even more seriously, the sacrificial connotation of "holocaust" also implies a third party to this ceremony, He to whom the sacrifice is offered: God, Himself... Why focus on a term that could be said to suggest that God and the Nazis were co-conspirators in the sacrifice of the Jews? (p. 200)
5. Whether [Elie] Wiesel actually was the first to employ "holocaust" in this manner or not, for all intents and purposes his adoption of the term was the single most important factor involved in legitimizing it in its current usage... And the motivation for Wiesel's use of "The Holocaust" has unmistakably religious/sacrificial overtones, as his own writings reveal. (p. 202)
6. The elemental *human* struggle manifest in this event can be properly grasped only if the Jewish genocide is kept ugly, ignoble, unheroic, punctuated by the screams of those who found themselves in mortal peril... A more humane model would see the Germans, even the Nazis, as ordinary human beings, who showed in the Jewish genocide that ordinary people in certain circumstances are capable of extraordinary cruelty. (p. 207)
7. The truth is that 11 million people were killed by the Nazis in the concentration camps. Nearly half of these are excluded in most characterizations of "The Holocaust," and this seems to imply that Gentile deaths are not as significant as Jewish deaths... [W]hen Jews urge each other, "Never Again!" the sub-text is really more, "Never again *for us*!" This stress can have a subtle effect of desensitizing the Jewish community to the suffering of others as the community takes whatever steps it feels are necessary to insure its own survival. (p. 208)
8. The time has come for what happened to the Jews in the first half of the twentieth century to be placed in a more dispassionate perspective. The Jewish genocide needs to be humanized; its saints and devils need to be demythologized back into the mere people that they always were, its message of survival must be shared with all who have suffered and will suffer. (p. 209)

I cite their observations to remind all of us of the power inherent in the words we choose, both to confirm and to disconfirm, and not only in the case of the Holocaust/*Shoah* but genocide as well – *before* we turn to the "Problems, Issues, Concerns Associated with *Teaching* the Holocaust – AND Genocide!"[2] As educators – and students – collectively, we have the moral and intellectual responsibility to be thoroughly grounded in the *reality* of the historical facts that continue to elicit our interest and demand our attention. And with that knowledge comes the commensurate responsibility to defeat those who continue to deny these histories – not directly, because those who hold hard and fast to denialism will not change, and such direct confrontations accomplish nothing – but to the unsuspecting who, with little knowledge, raise questions worthy of proper answers and deserve our best. And, yes, where the deniers enter the public arena – be it the classroom, the campus, the media – creative responses on the part of those capable of providing those answers must be forthcoming.

"Worth Thinking About"
We have seemingly ignored Justice Jackson's dire warning as, post-World War II, the human community has experienced genocides in Cambodia/Kampuchea, Bosnia, Rwanda, and now Darfur. One is reminded of the unknown critic's seemingly accurate comment, "History teaches us that history teaches us nothing!" One implication, therefore, of the consequent tragedy of the Holocaust/*Shoah* is that its horrors continue to be ignored, the human toll on men, women, and children forgotten; and nation-states continue to allow the corrupt access to corridors of power to practice their genocidal agendas.

Many of us remain in debt to Elie Wiesel (b. 1928), whose writings have put the Holocaust/*Shoah* before the world community and whose stories and parables remind us of the power of literature to evoke responses in all of us. And yet, it is truly troubling, as Garber and Zuckerman correctly note, that the attribution of the term "Holocaust" itself – whether self-perceived or other-perceived – is the wrong term and opens doors to religious and theological misunderstandings that are better not raised because they are the wrong understandings.

There is another person to whom we must remain indebted if we are to address these words of meaning, "Holocaust" and "genocide." And that is Raphael Lemkin (1900–1959). According to the Babylonian Talmud (Sanhedrin 4:8 [37a]), "Whoever saves a life, it is considered as if he saved an entire world." This Polish-American Jew, lawyer and scholar, survivor and escapee from the Holocaust/*Shoah*, who lost forty-nine members of his own family, through his coinage of the word "genocide" gave the world a singularly unique gift: the opportunity to prevent the crime of genocide and punish those guilty of such a crime. That the world continues to reluctantly accept the gift, as evidenced by international failures in the cases of Rwanda and now Darfur, and less so in the case of Bosnia, speaks volumes. However, by doing so, this above Talmudic reference certainly must apply. We will never know how many lives have been saved, how many genocidal actors consciously chose not to participate in these barbarities because knowledge of criminal punishment for such behavior was part of their consciousness. If only one since the world-consciousness of the term, then Lemkin, indeed, has saved the entire world.

Holocaust and Genocide: The Origins of Our Terms

As is now universally accepted, etymologically, from the Hebrew of *olah* came the Greek *holocaustos* came the Latin *holocaustum* came the English *holocaust* (note the small "h") came Wiesel's and others' <u>*The Holocaust*</u> (specifically referencing the genocide of the Jews during the Second World War), and perhaps somewhat ironically full-circle came the Hebrew *Shoah*.

Far easier is the etymological origin of our word "genocide," as Lemkin himself, its author, informs us. It comes from the Greek *genos* (race, tribe) + Latin *cide* (killing). Among the verbal tragedies, again as Garber and Zuckerman note, has been the exclusion of the one other population group marked for extinction/ extermination/ annihilation, the Roma, by the use of the term "Holocaust." This is made all the more significant by the fact that in the language of the Roma peoples they themselves have their own word to describe their tragedy: *Porajmos*: "the attempt by the Nazis to exterminate most of the Roma peoples of Europe as part of the Holocaust/*Shoah* during the Second World War. Figures range from 220,000 to 1,500,000 murdered between 1933 and 1945." Alternative terms found in the Roma language are both *Samudaripen* ("mass murder") and *Kali Traš* ("black fear").

Even more pointedly, however, has been the failure on the part of some Jews, some Jewish communities, some Jewish organizations, and some Jewish agencies to build bridges of solidarity with other victims of genocide and to privilege its own victims above those of others. Thankfully, this is beginning to change.

Genocide the Word

According to Raphael Lemkin, in his magnum opus, *Axis Rule in Occupied Europe: Laws of Occupation, Analysis of Government, Proposals for Redress*,[3] genocide is "a new term and new conception for destruction of nations." Indeed, he writes:

> By 'genocide' we mean the destruction of a nation or of an ethnic group. This new word, coined by the author to denote an old practice in its modern development, is made from the ancient Greek word *genos* (race, tribe) and the Latin *cide* (killing), thus corresponding in its formation to such words as tyrannicide, homicide, infanticide, etc.*

... a coordinated plan of different actions aiming at the destruction of essential foundations of the life of national groups, with the aim of annihilating the groups themselves.

*[Another term could be used for the same idea, namely, "ethnocide," consisting of the Greek word *ethnos* (nation) and the Latin word *cide*.]

In that same chapter nine of *Axis Rule in Occupied Europe*, Lemkin wrote:

As far back as 1933, the author of the present work submitted to the Fifth International Conference for the Unification of Penal Law, held in Madrid in October of that year in cooperation with the Fifth Committee of the League of Nations, a report accompanied by draft articles to the effect that actions aiming at the destruction and oppression of populations (what would amount to the actual conception of genocide) should be penalized. The author formulated two new international law crimes to be introduced into the penal legislation of the thirty-seven participating countries, namely the crime of barbarity, conceived as oppressive and destructive actions directed against individuals as members of a national, religious, or racial group, and the crime of vandalism, conceived as malicious destruction of works of art and culture because they represent the specific creations of the genius of such groups. Moreover, according to this draft these new crimes were to be internationalized to the extent that the offender should be punished when apprehended, either in his own country, if that was the situs of the crime, or in any other signatory country, if apprehended there.

This principle of universal repression for genocide practices advocated by the author at the above-mentioned conference, had it been accepted by the conference and embodied in the form of an international convention duly signed and ratified by the countries there represented in 1933, would have made it possible, as early as that date, to indict persons who had been found guilty of such criminal acts whenever they appeared on the territory of one of the signatory countries. Moreover, such a project, had it been adopted at that time by the participating countries, would prove useful now by providing an effective instrument for the punishment of war criminals in the present world conflict. It must be emphasized again that the proposals of the author at the Madrid Conference embraced criminal actions which, according to the view of the author, would cover in great part the fields in which crimes have been committed in this war by the members of the Axis powers. Furthermore, the adoption of the principle of universal repression as adapted to genocide by countries which belong now to the group of non-belligerents or neutrals, respectively, would likewise bind these latter countries to punish the war criminals engaged in genocide or to extradite them to the countries in which these crimes were committed. If the punishment of genocide practices had formed a part of international law in such countries since 1933, there would be no necessity now to issue admonitions to neutral countries not to give refuge to war criminals.[4]

United Nations Convention on the Prevention and Punishment of the Crime of Genocide (December 10, 1948)

This is the actual wording of what has now come to be called the "Genocide Convention," as first proposed by Lemkin and ultimately passed by the United Nations. Its story is a maze of intrigue among the member nation-states, not always positive, as even while ratifying it, no member wanted to see itself in a vulnerable position, including both the Soviet Union in the aftermath of its collectivization in the Ukraine, and the United States in its then still unresolved racial difficulties.[5] It remains an imperfect document, to be sure, but it is still the only legal definition of genocide having international teeth. (Each of these sections of the Genocide Convention, as well as its history, are worthy of teaching opportunities.)

- **Article I:** The Contracting Parties confirm that genocide, whether committed in time of peace or in time of war, is a crime under international law which they undertake to prevent and to punish.
- **Article II**: In the present Convention, genocide means any of the following acts committed with intent to destroy, in whole or in part, a national, ethnical, racial or religious group, as such:
    - (a) Killing members of the group;
    - (b) Causing serious bodily or mental harm to members of the group;
    - (c) Deliberately inflicting on the group conditions of life calculated to bring about its physical destruction in whole or in part;
    - (d) Imposing measures intended to prevent births within the group;
    - (e) Forcibly transferring children of the group to another group.
- **Article III**: The following acts shall be punishable:
    - (a) Genocide;
    - (b) Conspiracy to commit genocide;
    - (c) Direct and public incitement to commit genocide;
    - (d) Attempt to commit genocide;
    - (e) Complicity in genocide.

- **Article IV**: Persons committing genocide or any of the other acts enumerated in article III shall be punished, whether they are constitutionally responsible rulers, public officials or private individuals.

The limiting definitions of what constitutes a group – "national, ethnical, racial or religious" – remains one of the most contentious issues with regard to this Convention. Of late, it was used in the "Report of the International Commission of Inquiry on Darfur to the United Nations Secretary-General" of January 25, 2005 to deny the genocide in the Sudan in stating that the issue at hand was that of tribes, and tribes are not one of the protected categories.

Secondly, to our U.S. shame, almost forty years later our own country ratified the Convention under then-President Ronald Reagan (1911–2004), and it was earlier used against then-President Richard Nixon's (1913–1994) protestations against the communist Chinese human rights record.

The Eight Stages of Genocide

According to Gregory Stanton, immediate past president of the International Association of Genocide Scholars, and creator and maintainer of the website www.genocidewatch.org, there are eight stages of genocide which follow something of a sequential path, though not hard and fast, but, rather, bleeding into each other. (An extended discussion of each occurs on the website). They are:

- **Classification**: All groups, societies, and nation-states distinguish between themselves and others, i.e., "us versus them." The initial task must thus be to universalize the common community of persons so that distinctive sub-categories of persons do not become initial warrants for genocide, as they have in the past.
- **Symbolization**: Symbolically giving identifiers to various persons and/or groups is a step on the road to genocide, especially when those identifiers negativize those persons and/or groups (e.g., the yellow star insisted upon by the Nazis for the Jews). Such negativizations can be thwarted by legally preventing them.
- **Dehumanization**: Primarily through the use of various media, hate speech denigrating the object group is a true genocidal factor as the various outlets (radio, television, newspapers, movies) consistently portray the group to be destroyed as less than fully equal and fully human, thus easing the process of genocidal murder.
- **Organization**: Almost always state-sanctioned, genocide is an organized activity, sometimes employing the already-existent military and governmental apparatus and, at other times, calling into being a

271

paramilitary or military force to do the work. Such "unofficial" groups should be outlawed nationally and condemned internationally.

- **Polarization**: In order for genocide to take place, the victim group or groups must be separated from the perpetrator group or groups. This can be done by forbidding intermarriage (as was the case in Nazi Germany), also ghettoizing the former, as has been done throughout history as a prelude to their destruction. Support for various human rights groups under law is a strategy to prevent such victimization.

- **Preparation**: As part of the organizational and systematization process, once identified, lists of victims (usually in positions of leadership) are drawn up and the net of genocidal destruction is cast wider and wider to include more and more of the victim group in its maw. It is at this point that the international community of nation-states must have the political will to intervene before genocide becomes a reality.

- **Extermination**: As in most group processes, once the killing spree of genocide has begun, it takes on a life of its own, and continues until either the goal of total extermination or annihilation is achieved, or intervention on the part of other nation-states occurs to bring it to a conclusion. After the fact and after the energy of genocidal violence has been spent, the work of aid and reconciliation on the part of other nation-states remain primary tasks.

- **Denial**: Following the events of the genocide, and sometimes continuing for many, many years (e.g., the Armenian genocide and the Holocaust or *Shoah*), the perpetrators will take massive steps to hide the evidence of their deeds. Tribunals must, therefore, be in place to try those responsible. Years later, others not necessarily physically associated with the events themselves, out of a desire to rehabilitate the perpetrator nation-state and/or its leadership, will continue to deny that the historical events were as others have recorded them, challenging the historical record, arguing against the implementation of the definition of genocide itself. Elie Wiesel himself has suggested that the deniers murder the victims a second time by their denial.[6]

For Genocide to Occur...

According to M. Hassan Kakar, in his book *Afghanistan: The Soviet Invasion and the Afghan Response, 1979–1982*:[7]

> For genocide to take place, there must be certain preconditions. Foremost among them is a national culture that does not place a high value on human life. A totalitarian society, with its assumed superior ideology, is also a

precondition for genocidal acts. In addition, members of the dominant society must perceive their potential victims as less than fully human: as "pagans," "savages," "uncouth barbarians," "unbelievers," "effete degenerates," "ritual outlaws," "racial inferiors," "class antagonists," "counterrevolutionaries," and so on. In themselves, the conditions are not enough for the perpetrators to commit genocide. To do that – that is, to commit genocide – the perpetrators need a strong, centralized authority and bureaucratic organization as well as pathological individuals and criminals. Also required is a campaign of vilification and dehumanization of the victims by the perpetrators, who are usually new states or new regimes attempting to impose conformity to a new ideology and its models of society.

Genocide, thus, is a process, not an instantaneous moment with a long and dishonorable history, as the following charting out informs us. In the classroom in particular, each of these historical cases is fully worthy of study, though given the realities of classroom time, it would be humanly impossible to examine them all. Thus, an alternative would be for the instructor to familiarize himself with all of them and allow the students to select their own for study and brief classroom presentations.[8]

I. Genocides in Antiquity

•Ai, •Amalekites, •Asine, •Askra, •Canaanites, •Etruscans, •Hittites, •Hurrians, •Lydians, •Medes, •Melos, •Minoans, •Mycenae, •Parthians, •Pisatis, •Plataia, •Skione, •Sybaris, •Tiryns, •Torone, •Troy

II. Genocides during the Middle Ages

•Genghis Khan (1162–1227), •Tamerlane (1336–1405), •First Crusade (1096–1099), •Second Crusade (1147–1149), •Third Crusade (1189–1192), •Fourth Crusade (1202–1204), •Albigensian Crusade (1209–1229)

III. Genocide in the Early Modern and Modern Periods

•Armenians (~1,500,000 deaths), •Aztecs (?), •Bosnians-Croats-Serbians (~200,000 deaths), •Cambodians (~2,000,000 deaths), •Caribs (?), •Chinese (~300,000 deaths), •Darfurians (~400,000 + deaths), •Herreros (~75,000 deaths), •Huguenots (~70,000 deaths), •Jews (~6,000,000 deaths), •Roma (~1,500,000 deaths), •Rwandese (~800,000 deaths), •Tasmanians (~8,000 deaths), •Ukrainians (~700,000 deaths), •Vendéans (~450,000 deaths), •"witches" (?)

Always remember that even these numbers in this last set of genocides are not numbers but human beings – men, women, and children – whose lives were snuffed out not because of something they did, but who they were.

Problems, Issues, Concerns

Like everything else we human beings create, words, too, as Garber and Zuckerman have pointedly indicated, can be abused. Here, in microcosm, are some examples of linguistic abuse applied to both "Holocaust" and "genocide," and thus they must be kept in mind as we enter our classrooms and see and listen to our media. Such linguistic abuses must be challenged if the words we use to describe these horrors are to maintain their integrity, not only in our schools but in our communities as well. Each and every one of them on the list contains the understood phrase either "… of the Holocaust/*Shoah*" or "… of genocide."

Anthropologization/Dehumanization: Turning the events of the Holocaust/*Shoah* or any other genocide simply into an academic exercise whereby one studies human cultures and fails to see in the events themselves the destruction of human beings;

Appropriation/Misappropriation: Using the example of the Holocaust/*Shoah* for purposes irrelevant to its historicity – e.g., the ever-contentious abortion debates;

Christianization/Theologization/Mythologization/Demonization/Satanization: Seeing the Holocaust/*Shoah* as somehow "more than" an historical event perpetrated by ordinary human beings, neither demi-gods nor demi-satans (as Garber and Zuckerman correctly remind us) and reading into the event meanings other than the reality of what transpired;

Contemporization: Drawing false parallels between contemporary events – genocides in Bosnia, Rwanda, Darfur – and the Holocaust/*Shoah*, leading to misreading the reality of the events themselves;

Dejudaization/Delegitimization/Denialization: The attempts by those antisemites who regard the reality of the Holocaust/*Shoah* as false, or worse, non-existent history to serve Jewish and/or Israeli agendas. In this context, one must also make mention of the continuing Turkish (and others, including a small coterie of American academics) efforts to deny the Armenian genocide;

Parochialization: Advancing the Holocaust/*Shoah* to the exclusion of other genocides, both historical and contemporary in both Jewish (and other) communal endeavors, as well as in educational contexts.

Politicization: The use of the Holocaust/*Shoah* or any other genocide by any parochial community to advance other agendas unrelated to the specificity of the historical events themselves, e.g., comparing Yasser Arafat (1929–2004) or Mahmoud Ahmadinejad (b. 1956) to Hitler; trying to convince Jewish communities in both Israel and America that a "second Holocaust" is just around the corner;

Trivialization/Routinization/Marginalization: Seeing either the Holocaust/*Shoah* or any other genocide merely as examples of "humanity's inhumanity to itself," again denying the specificity of what actually transpired;

Universalization: Ignoring the specificity of the Holocaust/*Shoah* – the victims were not simply human beings; they were Jews and it was for that reason that they were the Nazis' primary victims;

Victimization/Memorialization: Falling into the trap of misreading the story of Jewish history as one of unbroken sadness – what the late Columbia University Professor Salo Baron (1895–1989) called the "lachrymose view of Jewish history" – and consistently ignoring the intellectual creativity and productivity throughout much of Jewish history.

The Challenge: What are YOU going to do about Genocide?

Words do not kill people. Yet they begin a process of dehumanization of others which leads to the collective horrors we now label "Holocaust," "genocide," and/or "ethnic cleansing." Thus our first line of defense is the education of others, especially but not solely the young people entrusted to our care, to be linguistically sensitive to the words we use in classifying those who are not like us, whose cultural, religious, social practices, etc., are different than our own. In that process of education comes both a moral and ethical responsibility to speak out when those in power denigrate those in our midst who have little or no power themselves, who are denied access to such corridors, and are consistently devalued and maligned in our media. Secondly, we who are educators are, definitionally, role models whether we wish to affirm it or not. How we conduct ourselves in the face of such horrors says more to our students ofttimes than our words. If we join anti-genocide organizations, we give our students an avenue to channel their anti-genocide energies. If we write letters or emails to our congresspersons, we teach our students that government is a primary responsibility of all our citizenry, especially when decisions at the highest levels result in the deaths of untold numbers. We as educators thus bear a primary responsibility to break into the cycle of violence known as genocide.

Questions

1. *Among the terms used to describe the murder of Jews during the Second World War (1933–1945) have been "the Holocaust," "Ha-Shoah," "the Jewish Holocaust," "the Nazi Holocaust," and "Judeocide." Which term do you feel best expresses your own thinking and understanding of this event? Why so? Be prepared to defend your choice with illustrative examples.*

2. Raphael Lemkin stated in his footnote to his chapter on genocide in Axis Rule in Occupied Europe (1944) *that he was apparently comfortable with either "genocide" or "ethnocide" to describe the events he was describing in that chapter. Given everything that has transpired since the adoption of the 1948 United Nations Convention on the Punishment and Prevention of the Crime of Genocide – including the important Whitaker Report of 1985 (www.preventgenocide.org/prevent/UNdocs/whitaker) – which term do you feel best describes this ongoing collective human tragedy? As above, be prepared to defend your choice with illustrative examples.*

3. *Scholars and others continue to use the Holocaust/*Shoah *as the "yardstick" by which to evaluate all other cases of genocide, primarily because of its exhaustive documentation. Given the different cases of genocide that you have examined and will examine, does this comparison continue to make sense? Why or why not?*

4. *Among the most contentious issues surrounding the Holocaust/*Shoah *is that of uniqueness – what the late Emil L. Fackenheim (1916–2003) called "unprecedented." Where do you stand on this issue? Be prepared to defend your position with illustrative examples.*

Bibliography

Alexander, Jeffrey C., et al. *Remembering the Holocaust: A Debate*. New York and Oxford: Oxford University Press, 2009.

Bartov, Omer and Phyllis Mack, eds. *In God's Name: Genocide and Religion in the Twentieth Century*. New York and Oxford: Berghahn Books, 2001.

Bloxham, Donald. *The Final Solution: A Genocide*. Oxford and New York: Oxford University Press, 2009.

Cooper, John. *Raphael Lemkin and the Struggle for the Genocide Convention*. New York: Palgrave Macmillan, 2008.

Goldhagen, Daniel Jonah. *Worse than War: Genocide, Eliminationism, and the Ongoing Assault on Humanity*. New York: Public Affairs, 2009.

Jacobs, Steven Leonard, ed. *Confronting Genocide: Judaism, Christianity, Islam*. Lanham: Lexington Books, 2009.

Jones, Adam. *Genocide: A Comprehensive Introduction*. London and New York: Routledge, 2006.

Mitchell, Joseph R. and Helen Buss Mitchell. *The Holocaust: Readings and Interpretations*. New York: McGraw-Hill/Dushkin, 2001.

Shaw, Martin. *What is Genocide?* Cambridge and Malden: Polity, 2007.

Stone, Dan, ed. *The Historiography of the Holocaust.* New York: Palgrave Macmillan, 2004.

Stone, Dan, ed. *The Historiography of Genocide.* New York: Palgrave Macmillan, 2008.

Totten, Samuel, ed. *Teaching About Genocide: Issues, Approaches, and Resources.* Greenwich: Information Age Publishing, 2004.

Totten, Samuel, ed. *Teaching and Studying the Holocaust.* Charlotte: Information Age Publishing, 2009.

Totten, Samuel and Paul R. Bartrop, eds. *The Genocide Studies Reader.* London and New York: Routledge, 2009.

Totten, Samuel, and William S. Parsons, eds. *Century of Genocide: Critical Essays and Eyewitness Accounts.* London and New York: Routledge, 2009.

Notes

1. *Modern Judaism*, 9 (2): 197–211.
2. It should also be noted at the outset that the term "Holocaust" is itself problematic, as Garber and Zuckerman note. Arising out of a religious context, it ultimately and historically meant a sacrifice given to God. Certainly no one would therefore conclude that the murders of so many Jews by the Nazis and their minions was a "gift" to a God whom the Nazis themselves rejected. Thus the Hebrew term *Shoah* – Devastation or Destruction – has gained currency among Jews, scholars, and others. While not arising from or laden with religious connotations, it, too, is somewhat problematic in that it pointedly addresses only the tragedy of the Jews, not that of the Sinti and Roma peoples who were also marked for annihilation. Thus, ultimately, there is no one universally accepted word to accurately label the non-military deaths of so many during the Second World War.
3. Raphael Lemkin, *Axis Rule in Occupied Europe: Laws of Occupation, Analysis of Government, Proposals for Redress* (Washington, D.C: Carnegie Endowment for International Peace, 1944), pp. 79–95.
4. Ibid., pp. 91–92.
5. The United States Senate ratified the "Genocide Convention" (as it has come to be called) in February 1986 by a vote of 83 to 11.
6. Stanton has prepared an excellent 50-slide PowerPoint presentation of the Eight Stages of Genocide for classroom use on his website www.genocidewatch.org.
7. Berkeley: University of California Press, 1995.
8. Two important books edited by Samuel Totten are *Teaching and Studying the Holocaust* (Charlotte: Information Age Publishing, 2009) and *Teaching About Genocide: Issues, Approaches, and Resources* (Greenwich: Information Age Publishing, 2004).

40 Years of Silence: An Indonesian Tragedy

■ ■ ■ ■ ■ ■ ■ ■ ■ ■ ■

Robert Lemelson

Semel Institute for Neuroscience, Center for Culture and Health,
University of California, Los Angeles, CA

Annie Tucker

Elemental Productions, Pacific Palisades, CA

In one of the largest unknown mass killings of the twentieth century, an estimated 500,000–1,000,000 people were secretly and systematically killed in 1965–1966, when General Suharto began a bloody purge of suspected communists throughout Indonesia in retaliation against an alleged communist-led coup.[1] In Bali alone, an estimated 80,000–100,000 people, or approximately 5–8 percent of the population, were killed between December 1965 and March 1966.[2] Thousands more were tortured, imprisoned, and sentenced to forced labor, with some being held under harsh conditions for up to a decade. The primary victims of this violence were Communist Party members, alleged communists, members of affiliated organizations, and those accused of being sympathetic to the communist cause. The perpetrators of violence included nationalist military and paramilitary forces, religious groups, those neighbors and family members who voluntarily informed on or attacked other villagers, and those who were forced into violent acts through threats of death or further violence and destruction.

Up until this time, the Communist Party, or *Partai Komunis Indonesia* (PKI), was an entirely legal political organization. In fact, as one of the largest parties in the nation, it supported and was supported by President Sukarno. However, in the growing anxiety of the cold war era, and growing dissatisfaction with Sukarno, the coup destabilized the nation. In the chaos of the weeks and months following these events, by framing the events to ostracize and blacklist those who were perceived as supporting the communists, Suharto rose to power as president of the New Order regime (1966–98).[3] The anti-communist stigma that the New Order perpetuated for decades extended not only to former PKI members, but also to their families, who were denied many civil rights. Until Suharto's fall in 1998, any public discussion of the events of 1965 that was at variance with the official government version was forbidden, and those who engaged in it were jailed or "disappeared." Any discussion, recognition, or memorializing of the mass killings that differed from the official state narrative was quickly suppressed.[4]

This monolithic state narrative was possible within Indonesia because the perpetrators remained in power for decades after the killings, but it also meant that the world knew very little of this horrific and tragic history, even though it was among the largest mass killings of the twentieth century. This brings to mind the quotation from Adolf Hitler, who, in planning the "Final Solution," stated, "Who remembers the Armenians?" His belief was that he could act with impunity because he believed no one remembered or chose to care about the Armenian genocide. It is only now, after the fall of the New Order regime in 1998 and the death of President Suharto in 2008, that Indonesians are beginning to speak out and come to terms with their complicated and painful history. This process is long overdue in modern Indonesia, yet vital to ensure that such events are never repeated. The "will to bear witness" active in the efforts to bring the mass killings of 1965 to wide attention is a necessary corrective to the silencing of millions. The film *40 Years of Silence: An Indonesian Tragedy* (2009)[5] represents part of the growing effort to not only break that silence, but also to situate Indonesia's mass killings within a global context of genocide and genocide studies and grasp modern-day Indonesia's potential for retribution, rehabilitation, and reconciliation.[6]

40 Years of Silence follows the compelling testimonies of four individuals and their families from Central Java and Bali, two regions heavily affected by the purge. As they tell their stories publicly for the first time, each family provides an intimate and frightening look at what it was like for survivors of the mass killings. In chilling detail, they describe the events of 1965 through their own experiences, reliving and reflecting upon the stigmatization and brutalization that they continue to endure on both the village and state levels. Over time, the survivors and their families attempt to find ways to deal with a tragedy that was not openly recognized by their neighbors, government, or the world.[7]

Through the film, viewers may become more aware of this tragic history from the perspective of the victims. However, beyond this specific historical case the film provides an understanding of the social, cultural, and personal repercussions of mass violence that can be broadly applied to trauma and genocide studies. It acknowledges the deeply personal aspects of these horrific struggles, traces the long-term effects of trauma through generations, and emphasizes the fact that trauma occurs within a specific social and cultural setting, which provides clues to interpreting its meanings and implications. It fosters an appreciation for the highly individual responses to violence and trauma, and the resilience factors that provide pathways to recovery.[8]

In considering the diverse perspectives from which to view trauma and its impacts, it is useful to consider how biological, clinical, and cultural approaches might work together to deepen our understanding of individual and collective responses to traumatic experiences such as genocide and mass killings. In the film, all four characters suffered trauma during the political upheaval in Indonesia in 1965. All experienced intense fear or terror witnessing family members being severely beaten, taken away, or killed. All have lived in a political climate, from 1965 through the late 1990s, in which their status as relatives of alleged Communist Party members made them continued targets for harassment, intimidation, violence, and discrimination. However, despite these similarities, the long-term outcomes they and their families have experienced are vastly different. Each of the characters' stories details their markedly different backgrounds and resources, which represent some of the diverse ethnic, cultural, and religious strands within the rich tapestry of Indonesian society, and which contribute to equally diverse experiences of trauma. Understanding these stories requires us to understand how they are embedded in – and emerge from – multiple contexts: biological processes of learning and memory; embodied experiences of injury, pain, and fear; the narrative trajectories of personal biography; the knowledges and practices of cultural and social systems; and the power and positioning of political struggles enacted on individual, family, community, and national levels.[9] Below, the main characters in the film are described, to point out both commonalities and differences between their personal biographies and the historical and political context in which their lives unfolded.

Budi[10]

Budi was initially referred to Dr. Mahar Agusno, a Javanese psychiatrist, by the staff of the orphanage where his parents had placed him to remove him from an environment of community and family violence. He explained, "I came to this home because I had… a rather complicated problem… My family was unjustly maltreated, slandered, terrorized (*keluarga saya dianiaya, difitnah gitu, diteror*). It was like that." Budi's father, Mudakir, had been imprisoned for being an alleged communist, and this event had devastating consequences for himself and his family.

Mudakir grew up in a poor village outside of Yogyakarta. He worked as a coffee salesman, fell in love with a woman from his village, and hoped to marry her. Unfortunately, the son of the village headman also desired her, and in the chaos of 1965, reported to the authorities that Pak Mudakir was a PKI activist. While Pak

Mudakir denied this, he was arrested and sent to a series of prisons where conditions were unbearable. He was frequently the target of beatings and violence, and said that he suffered multiple skull fractures. He was held for fourteen years, and yet his release led to more hardship: his ex-prisoner status meant that many jobs were closed to him, his activities and movements were restricted by the government, and his potential of finding a spouse was limited. Furthermore, he was broken-hearted to discover that his previous love interest had married the village headman's son. He found that he now more frequently lost control of his temper and flew into violent rages, a development he attributed to the harsh physical maltreatment he had received in prison.

Mudakir married Sumini, whose own father had also been imprisoned for alleged communism. Sumini bore the brunt of Mudakir's frequent violent outbursts along with her two sons, Budi and his older brother Kris. The family was continuously subjected to harassment, intimidation, and discrimination from the local community due to Mudakir's political status. Sumini was often sexually harassed by village men when her husband was away at work. Budi says that he was regularly mocked and avoided by other youth in the community, since he was as young as seven. When he was nine, he witnessed his seventeen-year-old brother Kris being attacked by his fellow villagers, stoned, beaten, stripped, and forced to walk naked on his hands. Sumini's attempts to report these incidents to local leaders were met by threats of sending her husband back to jail or endangering her family if she did "anything stupid." Thus, they moved to Yogyakarta for safety and in 2002 were told that villagers had destroyed their house.

Repetitive memories of such scenes led to much grief for Budi, accompanied by feelings of worthlessness, tension, and anger. Thoughts about these events were often associated with physical discomfort for the teen, and he suffered from feelings of physical heat, stabbing pains in his chest, shortness of breath, heart palpitations, and debilitating stomach cramps. Sometimes this distress would lead him to faint. His teachers noted that Budi would fall asleep at his desk. The nuns at the orphanage reported that he often awoke in the middle of the night calling out his brother's name, sometimes wracked by physical paroxysms that frightened them and led them to take him to the local hospital's emergency room. They had also on several occasions intercepted him standing on the edge of a nearby well, as he wrestled with his frequent suicidal thoughts. Based on all this information, Dr. Mahar diagnosed Budi with posttraumatic stress disorder, depression with psychotic features, and conversion disorder. He prescribed both pharmacotherapy and counseling.

Over time, the theme of revenge became prominent in Budi's everyday preoccupations, constituting a salient narrative arc linking his past, present, and future. When he first met Dr. Mahar in 2002, he felt that he had no future and imagined doing "evil things," saying he wanted "to assassinate, to torture… the way they did to my family members." Fortunately, as he enters adulthood he is finding newer and more socially acceptable ways of seeking this justice, particularly through the practice and ethos of martial arts. At first, Budi was drawn to the Japanese martial art Ninjutsu that he was introduced to through Manga and the movies. Then, in 2006, he began training in *pencak silat*, or Javanese martial arts. The combination of breathing exercises, meditation, and free fight have created a bodily, spiritual, and psychological outlet for coping with his emotions. Budi's yearnings for empowerment, revenge, and justice are slowly being channeled into visions of a more positive future. In more recent years, he has named peace and safety as the ultimate purpose of life, and characterized himself as a potential agent of justice.

Overall, by early 2007 Budi seemed to feel increasingly stable, confident, and in control. While cognitive and moral transitions accompanying his development were likely one source of these shifts, changes in sociopolitical circumstances also play a crucial role. Many of the events that initially traumatized Budi and his family occurred during a period of unrest following the Asian economic crisis, when there was an upsurge of local violence across numerous ethnic and religious divides, and ex-PKI members became convenient scapegoats. By the time of later interviews, this turmoil had eased slightly. Thus, Budi's sense of growing empowerment cannot be separated from the systematic changes that provided new structures of support, including legal recourse and a growing community of fellow survivors of political violence who are willing to share their perspectives with one another.

Kereta[11]

Pak Kereta was born in 1944 in a small rural village in central Bali. He lives in the house where he was born, has been a farmer his whole life, and has been married for over twenty-five years to a woman who is a member of his clan. They have two adult sons. At the age of twenty-one, he witnessed the massacre of several fellow villagers in the context of a political coup. Military and paramilitary forces purportedly belonging to the Indonesian Nationalist Party (PNI) entered his village looking for suspected members of the Indonesian Communist Party (PKI). A number of the villagers were singled out as PKI members and marched off to the local cemetery. Pak Kereta followed at a distance, along with a group of other villagers. He became terrified and felt sure that someone would hurt or kill him. He slipped away and climbed a tree; from there he witnessed the group being systematically hacked to death with machetes. Perhaps even more distressing, Pak Kereta also witnessed the torture and brutal murder of his own father just outside the family compound.

Soon after these horrifically traumatic events, Pak Kereta's long-standing problems with social withdrawal and fear began. He believes the constant terror he experienced in the wake of these murders weakened his life force. He began to have problems such as a loss of appetite, anxiety, heart palpitations, and insomnia. He felt an "inner pressure" weighing down his body, and lost his appetite. He had periods when he felt his mind go blank, and was frequently awoken by nightmares of being chased or people being butchered. Kereta became increasingly afraid of social gatherings and avoided public places and events.

Kereta married his wife in 1980. They had a son a year later, and then in 1984 they had a daughter. Unfortunately, the baby girl died soon after being delivered. Kereta describes this as the most difficult time in his life. In his grief he cried continuously. He also began seeing small, black figures, which he believed to be spirits known as the *wong samar*, or "the indistinct people," a commonly recognized form of potentially dangerous spirit in Bali. He first saw the *wong samar* while cutting the grass in the rice field, describing them as wandering over the grass and hiding in stagnant water. At first they made noises that he could not understand, but gradually the noises coalesced into words as they asked him, "Why don't you take care of yourself? Will you take care of us?" He felt the figures were competing with one another to enter his head, take possession of his body, and turn him into a communist.

Kereta would sometimes leave his home for days, hiding in remote rice fields or the deeply-cut canyons that crisscross the Balinese landscape. When he returned, he would explain to his family that he had been taken into the *wong samar* world and forced to marry a *wong samar* woman. He withdrew from his family and society even further, finally refusing to leave his room at all. At this point, his family took him to a *balian*, or traditional healer. According to the *balian*, his illness was caused by witchcraft, as the result of the ill wishes of unspecified village members. Pak Kereta stayed at the *balian*'s compound for a month to receive treatment.

Kereta's experiences with spirit beings gradually waned over time. When he did experience a relapse in symptoms, he would seek out different treatments, including further traditional healing and pharmacological interventions prescribed by psychiatrists at the Wanjaya and Bangli mental hospitals in Bali. He described long periods where he would not see or hear any spirits at all. However, during the national election campaigns in 2002–2003, when Indonesia elected its first-ever democratically elected president, the spirits returned. This time, they were asking Kereta to rejoin the Communist Party. In response he would wear a camouflage jacket and military helmet, and would sleep in his family temple courtyard. He believed these actions prevented the spirits from entering his body and forcing him to return to the PKI.

Kereta himself describes his illness as "*ngeb*," which has two distinct, but related, meanings and presentations in Balinese culture. *Ngeb* is an illness caused by witnessing something horrific, frightening, or bizarre. Seeing spirits, such as the *wong samar*, causes another variant of *ngeb*. As a result of these frightening or horrific experiences, sufferers put themselves in a self-imposed exile characterized by "muteness" (*membisu*) and lack of participation in the social world. Kereta believes his *ngeb* began with the witnessing of the massacre in 1965. Following the death of his infant daughter, his initial *ngeb* was compounded by visual and auditory hallucinations of the *wong samar* world.

While psychiatrists may refer to *ngeb* as mental illness, *ngeb* is also quite resonant with the Balinese practice of *puik*, intentional silence and social avoidance,[12] or a kind of social commentary indicating the person is *koh ngomong*, or literally "fed up of speaking."[13] This intentional silence was compounded by a national political culture that, until the fall of Suharto, made expressing distress and remembering 1965 a politically and socially dangerous, if not fatal, behavior. While it might seem obvious to outsiders that Kereta is a victim and survivor of a politically-based massacre, bordering on genocide, he is viewed by members of his community as being a perpetrator or instigator of the events of 1965, because he was a sympathizer with the Communist Party. Only in 2004 could his brother say that Kereta himself had been forgiven by villagers for causing the "disorder" of the events of 1965.

The silence of *ngeb* is reinforced by a cosmological context that leads to further suppression of social memory. *Ngeb* has been viewed as a means of political protest that can take two forms. One is the muteness that acts as a form of a resistance against political authority, in which the memorializing and even recall of a specific traumatic event, caused by state terror, has been suppressed. The other meaning of *ngeb* is a fear of memorializing or resisting cosmological authority, which, it is believed, causes the community to risk natural disasters, such as epidemics or volcanic eruptions. It is significant that Kereta has several friends who are similarly characterized as *ngeb*, and avoid social gatherings. His closest neighbor has symptoms very similar to his own, is also classified as *ngeb*, and also witnessed the events of 1965. Individuals with *ngeb* arising from 1965 can thus be seen as mute witnesses against the domination and control that the Suharto regime imposed on Indonesia following its ascendancy in 1965.

Lanny

Bu Lanny is a sixty-year-old, well-educated English teacher in Java, Indonesia. She was born into a socially respected, well-off Chinese-Indonesian family. Her father, Alex, was a prominent leader in the local Chinese Indonesian community and a successful businessman. Bu Lanny was very close to her father and describes herself as his favorite child. Alex owned several motorbikes, which was very rare at the time, and liked to show off little Lanny by having her ride these motorcycles with him. She described him as "my hero."

For several months after the 1965 coup, there were frequent riots led by youth brigades, paramilitary forces, and other groups associated with the PNI. Although few in Lanny's Chinese merchant community in Klaten were associated with the PKI, during this period more than 200 Chinese homes and businesses were burned, and numerous members of the Chinese community were arrested or disappeared. During one of these protests, hundreds of people surrounded Bu Lanny's house, throwing stones and axes and calling Alex's name. Shots were fired into the house, and the family hid in terror behind sandbags to avoid being killed.

For Bu Lanny, the most painful memory from this frightening event was her father's response to the violence. During the height of the terror, with the crowd shouting his name in anger, Alex ran away. Bu Lanny's last image of her father was of him leaning against a wall, hyperventilating in fear, having abandoned his family. Alex was picked up several weeks later and taken to a local internment camp near Klaten, where the family was able to see him one last time through the bars of his cell, and he ultimately "disappeared."

Witnessing her father's brutalization and imprisonment triggered a number of physical and psychological ailments for Lanny. She suffered from severe headaches, startled easily, panicked when she saw vertical lines or people in uniform, and often felt her heart beating rapidly. She became forgetful and could not remember people's names, even that of her desk-mate at school. She experienced episodes of mental "blankness" and would sometimes disassociate to the point where she would fall over while riding her bicycle, or find herself riding a motorcycle, not knowing how she got there or where she was going.

These personal struggles were in the context of the struggles of her family, who were suffering a financial crisis due to Alex's imprisonment and felt disconnected from the surrounding community, which included those who had organized the anti-Chinese campaigns. Her mother was distraught and unable to function, so Lanny bore the brunt of responsibility for caring for her younger siblings and the family business. Bu Lanny says that she reacted to this stressful situation – the emotional distress of her father's perceived cowardice, the pressure to keep her family together, and frustration at the injustices faced by her family – by becoming very angry and hateful. She was short-tempered, competitive, and obsessed with vengeance. However, Lanny had the support of her family members, who developed an enduring trust in each other. Through the encouragement of her grandmother, who always reassured her that her father was not a criminal but the victim of racism, she began to find ways to tell her story and come to peace with the sorrows she had suffered.

This way of coping helped her to survive, but also caused her great suffering until 1978, when she had a spiritual awakening. She had a profound experience of communicating with God, who promised he would always be with her and help her accomplish good things. This developed into a feeling of peace that led to an interest in Buddhism. In 1992, she had another compelling religious experience at a Buddhist meditation retreat in which she confronted some of her worst fears, embraced the impermanence of life, and found the key to her future work. She became a practicing Buddhist and founded a center for Buddhist meditation.

Once the New Order fell, Lanny and many like her began to take the first steps towards openly discussing the events of 1965. Despite the lingering political danger, Lanny has published her memoirs of the period and spoken about her experiences at public events and trauma training workshops for Indonesian professionals. Far from suppressing her memories of the events, she has found ways to make active use of them as historical testimony, evidence of her own resiliency, and still more importantly, as a basis for her conversion to Buddhism. This has made her a moving and effective teacher.

Lanny's history highlights the redeeming aspects of the will to bear witness that can be seen as crucial to the survivor's recovery. However, it should be noted that although this will may be a strong, perhaps universal, response in some people to forms of violence and trauma, its enactment and realization can take place only when political conditions allow it.

Degung

Degung Santikarma is an Indonesian anthropologist, journalist, and human rights activist from a high-caste Balinese family. He remembers enjoying a happy and well-off childhood. He was one of the first children in the neighborhood to have a car and he also enjoyed products from abroad, such as his coveted pair of waterproof swimming trunks. Degung was five years old in 1965. When the violence and chaos reached his village, at first he was too young to understand its implications; in fact, he remembers the thrill of houses burning and people crowded in the streets, and the novelty of being awake in the middle of the night and hiding in the temple. Gradually fear and horror took the place of excitement, however, as a beloved neighborhood doctor was killed and as Degung witnessed corpses piling up on the streets and riverbanks of his village.

Unfortunately, this danger would soon affect Degung's own immediate family. His parents were well educated and very politically active, often travelling outside the country to attend political conferences. His mother was renowned in the village for being a typist, which was associated with writing, a potentially subversive act in such volatile times. This activity made them targets of governmental violence. First, Degung's father was taken by the Nationalist Party for interrogation. Degung's aunt remembers her brother being paraded around town, called a criminal and a communist, and publicly humiliated. The family watched in fear and grief, but was unable to intercede. Ultimately, he was taken away and murdered. Degung's mother was a member of Gerwani, the women's organization affiliated with the Communist Party, and soon after his father's death she was also imprisoned. While in jail, she developed a relationship with a guard. This resulted in her being stigmatized by her family and accused of being a prostitute. Feeling shunned and threatened, Degung's mother left Degung with the family and married the prison guard. Members of Degung's extended family and village ostracized him as well, avoiding or taunting him because of his communist connections.

Degung felt deeply abandoned and rejected. Hoping to remove him from an upsetting situation and to help him reinvent himself without the stigma of being the son of communists, Degung's grandmother sent him to live with an uncle in Surabaya. The man was such a harsh disciplinarian that Degung ran away and found solace with a group of prostitutes who lived in the Wonokromo neighborhood. They cared for him, providing him with clothes and other necessities as they could. While Degung continued to attend school, he also lived as a street kid, surviving on food he had stolen himself. He said that he returned to Bali some years later as a "wild boy," but received some life-changing guidance from his uncle, who had also been imprisoned during the events of 1965. His uncle counseled him to remain dedicated to his education.

Degung went to college, where he learned about human rights and began activist work. He has also gone on to publish writing as an academic and a journalist. A significant part of his effort is to advocate for a more direct and open dialogue about the events of 1965; this in turn necessitates a more direct and open dialogue about the flows of power and political discourse in his native island of Bali and, more broadly, the country of Indonesia. Degung has been called a "maverick" for his writing and public speaking, which challenges stereotypes about Balinese life and boldly questions the status quo. Along with his wife, anthropologist Leslie Dwyer, he has written numerous articles about violence in Bali,[14] presented this work at national and international conferences, and engaged in public conversations and debates with other journalists and academics. Some of his works implicate globalized forms of commerce and international relationships that may perpetuate the silence around 1965. For example, Degung connects the mandates of a tourist economy, and its requisite demands of presenting Bali as a peaceful paradise with smiling inhabitants, with an enforced amnesia about past and present violence, unrest, or discontent on the island.[15]

Degung's case illustrates that to come to terms with the events of 1965 and resolve the grief they caused, dialogue must be engaged on personal, local, national, and international levels.

Discussion

For clinicians and others, a crucial aspect of these stories is captured by the diagnostic construct of posttraumatic stress disorder (PTSD). Such a diagnosis is helpful in that it may lead to specific guidelines for the prognosis and treatment of illness. But it can be argued that, in its very nature, psychiatric diagnosis decontextualizes or essentializes human problems, assuming that disorders can be generalized or treated similarly across diverse cultures or situations.[16] The diagnosis, with its use of the prefix "post" also fails to take into account the fact that episodes of violence and trauma may reverberate on multiple levels and persist through multiple generations. *40 Years of Silence* illustrates components of persisting and recurring trauma where the conditions responsible for the original trauma continue to exist, albeit in different forms. In Indonesia these conditions include an overt, lingering political threat; ongoing forced daily interaction with perpetrators of past violence; and cycles of familial instability, interpersonal prejudice, and domination. Instead of a discrete episode of trauma, there is layer upon layer of acute response to constantly changing threats – which may be real or imagined with equal effects.

Furthermore, the focus on personal pathology that PTSD suggests lacks a developed conceptual vocabulary for relational, social, communal, or cultural problems and de-emphasizes how trauma affects – and is affected by – families, kinship networks, and communities. *40 Years of Silence* encourages a consideration of some of these key issues of traumatic experience in the context of 1965, showing how these compelling factors may be even further compounded by cultural models of grief and suffering. For example, the complexity of remembering and forgetting in the Indonesian context is further deepened by prevalent cultural ideas about the harmful effects of expressing negative emotions or dwelling on painful events. Javanese and Balinese cultures value interpersonal harmony and therefore call for the management and regulation of strong or negative emotions.[17] Such cultural models provide their own locally coherent ways to orient, explain, and give meaning to traumatic events and their consequences.

Stories of trauma can be constructed for different purposes, whether these be to guide research or to enable people to live together despite the injuries of the past. The film clearly shows that what is at stake for individuals who have suffered trauma is usually much broader than any discrete psychiatric disorder, and the stories they have to tell encompass social and political dimensions that articulate with individual experience in complex ways. Although the suffering and impairment caused by trauma may be the primary focus for some individuals, in other cases the social, moral, and political dimensions of trauma are paramount, and the crucial questions center on how to make sense of violence and loss, and how to rebuild one's life and one's community in the face of stigmatization, discrimination, or genocide. Budi's case is compelling in the way it highlights the interactions between developmental changes, clinical symptoms, and familial and sociopolitical contexts. Kereta's case emphasizes the cultural specificity of trauma response and the potential for even disturbing symptoms of illness to act as a form of social and political resistance. Degung's case further situates this resistance within a context of activism and international networks of intervention. Finally, Lanny's case provides an example of how spiritual practice can provide a framework for healing and transformation.

Questions

1. *Memorializing Mass Killing*

   40 Years of Silence *suggests that grieving and healing processes were hindered by the state's control over the representation and memorialization of the events of 1965. It also clearly shows that giving voice to personal experiences of trauma or violence may be therapeutic for those who have suffered. However, the film also signals how complex this process of memorialization can be, due to such factors as multiple versions of past events and diverse personal experiences of trauma, a complex political history, cultural approaches to remembrance that favor silence, and present realities of social life where perpetrators and victims are still living in close proximity.*

   How can events of mass violence be successfully memorialized? Is it necessary that the remembrance occur on a national scale, or in concert with truth and reconciliation or retribution efforts? What role might the arts and/or media play in contributing to national or personal recovery from mass violence?

2. *Trauma in Context*

   All experiences of trauma occur within a specific social and cultural context. 40 Years of Silence *makes the point that in order to understand how best to treat victims of trauma, we need to have a clear understanding of their culture, history and social networks. Looking at the case studies shown in this film, identify some of the socio-cultural elements that affected each character's experience of trauma. How did these elements contribute to the experience, expression, repercussions of, and recovery from violence?*

   At the same time, 40 Years of Silence *highlights the importance of socio-cultural and psychological differences between subjects, even those coming from the same social and political contexts. It emphasizes the concept of personal agency and individual response to violence and recovery, and the possibility for improvement or a positive outcome over time. All four characters in this film find different ways to cope with their trauma without medication. What were some of the resilience factors that helped Budi, Lanny, Degung, and Kereta? How did each foster and express their "will to bear witness"?*

3. *Long-Term Outcomes of Trauma and Mass Killing*

> *Through its longitudinal perspective,* 40 Years of Silence *is able to illustrate some of the long-term effects and outcomes of political violence and trauma. Which aspects of suffering or grief lessen with time? What problems or challenges persist? How do different generations face and cope with the fallout of violence? What aspects of traumatic memory continue to resonate on personal, familial, collective, national, and international levels, and what opportunities are there for intervention at each of these levels?*

Bibliography

Cribb, Robert, ed. *The Indonesian Killings of 1965–1966: Studies from Java and Bali.* Clayton: Centre for Southeast Asian Studies, Monash University Australia, 1990.

Cribb, Robert and M. Ford, eds. "The Killings of 1965–66." *Inside Indonesia* 99 (January–March 2010). http://insideindonesia.org/content/view/1278/178/.

Dwyer, Leslie. "The intimacy of terror: Gender and the violence of 1965–1966 in Bali, Indonesia." *Intersections: Gender, history, and culture in the Asian context*, 10 (August 2004).
http://wwwsshe.murdoch.edu.au/intersections/issue10/dwyer.html.

Dwyer, Leslie and Degung Santikarma. "When the world turned to chaos: The violence of 1965–66 in Bali, Indonesia." *The Specter of Genocide: Mass murder in historical perspective*. Eds. Robert Gellately and Ben Kiernan. New York: Cambridge University Press, 2003.

Dwyer, Leslie and Degung Santikarma. "Speaking from the Shadows: Memories of Massacre in Bali." *After Mass Crime: Rebuilding States and Communities*. Eds. B. Pouligny, S. Chesterman, & A. Schnabel. Tokyo: United Nations University Press, 2006.

Kirmayer, Lawrence J., R. Lemelson, and M. Barad, eds. *Understanding Trauma: Integrating Biological, Clinical, and Cultural Perspectives*. New York: Cambridge University Press, 2007.

Lemelson, Robert, L. Kirmayer and M. Barad. "Trauma in Context: Integrating Biological, Clinical, and Cultural Perspectives." *Understanding Trauma: Integrating Biological, Clinical, and Cultural Perspectives*. Eds. Laurence J. Kirmayer, Robert Lemelson, and Mark Barad. New York: Cambridge University Press, 2007: 451–474.

Lemelson, Robert, N. Supartini and E. Ng. "Anak PKI: A longitudinal case study of social ostracism, violence, and bullying on an adolescent Javanese boy." *Formative Experience: The Interaction of Caregiving, Culture, and Developmental Psychobiology*. Eds. Carol M. Worthman et al. New York: Cambridge University Press, in press. 378–389.

Lemelson, Robert and L. K. Suryani. "The Spirits, Ngeb, and the Social Suppression of Memory: A Complex Clinical Case from Bali." *Culture, Medicine, and Psychiatry* 30 (2006): 389–413.

Robinson, Geoffrey. *The Dark Side of Paradise: Political Violence in Bali*. Ithaca: Cornell University Press, 1998.

Roosa, John. *Pretext for Mass Murder: The September 30 Movement and Suharto's Coup D'Etat in Indonesia*. New Perspectives in SE Asian Studies. Madison: University of Wisconsin Press, 2006.

Santikarma, Degung. "Koh Ngomong, the Balinese Tactic and Spirit of Resistance." Fourth International Bali Studies Conference, Sydney University, 1995.

Santikarma, Degung and Leslie Dwyer. "Posttraumatic Politics: Violence, Memory, and Biomedical Discourse in Bali." *Understanding Trauma: Integrating Biological, Clinical, and Cultural Perspectives*. Eds. Robert Lemelson, L. Kirmayer and M. Barad. New York: Cambridge University Press, 2007: 403–432.

Wardaya, Baskara T. *Supersemar Revealed! From the CIA to the Creeping Coup D'Etat Against Bung Karno*. Jakarta: Galang Press, 2006.

Zurbuchen, Mary. "History, Memory and the "1965 Incident" in Indonesia." *Asian Survey* 42.4 (2002): 564–581.

Notes

1. Robert Cribb, ed., *The Indonesian Killings of 1965–1966: Studies from Java and Bali* (Clayton: Centre for Southeast Asian Studies, Monash University Australia, 1990).
2. Geoffrey Robinson, *The Dark Side of Paradise: Political Violence in Bali* (Ithaca: Cornell University Press, 1998).
3. John Roosa, *Pretext for Mass Murder: The September 30 Movement and Suharto's Coup d'Etat in Indonesia*, (New Perspectives in SE Asian Studies, Madison: University of Wisconsin Press, 2006).
4. Mary Zurbuchen, "History, Memory and the '1965 Incident' in Indonesia," *Asian Survey* 42.4 (2002): 564–581; Robert Cribb and M. Ford, eds., "The Killings of 1965–66," *Inside Indonesia* 99 (January–March 2010), http://insideindonesia.org/content/view/1278/178.
5. More information about *40 Years of Silence* can be found at www.40yearsofsilence.com. The film is available through Documentary Educational Resources, www.der.org, and through Amazon.com.
6. Annie Pohlman, "*Testimonio* and Telling Women's Narratives of Genocide, Torture and Political Imprisonment in Post-Suharto Indonesia," *Life Writing* 5.1 (April 2008): 47–60; Katharine McGregor, "Sensitive Truths," *Inside Indonesia* 99 (January–March 2010), http://insideindonesia.org/content/view/1271/47/; Dahlia Gratia Setiyawan, "Terror in Tandes," *Inside Indonesia* 99 (Jan–March 2010), http://insideindonesia.org/content/view/1279/47/.
7. *40 Years of Silence* was based on over 400 hours of anthropological interviews, from 1997–2006, conducted by the first author as part of a larger research project on culture and mental illness in Indonesia.

8. Additional information and discussion about each of the case studies addressed below can be found in the film's study guide, available at http://www.40yearsofsilence.com/page/study-guide.

9. Robert Lemelson, L. Kirmayer, and M. Barad, "Trauma in Context: Integrating Biological, Clinical, and Cultural Perspectives," *Understanding Trauma: Integrating Biological, Clinical, and Cultural Perspectives*, Laurence J. Kirmayer, Robert Lemelson, and Mark Barad, eds. (Cambridge: Cambridge University Press, 2007), pp. 451–474.

10. A more in-depth consideration of Budi's case can be found in Robert Lemelson, Ninik Supartini and Emily Ng, "Anak PKI: A longitudinal case study of social ostracism, violence, and bullying on an adolescent Javanese boy," *Formative Experiences: The Interaction of Caregiving, Culture, and Developmental Psychobiology* (Cambridge University Press, Forthcoming March 2010), pp. 378–389.

11. A more in-depth consideration of Kereta's case can be found in Robert Lemelson and L. K. Suryani, "The Spirits, Ngeb, and the Social Suppression of Memory: A Complex Clinical Case from Bali," *Culture, Medicine, and Psychiatry* 30 (2006): 389–413.

12. Margaret Mead and Gregory Bateson, *Balinese Character* (New York: New York Academy of Sciences, 1942); Clifford Geertz, *The Interpretation of Cultures* (New York: Basic Books, 1973).

13. Degung Santikarma and Leslie Dwyer, "Posttraumatic Politics: Violence, Memory, and Biomedical Discourse in Bali," *Understanding Trauma: Integrating Biological, Clinical, and Cultural Perspectives*, Robert Lemelson, L. Kirmayer, and M. Barad, eds. (Cambridge: Cambridge University Press, 2007) pp. 403–432.

14. Leslie Dwyer and Degung Santikarma, "When the World Turned to Chaos: The Violence of 1965–66 in Bali, Indonesia," *The Specter of Genocide: Mass Murder in Historical Perspective*, B. Kiernan and R. Gellately eds. (New York: Cambridge University Press, 2003); Leslie Dwyer and Degung Santikarma, "Speaking from the Shadows: Memories of Massacre in Bali," *After Mass Crime: Rebuilding States and Communities*, B. Pouligny, S. Chesterman, & A. Schnabel, eds. (Tokyo: United Nations University Press, 2006).

15. Degung Santikarma and Leslie Dwyer, "Posttraumatic Politics," 2007.

16. Lemelson, Kirmayer, and Barad, "Trauma in Context," 2007.

17. Unni Wikkan, *Managing Turbulent Hearts: A Balinese Formula* (Chicago: University of Chicago Press, 1990); Douglas Hollan and Jane Wellenkamp, *Contentment and Suffering: Culture and Experience in Toraja* (New York: Columbia University Press, 1994).

40 *Years of Silence* in the Context of Suharto's Brutal Reign

James G. Paharik

Associate Professor of Sociology,
Seton Hill University, Greensburg, PA

Robert Lemelson's film *40 Years of Silence: An Indonesian Tragedy* compellingly describes the lingering pain produced by the mass murders that accompanied General Suharto's sudden seizure of power in the mid-1960s. The violence did lasting damage to individuals, families, and communities, and was compounded by the decades-long suppression of public inquiry into the reasons behind the widespread killings. Even today, as researchers like Lemelson are learning more about the victims of those atrocities, many questions about the nature of the crimes and the motives of the perpetrators remain unanswered.

One of the most basic of those questions would seem to be whether or not the murders, which claimed the lives of hundreds of thousands of Indonesians between October 1965 and March 1966, constitute genocide. Yet even on this topic there is ambiguity. A primary reason for the uncertainty is not in this case simply lack of information, but the fact that those believed to be communists were the primary target of the violence. The difficulty is that as a group that shares a political orientation, communists do not fall clearly within the boundaries of the United Nations Convention of 1948, which states that genocide is "the intent to destroy, in whole or in part, a national, ethnical, racial or religious group."[1] In light of this, scholars who have been reluctant to label the murders genocide have described them in various ways, such as "the Indonesian massacres," "mass killings," "politicide," or simply "the Indonesian killings of 1965–66."[2]

On the other hand, many others have argued that the language of the U.N. Convention is inappropriately restrictive. They have pointed out that literal application of the resolution would exempt other purges directed at political parties or classes from the charge of genocide, including those committed in Stalin's Soviet Union and by the Khmer Rouge. In fact, the original draft of the U.N. resolution did include "political groups" among the list of victims of genocide, but the category was removed due to pressure by the Soviet Union and its allies.[3] Scholars who maintain that groups targeted on the basis of political or class affiliations can also be the victims of genocide have, therefore, tended to place the 1965–66 Indonesian murders among the genocides of the twentieth century.[4]

In evaluating the nature of the atrocities, it is important to begin with the recognition that the murders in Indonesia during this period are indeed comparable, in terms of both numbers and types of victims, to other cases of genocide. However, identifying an act as genocide requires inquiring beyond numbers and targeted populations to consider the nature and the aims of the perpetrator. In order to fully understand the murders of 1965–66, then, it is necessary to place them in the context of Suharto's thirty-two-year reign, rather than approaching them as an isolated event. From that perspective, we may then inquire into whether Suharto's Indonesia resembled other regimes that perpetrated genocide.

Genocides during the past century have been almost exclusively the work of states that have used them to achieve policy objectives. The definition of genocide as "politically sanctioned mass murder" that is "intended to serve the ends of the state" effectively encapsulates the nature of a wide range of genocides, including the Armenian genocide, the Holocaust, and genocides in the Soviet Union, Cambodia, Bosnia, and Rwanda.[5] To what extent was this true of the murders of 1965–66 in Indonesia?

In the following pages, I argue that when the Suharto years are viewed in their totality, it becomes evident that the anti-communist purge was part of a pattern of brutality by a regime whose basic mode of operation resembled in many respects those of the states listed above. In its use of propaganda, relentless authoritarianism, the employment of mass murder as an instrument of state policy, and in blatantly placing the interests of its leaders above the well-being of the nation, Suharto's Indonesia exhibited characteristics typical of genocidal states.

Demonization and Oppression

Propaganda plays an integral role in genocide; states disseminate propaganda to both demonize their enemies and to present themselves in an idealized light. General Suharto rose to power in the aftermath of the murder of six high-ranking officers in the early morning hours of October 1, 1965. Suharto and his allies portrayed the murders as an "attempted coup" and themselves as the true defenders of the state. Though the murders were likely carried out by a small cadre within the military, Suharto used them as a pretext for launching a massive purge of members of the Indonesian Communist Party (PKI) and suspected sympathizers, who were said to be responsible for the killings.[6] Public anger was stoked by lurid rumors that the officers had been tortured and castrated by communist women, and that communist troops were preparing a bloody revolutionary overthrow of the government.[7]

This propaganda was used to rationalize the murders not only of PKI members but of many other persons, including teachers and artists, who were thought to have "leftist" leanings. The killings were swift and brutal; within six months, hundreds of thousands of people were dead. Collective punishment was inflicted in many areas; in some regions believed to be communist, the entire population of villages was exterminated.[8] Hundreds of thousands who were not killed were tortured or imprisoned, including on the infamous Buru Island.[9] In a process that would be repeated in later purges carried out during the Suharto regime, sexual torture and rape were common. In this case, women who were suspected of having a connection to the communist Gerwani, or Indonesian Women's Movement, were especially targeted.[10]

Propaganda in Suharto's regime not only served to legitimize the assault on communists but to inspire confidence and support in Suharto's leadership. Communism was vilified as a foreign ideology which had "infected" the nation; it had to be cleansed so that Indonesia could return to its authentic cultural roots.[11] Suharto's "New Order" was said to embody the true Indonesian way of *pancasila*, which was oriented toward order, harmony, progress, and patrimonial leadership.[12] It fell to General Suharto, who styled himself as the "Father of Development," to teach the people how to be true to their Indonesian character and to lead them toward a more prosperous future.[13]

The reality of life under Suharto was, however, sharply at odds with this utopian imagery. Throughout its long existence, the Suharto regime maintained its antagonism toward Indonesians with "communist" sympathies. Even after spending years and sometimes decades in prison, those accused of being communists, along with their families, continued to suffer persecution. Their property, which was almost invariably confiscated by the state, was not returned; they were barred from employment in many fields, often were not allowed to travel freely within the country or permitted to travel abroad, and were subject to persistent surveillance. Those who had escaped the genocide by fleeing to other countries were not permitted to return home.[14]

However, purported communists were not the only citizens who were oppressed by the state. In Suharto's New Order, the shifting definition of "leftists" was broad enough to include virtually any critics or opponents of the regime. The state used the charge of "communism" as a means of enforcing obedience to its dictates; patriotism was equated with support for Suharto's policies. Strikes became illegal, and rival political parties were banned on the grounds that they were contrary to the principles of *pancasila*; the media, too, came under state control.[15] Listening to certain kinds of music, reading "subversive" books, and even writing graffiti or wearing T-shirts with symbols or slogans that implied any criticism of the government or Suharto could result in arrest and imprisonment.[16]

Ominously, the Suharto regime employed both legal and extra-judicial means of exerting its might against citizens. In addition to the intervention of its powerful regular forces (ARBI) in domestic policing, it made use of Special Forces known as the Kopassus for assassinations of suspected insurgents. Even more disturbingly, shadowy "death squads" served the regime frequently during Suharto's reign, as in the massacres of 1965–66, at "election" times when Suharto and his party were invariably returned to office, and in the bloody assaults on Irian Jaya and East Timor.[17]

Mass Murder as State Policy

In terms of the numbers of people killed, the anti-communist genocide of the early months of Suharto's regime was its largest venture in mass murder, but it was only the first of several campaigns where mass killing, torture, and imprisonment of civilians was used to achieve political ends. In the regions of Irian Jaya and East Timor, Suharto's military engaged in protracted occupations that entailed horrific violations of human rights. It is important to note that these military interventions had nothing to do with opposing communism. Instead, the violence was designed to subdue and subjugate the populations of these areas so that the state, along with Suharto himself, could increase in wealth and power.

Under Suharto, Indonesia forcibly annexed West Papua, New Guinea, a territory that is geographically and culturally part of Melanesia. Though it had no historical connection to Indonesia, the territory was claimed by Suharto and renamed Irian Jaya. Beginning in the late 1960s, a rapid and highly destructive pattern was inaugurated that included: massive confiscation of land; dispossession and displacement of indigenous populations; waves of immigrants from Indonesia who dramatically altered the demographics of the region; reckless plundering of natural resources; the imposition of Indonesian language and culture on the population; the undermining of indigenous cultures; and violent suppression of resistance.[18] As in other areas of the country, the Suharto government prevented freedom of speech and political expression in Irian Jaya, and dealt with any show of resistance swiftly and harshly. Military violence against non-combatants was pervasive; attacks on women were brutal and systematic, and included rape, sexual mutilation, and murder.[19]

West Papua is an area rich in resources such as copper, gold, and lumber. The Suharto government reaped huge profits from clearing the rainforests and from the extraction of minerals; it invested in copper smelters and paper mills to process the raw materials, and constructed dams and hydroelectric plants. Yet from all of this economic development, very little benefit accrued to Papuans in the form of employment or public resources.[20] At the same time, a disastrous consequence of the rampant logging and other activities was the destruction of the habitats of many indigenous tribes, placing in severe jeopardy the cultural survival of as many as one million Papuans.[21]

Many of the above methods were again followed by Suharto's regime in the conquest and subjugation of East Timor. East Timor was a Portuguese colony that was granted independence in 1974; in the months following independence from Portugal, a nascent autonomous leadership emerged. Suharto, however, was determined to gain control of the region, and soon launched an invasion. Throughout the remainder of his years as head of state, Indonesia waged a deadly military campaign against the people of East Timor.

Indonesian troops in East Timor implemented a ruthless strategy of "encirclement and annihilation." The process began with aerial bombings and proceeded with the burning of fields and villages. Once flushed into the open and surrounded, residents were captured. The lucky ones were forced to leave the area; others were tortured, sent to internment camps, or executed.[22] Over the course of the twenty-four-year occupation of East Timor, Indonesian forces murdered thousands of people, and many thousands more died as a result of starvation and mistreatment in prison camps. Indeed, a recently completed, comprehensive United Nations report concluded that a total of more than 180,000 civilians perished as a direct result of the Indonesian actions, which represents an astonishing one-third of the pre-invasion population[23]

Though Indonesian troops faced some limited resistance from badly outnumbered Timorese forces, Indonesian soldiers in East Timor, as elsewhere, engaged in actions that represent an atrocious violation of the rules of combat. Napalm and other chemical weapons poisoned the food and water supplies in many parts of the country. Civilians were tortured, mutilated, and publicly murdered in hideous ways, such as being burned alive or beheaded.[24] Again, as in the regime's other campaigns of violence, the brutality directed against women was an integral part of the military plan. Indonesian troops engaged in rape as a weapon of war, establishing "rape houses" where victims were repeatedly assaulted. In addition to the beatings and rapes by soldiers, there is evidence that East Timorese women were violated in a quite different way in Indonesian-run hospitals and clinics, which sometimes administered birth control drugs without consent; some women were also sterilized against their will.[25] Forced birth control and forced sterilization constitute a violation of the United Nations Convention on Genocide, which prohibits "actions intended to prevent births" within a population.

Suharto's Predatory Rule

There is sometimes a temptation to try to explain the horrific actions of genocidal states in terms of their ideological principles. If the antisemitism of the Nazis led them to murder Jews and the anti-capitalism of the Soviets guided their purge of the bourgeoisie and the "kulak" class, perhaps, it might be reasoned, it was Suharto's anti-communism that led to the genocide of 1965–66. In fact, the history of the Suharto regime tells quite a different story. The publicly-annunciated anti-communism of the regime was to a significant extent a matter of propaganda and expedience rather than an expression of ideological conviction. Anti-communist ideology was highly effective in mobilizing support both domestically and internationally; despite its horrendous record of human rights violations, Suharto's Indonesia received consistent and enthusiastic backing from Western nations, particularly Australia and the United States.[26] At the same time, by so decisively and brutally moving against the PKI, Suharto eliminated a potential rival for power.

As with other genocidal states, then, Suharto's Indonesia moved from one group of victims to another as the need to eliminate or subjugate them arose. Just as Stalin, for example, shifted from class warfare to purges of ethnic groups and then to murders of those who might challenge his leadership of the Bolshevik Party, Suharto directed the wrath of the state against any faction that he believed posed an obstacle to increasing his power. The only principle that unites the seemingly disconnected campaigns of violence against communists and the people of Irian Jaya and East Timor is that these actions were judged to be in the interests of Suharto and his regime.

In following its ruthless self-interest, Suharto's state wrought havoc not only on particular groups inside and outside the country, but on the nation as a whole. As a predatory ruler, Suharto did not distinguish between the interests of the state and his own self-interest.[27] The major policies Suharto pursued, from eliminating internal opponents to invading other nations, invariably bolstered his own personal wealth and power. The Suharto government personified what Indonesians term KKN, for *Korrupsi, Kollusi, Nepotisme* (corruption, collusion, nepotism). Though Suharto is sometimes described as having been "pro-capitalist," during his rule the state greatly expanded its control over the economy through ownership of businesses and protectionist legislation. In many cases, the state passed laws to ensure that certain companies owned by Suharto or his relatives had a monopoly on the market. For example, Suharto's cousin and two of his sons benefitted greatly from their exclusive control over the import of plastics into the country.[28]

Indeed, so successful was Suharto's manipulation of the market that at one point he was the sixth wealthiest person in the world. He amassed a fortune worth an estimated $16 billion, yet even that gargantuan sum represents only a portion of the wealth of the nation that found its way to his personal treasury and into the hands of his wife, six children, and assorted family members.[29] As the public's attention to his astounding wealth grew, Suharto became defensive. When *Time* magazine's Asia edition cited a World Bank report identifying Suharto as one of the worst examples of an embezzling leader of a developing nation and estimated the worth of his family at

$15–35 billion, Suharto sued. The Indonesian Supreme Court determined that Suharto's reputation had indeed been tarnished and ordered the magazine to pay him over $100 million in damages (*Time* appealed the ruling).[30]

During his years in power, Suharto was often popularly imagined as a shadowy "puppet-master" who controlled the fate of the nation but was largely invisible. The efficacy of his regime in stifling political discussion and disguising its objectives and actions made it impossible for Indonesians to gain a clear sense of the terrible events of that period. In Western nations, too, the vision of many was clouded by the sympathetic light in which Suharto was cast by politicians and most of the media. However, since the end of his rule it has become increasingly possible to gain a more accurate view of the nature of General Suharto's regime. Mainstream reporting is now significantly more critical than it was during the height of the New Order. By the time of his death in 2008, articles were more likely to emphasize Suharto's avarice and authoritarianism than his economic achievements.[31]

Robert Lemelson's work with survivors is a vital part of the long overdue movement to honestly confront the terrible damage done by the Suharto years. Only when the truth is told can the healing of individuals, families, communities, and the nation as a whole begin.

Questions

1. List two views of the definition of genocide that were discussed in this article. Based on what you have read, which view do you support and why?

2. The article points out that the Suharto regime used propaganda both to attack certain groups and to present the regime in a positive light. Describe this dual use of propaganda.

3. Nazi Germany's victims included Jews as well as other groups; the same was true of the Soviet Union under Stalin, Cambodia under Pol Pot, etc. How would you list and describe the victims of the violence in Indonesia?

4. The violence under Suharto was particularly disturbing because of the way it targeted women, and because many acts were deliberately carried out in public. What do you think the military purpose of this kind of violence was?

5. Many nations of the West were quite friendly toward, and supportive of, the Suharto regime, despite its record of human rights violations and its corruption. What factors could help to explain this anomaly?

Bibliography

Bertrand, Jacques. *Nationalism and Ethnic Conflict in Indonesia*. Cambridge, UK: Cambridge University Press, 2004.

Bourchier, David and Vedi R. Hadiz, eds. *Indonesian Politics and Society: A Reader*. New York, NY: RoutledgeCourzon, 2003.

Cribb, Robert. "From Petrus to Ninja: Death Squads in Indonesia." *Death Squads in Global Perspective: Murder with Deniability*. Eds. Bruce B. Campbell and Arthur D. Brenner. New York: St Martin's Press, 2000: 181–202.

Cribb, Robert. "The Indonesian Massacres." *Century of Genocide: Critical Essays and Eyewitness Accounts*. Eds. Samuel Totten, William S. Parsons and Israel W. Charny. New York, NY: Routledge, 2004: 233–264.

Cribb, Robert. "The Indonesian Genocide of 1965–66." *Teaching about Genocide: Issues, Approaches and Resources*. Ed. Samuel Totten. Greenwich, CT: Information Age Publishing, 2004: 133–142.

Dwyer, Leslie and Degung Santikarma. "'When the World Turned to Chaos': 1965 and its Aftermath in Bali, Indonesia." *The Specter of Genocide: Mass Murder in Historical Perspective*. Eds. Robert Gellately and Ben Kiernan. Cambridge, UK: Cambridge University Press, 2003: 289–306.

Heryanto, Ariel. "Where Communism Never Dies: Violence, Trauma and Narration in the Last Cold War Capitalist Authoritarian State." *International Journal of Cultural Studies* 2.2 (Aug 1999): 147–177.

Robertson-Snape, Fiona. "Corruption, Collusion and Nepotism in Indonesia." *Third World Quality* 20.3 (Jun 1999): 589–602.

Simpson, Brad. "'Illegally and Beautifully': The United States, the Indonesian Invasion of East Timor and the International Community, 1974–76." *Cold War History* 5.3 (Aug 2005): 281–315.

Smith, Roger W. "State Power and Genocidal Intent: On the Uses of State Power in the Twentieth Century." *Studies in Comparative Genocide*. Eds. Levon Chorbajian and George Shirinian. New York, NY: St. Martin's Press, 1999: 3–14.

Wieringa, Saskia. "The Birth of the New Order State in Indonesia: Sexual Politics and Nationalism." *Journal of Women's History* 15.1 (Spring, 2003): 70–91.

Notes

1. Frank Chalk and Kurt Jonassohn, *The History and Sociology of Genocide: Analyses and Case Studies* (New Haven, CT: Yale University Press, 1990), p. 10.
2. Robert Cribb, "The Indonesian Massacres" in Samuel Totten, William S. Parsons and Israel W. Charny, eds., *Century of Genocide: Critical Essays and Eyewitness Accounts* (New York, NY: Routledge, 2004); Anthony Deutsch, "Survivors Describe Mass Killings under Indonesian Dictator Suharto," *The Irrawaddy News Magazine*, Jan. 29, 2008; Charles Coppel, "1965 Genocide of Indonesian Chinese Did Not Occur," *Eureka*

Street, 16, September 4, 2006 argues that the killings should properly be called "politicide"; Robert Cribb, ed., *The Indonesian Killings of 1965-66: Studies from Java and Bali* (Clayton, Australia: Monash University Centre of Southeast Asian Studies, 1990).

3. Chalk and Jonassohn, *The History and Sociology of Genocide*, p. 10.

4. Ibid, pp. 378-383; Eric Weitz, *A Century of Genocide: Utopias of Race and Nation* (Princeton, NJ: Princeton University Press, 2003), p. 9. In his recent work, Cribb has also referred to the killings as genocide, see Robert Cribb, "The Indonesian Genocide of 1965-66" in Samuel Totten, ed., *Teaching About Genocide: Issues, Approaches, and Resources* (Greenwich, CT: Information Age Publishing, 2004), pp. 138-140.

5. Roger W. Smith, "State Power and Genocidal Intent: On the Uses of Genocide in the Twentieth Century" in Levon Chorbajian and George Shirinian, eds., *Studies in Comparative Genocide* (New York, NY: St. Martin's Press, 1999), p. 3.

6. Cribb, "The Indonesian Genocide of 1965-66," p. 135. Cribb points out that while membership in and support for the PKI were strong, the PKI posed no military threat to the Sukarno regime.

7. Cribb, "The Indonesian Massacres," p. 236.

8. Cribb, "The Indonesian Genocide of 1965-66," p. 136.

9. Thomas Fuller, "Suharto's Gulag," *New York Times*, March 15, 2000, http://www.nytimes.com/2000/03/15/news/15iht-jak.2.t_0.html?pagewanted=1.

10. Annie Pohlman, "Women and the Indonesian Killings of 1965-1966: Gender Variables and Possible Directions for Research," Conference Proceedings of the Asian Studies Association of Australia, 2004, pp. 8-9; Saskia Wieringa, "The Birth of the New Order State in Indonesia: Sexual Politics and Nationalism," *Journal of Women's History* 15.1 (Spring, 2003): 75-78.

11. Leslie Dwyer and Degung Santikarma, "'When the World Turned to Chaos': 1965 and its Aftermath in Bali, Indonesia," in Robert Gellately and Ben Kiernan, eds., *The Specter of Genocide: Mass Murder in Historical Perspective* (Cambridge, UK: Cambridge University Press, 2003), pp. 295-297.

12. David Bourchier and Vedi R. Hadiz, eds., *Indonesian Politics and Society: A Reader* (New York, NY: RoutledgeCurzon, 2003), pp. 8-9.

13. Weitz, in *A Century of Genocide: Utopias of Race and Nation*, has shown that such state-generated myths that envision a bright future only for certain segments of the populations are common to genocidal regimes.

14. Rob Goodfellow and M. Dwi Marianto, "Buajingan! Indonesian Art, Literature, and State Violence around the Downfall of President Soeharto," in David E. Lorey and William H. Beezley eds., *Genocide, Collective Violence, and Popular Memory: The Politics of Remembrance in the Twentieth Century* (Wilmington, DE: Scholarly Resources, 2002), p. 126; David Hill, "Knowing Indonesia from Afar: Indonesian Exiles and Australian Academics," Conference Proceedings of the Asian Studies Association of Australia, 2008.

15. Adam Schwarz, "Indonesia after Suharto," *Foreign Affairs* 76.4 (Jul/Aug 1997): 123-124; Duncan McCargo, "Killing the Messenger: The 1994 Press Bannings and the Demise of Indonesia's New Order," *Harvard International Journal of Press/Politics* 4.1 (Jan 1999): 30-32.

16. Ariel Heryanto, "Where Communism Never Dies: Violence, Trauma and Narration in the Last Cold War Capitalist Authoritarian State," *International Journal of Cultural Studies* 2.2 (Aug 1999): 157-164.

17. Robert Cribb, "From Petrus to Ninja: Death Squads in Indonesia," in Bruce B. Campbell and Arthur D. Brenner, eds., *Death Squads in Global Perspective: Murder with Deniability* (New York: St Martin's Press, 2000). For a discussion of how Suharto's regime sought to evade responsibility for military abuses, see John Virgoe, "Impunity Resurgent: The Politics of Military Accountability in Indonesia, 1998-2001," *Asian Affairs* 39.1 (Mar 2008): 95-98.

18. This list invites comparison with actions undertaken by other genocidal states, including Nazi Germany, whose aggressive search for *Lebensraum* included the repopulation or "Aryanization" of areas to the east.

19. Stuart Kirsch, "Rumour and Other Narratives of Political Violence in West Papua," *Critique of Anthropology* 22.1 (Mar 2002): 64-67. For this reason, the Suharto government strictly limited the access of reporters to Irian Jaya; those who did enter the region were often threatened or attacked by soldiers. See Russ W. Baker, "The Deforesting of Irian Jaya," *The Nation*, Feb. 7, 1994, p. 163.

20. Jacques Bertrand, *Nationalism and Ethnic Conflict in Indonesia* (Cambridge, UK: Cambridge University Press, 2004) p. 151.

21. "Indigenous Peoples – The Anti-Slavery Approach," *Cultural Survival Quarterly* 8.4 (Winter, 1984).

22. Bertrand, *Nationalism and Ethnic Conflict in Indonesia*, p. 138. See also John Pilger, "Land of the Dead," *The Nation*, April 4, 1994, pp. 550-552.

23. Sian Powell, "UN Verdict on East Timor," *The Australian*, January 19, 2006.

24. Ibid.

25. Christine Mason, "Women, Violence, and Non-Violent Resistance in East Timor," *Journal of Peace Research* 42.6 (Nov 2005): 743-745.
26. Brad Simpson, "'Illegally and Beautifully': The United States, the Indonesian Invasion of East Timor and the International Community, 1974-76," *Cold War History* 5.3 (Aug 2005): 291-298; Paul Paolucci, "Classical Sociological Theory and Modern Social Problems: Marx's Concept of the Camera Obscura and the Fallacy of Individualistic Reductionism," *Critical Sociology* 27.1 (Jan 2001): 83-87.
27. Anna Grzymala-Busse, "Beyond Clientelism: Incumbent State Capture and State Formation," *Comparative Political Studies* 41.45 (Apr 2008): 645-646.
28. Fiona Robertson-Snape, "Corruption, Collusion and Nepotism in Indonesia," *Third World Quality* 20.3 (Jun 1999): 594.
29. "Suharto," *The Economist*, Feb. 2, 2008: 97.
30. "Time and the Dictator," *New York Times*, December 29, 2007: 16.
31. Seth Mydans, "A Dying Suharto Avoids Answering for Crimes," *New York Times*, January 20, 2008: 10; "Epitaph on a Crook and a Tyrant," *The Economist*, February 2, 2008: 14.

Indonesian Politicide:
A Review of Robert Lemelson's Film
40 Years of Silence: An Indonesian Tragedy

■ ■ ■ ■ ■ ■ ■ ■ ■ ■

Michael Cary

Professor of History and Political Science,
Seton Hill University, Greensburg, PA

A recent documentary, *40 Years of Silence: An Indonesian Tragedy*, directed by Robert Lemelson and released late in 2009, is a complex film. Its title derives from an event heretofore little understood in the West, the genocidal murder of up to one million Indonesians, on the islands of Java and Bali, in 1965 and 1966. More than a documentation of a tragedy, this film provides educators and researchers with a valuable tool for exploring the complicated issues surrounding the all-too-common[1] events of political repression, mass killings, and political exile, as well as the damaging effects of such events over the long term on human psychology and culture. As a case study, it also illustrates possible obstacles and pathways to reconciliation after tragedy.

Dr. Lemelson, who directed this film, is a psychological anthropologist, and the film emerges from his "psychocultural"[2] research in Indonesia. Stories told by four families, victims of the violence of the Thirtieth of September Movement of 1965, are at the heart of this project. Early in the film, on camera, Lemelson indicates his orientation toward the individual personality affected by culture and change: "We need to have a sufficient understanding of history and politics and culture as reflected through their experience and understood by them." Thus, the stories of the four families are interwoven with the larger history of the genocide/politicide[3] in Indonesia in 1965–1966, and with ripples of successive, derivative events. Each of the four case studies is presented, through interviews illustrated with historical news footage, in historical order, beginning with an exploration of how their lives were lived in the time prior to September 30, 1965. Next, their experiences during those years of genocide are related, followed by an examination of the long, repressive years of suffering and silence. Finally, the film looks at some changes that have come to Indonesia in the years after Suharto's resignation in 1998, a period when the long-hidden truth about the events of 1965 is gradually emerging.

Watching the film, we become acquainted with intimate details of tragic lives – lives lived out in sadness, but also with courage and in modest dignity. In communicating these qualities, *40 Years of Silence* elevates its protagonists above the status of victim, thereby infusing the film with hope. In any study of genocide, realistic hopefulness is a precious thing that we need to recognize and claim.

Beyond the psychocultural insights, Lemelson documents political events of 1965–1966, using interviews with academic researchers to tell the story of how a military coup d'état, planned and executed by Indonesian Army officers, was blamed instead on the Indonesian Communist Party (PKI) and used to rationalize the execution of thousands of purported PKI members or supporters. In so doing, the film takes its place as an important historical and political document, valuable for getting the word out about this disturbing event in recent world history.

Reflecting upon the events portrayed in *40 Years of Silence*, along with similar events from Cambodia, Rwanda, Bosnia, Sudan, and other places, two things become clear. First, despite statements of "Never Again" after the Holocaust, genocide recurs with disturbing frequency, and policymakers are seldom moved into action to prevent, interrupt, or punish that crime. Second, because of this, it becomes imperative to take a comparative approach to the study of genocide and politicide. A comparative approach can address conditions and issues that have often remained ignored in the past, including the possibility that non-state actors can be the perpetrators of efforts to destroy rival ethnic and/or political groups, as occurred in Bosnia in 1992–1993.[4] More important, a comparative approach can substitute an empirical definition of genocide/politicide for a legalistic one (as that deriving from the U.N. Convention), thereby taking advantage of the strengths of social science analysis. The goal is to develop and refine "warning systems to detect humanitarian disasters in the making."[5] *40 Years of Silence* provides more testimony in support of this imperative.

Another strength of Lemelson's film is as a case study in propaganda. Propaganda enabled the Nazis to persuade millions of German citizens that Jews, by their very existence, constituted a dire threat to them and ought to be exterminated. Similarly, in Indonesia, propaganda turned truth into a lie, blaming the PKI for murders it had nothing to do with, and making heroes of the actual murderers. The pervasiveness of anti-PKI propaganda becomes clear from watching the film. Viewers observe a massive monument dedicated to the martyrs and "heroes" of the Thirtieth of September

Movement. They are shown images of the fraudulent dioramas in Indonesian museums depicting PKI murder. Also presented are excerpts from an anti-PKI propaganda film that Indonesian students were required to view repeatedly over the course of their education. Also indicative of the scale of the propaganda effort is news footage showing President Suharto presiding at an elaborate commemorative ceremony, held on September 30th each year on the site of the September 30th murders, and pushing the same anti-PKI message.

As political history, *40 Years of Silence* is narrowly conceived, limiting its attention to the political genocide in Indonesia in 1965–1966. Absent is any attention to the genocide on East Timor, which Indonesia claimed in 1975. Between 100,000 and 200,000 East Timorese, of a population totaling fewer than 700,000 persons, died in that event.[6] This absence in no way lessens the power of the film. However, because the United States has been implicated in its support for the invasion,[7] and was providing military assistance to the Suharto regime, this absence should be noted for the record.

Another possible criticism might concern the significance of religious difference in the Indonesian genocide. The majority of the population of Indonesia is of the Islamic faith, but many of the PKI were either not religious or were not Islamic. The religious factor is not ignored in the film, but perhaps could use more development, as it remains unclear.

On balance, *40 Years of Silence* breaks new ground, both in its subject matter and in its psychocultural approach, and is certain to have a lasting impact in the field of genocide/politicide studies.

Questions

1. *The United Nations Convention on the Prevention and Punishment of the Crime of Genocide defines genocide as a crime committed against "a national, ethnical, racial or religious group." Should that definition be expanded to include other groups, and what kind of characteristics might identify such groups?*

2. *Victims of genocide include many individuals who have survived the killings, including victims who have been physically injured but not to the point of death, as well as the relatives and communities affected by the violence and strife. In what ways might the harmful experiences of such "collateral" victims be **magnified** when the group responsible for genocide remains in power, as was the case in Indonesia, for many years following the event?*

> 3. *The United Nations' anti-genocide Convention is best suited for addressing genocide committed by governments. Can genocide also be committed by actors **not** acting on behalf of an existing government? If so, how might that kind of genocide be confronted or addressed?*

Bibliography

Cribb, Robert. "The Indonesian Massacres." *A Century of Genocide: Critical Essays and Eyewitness Accounts.* Eds. Samuel Totten, William S. Parsons and Israel W. Charny. New York: Routledge, 2004: 233–260.

Dunn, James. "Genocide in East Timor." *A Century of Genocide: Critical Essays and Eyewitness Accounts.* Eds. Samuel Totten, William S. Parsons and Israel W. Charny. New York: Routledge, 2004: 263–293.

Harff, Barbara. "No Lessons Learned from the Holocaust? Assessing Risks of Genocide and Political Mass Murder since 1955." *The American Political Science Review* 97, no. 1 (2003): 57–73.

Kiernan, Ben. *Blood and Soil: A World History of Genocide and Extermination from Sparta to Darfur.* New Haven: Yale University Press, 2007.

Lisson, David. "Defining 'National Group' in the Genocide Convention: A Case Study of Timor-Leste." *Stanford Law Review* 60, no. 5 (2008): 1459–1490.

Porpora, Douglas V. *How Holocausts Happen.* Philadelphia: Temple University Press, 1990.

Schabas, William A. *Genocide in International Law: The Crimes of Crimes.* Cambridge: Cambridge University Press, 2000.

van Schaack, Beth. "The Crime of Political Genocide: Repairing the Genocide Convention's Blind Spot." *The Yale Law Journal,* 103, no. 7 (1997): 2259–2291.

Notes

1. Since World War II, after the Holocaust and the Nuremberg trials, at least 12 million and as many as 22 million non-combatants have died in nearly fifty episodes of genocide, according to research conducted with the assistance of the CIA. See Barbara Harff, "No Lessons Learned from the Holocaust? Assessing Risks of Genocide and Political Mass Murder since 1955," *The American Political Science Review* 97, no. 1 (2003): 57–73.

2. According to his UCLA website (www.cns.med.ucla.edu/Bios/LemelsonR.htm) entry, Dr. Lemelson is the founder and president of the Foundation for Psychocultural Research (The FPR).

3. The term "politicide" is made necessary and useful by the wording of the U.N. Genocide Convention because that document limits its definition of genocide to "national, ethnical, racial, or religious groups" and does not include groups of victims whose victimhood derives from their political affiliations or actions. In her study of genocides and politicides occurring between the years 1955 and 2001, Harff identifies thirty-seven such events. Of those, thirty-two are classified as involving politicide, Harff, op.cit., p. 60.

4. Harff, p. 58.
5. Harff, p. 57.
6. Sian Powell, Jakarta correspondent, "U.N. Verdict on East Timor," *The Australian*, January 19, 2006, reprinted on the Yale University Genocide Studies website, http://www.yale.edu/gsp/east_timor/unverdict.html
7. Numerous supporting documents are available online from the National Security Archive of George Washington University, http://www.gwu.edu/~nsarchiv/NSAEBB/NSAEBB174/index.htm.

40 Years of Silence:
Some Comments for Discussion

■ ■ ■ ■ ■ ■ ■ ■ ■ ■ ■

Carol Rittner, R.S.M.

Distinguished Professor of Holocaust & Genocide Studies,
Dr. Marsha Raticoff Grossman Professor of Holocaust Studies,
The Richard Stockton College of New Jersey, Pomona, NJ

Forty years of silence is a long time – biblically long, as long as the Jews were wandering in the desert, trekking after Moses and Aaron, looking for "the promised land," looking for some respite from all they had experienced as they fled from Pharaoh and his soldiers. Like so many others, I came to the study of "general" genocide, if I can put it that way, through my study of a "particular" genocide – the genocide of the Jews during World War II and the Holocaust. Thus, many of my points of reference, my images, are Holocaust-related, often "Jewishly" related. When I say "forty years of silence," it is hard for me **not** to think about Jews wandering in the desert, not to mention the nearly forty years after 1945 – the year that marks the end of World War II, the Holocaust, and the Nazi concentration and death camps – when so many Jews metaphorically wandered in a desert of silence until people, Jews and non-Jews alike, were more willing to "listen" to survivors of the Holocaust talk about and commemorate their dreadful experiences.

While the experience of Indonesians who survived the massive 1965–66 purge of communists and their sympathizers in Indonesia is not totally analogous to the experience of the Jews who survived the Holocaust, there are some points of near similarity. For example, like Holocaust survivors who after 1945 were subtly, or not so subtly, "pressured" by the Jewish community in parts of the world that did not directly experience the Nazi terrors and horrors to "get on with their lives," survivors of the 1965–66 Indonesian mass-killings were absolutely *forbidden* by a ruthless, authoritarian government, headed by a ruthless, authoritarian dictator – General Suharto – from either recognizing, speaking, discussing, or memorializing the mass killings and brutalization they had experienced, *if their memories of it* differed in any way from Suharto's official state narrative.[1]

As for those of us living in America, if we are old enough to remember 1965–1966 and the years following the purge of communists in Southeast Asia, this part of the world was increasingly seen as vital to American national interests, which were, to say the least, anti-communist. Getting rid of a few hundred thousand communists, particularly if we Americans did not have to do it, was, to quote *Time* magazine, "The West's best news for years in Asia."[2]

40 Years of Silence: An Indonesian Tragedy is about a part of the world, a political situation, and a people about which many of us may be unfamiliar. At least, I do not know as much about Indonesia and its 1965–66 horrors – *genocide* – as I know about the Holocaust, the 1994 genocide in Rwanda, or even about the mass slaughter of the Bosnian Muslims in former Yugoslavia during the 1990s. I suspect it may be the same for many of us who teach mostly about the Holocaust or about the more recent genocides of the 1990s. I would like to make two suggestions, particularly for teachers who decide to use *40 Years of Silence* in the classroom, whether at the high school or college level:

- Make liberal use of maps so as to locate for students the part of the world discussed in the film; and,
- Identify some of the major political figures, both in Indonesia and beyond, who had an impact on what was happening in Indonesia in 1965–66.

For example, there is **President Lyndon Johnson** (1908–1973), the 36th President of the United States (1963–1969). We do not hear about him in the film, but I do think it is important for us to recall that he was the President of the United States in 1965–66. I think it is also important to know that American involvement in the Vietnam War was significantly "heating up" in the 1960s. That war, if you remember, was being fought at a time when American foreign policy was still heavily influenced by the so-called "domino theory," a foreign policy theory popular during the post-World War II era, even into the 1980s, that speculated that if one land in a region came under the influence of communism, surrounding countries in the region also would fall under communist influence, like a row of falling dominos.[3] Knock one domino – country – down and the others fall as well. Likewise, it is probably also good to keep in mind that in the middle to late 1960s, the United States was pitted against the communist regime of North Vietnam in a war that was being fought to keep South Vietnam – and the rest of Indo-China – from going communist, or, at least, that was part of the rationale for our military involvement in that part of the world. During much of the time when the United States was being drawn deeper and deeper into that conflict, Lyndon Johnson was President of the USA.

Sukarno (1901–1970) is another important political figure we should know. He was the first President of Indonesia, having helped Indonesia win its independence from the Netherlands after World War II. President from 1945 to 1967, Sukarno presided with mixed success over the country's turbulent transition to independence. He was forced out of power by one of his generals, Suharto, who formally became President in March 1967.[4]

General Suharto (1921–2008) was born in a small village near Yogyakarta, during the era of Dutch colonial control. He joined the newly-formed Indonesian Army and rose to the rank of Major General. An attempted coup on September 30, 1965 was countered by Suharto-led troops. He took control of the army, and the coup attempt was blamed on the Indonesian Communist Party. The army, led by Suharto, engaged in a violent anti-communist purge, which killed more than half a million people. He became president of Indonesia in March 1967, holding office until 1998.[5]

In addition to individuals who may have had an influence on Indonesia and the 1965–66 tragedy there, it also is important to know a little about two of the major organizations. There was the **PKI** (*Partai Komunis Indonesia*, Indonesian Communist Party), which was the largest communist party in the non-communist world and a major contender for power in Indonesia. The PKI was loathed by many in the Indonesian Army because of its involvement in a revolt against the fledgling Indonesian Republic during its war for independence from the Netherlands following World War II.[6] In addition, one should know a little something about **Gerwani**, or the Indonesian Women's Movement. It was a communist-aligned women's organization. In 1965–66, and even in following years, Gerwani members "became the target of anti-communist fervour directly following the [military] Coup and the military's media campaign"[7] in 1965.

As I watched the film *40 Years of Silence: An Indonesian Tragedy*, I could not help but reflect on a question I often ask students: **Is prejudice a prelude to genocide?** In other words, does what we think about others influence how we treat others? It was Abraham Joshua Heschel who said that the Holocaust did not begin with Auschwitz. The Holocaust began with words, with ideas about others, with ideas about Jews and Gypsies (the Roma and Sinti), with ideas about the handicapped and people who were considered less than perfect in the Nazi worldview.

The massive killings in Indonesia did not ***begin*** with the wholesale slaughter of villagers in Central Java, or on the island of Bali. The killing of communists and communist sympathizers also began with words, with ideas. In his new book, *Worse*

Than War: Genocide, Eliminationism, and the Ongoing Assault on Humanity, Daniel Jonah Goldhagen writes:

> Ideologies, ideas and values, beliefs about other people and the world, prejudices and hatreds, these are the things, mechanisms – call them what you will – that have moved the perpetrators of these and many other mass murders and eliminations. The people slaughtering, eliminating, and inflicting immense suffering on other people, upon millions of children, have been motivated by their beliefs about the victims and about the treatment or punishments they justly deserve. Mass murder begins not in abstract structures or inchoate psychological pressures, but in the minds and hearts of men and women.[8]

Why mention this? Because as you think about this film, *40 Years of Silence*, I want you to think about the prejudice that was so rampant in the Western World in the 1950s, '60s, '70s, and '80s against anything and anyone labeled "communist". Think about that even as you also reflect on the rabidly anti-communist Indonesian military and the brutalization victims suffered at their hands. Also consider the silence and inaction of the Western World, particularly the silence and inaction of our own United States of America in 1965–66, as hundreds of thousands of Indonesian communists were kidnapped, arrested, tortured, and killed. Isn't this an example of "bystander behavior"? Mix into that reflection what the victims and their family members in the film tell the viewer about the stigmatization they and their families endured then, and continue to endure even up to the present time.

Many of the analyses of the 1965–66 Indonesian massacres that I read stressed the role of ordinary Indonesians in killing their communist neighbors. Does this not raise the same issues as the Holocaust, the same issues as the genocidal conflict in former Yugoslavia, and the same issues as the 1994 genocide in Rwanda? That is: How do "ordinary people," former neighbors, friends, even in-laws become such willingly "ordinary executioners"? Surely the initiative for such "ordinary evil," if I can put it that way, has to come from somewhere, perhaps from how political, religious, and civic leaders, not to mention the media, demonize the "other," whether that "other" is a European Jew, a Bosnian Muslim, a Rwandan Tutsi, or an Indonesian communist?

The *40 Years of Silence* website notes that one of the themes "in the film is the multigenerational effects of the killings of 1965."[9] I am not a psychologist, nor am I a psychiatrist, so I am not able to comment on the psychological effect of the killings, but one thing that struck me after seeing the film, thinking about it, and doing some research to try to learn more about what happened in Indonesia more than four decades ago, is the realization that many of these "ordinary killers" were drawn from religious groups – Muslim, Hindu, and Christian – and were armed, trained, and

CAROL RITTNER

authorized by the Indonesian Army to engage in their murderous work.[10] This realization provokes in me the same questions that studying about the Holocaust, studying about former Yugoslavia, and studying about Rwanda in 1994 provoke: What happened to the Golden Rule? What happened to "Do unto others as you would have them do to you?"

All of our religious traditions – Muslim, Hindu, and Christian – preach some variation of the Golden Rule, and all of our religious traditions say that there is no higher rule of life. Why is it, then, that multigenerational religious teaching has been unable, generally speaking, to inoculate ordinary people around the world against prejudice, demonizing, torturing, and killing? How, and why, have we religious people failed?

Finally, a word about what is not so prominent in the film *40 Years of Silence: An Indonesian Tragedy*, but that, without a doubt, was a major part of the Indonesian tragedy of the 1960s: sexual violence against women. No matter the conflict, no matter the war, no matter the genocide, women are always targeted in a sexual manner. I do not say this in order to argue that women suffered more than men, or more horribly than men, but only to point out that women are particularly vulnerable during periods of mass killing. Sexual violence was part and parcel of the brutalization, horror, and massive killing in Indonesia. As Annie Pohlman writes, women are always and "especially at risk to abuses of their sexuality, namely rape, pregnancy, abortion and sexual humiliation, and of their gender-defined roles of maternal responsibility…" They are also particularly vulnerable "through their children."[11]

Although Pohlman says that there still are not many accounts by Indonesian women available, I suspect this is both because of the general repression/suppression enforced by the Suharto government when it came to talking about one's experiences during the 1965–66 communist purge in Indonesia, but also because of the natural hesitancy of women to talk about experiences of sexual humiliation. We know that "members of the Communist-aligned women's organization, Gerwani, were abused and murdered."[12] They were the target of anti-communist actions following the attempted coup in 1965, and they also were the target of the Indonesian military's media campaign.[13] The few accounts of what happened to women during the massive killing in Indonesia, "mention that female victims were raped/gang-raped before being killed." These accounts also say that singling out Gerwani members during the massacres was the norm, and

> that a common form of torture was to insert different objects into the woman's vagina, such as 'a sharpened bamboo pole', 'long knives until their stomachs were pierced' or iron rods. The other forms of sexual torture carried out against women victims included cutting off their breasts/nipples, after having been 'raped many times'.[14]

These most intimate and difficult memories of women and girls also need to be collected and preserved. Those of us who research and write about women during the Holocaust and other genocides, particularly post-Holocaust genocides, have read such accounts of gender-specific torture and killing over and over again. We know that whenever a region or country is seized by violence women are prey, and we also know that rape and sexual abuse of women are not by-products of war but increasingly are used as a deliberate military strategy, if not to annihilate the enemy, certainly to humiliate and harm the enemy through women, who are seen as the reproducers and carers of the community.

Lastly, as you think about this film, it seems appropriate to offer a few words about memory, for the film *40 Years of Silence* is a film about memory, and as Elie Wiesel, a memory-keeper par excellence, often says, "If we stop remembering, we stop being."[15] However, it is not enough to just talk about "[t]he existence of memory... Memory alone is insufficient for our needs."[16] It all depends on what kind of memory we keep, and what we do with memory. We must keep alive memory that is lucid, candid, and truthful about horrific events, and we must use that memory as a shield, as a reminder, in the words of Yehuda Bauer, that we must

- Never be a victim,
- Never be a perpetrator, and
- Never, but never be a bystander.

And we must keep alive memory of such horrific events as a shield against the possibility of such horrific things ever happening again, against any people, in any part of the world.

The rhetoric is easy, but the challenges are profound. To paraphrase slightly Holocaust scholar John K. Roth, a film like *40 Years of Silence: An Indonesian Tragedy* can play an immensely important part to sensitize the conscience of individuals, and thereby to keep us more conscientious than we might otherwise be when we are tempted to turn our back on prejudice, demonization, hatred, torture, and murder.[17] If this film has the power to do that, the memories of these men and women in *40 Years of Silence: An Indonesian Tragedy* will serve as a powerful motivator for protecting the human rights of all people, including "the other." And their memories will bear witness for the living, and for life.

Questions

1. *What impact did America's anti-communist foreign policy during the late 1940s, 1950s, and 1960s have on how the USA responded to the horrific events happening in Indonesia in 1965 and 1966?*

> 2. *What impact, for good and for ill, does religion, religious belief, and the attitudes of religious leaders have on how religious believers respond to, or fail to respond to, how "others" are being treated by those in power? Explain.*

> 3. *What accounts for the fact that the experiences of women during horrific conflicts are so often overlooked and undervalued? What, concretely, can be done to remedy this oversight?*

> 4. *Why is it important to encourage survivors of massive conflicts, wars, and genocide to "speak their truth"? How can those who listen to survivors speak actually "hear" what they have to say? What is the difference between "listening" and "hearing"?*

Bibliography

Adam, Asvi Warman. "The History of Violence and the State in Indonesia." CRISE Working Paper No. 54, June 2008. Queen Elizabeth House, University of Oxford.

Cribb, Robert. "Genocide in Indonesia, 1965–1966." *Journal of Genocide Research* (Great Britain), 3(2) (2001): 219–239.

Fein, Helen. "Revolutionary and Anti-Revolutionary Genocides: A Comparison of State Murders in Democratic Kampuchea, 1975 to 1979, and in Indonesia, 1965 to 1966." *Comparative Studies in Society and History*, 35(4) (1993): 796–823.

King, Seth S. "The Great Purge in Indonesia." *New York Times Magazine*, 1966: 25, 89–94.

Moser, Don. "Haunted Face of a Red Defeat." *Life Magazine*, 66(1), 1966: 24–33.

Notes

1. Various estimates of the number of Indonesians killed in 1965–66 – even as late as 1969 – by the Indonesian Army, in their attempt to purge Indonesia of communists and communist sympathizers, range from 78,500 to 3,000,000 (see further, Annie Pohlman, "Women and the Indonesian Killings of 1965–1966: Gender Variables and Possible Directions for Research" on the website for the 15th Biennial Conference of the Asian Studies Association of Australia, Canberra, June 29–July 2, 2004; see also, "Genocide and Crimes Against Humanity | Indonesia," http://www.enotes.com/genocide-encyclopedia/indonesia/print; accessed September 21, 2009. I am using the figure of 500,000–1,000,000 cited in the website, "40 Years of Silence: An Indonesian tragedy," www.40YearsOfSilence.com.
2. See further, "Genocide and Crimes Against Humanity | Indonesia," par. #8.
3. Wikipedia, "Domino Theory," http://en.wikipedia.org/wiki/Domino_theory.
4. Wikipedia, "Sukarno," http://en.wikipedia.org/wiki/Sukarno.

5. Wikipedia, "Suharto," http://en.wikipedia.org/wiki/Suharto.
6. See further, "Genocide and Crimes Against Humanity | Indonesia," pars. #1, 4.
7. Pohlman, "Women and the Indonesian Killings of 1965–1966," p. 8.
8. Daniel Jonah Goldhagen, *Worse Than War: Genocide, Eliminationism, and the Ongoing Assault on Humanity* (New York: Public Affairs, 2009), p. 216.
9. www.40YearsOfSilence.com, p. 2.
10. "Genocide and Crimes Against Humanity | Indonesia," par. # 9.
11. Pohlman, "Women and the Indonesian Killings of 1965–1966," p. 3.
12. Ibid., p. 8.
13. Ibid.
14. Ibid., p. 9.
15. Elie Wiesel, "Let Him Remember," in *Against Silence: The Voice and Vision of Elie Wiesel*, 3 vols., ed. Irving Abrahamson (New York: Holocaust Library, 1985), 1: p. 368.
16. John K. Roth, "The Ethics of Memory: Reflections on the Holocaust at the Threshold of the 21st Century," in *The Pall of the Past: The Holocaust, Genocide and the 21st Century*, ed. Marilyn Nefsky, (Merion Station, PA: Merion Westfield Press International, 2000), p. 15.
17. Ibid., p. 17.

APPENDIX

Dr. Ethel LeFrak

....

A graduate and trustee of Barnard College, Ethel LeFrak has been active as a trustee or member of the board of directors of many cultural, philanthropic, educational, and medical institutions, including serving as a trustee of the Cardozo Law School, vice-president of the Little Orchestra Society, trustee of the Carnegie Council for Ethics in International Affairs, trustee of the Albert Einstein Medical College, and patron of the Asia Society.

A member of the Metropolitan Opera's "Golden Horseshoe" and "Opera Club," Ethel LeFrak also has been a patron of the Lincoln Center, a conservator of the New York Public Library, a member of the Council of the Salk Institute, and a member of the Board of the United Nations International Hospitality Committee – which was instrumental in having her and her husband, the late Dr. Samuel J. LeFrak, honored with the United Nations' "Distinguished Citizens of the World" Award in 1994.

Among the many institutions recognizing the philanthropic generosity of the Samuel J. and Ethel LeFrak Foundation are the Guggenheim Museum of the City of New York, Temple Emmanu-El on New York's Fifth Avenue, Queens College, the Smithsonian National Museum of American History in Washington, D.C., the Pratt Institute, Barnard College, and the American Museum of Natural History of New York.

Mrs. LeFrak also generously donated a large gift to the Albert Einstein College of Yeshiva University.

With her husband, Dr. Samuel LeFrak, Ethel LeFrak co-authored two books on their family art collection: *Masters of the Modern Tradition* and *A Passion for Art*. The LeFrak collection has been hailed by *Art & Antiques* magazine as being one of America's top 100 collections.

In 1996, Mrs. LeFrak was awarded a Doctor of Humane Letters, *honoris causa*, from Seton Hill University. In 1998, Marymount Manhattan College also presented her with a Doctor of Humane Letters, *honoris causa*.

About The Ethel LeFrak Holocaust Education Conference and Student Scholars of the Holocaust Fund

In 2008, noted New York philanthropist Ethel LeFrak made a generous donation to Seton Hill University's National Catholic Center for Holocaust Education (NCCHE) to endow The Ethel LeFrak Holocaust Education Conference and create The Ethel LeFrak Student Scholars of the Holocaust Fund. The triennial Holocaust Education Conference of the National Catholic Center for Holocaust Education – now known as The Ethel LeFrak Holocaust Education Conference – seeks to enhance Catholic-Jewish understanding by "educating the educators" in the hope of reaching the whole of humanity. The conference equips teachers and faculty members, especially those at Catholic institutions to enter into serious discussions on the causes of antisemitism and the Holocaust, and to write and deliver papers that shape appropriate curricular responses at Catholic institutions and other educational sites. The Ethel LeFrak Holocaust Education Conference Endowment Fund supports the appearance at the conference of national and international speakers, sponsors the art, music, and film events that accompany the conference, and underwrites the publication of The Ethel LeFrak Holocaust Education Conference Proceedings.

The Ethel LeFrak Student Scholars Fund provides annual scholarships to support Seton Hill student participation in the following activities: the Summer Institute at Yad Vashem, the Holocaust Remembrance Authority in Israel; The Ethel LeFrak Holocaust Education Conference; the Genocide and Holocaust Studies Program at Seton Hill; and activities relating to international travel, Jewish-Catholic traditions, and readings and research to advance understanding of significant Holocaust issues, past and present. In addition, The Ethel LeFrak Outstanding Student Scholar of the Holocaust Award in the amount of $1,000 will be presented annually to the Seton Hill student who writes a reflection paper that best demonstrates a keen and advanced understanding of the lessons of the Holocaust or another specific act of genocide.

About The Ethel LeFrak Outstanding Student Scholar of the Holocaust Award

NCCHE benefactor Ethel LeFrak, of New York, New York, created The Ethel LeFrak Outstanding Student Scholar of the Holocaust Award to recognize the Seton Hill University student who writes a reflection paper that best demonstrates an advanced understanding of the lessons of the Holocaust.

The director(s) of the National Catholic Center for Holocaust Education and faculty teaching in Seton Hill University's Genocide and Holocaust Studies Program select the winning paper for this annual award begun in 2009.

All students selected to receive the award will have their papers included in the proceedings of The Ethel LeFrak Holocaust Education Conference, which are published on a triennial basis. Additional recognition includes a $1,000 award presented during a Center-sponsored event and publication of an excerpt in the *Setonian*, Seton Hill's student newspaper.

Michelle Horvath, a graduate student in Seton Hill's Genocide and Holocaust Studies Certificate Program and a history teacher at Saucon Valley High School in Springtown, Pennsylvania, received the inaugural Ethel LeFrak Outstanding Student Scholar of the Holocaust Award during The LeFrak Holocaust Education Conference in October 2009. Horvath received her award for her paper "Passivity of the 'Ordinary' German: Factors Leading to the Evolution and Implementation of the Final Solution."

Jennifer L. Goss, also a graduate student in Seton Hill's Genocide and Holocaust Studies Certificate Program and a social studies teacher at Fleetwood Area High School, Fleetwood, Pennsylvania, received the second award, which was presented during the University's annual *Kristallnacht* Remembrance Service in November 2010. "Children and the Holocaust: Universal Aspects" is the title of her award-winning paper.

ACKNOWLEDGEMENTS

No publishing project is ever completed without an enormous amount of help from many people, so we would like to thank the many who helped in one way or another with advice, assistance, and support as we completed this project:

Dr. JoAnne W. Boyle, Seton Hill University President, who has supported the National Catholic Center for Holocaust Education (NCCHE) and its work from the very beginning;

The NCCHE Advisory Board, especially Rev. John T. Pawlikowski, O.S.M., Ph.D., Chair, and members of its Steering Committee;

Sister Gemma Del Duca, S.C., Ph.D., NCCHE Co-director in Israel, and Sister Noël Kernan, NCCHE Co-director Emerita, and Wilda Kaylor, NCCHE Associate Director at Seton Hill University, whose invaluable help enabled us to "get this volume done";

Sister Lois Sculco, Vice President for Mission and Student Life at Seton Hill University, and the many Seton Hill University administrators, faculty, professional staff, employees and students, who supported this endeavor in various ways;

The Pennsylvania Holocaust Education Council (PHEC);

Glen Powell, who carefully and creatively designed the cover and the book's contents;

Laurel Valley Graphics, our printer, who helped to bring this publishing project to final completion;

And, finally, but not least, we thank the contributors to **Learn. Teach. Prevent.** Their willingness to "polish" their presentations into essays, and cooperation in meeting our deadlines made our task much easier. We thank them, and all who contributed in any way to **Learn. Teach. Prevent.**

Carol Rittner, R.S.M., Editor
Wendy Whitworth, Managing Editor

Index

emigration to, 182; Indonesia and, 298
University of Southern California, 122, 162, 265
USHMM, see United States Holocaust Memorial Museum
Uszod, Hungary, 105

Vanczak family, 111, 116, 117, 118, 119, 120, 121
Varga, Bela, 111
Vatican, 26, 32, 34, 111; Vatican II, 21, 25, 27, 41, 59, 69, 72–3, 75; Jews and, 71
Veesenmayer, Edmund, 119
Versailles, Treaty of, 82, 90
Veterans' Museum, USA, 204
Victims, 17, 150, 168; child victims, 168–177; Indonesia, 279; numbers of, 165
Video conferences, use of, 230, 233–39
Video testimonies, survivors and, 145, 165
Vienna, Austria, 121
Vietnam, North, 310; South, 310; War, 75, 309–10
Vilnius, Lithuania, 104
Vogel, Judith A., 168–177
Voices Project, 165
Vos, Johtje, 164
Vrba, Rudolf, 103, 106, 108
Vrbova, Gerta, 106, 107, 108

Waldheim, Kurt, 90
Wall Street Journal, 50
Wallenberg, Raoul, 107, 111, 113, 116, 119, 120, 121
Wanjaya hospital, Bali, 283
War & Genocide, 203
War Child, film, 193

Warsaw Ghetto, 170, 181
Washington, D.C., 21, 132, 164, 203, 204, 257, 318
Waterson, Robert A., 153–161
We Believe series, 42
We Remember: A Reflection on the Shoah, 22, 68, 189
Weber, Mark, 134
Weimar Republic, 82, 191
Weiss, Dr., 189, 192
Weiss, Manfred, 117, 118
West Papua, New Guinea, 296
Western Connecticut State University, USA, 137
Western Wall, Jerusalem, 29
Wetzler, Alfred, 103, 106, 107
White Rose movement, 251–261
Whitwell, Tennessee, 52
Whitworth, Wendy, 7
Wiernik, Yankiel, 205
Wiesel, Elie, 16, 17, 81, 90, 108, 109, 180, 182, 205, 266, 267, 268, 272, 313
Wiggins, Grant, 145, 146, 147
Wikipedia, 230
Williamson, Bishop Richard, 21, 32, 35
Wilno, Poland, 104
Wittenstein, George J., 254–56
Wittenstein, Jürgen, 252
Wojtyła, Karol Józef, 27, 28; see also John Paul II
Women, sexual violence and, 295, 296, 297, 312, 313; sterilization of, 297
Wonokromo, Indonesia, 287
Workers, Catholic Church and, 70
World Bank, 298
World religions, 46–55
World Trade Center bombing, 52
World War 1, 82, 84, 89, 90, 106
World War II, 2, 3, 9, 16, 41, 58, 63, 90,